Counseling Powers and Passions

MORE COUNSELING TECHNIQUES THAT WORK

Foreword by
H. Allan Dye

JOHN VRIEND

Copyright 1985© by the American Association for Counseling and Development

American Association for Counseling and Development
5999 Stevenson Avenue
Alexandria, Virginia 22304

Dedication

This book is a requiem

for

a great lady, Anne Lakeman Vriend, 1895-1985, who consistently taught her son, throughout her long tenure on planet Earth, that a human mind and a human life are sacred, to be prized above all else, and it is

for

Timothy Broe, Nancy Jo Condland, Frederick L. Cohen, Jerry A. Dancik, Ann Frasier, Walter J. Goldsmith, Joan Haas, Lillie M. Jackson, Mary Klym, Robert Klym, Patricia Lodish, Wilbert J. Mc-Clure, Robert M. Meisner, Bruce Peltier, Richard Rubinstein, Donna Sutherland, Roxanne C. Wilson, and especially, June E. Polatsek, all of whom have taught the author and know that a book is the product of a living mind.

Table of Contents

Foreword

This book is a sequel to *Counseling Techniques that Work*, a highly successful book by Wayne W. Dyer and John Vriend, first published in 1975. That book was acclaimed for its utility and readability and because the authors were successful in achieving what they set out to do. Two experienced counselors described in direct, uncomplicated language an array of effective methods and strategies for working with clients and groups of clients. Because that book was regarded by practitioners as a genuine contribution to the field, the American Association for Counseling and Development has decided that the spirit and form of the original should be continued.

And so it has been. This book, too, is a compilation of methods, techniques, and strategies for counseling individuals and groups of individuals. The range of specific topics is broad and, as before, each subject is accompanied by straightforward discussion of philosophical considerations (beliefs and assumptions about human nature and learning), rationale and objectives (what is to be accomplished at this time with this client), and methods (what can be done that will achieve the present counseling goal). In addition to offering his own creative responses and interventions, Vriend regularly encourages us to discover our own ways of effectively responding to counseling challenges and opportunities. The writing is instructional, encouraging, richly provocative, and delightfully entertaining.

As you read the following pages you will discover that John Vriend is a man of passions, that he cares deeply about many things. Prominent among these are counseling and writing, and he is a master at both. He is also possessed of an enormous curiosity, a will to know and understand. He is as committed to discovering what others have learned as he is to presenting his own view of the world, perceptions he has accumulated during a successful career as a counselor, counselor educator, consultant, and writer. Along the way he has also been a railroad dining car steward, a carrier-based divebomber pilot, undergraduate student, junior high school English teacher, graduate student, and officer in several professional associations, most recently President of the Association for Specialists in Group Work, a division of the American Association for Counseling and Development.

Vriend's lifelong passion for language and ideas about the human experience has had a directing influence, drawing his attention into any realm where there might be an alert mind, a worthwhile thought, a practical method. In documenting and illustrating his thoughts, he refers to other counselors and therapists, as one would expect, and in so doing provides validation that is internal to the field and familiar to most readers. In addition to such peer confirmation, we are often treated to an ecumenical view of life as represented by philosophers, futurists, economists, anthropologists, political scientists, novelists, and poets. If these broadly cited thoughts are a fair example, it may be that the proper fields of study for aspiring counselors are philosophy and literature, for the perspectives included here provide intellectual texture not often found in the literature of counseling, much of which has derived from psychology and education. Vriend thus reminds us that who we are and what we do are part of the larger scheme, that there are universal definitions of logic, common sense, striving, fear, and courage. He points out that across time and fields of endeavor we humans are more alike than different, regardless of such circumstantial factors as sex, age, vocation, race, era, and status. The lesson here for counselors is that meaning and identity are sought by every individual and that satisfying definitions are always personal.

Creativity is a frequent theme, one that is discussed and demonstrated throughout. It is promoted as a resource of power for both client and counselor that often remains untapped because its nature is not well understood. A popular conception is that creativity is a gift, is inborn, that one either does or does not have it. Vriend's observation, however, is that all of us can be more creative, not so much by trying as by allowing, once role and attitudinal fetters have been removed. The key, he alleges, is to understand that creativity cannot be directly sought; it is simply the by-product of authenticity accompanied by energy. Examples of the author's creative efforts in the form of ideas, strategies, even forms, are available in large number, along with suggestions for acquiring creative habits and behaviors.

Vriend is an unyielding pragmatist. His constant, fundamental objective is the improvement of counseling effectiveness. In order to act more effectively it is first necessary to understand differently, more correctly, or thoroughly. Thus, the material in this book is of two major types. Some chapters are almost exclusively theoretical in nature whereas others primarily consist of practical suggestions and descriptions of methods, techniques, and strategies. In both Part I devoted to individual counseling and Part II to group counseling he has made powerful contributions to our understanding of critical processes, while also providing illustrations of how greater goals may be achieved.

There is a custom among reviewers from academic settings, when they are enthusiastic about something they have read, to report that the selection "... will be required reading by my students." This sounds like a punishment. For any who prefer giving gifts of enlightenment to their protégés, however, they might well recommend Chapter Three, "Twenty Postulates of an Emotions Theory for Counselors" and Chapter Nine, "The One And the Many." The thinking and writing in these chapters are directed to topics that are foundational to counseling but that have rarely been treated with such insight and skill. Emotions are of tremendous importance in the theory and practice of counseling, yet in the literature there is a large, gaping hole where a functional description of emotions should be. In Chapter Three, Vriend presents 20 postulates that describe what emotional behavior is, its origins, how emotions are related to but different from thought and sensation, and how they can be modified. This chapter will be warmly received, read with appreciation by novices and veterans alike. Counselors will find these postulates useful in predicting and explaining client behavior and in developing effective interventions.

Chapter Nine is a discussion of the classic dilemma in group counseling and therapy, the pressure to conform while seeking greater individual identity. In this case as well, students, practitioners, and authors are aware of the problem and, like the weather, everyone talks about it. Vriend's treatise here is a thorough, insightful view of the phenomenon from both the general and group counseling perspectives. What makes this chapter uncommonly valuable is his explanation that the pressure to conform is not a unique characteristic of the counseling group, a notion that is widely held. Rather, he assures us, conforming is a common, necessary, and potentially growth-promoting process in which we all engage daily. It is the *habit* of conforming on the part of clients and counselors alike that must be guarded against, especially in the group. The implications are made clear by description and illustration. Readers with professional interest in group counseling will find this chapter to be extraordinarily useful.

Across the breadth of subjects and within the depths of the author's understandings there is a message in this book: If we are to be effective, we must care about ourselves, our clients, our work. We must be aggressively curious in understanding what we do and courageous in becoming able to do it. There are broad guidelines, some of which are presented here, but no blueprint. Instead, there is an infinite number of patterns, one for each of us to create from our own passions and energies.

H. Allan Dye
Purdue University
New Year's Day, 1985

Introduction

In order to say Hello, you first get rid of all the trash which has accumulated in your head ever since you came home from the maternity ward, and then you recognize that this particular Hello will never happen again. It may take years to learn how to do this.

—*Eric Berne*[5]

A s this book is being published, so too is the third edition of *Counseling Techniques That Work*, a book that Wayne Dyer and the author wrote and first issued in 1975.[6] That book, we have been told many times by many different people, is a counseling classic. We have no reason to doubt it. *Counseling Techniques That Work* has continued to be a best seller in the counseling field through numerous printings. What it contains is timeless, neither dated nor dependent upon changes in the counseling field. We see no reason to revise it.

What continues to account for the success of *Counseling Techniques That Work*? Hundreds of readers have taken the time to tell us, both in person and by letter, that it has solid usefulness for them. They appreciate its practicality, its lively, down-to-earth writing, and its appeal to and concern for the counseling practitioner.

This book, *Counseling Powers and Passions*, is its sequel. Subtitled *More Counseling Techniques That Work*, it builds upon the operational ideology of its predecessor, expands on concepts, and introduces a variety of additional techniques. It has a similar format: The second part of the book, which is on group counseling, assumes a counselor who functions according to the theoretical and operational modes and manners presented in the first part, which deals with individual counseling.

This book is about powers and passions in counseling, the power to do and the passion that accompanies doing what is well done. Counselors seek powers that will enhance their work, knowing the low feeling of powerlessness, knowing the sinking of the professional spirit that comes with impotence in the face of a client they fail to serve, when as self-advertised helpers they can think of no further help to give to another who is crying out in pain. This book is about the power of thought and about the power of passion, and it is about passion itself: where it comes from, how it works, and how it induces emotional well-being. It contains a full-blown theory of emotions for counselors, and as the quotation has it, "What can be more practical than a good theory?" It also contains a smorgasbord of useful counseling techniques.

What after all is a technique, we can ask, if not both a power and a passion, both the ability to act in a given way and the will to carry out the action with feeling? It is the strength and the glory of a beneficial force within us. What is a technique? Why, it is the method, the skill, the design that enlarges us. The more techniques we know, the greater our powers will be, and the more passion we can bring to our work. A technique sits in the mind. It is a given planned performance. It is a technology. A technique is the program in the computer. It is owned. It activates the instrument of the self in a certain way, one way one time for one purpose under given stimulus conditions, another way at a different time for different purposes under different conditions. A technique is neither a tool nor a utensil. One cannot go shopping for techniques the way one goes through the hardware store choosing tools for particular jobs—tools which are then stored in the garage or basement until needed for a similar job. Techniques are not utensils, knives, forks, spatulas, the armamentarium of the kitchen. One acquires a technique and stores it in the head. A technique governs a person in a certain way when that way is called for. A technique is absorbed, owned, on call, at the ready. A technique requires nothing external.

The individual who has a technique can not only put it to use, but can produce a blueprint of it, can communicate it, can model it for others. A technique is the intelligence behind the behavior. Techniques can be improved, modified, tightened up, and made more efficient through practice. They are skills and methods of doing and being that can be perfected and mastered.

When it is understood what purposes techniques serve, when they work and whey they do not, when they bring about the desired effect, then the choice to use a particular technique is a judgment. A technique may be owned but used improperly, the result of ill-informed judgment or lack of judgment. Making a judgment to use a technique is not the technique itself.

Competence includes the concept of judgment. Maturity, the result of experience, sharpens judgment. When we say that a person shows mature judgment we mean that he or she is discriminating, thoughtful, has considered alternatives, has applied criteria and principles before choosing a certain technique. Such a person doesn't "go off half-cocked" or "shoot from the hip." Such a person possesses patience and control. Such a person focuses outward, using an informed intelligence to make operational decisions, forgetting vested self-interests, completely at the service of another.

Techniques in counseling are used to engage individual clients or members of a group in certain ways for certain ends. Counselors are familiar with these techniques, have used them before, and can predict what effects their use will bring about.

When techniques are disparaged ("He's always trying new techniques." "She thinks her technique is what makes the difference." "It's all in his technique.") as being shallow or equated with flair or style, the chances are that the techniques in question are not sufficiently owned, sufficiently integrated into an overall operational philosophy. If the spotlight heightens technique to the extent that the process of counseling is secondary, then we may say that a part is overshadowing the whole, calling undue attention to itself.

One can favor certain techniques and overuse them, use them in every case rather than only when appropriate, rendering simplistic what is complex. The danger is "formula" counseling. Some trainers and educators "sell" such a party line, endeavoring to reduce counseling to a series of well-executed techniques, the exact danger, it would seem, in the mechanistic tenets of behaviorism, where a closed-system of reinforcement schedules will produce desired outcomes. The lure of the simple is the desire to acquire a set of techniques that will fit all clients, that will make do in all cases. Such a belief presupposes a truncated view of human nature. Techniques not sufficiently integrated into a large scheme of understanding and purpose are like empty exercises, calisthenics, those routinized physical movements done for their own sake (because physical activity is good for the physical system), rather than for a purpose beyond and external to the self, as meaningful work or sport.

Like *Counseling Techniques That Work*, this book has been written for counseling practitioners, counselors working in every imaginable setting with every conceivable kind of client population, and for those training to become practitioners. The central focus is practicality, reality-based straight talk about the world of counseling as it is, not how it should be or might be in some idealistic wonderland. Although what the effective counselor does is often invoked as a standard, a moral is neither drawn nor implied that someone whose performance does not yet meet such a standard is somehow tainted or inferior. Effective counseling is such a difficult undertaking that none of us can expect to be proficient in every phase of our calling, to provide the ultimate helping answer for all people we serve. We do our best and keep learning. And learning. There is so much to learn.

The "we" in this book refers variously to "us" as practitioners, co-workers in the field, aggressive strugglers after truth and greater professional proficiency, and to "us" as members of the total human community. Reader and author are in the same boat, afloat on the same river. That is our bond. If and when the author has chosen to set himself apart, it is to own a statement, a bias, a point of view perhaps too controversial to ascribe to or project onto his fellow practitioners.

"For whom am I writing this book?" is a question that troubles many writers even before they set pen to paper, fingers to the typewriter, or, these days, to the computer keyboard, and it haunts them all along the line to the final period. It troubled Ralph Waldo Emerson back in 1848, and he discussed it in his *Journals*:

> Happy is he who looks only into his work to know if it will succeed, never into the times or public opinion; and who writes from the love of imparting certain thoughts and not from the necessity of sale—who writes always to the unknown friend.[7]

The author has taken his cue from Emerson and it has guided him. The friend he has imagined is a counselor, or is studying to be a counselor, an enthusiastically committed person always endeavoring to be more skilled and competent, someone wholly committed to becoming as effective as possible, someone who sees this calling as gratifyingly significant among many possible occupational choices, someone who works hard at self-development. Certainly the author's friend is a good or outstanding learner, not only about counseling but about all of human nature, about any and every feature of human life. His friend is open-minded, of generous spirit, not prudish, boring, or dull. Rather, his friend is lively, engaged, ready to laugh, a joyous companion, full of understanding about life's balances. The author's friend is always ready to give him "space," to allow him his eccentricities, to hear him out, to disagree reasonably.

Now that the writing is done, this unknown reader friend is better known, as she or he has all along been a much treasured companion. When it is time to write again, the author knows his friend will sit across from him, be patient when his ideas require a long time to unravel, laugh with him when he makes a joke, gets off a good pun, or satirizes some pomposity in the field. There are even those times, those peak times, when his friend will applaud and say "That needed to be said, *mon ami*, and you have said it *par excellence!*"

Pains have been taken to make this a readable book, a lively book designed to wake up a reader, not to put him or her to sleep. It therefore contains much that orthodox thinkers in the field might judge to be unorthodox, some ideas that border on blasphemy, some that are heretical, and many that are at least controversial. An effort has been made to create tension in the writing, to make cold wires crackle with new electricity, to jolt worthy but dormant and undervalued ideas to wake up and zing. Writing has tension when things are not settled, when one cannot predict down what track a train of thought is headed. Surprises as well as amusement and laughter await the reader herein. If it is discernible here and there that the author has written with tongue in cheek, it will come as no surprise that he identifies more easily with an H.L. Mencken than with some more rabbinical purveyor of the good word. Said Mencken when he introduced a collection of his own writings:

> Those who explore the ensuing pages will find them marked by a certain ribaldry, even when they discuss topics commonly regarded as grave. I do not apologize for this, for life in the Republic has always seemed to me to be far more comic than serious. We live in a land of abounding quackeries, and if we do not learn how to laugh we succumb to the melancholy disease which afflicts the race of viewers-with-alarm. I have had too good a time of it in this world to go down that chute.[8]

Is life comic or tragic? The pendulum swings, but the author, at least, is squarely on the side of life as an ongoing comedy. So much of what most folks take seriously is thoroughly absurd, particiularly when they take themselves too seriously. And when clients are unable to laugh or to be amused, when they cannot appreciate the nonsensical nature of so much of what happens in their lives, it is a diagnostic sign of pathology as potent as any other indicator one could cite.

There are many "respects" in the coming pages. The reader will find a profound respect in this book for the mind, that most human part of human nature, the human mind as an entity at which to marvel, great minds of our contemporaries and of those who came before us, the mind of every citizen, the reader's mind, all human minds. Our minds enhance our lives. How we use our mental gifts determines all else. We live in our minds. Our powers and passions reside there. All else in life flows from what we know, what we have stored in our minds, and from how we think. Unless we are successful in helping clients to "change their minds," our efforts in counseling are ineffective, if not entirely wasted.

The preeminent regard for mind is a theme that salts and peppers every meal on this book's menu.

This book contains a healthy respect for history, the recent past, and the historical context in which we currently live, as well as for the history carried within every client. Frequently expressed in these pages is the idea that effective counseling cannot take place in a sterile laboratory setting in which the counselor is oblivious to a client's formative past or cultural influence. We are all shaped and moved by the times in which we live. None of us live in a void. We live in a river of time, the depth and character of the water influencing us, the current determining our pace relative to what is happening on the banks of both sides, the adventures, the dangers, the pleasures there engaging us, the sky and weather meeting out conditions of passage. We can abstract ideas, but we cannot abstract ourselves or our clients from the real contexts of our time on earth.

There is a commodious, a religious respect in this book for language and its uses, for writing, for oral communication, for the mother tongue, for words and sentences in which we formulate and express our ideas, for how we manifest our powers and passions. Our least utterings are a miracle, for it is through language that we transcend ourselves, that we represent and symbolize our worlds, that we climb above life on the material plane and interact as spiritual beings. It is through language that we are able to enter each other's heads, that we are privy to the sanctum sanctorum that every mind is. This is true even for enlightened living within our own minds, how we express the world and ourselves to ourselves. We are language-using creatures raised far above animality by this gift. The dead speak to us through the language records they have bequethed us. We can know them *personally* without their material presences. They have transcended their own time on earth when they come alive once more in us. What could be more miraculous, more spiritual than this? That person who takes language for granted, who fails to see and understand its enormity in our lives, can be counted as short-sighted.

In this book the reader will discover a respect for knowledge, for all knowledge anywhere, but especially for whatever knowledge lies beyond the purview of what is normally construed as "the literature in the field." It is not simply a show of humility to say that all the knowledge that is pertinent to what counselors do is but a small fraction of all that is known. It is the recognition that in the entire scheme of things, in the legacy of wisdom we all can share by availing ourselves of any part of the immense written record of our species, what constitutes counseling knowledge as exemplified in books and journals is but a minnow in a vast unexplored ocean where whales migrate, porpoises cavort, sharks hunt, and who knows how many other species of sea-life flourish. Ours is a young discipline, fraught with error, populated with do-gooders, message-repeaters, and a relatively small troop of hard thinkers humbled by the fact that they know so little about what works and what doesn't in counseling. Our common counseling knowledge is so picayune because human nature, any particular person's make-up, is so complex. We must cross over the borders of our own jurisdictions to understand every client, and our understanding is always partial. That we do not understand ourselves helps us to appreciate the impossibility of completely understanding any other person. Thus, effective counselors are knowledge-seekers, finding new facts, new ways to think and act wherever they go and wherever they look. To know all there is to know is to be God, a dangerously unethical role for any counselor to aspire to.

Finally, one will find a paramount respect for counseling in this book as being the "heart of the matter." Not a hierarchical respect, one that looks upward from a position at the bottom rung of an occupational prestige ladder that includes social workers, psychologists, psychotherapists, psychoanalysts, and psychiatrists and how these professionals view their disciplines, but a straightforward respect for counseling and counselors as their equals. If a counselor knows all that these professionals know, is he or she then no longer a counselor? Only if a new title is sought, another name. When this is the case it seems to the author, at least, that its owner covets a perceived status: If one is only a counselor, that is not good enough. But isn't this simply poppycock? If our professional home lacks worthiness, it is up to us as a group to enhance it. It will be through the eyes of the general public as well as through the eyes of other professional groups that our status will gain elevation, and this will come from esteem for who we are and what we can do. Our best practitioners must remain counselors with a reputation for excellence.

Having said this, let us also acknowledge the dangers in professionalization. The professions breed homogeneity. Differences are smoothed out and tend to be reconciled and accommodated. The central tendency is toward orthodoxy. A body of conventional wisdom accumulates, preferential methodology becomes formalized and institutionalized. This process is analogous to the search for truth in the hard sciences such as mathematics, chemistry, physics, and biology, where accurate descriptions of reality are recorded and physical laws that advance knowledge and technology are discovered. In the physical sciences there is always the frontier between what is known and what is unknown. Knowledge is more reliable because it has its objective proofs. In the helping professions, however, the tests for reliability and best practice are infrequently objective, and here is where the analogy with the hard sciences weakens. Best practice is determined by consensus or majority rule. A tradition builds. A vast investment is made in the establishment and maintenance of particular training programs, procedures, rituals, rights, privileges, and organized practices. Newcomers to a profession become indoctrinated in the large body of ways and means identified with the professional area. In any established profession differences are more threatening to the status quo than they are challenging or refreshing. It is at this point that the truth hurts. This is what John Milton had in mind when he wrote, "Truth . . . never comes into the world, but like a Bastard, to the ignominy of him that brought her forth."[9]

Differences of opinion, new ways of viewing phenomena, divergent ideas about how to proceed, and ideas based on a different order of values tend to come from *outside* the professional ranks. By virtue of their training, longevity, and natural desire to advance within the ranks, professionals in a given area are conditioned to see and think within parameters that mitigate against the recognition and acknowledgement of perceptual differences. Outsiders unaffiliated with in-group factions see the profession critically, question practices and rationalizations, and from their foreign orientations offer new ways of seeing and judging. When their criticisms and offerings are threatening, insiders consolidate and defend, furthering homogeneity. A common foe generates cohesion in the ranks.

This trend toward orthodoxy in human affairs and institutions is a well-known phenomenon. It pertains in religion, the arts, politics, in practically every area of communal endeavor. It has its virtues and drawbacks for both insiders and outsiders. An analogy with genetics provides us with a metaphor: the concept of inbreeding and cross-fertilization. In universities, which are freer of the profit motive than are most social institutions, cross-fertilization and the influx of new blood and new ideas is a common occurrence; the internal rules against the dangers of inbreeding are generally followed. Professional, craft, and labor groups, on the other hand, are concerned about a guaranteed livelihood for members, seek to consolidate their gains through organizational activities that include control over entry into the field, training programs, requirements for practicing, licensing, fee-setting, and determining the market for their services. Inbreeding creeps in. Restraint of trade, a closed market, governance of members, ethical codes, and ideational orthodoxy all tend to diminish free inquiry and to muffle internal dissent. These ends are not the result of Machiavellian plotting, of schemes developed in closed boardrooms by a hierarchy of powerful string-pullers. This is simply how professional bodies evolve. In the early stages, lively experimentation, wide divergence in practices, an open market, and a lack of tradition and authority characterize a burgeoning profession. As the enthusiasm to try something new and the excitement and creativity wane, however, the professional stalwarts take over and organize the operation; they bring stability through institutionalization.

It is not the author's purpose to determine and evaluate where counseling stands in its development as a profession, nor even to argue that it has attained such status. In any comparison with more established professional groups (law, medicine, accounting), it can be said to lack certain representative features. What the author sess as important to bring out from the wings and place at center stage here is the very idea of differences of opinion about counseling as a professional practice. What may be identified as the mainstream in the discipline, the field, the literature, seems to the author's mind to be impoverished by divergent points of view. As a consequence, one that is reflected in many ways in this book, he has gone outside the customary literature of the field and sought authority for his opinions from many responsible thinkers not ordinarily associated with counseling. Certainly many of his ideas may thus appear heretical, and if he has failed in his efforts to justify the inclusion of an uncustomary way of viewing some aspect of counseling, it has not been for want of enthusiasm. Along with John Milton again, he can say,

> And though the winds of doctrine were let loose to play upon the earth, so truth be in the field, we do injuriously by licensing and prohibiting to misdoubt her strength. Let her and falsehood grapple; who ever knew truth put to the worse, in a free and open encounter?[10]

The author's motives are simple enough. By virtue of his own reason and experience he cannot view what counselors do as carved in stone. Counseling is so difficult because human beings are so diverse in their beings, their histories, and the contexts in which they live, because the human mind is so complex, because the process of effective counseling requires so much understanding of how thought impinges on and determines behavior, because the *means* by which counselors provide service—the use of verbally expressed language—is so complicated and multi-leveled, to name only some prominent reasons. In many places in this book it is his intention to poke at complacency and to bestir new dialogue over issues of theory and practice which, to his mind, are far from settled. And he does this as an insider, one who is self-critical, one who welcomes controversy, one who is sounding alarms here and there for his professional family against the dangers of inbreeding, of taking ourselves too seriously, of sanctifying false gods, of isolating ourselves from all those realms of intellectual inquiry that pertain to our professional pursuits and interests.

Following in the footsteps of *Counseling Techniques That Work*, this book has a similar design, partly about individual counseling and partly about group counseling. It builds upon principles of personal mastery counseling put forth in the original work and in the cassette tape series, "Counseling for Personal Mastery."[11] The operational counseling philosophy espoused here is consistent with these earlier works. This book is their partner, but it can also stand alone. It addresses new areas of import to practitioners and extends those introduced previously.

Although numerous specific techniques are presented in the territory ahead, these hardly compose the essence of what the reader will encounter. Essentially this is a book of essays wherein the author has taken the stance of: "Let us reason together, fellow practitioner, about what we see as vital to our welfare as counselors seeking to be as effective in our work as we can be." Here the reader will find answers to relevant questions that are not always lined up on the side of what is already known or agreed upon by leaders in the field, another source of the tension alluded to above. The spaciousness of an entire book permits the development of ideas, the presentation of arguments in favor of some strong opinions which, it is fervently desired, the reader will embrace as *un*common sense, and the author has taken advantage of this opportunity.

If there is an overriding appeal in *Counseling Powers and Passions*, it would be this: Counselor, become more mindful. As counselors we succeed more when we are more mindful. Becoming more mindful of ourselves, our lives, our behaviors and more mindful of our clients, their lives, their behaviors is what there is to mind in our work. If we are minding our business, there is much, oh so much, to bear (and bare) in mind.

John Vriend
Southfield, Michigan
Thanksgiving Day, 1984

NOTES

1. Russell, B. (1919). *Proposed roads to freedom—anarchy, socialism, and syndicalism.* New York: Henry Holt, pp. 186–187.
2. Coles, R. (1978). *Walker Percy: An American search.* Boston: Little, Brown, p. 14.
3. Nisbet, R. (1982). *Prejudices: A philosophical dictionary.* Cambridge: Harvard University Press, p. 179.
4. Malamud, B. (1952). *The natural.* New York: Pocket Books, p. 143.
5. Berne, E. (1972). *What do you say after you say hello?* New York: Grove Press, p. 4.
6. Dyer, W. W., & Vriend, J. (1975). *Counseling techniques that work: Applications to individual and group counseling.* (3rd ed.). Washington, DC: American Personnel and Guidance Association.
7. Emerson, R. W. (1926). In B. Perry (Ed.), *The heart of Emerson's journals.* Boston: Houghton Mifflin, p. 231.
8. Mencken, H. L. (1949). *A Mencken chrestomathy.* New York: Knopf, p. vii.
9. Milton, J. (1956). The doctrine and discipline of divorce. In J. M. Patrick (Ed.), *The prose of John Milton.* New York: New York University Press, p. 145. (Original work published 1643)
10. Milton, J. (1956). Areopagitica: A speech for the liberty of unlicensed printing. In J. M. Patrick (Ed.), *The prose of John Milton.* New York: New York University Press, p. 327. (Original work published 1642)
11. Vriend, J., & Dyer, W. W. (1974). *Counseling for personal mastery: A cassette tape series.* Washington, DC: American Association for Counseling and Development.

Those whose lives are fruitful to themselves, to their friends, or to the world are inspired by hope and sustained by joy: they see in imagination the things that might be and the way in which they are to be brought into existence. In their private relations they are not pre-occupied with anxiety lest they should lose such affection and respect as they receive: they are engaged in giving affection and respect as they receive freely, and the reward comes of itself without their seeking. In their work they are not haunted by jealousy of competitors, but are concerned with the actual matter that has to be done. In politics, they do not spend time and passion defending unjust privileges of their class or nation, but they aim at making the world as a whole happier, less cruel, less full of conflict between rival greeds, and more full of human beings whose growth has not been dwarfed and stunted by oppression.

—**Bertrand Russell**[1]

Unquestionably Kierkegaard is gloomy as he surveys mankind, and there is implicit in his "stages" a pessimism with respect to most of us: we are victims of what, eventually, bores us; or we try hard to live decent and generous lives, but end up entirely missing the point of "existence." Kierkegaard regarded most of us without detachment, perspective, judgment—as the blind leading the blind. We live on an insignificant cinder, whirling through the universe, and soon enough, perhaps, not only will each of us die, but the cinder, too, will lose its glow, give out and crumble—again, dust to dust. Meanwhile we strut, boast, make all too much of ourselves, and, lest there be any gnawing doubts or second thoughts, resort to various forms of psychological anesthesia. For Kierkegaard, one of them is any political, psychological, or philosophical theory which claims to have figured out what is and what will be—thereby encouraging a fool's paradise. Pure whistling in the dark—that is what he thought of all such efforts. There is no real propsect, he believed, for lasting social cohesion; nor is man perfectable. The future is as bleak as the past was wretched. But some try at all costs to live it up, dance "the whole night through," and others kid themselves with that craven sly instrument—the human mind and its bag of tricks. Still, there is that mind, and it does indeed set us apart, distinguishes us from all other life on this planet.

—**Robert Coles**[2]

Thanks to Freud, it has been joked, when a person thinks a thing, the thing he thinks is not the thing he thinks he thinks but only the thing he thinks he thinks he thinks.

—**Robert Nisbet**[3]

We have two lives, Roy, the life we learn with and the life we live after that. Suffering is what brings us toward happiness.

—**Bernard Malamud**[4]

Part I

Individual Counseling

Counseling is herein understood as predominantly verbal action that transpires between a professional and a client, the latter seeking a service that must be created and tailored to fit. The action arises from the professional's thought, from previously acquired knowledge about service techniques, and from the acquisition, digestion, and reflection upon the peculiar data the client supplies. Other action arises from the client's thought, what the client thinks about the experience, choses to disclose, decides to do. This interaction may or may not be enjoyable, productive for either party, or long-lasting. It all depends on what is communicated between them as they grope their way along.

1

Personal Mastery Counseling: Steps in the Process

My investigations on self-actualization were not planned to be research and did not start out as research ... When you select out for careful study very fine and healthy people, strong people, creative people, saintly people, sagacious people—in fact, exactly the kind of people I picked out—then you get a different view of mankind. You are asking how tall can people grow, what can a human being become?

—Abraham Maslow[1]

What is personal mastery counseling? *Personal mastery* is admittedly an umbrella term similar to (if not a synonym for) such global concepts as self-actualization, self-fulfillment, even personal happiness or the realization of one's full potential. But there is one important difference. By alluding to mastery it is inferred that levels exist at which an individual is less than masterful. The concept represents a totality, the sum of an infinite number of parts. Under the umbrella of personal mastery taken as a whole are all the possible behaviors that human beings have the power to develop to mastery. We all have the capacity to choose particular behaviors that we want to acquire or upgrade. In this sense personal mastery is not unlike self-actualization. In personal mastery counseling, however, we are more cocnerned with the identification of specific behaviors to master than with the acquisition of traits and characteristics. The thrust is for identifying and putting into operation what has lain dormant.

Behind the concept of personal mastery is the question Abraham Maslow asked. In essence he said, "Why are psychologists so preoccupied with studying the normal and abnormal, in trying to find ways to bring the abnormals up to the norm, whatever that is? Why not look at the other end of the human development continuum and study human beings who excel in their personal living? Then, if we learn how to do so from these folks, we can help everyone to improve, to grow, to live their lives more effectively, more happily. We can raise the norm." And because these individuals obviously got there on their own, without the intervention of counselors, therapists, and similar helpers, Maslow concocted the term *self-actualized.* It was a fantastic lure, perhaps even a threat to the helping professions. You can actualize yourself. Haven't others done it? Who needs a counselor, a therapist, or a psychiatrist, preoccupied as they tend to be with sickness, inadequacy, and deviations from the norm?

Maslow himself, of course, understood that his study of those whom he singled out as self-actualized could not be made to fit the rigorous parameters of the scientific method, that vaunted and guarded system of thought in which any social or behavioral scientist must work to receive peer approval. Though Maslow apologized profusely for this, he fumbled merrily ahead anyhow. Although others had wandered there from time to time, he found himself in an unmapped section of the forest and it was up to him to become the cartographer of its landmarks and to do his own trailblazing. His delineation of the characteristics of self-actualized persons tells the story of his search and provides the basis for personal mastery counseling. He has pointed the way for us, his heirs.[2]

Let us take just one of Maslow's important characteristics of self-actualization as an example: humor. If it is true that self-actualized people have a sense of humor, can laugh at the comedy that others create as well as creating their own, does not their modeling show that any one of us can learn to do as much, desiring as we do to live more effectively? What is this prized sense of humor? One is not born with it. One does not get spanked into the world and immediately begin laughing at the folly of the human experience. It is particularized *behavior*, present at a certain time and place usually in the company of particular others: All behavior is learned. It is mental behavior first, followed by attending emotional and physical behavior. Behavior can be studied and imitated, its essence understood, its principles learned, and its processes incorporated by another who also chooses to acquire it. For whatever reason, we *learn* how to respond to the funniness in others and to be funny ourselves. We *learn* how to worry or to be free of worry, to criticize or to be free of any desire to do so, to feel happy, sad, even depressed. The basic truth about being human is that we are born with no knowledge and very little ability, and we must learn everything.

"True," says Albert Ellis, in a critical reaction to this idea. "But we seem to be born with very strong predispositions to learn certain things (e.g., to love and be bigoted) and to resist learning other things (e.g., to be independent and self-disciplined). Personal mastery counseling seems to ignore our biological tendency to be irrational and self-defeating in many respects; and therefore it is sometimes not as realistic as it could be."[3]

If we accept the premise that we are genetically predisposed to be irrational, to favor and learn crazy ways of living rather than to make more sensible use of our minds, it follows that despair, cynicism, and acceptance of an inability to transcend our self-defeating natures will too frequently be the result. No doubt irrationality is widespread, but it is hardly universal. To paraphrase Abraham Lincoln, we can undoubtedly expect that some of the people are crazy (engaging in neurotic or psychotic behavior) all of the time, and all of the people are crazy some (most?) of the time, but not all of the people are crazy all of the time. If irrationality is not seen as universal or biological, how are we to account for its pervasiveness? In their book, *The Adjusted American: Normal Neuroses in the Individual and Society*, Snell and Gail Putney contribute a telling answer to this question.[4] We can account for irrationality on a cultural basis. Society is crazy, and if we live in it we will learn its crazy ways. They quote Friedrich Nietzsche: "Insanity in individuals is something rare—but in groups, parties, nations, and epochs, it is the rule."[5]

This is another way of saying that a person who hears a different drummer, in Thoreau's phrase, is likely to be perceived by the majority as having strange digressions of the mind when that mind is actually functioning more rationally than theirs. The issue has to do with conformity.

Presuming that we are willing to stand up to the consequences of our acts, to weather the gaff from relatives, companions, co-workers, and acquaintances who pressure us to be like they are, why not master those behaviors that are rational and benefit us, help us to be happy, prosperous, capable, rather than those that harm us, cause our unhappiness, and prevent us from accomplishing our desired ends? This is a rhetorical question with a simple answer: We do not know how, we do not want to exert ourselves enough or to take the time to do so, or we are not convinced that it is worth doing. The personal mastery counselor, in contrast to the average citizen, is convinced that it is worth doing, has taken the time to do it, and knows how. These counselors have learned ahead of their clients how to perform or behave in any dimension of personal mastery on which the counseling focuses.

The concept of a personally masterful, self-actualized, or fully-functioning individual is an idealization, of course, a vision of perfection not attainable in a hundred lifetimes. But that vision provides us with direction for growth and determined self-enhancement in place of the willy-nilly opportunistic development that is the result of following our cultural and social noses. Effective counselors understand this. They constantly work to increase their empirical comprehension and capability in more and more areas not only for the sake of their clients, but first and foremost for their own sakes in their own lives. They practice what they preach. They are neither quacks nor fumblers in the dark. Whether they are autodidacts or have been taught by others, they have aquired learning and can articulate and give it away. The skills effective counselors have are specifiable, teachable, and valuable to anyone. These counselors are experts in effective, masterful human living, at least in the dimensions in which they propose to serve their clients, and they are experts in the special teaching skills that compose the counseling process.[6]

BEHAVIOR

Any embodiment of a process requires that operational principles and steps be explicated. This process applies to personal mastery counseling. In *Counseling Techniques That Work* an operational definition of counseling and the assumptions behind it were delineated. The purpose here is first to present some related fundamental understandings about be-havior and then to break down the operational definition of counseling into its sequential steps to illuminate the forms of each in actual practice.

Behavior is a useful word made less useful by the supposition that all who encounter it are knowledgeable about its meaning. It carries the flavor of concreteness. As a noun we assume it refers to any human action. When we use it as a modifier, again human activity is presumed. Behavioral science implies the study of how human beings behave. When we say that the desired outcome of counseling is positive behavioral change, we all assume that we know what that is, that we can cite instances of such change. Accompanying the idea of behavior as we generally understand it is its observability, even its measurability.

If we put aside human behavior for a moment and see how behavior is observed in any nonhuman environment, the same understandings apply. We study plant and animal behavior. We study the behavior of inanimate objects, of machines, of elements in nature, even of natural forces such as the weather, the currents in oceans, and the movements of heavenly bodies. We observe the behavior of particles in nuclear fission. *Behavior* is a modern word that connotes scientific experimen-tation and observation and the collection and analysis of data. It is a word we have elevated to a high status and we have duly paid homage to it.

In so doing we now circle it somewhat awesomely as though it is an established shrine, perhaps only treating it contentiously when we con-sider it as a sect in psychology, as the school of behaviorism that is founded on the elaborations of reinforcement theory. Psychology itself, once a branch of philosophy that had as its province the study of the mind, now is a discrete discipline whose province is the study of human behavior.[7] And there can be a psychology of any particular enclave of human behavior: occupational psychology, industrial psychology, the psy-chology of sports, of love, of humor, of salespersonship—whatever. This stance of treating behavior as an understood and established entity has permeated the conventional wisdom of our times.

In personal mastery counseling, however, behavior is seen as divisible into three categories: *mental* behavior, *emotional* behavior, and *physical* behavior. Thinking, or whatever term we choose to signify the activities of the mind, is mental behavior. Although we cannot directly observe these mental operations, their existence is hard to dispute. The nature and forms of mental behaviors are more disputable, and many theories and much speculation abound on how the mind works. It is important for personal mastery counselors to remember, however, that both emo-tional and physical behavior result from mental activity.

This is to note that whatever we feel and however we cause our bodies to act are the direct consequence of what the mind commands. Emotional behavior, discussed at length in the following chapter, comprises the physiological reactions we have to thoughts, whether our thoughts are conscious, subliminal, preconscious, or unconscious. We feel all the time; we have body states that are ongoing but they are seldom homeostatic; they are governed at every turn by whatever mental behaviors are currently prevailing. The exception to this rule of visceral and somatic states being governed by mental activity is when bodily processes are altered by externally introduced substances, and even then feelings are complicatd by the effects of our thinking. What we can say with certitude is that our emotional behavior and our physiological reactions are in attendance at all times to what is happening in our minds.

Our physical behavior, too, is in attendance. This is to say that how we act—including the most minute action of flicking an eyelash, slightly frowning, or wiggling a toe—is governed by mental processes. Even when how we act seems to be out of control or involuntary, the activity in the mind is playing its part in determining the nature of the physical action. A causal realtionship exists between mental behavior and the resulting emotional and physical action. To say that we are stimulus/response organisms and that observable (physical) behavior is the result of external prodding, which is the basic idea of reinforcement learning theory, is to ignore the role the mind plays in determining behavior. If a subject has a predictable response to a given stimulus, the subject's mind is conditioned—programmed, if you will—to direct the body to behave in the predicted way. The *seat* of the behavior is in the mind. Even when positive reinforcers are used successfully to engender desirable new behavior and thereby extinguish the undesirable previously learned response, success is due to the subject's *thinking* about the value of the reinforcer.

Reinforcers work with animals. Although it is certainly valid that humans are animals, it is also true that they can modify and even pervert any animal function or tendency by their own mental intervention. When reinforcement techniques are successfully invoked, the process simultaneously reinforces nonthinking—the underplaying, belittlement, or circumvention of the mind. Using animal behavior as a practical analogy for human behavior is a dangerous inclination against which Arthur Koestler has been warning us for a long time.[8] He calls this view *rattomorphic*, based on the laboratory experimentation of psychologists with rats, rabbits, pigeons, and other animals, and laments the transference of behavioral-change procedures so discovered to various aspects of community life among human beings.

The usefulness of dividing behavior into mental, emotional, and physical categories for effective counseling lies chiefly in the emphasis on *mental* behavior. What happens in the mind precedes what happens emotionally or physically, but that process cannot be observed. We can observe only affects and effects. In most cases we must infer what mental behavior is going or has gone on, what conscious thoughts or what mental programming is responsible for what we can observe. This is extremely difficult, given the complexity of the workings of anyone's mind, and given the fact that so much more is stirring in the mind than what an individual communicates verbally. Most people cannot figure out how their own minds are working in any particular circumstance; they are unaware of the complications of motivation, early programming, mind/body interaction, impulses, drives, and a host of other considerations.

Most counselors want to *simplify* the counseling process, to reduce the intricate business of helping clients to a set of learnable operations that will be applicable to all case circumstances and produce results. Therapy theorists have been trying to oblige and accommodate this understandable desire to simplify in every way they can. Yet, each theory is lacking in comprehensiveness because the minds of human beings are such marvelously complex instruments. At best each theory provides the counselor with only part of the answer and relatively few insights about how to proceed under certain restricted conditions in certain cases. Every counselor must of necessity become a lifetime student of the human mind, of how it works and of how it differs in each of us if we are to achieve increasingly greater counseling competence.

Another practical way to use the concept of behavior is to attach the word itself to specific acts that clients manifest. One purpose in doing this is to separate the person from the behavior. Thus, a person is not "stupid" when he or she engages in stupid behavior, nor a "klutz" when klutzy behavior occurs. But these are pejorative valuing terms even for labeling behavior. Better that they are scuttled and more objective descriptions used, such as "tripping behavior" or "fumbling behavior" for klutziness. ("You seem to manifest this fumbling behavior only when you are in the company of others, not when you're alone. You hurry yourself when others are watching and, no doubt, judging you, is that it?")

Another purpose for attaching the word *behavior* to given client actions has to do with accurate labeling.[9] When the elimination of particular behavior is sought, or when *any* behavior is deemed worth focusing upon in counseling, then its specific and accurate labeling clarifies communication about it and enhances the goal-setting process. "Swearing-in-front-of-your-mother behavior" is more specific than "swearing behav-

ior." Counselors can train themsleves productively to think in such labeling ways; they can invoke "labeling behavior" frequently for telling
results. Thus it readily occurs to them to say "blaming behavior," "fault-
finding behavior," "self-downing behavior," or a thousand other appellations that help clients to a particular the behavior, to take responsibility
for it, and to realize that they can wear the behavior or discard it just as
they can put on and take off a pair of shoes.

Before moving on from this consideration of behavior, let us be aware
that there is one more way to view it. If we presume any behavior to be
performed at different levels of effectiveness, then a quintet of descriptors
diagnostically assists us in locating any behavior on a performance continuum. These five descriptors: panic, inertia, striving, coping, and mastery constitute criteria for judging behavior in any area.

1. *Panic behavior:* The person in a state of panic is incapable of self-
   help and is literally acting out of control, thus beseeching others
   to intervene.
2. *Inertia behavior:* The inert person shows no movement, is stuck,
   but is better off than the person who panics.
3. *Striving behavior:* The person who is striving to achieve is better
   off than the inert person, but striving doesn't mean that attempts
   to change are leading anywhere, that performance is making a difference.
4. *Coping behavior:* This behavior is helping its owner to adjust, to
   "make it," to "hang in there," but there is room for improvement;
   better than striving, coping denotes performing in ways that produce minimally acceptable results.
5. *Mastery behavior:* This behavior refers to what is effective in any
   given situation and can hardly be improved upon. A person "at
   mastery" has the sense of being in full control, "on top of things,"
   and is aware of having several if not many options.

This five-step view of behavior can be applied to any dimension of
human activity. One can, for example, judge a marriage or a job using
these benchmarks, noting when a person's behavior in either context is
panicky or inert or striving or coping or at mastery. The criteria can be
applied to any physical task, such as swimming or riding a horse, as well
as to emotional or social behavior. If, for example, one imagines a student
giving a speech in a class, one could picture how the speech-making
behavior would look at any one of the five levels of performance, from
being stage-struck and mutely panicky to being articulate, entertaining
and in full control of an audience. Using these descriptive criteria not

only helps the counselor to formulate more concrete and practical diagnoses of particular behaviors, but also to provide clients with more objective scale points for locating their levels of performance. In *The Sky's the Limit* Wayne W. Dyer has presented a comprehensive view of myriad commonly important life-behaviors by analyzing them from the perspective of panic-to-mastery. His chart describing 37 of these behaviors, catalogued according to this performance scale, provides a useful service for counselors.[10]

Finally, it must be said about behaviors that we don't *un*learn those that are self-defeating, ineffective, or harmful. We simply replace them with freshly learned alternate behaviors. If we hold with learning psychologist John B. Carroll that at least 90% of our clients have the aptitude to master any task that might be the called-for outcome in counseling, then, rather than despairing that our clients do not achieve their goals, we will see our own professional abilities and interventions as inadequate and in need of upgrading. Carroll considers *time* as the truly significant variable in learning and defines aptitude as "the amount of time required by the learner to attain mastery of a learning task." And he defines perservance, seen as crucial as aptitude, as "the time the learner is willing to spend in learning."[11] This is another way of saying that "practice makes perfect." Our clients, however, must be dedicated to doing the work, and some will take much longer than will others in attaining mastery, if that is their goal.

STEPS IN THE COUNSELING PROCESS

Presented in *Counseling Techniques That Work* is a carefully thought-out operational definition of counseling.[12] It is our purpose here to break down that definition into its component steps and to expand on each of these, treating each as a unit in the process that calls for particular counselor skills and interventions. Any process considered in the abstract is difficult to envision operationally, even when the operations apply to concrete objects. Such is the case in the assembling instructions that accompany certain store-bought goods, especially those that come from a land where the manufacturers aren't familiar with the peculiarities of English. When such operations are to be applied in a human interactional context, the difficulties pyramid and frequently cause an impasse: The process bogs down and stalls. In counseling, particularly for the less experienced, this often happens. But the counselor who has a tight grasp on procedure, knowing what will be accomplished at each point along the way, is less likely to go off on a spur track or encounter a barrier. Then, too, a firm conviction on how the counseling will go is necessary for declaring to any client what services can and will be delivered. Clients cannot be expected to know how counseling works, yet they have a right to know what to expect, and the effective counselor will be able to articulate what the experience will be like.

The descriptive definition of counseling presented in *Counseling Techniques That Work* is here broken down into nine steps. These include: (1) exploring—for the sake of determining where to spend counseling time and focus; (2) identifying and labeling self-deafeating behaviors; (3) providing insight—helping clients to understand the psychological maintenance system of self-defeating behaviors and why they have persisted; (4) making decisions to change thinking, feeling, and doing behaviors; (5) identifying alternate behaviors—possible replacement behaviors of a more self-enhancing character; (6) setting goals to adopt behavioral alternatives; (7) practicing the new behaviors in the counseling session wherever possible; (8) detailing the psychological homework to be done between sessions; and (9) evaluating what has transpired between sessions. Below, each is discussed in sequence.

1. *Exploration.* The first business in the initial encounter between professional and client has to do with setting the terms and conditions of the counseling, defining the services available, getting a commitment from the client, checking on how the client got there and what the expectations are, checking on previous counseling experiences, all the while correcting client distortions and shaping an understandable and reasonable picture of what will happen as the counseling progresses and how it will happen.[13] These essential components of an initial interview can take place at any time during that session and, when done efficiently, allow plenty of time for the counseling itself to begin at the first step: exploring to determine where to focus counseling efforts. The counselor wants to know, "Where can I go to work and make a productive difference?" The answer to such a question comes from having elicited enough data about the client's present ways of functioning to make a determination.

The counselor usually, if not always, provides services to a client in a time-frame. This is the way a competent counselor's mind is set: "I have a finite number of contacts for a finite number of hours with Laurel. Of what help can I be to her in that time? I need to establish priorities, to decide how the time might most productively be consumed. I know what I can best deliver. For Laurel, I need to decide *what* to deliver, where to begin, how to proceed. I cannot make such a decision without Laurel

13

showing me how she functions, what and whom she contends with, what her struggles are like on a daily basis, what she thinks, feels, and does, where her head and heart are, what her goals and aspirations are, how and if she gets joy and love, what is blocking her, what is going on in her mind that she feels so frustrated and despondent. I cannot expect Laurel to know what it is that I want, what information I require to make a decision of how to help to her. She has her notions, and these will come out. But she has no notion of what to tell me about herself that will help me to know how I can best serve her in the time available. That's my job. I will help her to provide me with the pertinent information."

Regardless of what has transpired previously, when it comes time to get down to the business of actual counseling, exploring for the sake of gathering pertinent data is the first step in the process. This step is not always formalized, if indeed it ever can be. Nor is this step ever finalized; data collection continues during the entire tenure of the counseling. As counselors we try to *know* our clients, and we know them more with each contact as they disclose more about themselves and emit more behaviors during the interpersonal action of the sessions. Their natures unfold in much the same way as those of major characters in a well-constructed novel. As in a novel, events and circumstances clients face and live through, including revelations about their past and even how they deal with conselor confrontations, often cause revisions of how the counselor sees or knows them.

In certain agency settings there are formal intake procedures. The counselor must establish a case file, accumulate specific case information, and make case notes according to formalized questionnaires and office paper-flow routines, much like the model physicians and hospitals use in detailing a patient's medical history. Elaborately constructed questionnaires frequently waste time and are abusive to clients, each of whom is unique and occupies a personal world different from that of any other individual. Perhaps such procedures cannot be avoided due to agency funding policies or eligibility for services, and the effective counselor will comply with the procedures while simultaneously seeking to modify them to serve exploratory purposes more realistically. The question becomes: What data ought to be gathered and how does the counselor go about gathering it? Since every client is different, no single format works for all clients. An effective counselor, therefore, uses many investigatory paths that yield data relevant to counseling-focus decisions. The focus chosen depends on what the client expects to get from the counseling and on the understanding between client and counselor about how the counseling time is to be spent.

The list of exploratory leads that follows is far from exhaustive. And let us emphasize "leads" even though most are presented in interrogatory form. Beginning counselors ask endless questions, not knowing how to deviate into other productive interactional modes—reflecting, clarifying, interpreting, hypothesis-testing, restating, summarizing, reviewing—the gamut of interventional options available to counselors. There is much room in the data-collection process for creativity.

- What is a running account of a typical day or week like for Laurel? Who is in it? Who counts? What pressures does my client face? What tasks? "If I were your shadow or invisible, Laurel, and I followed you around on a typical day, what would I see? Start with waking up in the morning. Where are you?"

- Does Laurel have any physical dysfunctioning? What about eating, sleeping, elimination processes, tension, exercise, use of medication, menstrual cycles, and visits to doctors? What is Laurel's general heatlh? When did Laurel last take sick leave from work? What illnesses has Laurel had in the last 5 years?

- Who are the people in Laurel's world that matter to her or care about whatever happens to her? "Who's the most important person in your life right now, Laurel? Who's second? Third? ... Tenth?" Does Laurel put herself into this line-up? What criteria does she use to determine importance?

- Where is Laurel developmentally? At every life stage each of us has to deal with circumstances peculiar to that stage. How is Laurel handling the appropriate and crucial developmental tasks in the stage she now occupies?

- What negative emotions are now prevalent or dominate Laurel's life? What are her emotional ups and downs? Let me feel Laurel's pulse in the major categories of guilt, worry, frustration, boredom, fear, anger, depression—all the negatives. Let me see where Laurel feels "up," gets satisfaction, is pleased, happy, glows, anticipates pleasure, has fun—the positive areas.

- Where is Laurel in the love dimension? To whom does she give love? From whom does she get it? What does the word connote for her? What skills does she have in love-giving and love-getting? Does she love nature, reality, people, ideas, herself?

- How do others see Laurel? Is she likable? Good company? A work horse? Too self-sacrificing? Frivolous? Unreliable? How do I see her? Among Laurel's intimates, what is she known for?

- Where is Laurel in the pecking order? In the family? At work? In every social context? Who is allowed to peck her? Whom does she peck? Whose decisions does Laurel follow? What is her relative degree of autonomy and power?

- How does Laurel manage time? Does she take on too much? Does she waste time? Does she live in time-pressured ways? What are the schedules she keeps?

- How does Laurel manage money matters? Does she have money sense? Is she in debt? What is she saving for? Do others manage her financial affairs? What does she spend her money on?

- Because the absence of laughter and a sense of humor represents psychic pathology, I want to know if there is any humor and laughter in Laurel's life. Can I make her laugh? Let me test this out right in the counseling. What does she laugh at?

- Is Laurel getting good mileage out of her smarts? Is she alert to what is going on right in this room, to what her surroundings are like? From the questions she asks, I can get a feel for how her mind is clicking away. How functional is her intelligence? Is she logical, following leads from her head, or emotional, following leads from her heart? Does she base her conclusions on evidence or on faith in make-believe handed-down untruths? When I confront her with evidence or logic, what does she do with it?

- What are Laurel's dreams and desires? What are here fantasies? Does she know what she wants, or only what she doesn't want and is sick of? Are her wants dependent on what she can make happen or on what others must do to supply them?

- Does Laurel have any goals she is working on independently of the counseling? What are these? What is her track record of goal-setting and working toward her goals? Does she have any notion of setting behavioral goals for herself, working on herself to change her behavioral ways?

- Laurel has told me who the important people are in her world. Now let me gauge how her relationship with each is going. Is she troubled about any one of them? Is she getting what she wants from each? Where one of them is sticky, does she know what is gumming up the works?

- How does Laurel handle new situations? With people? With work and other environments? How good is she at causing and handling change? How adaptable is she?
- Who knows that Laurel has come for counseling? What investment does any third party have in the outcome? To whom is she beholden?
- What defenses does Laurel put up? What forms do they take? Can I figure out what she is defending against? Do her defenses work for her? Are they necessary to keep her on an even keel in stormy situations? Does she lower her defenses in the counseling? What can I try to test this out?
- What are Laurel's work circumstances? What kind of worker is she? What is her employment history? When unemployed, what activity does she consider to be work? What does work mean to her?
- What are Laurel's play circumstances? What does she consider play to be? When, where, and with whom does she play?
- What moral considerations govern Laurel's living? What does she see as her duties and obligations? What actions would go against her moral code? How does religion fit into this picture?
- What events in the last 5 years of Laurel's life have made a big difference to her, caused her to change, were hard to handle, were ecstatically rewarding? What achievements helped her to feel proud?
- What kind of communicator is Laurel? What are her strengths and weaknesses in using language? How aware is she of these? How important is communication to her? Does she see her verbal behavior as something she can alter and upgrade?
- How does Laurel think and feel about pain and death? Do thoughts about her own mortality govern her behavior in any way?
- How does Laurel handle solitude? Is she afraid to be alone? Does she engage in activities worthwhile to her that require privacy? What does she do when she's alone? Does she feel lonely a lot? Is she good company for herself?
- How attractive to others does Laurel feel she is? What about herself does she think is attractive and unattractive? What personality traits does she think she has that are positive and negative?

This list of 26 veins to mine "in going for the gold," as one colleague describes the exploratory process, gives some idea of the scope of possibilities, and of the number of important dimensions to explore about a client's life. Counselors without an appreciation for the full spectrum frequently get stuck in helping a client to make decisions about where to focus in counseling chiefly because they do not take responsibility for canvassing enough facets of the client's world; they play nursery tunes instead of fingering the full range of the piano keyboard. Most clients have neither time nor inclination to explore in much breadth or depth, their reason for seeking counseling being narrow in the first place. But where this is not the case, it behooves the effective counselor to have a protraction of ideas about which keys to strike, a feel for the elongated scale of all the significant life-melodies that may be orchestrated.

2. *Identifying and labeling self-defeating behaviors.* The concept of self-defeating behavior has been around for so long that most users of the code-word take it to be a self-evident phenomenon. But this is hardly the case. Others inform us that a certain action or activity is self-defeating and we say, "Yeah, yeah, I know. That's the way I am. That's me. I've always been like that," as though this explanation ends the matter. In a sense, usually a socially accepted sense, it does. The observation is perceived as a kind of criticism and dispensed with, warded off by reference to a fixed make-up, as though personality or character were formed long ago and now must be borne throughout the remainder of life. Many such disruptive behaviors were learned in infancy, childhood, or adolescence and have neither been discarded as inappropriate or no longer useful, nor upgraded to meet adult requirements. A client who does not believe that a particular behavior can be changed is unwilling to invest time and energy in working on it. For most clients some counseling time, therefore, must be spent in helping them to see that they are *choosing* the behavior in every instance of its manifestation. Most people are not convinced that they have choices.

Although the term *self-defeating behavior* is here used to describe a category, it must be emphasized that this category includes the *absence of self-enhancing behavior* as well. In counseling we always arrive at the point where some desired behavior is identified and sought out. If Laurel repeatedly gets into situations where she takes no action and loses as a result, in situations where others exhibit a variety of positive actions that are self-promoting, then it is up to Laurel to acquire similar new behaviors where before she had none. In this sense Laurel's non-action under certain stimulus conditions is self-defeating. What is true in these situations, though, is that there is mental and emotional behavior within Laurel that a counselor can smoke out. What self-defeating thinking is combusting in Laurel's head at the time?

Counselors frequently advertise their services as being beneficial to anyone and everyone (this is particularly true, for example, of school counselors), and so will see clients who claim with relative validity that they have no problems, are untroubled, that their lives are going fine, that they have no self-defeating behaviors. Under these circumstances the counselor in search of pathology alienates the client. If the counselor is aware that a client is performing well and on all fronts propagating self-enhancing behaviors, then the exploratory process becomes one of hunting for those areas where the client wants to grow and develop. We reserve the concept of perfectablity for deities. Human beings are never finished products. Although not knowing how to speak Spanish in no way hurts Laurel, if she acquired the ability her existence would be improved. The same may be stated of how she performs in her personal relationships.

Clients have general notions about the behavioral arenas in which they wish to work. Most arrive in counseling because of intense dissatisfaction, pain, even fear. But they are unaccustomed to examining the dynamics of the part they play in their life circumstances; in most cases they don't know how to take apart and analyze their behavior. A raft of particular mental, emotional, and physical behaviors accompanies the concepts of shyness, laziness, tiredness, impulsiveness—or any other global self-designations of behavior clients complain about. It is the counselor's task, then, to help the client sort out and specify the behaviors that account for such summarizations. The concept of cause and effect is important here; the counselor must trace backwards from what actually happened to the triggering impetus and build-up of the behavioral event. And because most behavioral areas clients want to work in involve interaction with others, a counselor is forced to make appraisals and judgements about how clients read the social contexts in which a set of behaviors appears dysfunctional.

3. *Providing insight.* Ineffective counselors often ignore or underplay this step, yet it is crucial for clients. They are reluctant to make a commitment to change if they fail to understand why their self-defeating behavior has persisted for so long. Many clients implore counselors to tell them *why* they act in certain self-defeating ways, and counselors who are unaware of the dead-end trap into which such an investigation leads tend to fall in line with the idea of its importance. "If only I could find out *why* I do this, I could cut it out" is the belief, and the hunt for origins begins. Insight and self-understanding are vital to exercising control and making conscious choices to act in ways conducive to social success, equilibrium, and happy feelings, but the insight does not come with answers to "why" questions.

Rather, the question in the counselor's mind about any behavior has to do with payoffs: What does my client get out of acting in this way?

What psychological or social rewards, however seemingly undesirable or neurotic, help this behavior to persevere? What payoffs maintain the behavior?

A client, for example, complains of headaches for which no physical cause can be found. When do they occur? Who knows about them? What does the client do when they attack? It generally turns out that the client is able to receive sympathetic attention from others for being in pain, or at least is excused by others for not participating in whatever activity is going on. The headache gives its owner license to act withdrawn or even irritable. The client retreats from work, perhaps even to nap or escape to more pleasant comforts. A headache permits self-pity, gives its host the right to be self-attending or indulgent. Headache behavior has innumerable payoffs, some of which are bizarre: "I deserve to hurt, to be punished like this for being such a bad person." When the psychological maintenance system is thoroughly examined in a particular case, even such apparently involuntary behavioral phenomena as this turn out to serve a client's unconscious wishes. This is true of all emotional behaviors that clients believe they have neither caused nor invited. We get something out of anger, depression, fear, boredom, worry, guilt, or whatever. Every behavior works for us on some level.

When clients understand what a certain behavior has been doing for them, how it has served a variety of ends, they are more likely to be ready to change it. In a sense they have been functioning subconsciously in a conditioned fashion, and when they become aware of what their payoffs are they begin to see that other behaviors will do the job more effectively without the accompanying pain or other unpleasant consequences.

A major implication of this step in the counseling process can be noted here: The more perceptive and insightful the counselor is about behavioral payoffs, the more accurate he or she can be in analyzing specific self-defeating behaviors clients display or reveal in counseling. Diagnostic skills in this dimension are what novice counselors tend to lack. Once they appreciate the concept, however, counselors work hard at analyzing behavior wherever they can observe it simply to increase their comprehension of how it is supported by the ends it serves. They become students of all behavioral dynamics.

In determining what payoffs a client receives from a particular self-defeating behavior, there are two major areas of productive inquiry: time and people.

- *Time.* If the client were not now engaged in self-immobilizing worry or any other behavior, how would he or she be using this time? What does the client gain by this behavior? What tasks are being put off or avoided?
- *People.* Who knows about the behavior? What is the client advertising to others about self? When the client behaves in this way, how do others respond? Is there a living-out of a self-fulfilling prophecy? Are others being manipulated as in the use of anger, for example?

4. *Decision to change thinking, feeling, and doing behaviors.* When clients have acquired insight by examining why they have continued to behave in self-defeating ways, they are in a receptive position to consider changing. A vital part of the insight is client acknowledgement of responsibility: "I did it. No one made me do it. It didn't come from outer space and attack me. I chose it. I always chose it in the past because it served me in some ways. But now I understand that I can act differently. I am no longer tolerant of this behavior. I want to change."

Whether a client has made a decision to change can only be determined a posteriori. We come to know a decision by its effects. Commitment to change is demonstrated by what a client does. This critical step in the counseling process must, therefore, be revisited if no client movement is observable. Frequently even if there is observable change, we cannot say a decision has been made because new behaviors require testing and repetition to endure. If after testing new ways a client finds them wanting in some regard, a reversion to the old familiar ways may quickly result.

5. *Identification of alternative behaviors.* Specific behaviors that a client wants to change have been identified and labeled. Now what? Whatever replacement behavior is to be tried must be pictured in the client's mind as something that will work. The client requires a realistic vision of seeing himself or herself acting differently. Too often counselors fall into giving advice at this step in the counseling process by saying what works for them, and the client rejects the suggestions. The counselor's implied injunction: "Be like me," doesn't work. Determining alternate ways to function in any human context is more spontaneously accomplished in a group where others can testify than it is in individual counseling. There is no ready-made shopping list for every client. The counselor checks out what the client has attempted or accomplished in the past. Is this client effective in adaptation, in creating change? What works for this client? Does the client look for extrinsic or intrinsic rewards? What are these? Can the client modify behavior when no one in the client's world will approve of the changes? Does the client understand

that others want the client to stay the same, because when the client changes, they then have to find new ways to interact and they, too, resist change?

When alternate behaviors are considered, they are more appealing to a client who has considered them as a result of the thinking that the counselor has helped to foster. There is a danger here of the counselor formulating the "fishing" expedition into a problem context for which there is a "solution." Any number of different ways of behaving are possible in most life contexts, few of which fit neatly as a solution. When clients are willing, it benefits them to do research, to talk to the folks in their worlds and observe how they function when viewed form perspectives learned in counseling.

6. *Setting goals to adopt behavioral alternatives.* So much has been written on effective goal-setting in counseling that it would be redundant here to launch into a detailed description of this important counselor skill. It is sufficient to say that when client goals are well-set they will meet seven basic criteria. The goals will be:

- high in mutuality of agreement between client and counselor as to their suitability.
- specific in nature.
- relevant to the client's self-defeating behavior.
- achievable and success-oriented.
- measurable and quantifiable.
- behavioral and observable by others.
- understandable and repeatable.[14]

The last criterion is often unstressed by counselors but is essential to goal-achievement. If a client cannot articulate satisfactorily what he or she intends to do, when, where, and with whom, then there is little likelihood that the goal will be met; either the client doesn't understand what to do or is insincere about intentions to carry out the action.

7. *Practicing the new behaviors in the counseling, if possible.* If we clearly divide goals into our three categories of behaviors—mental, emotional, and physical—then it becomes more apparent how a counselor would help a client to practice working on goals right in the counseling session. Mental behavioral goals involve self-talk, the logic of thinking, the use of the imagination, and such operations as analysis and setting priorities, meditating, problem solving, and much more. A counselor who has gauged the client's characteristically self-defeating ways of using the mind can create simulation exercises for new ways of thinking to elim-

inate error and acquire mentation skills. The same is true for working on upgrading feelings and eliminating negative emotions.

Physical behavioral goals in counseling most often involve other people, and both counselor and client can work in roles to simulate likely interactional contexts the client might encounter.[15] In any evaluation of such simulation, it is important to notice what mental and emotional behaviors accompany the interaction.

Although it is outside of the counseling—in the client's real world where everything counts—that new behaviors are tested and shaped, a client who has gone through some trial runs within the counseling has some advantage over not having tried out the new behaviors at all. Practicing is a confidence-builder. It also teaches a client how to use a counselor as an accepting, reliable critic and a supportive consultant.

8. *Detailing psychological homework to be done between sessions.* Too often counselors see the concept of homework as *what the teacher assigns* and then behave similarly, even using the word itself when checking out with a client what he or she will do between sessions. Most young people dislike or detest homework because it usually means rote and drill and implies the imposition of a joyless sense of order totally lacking in any promise of fun. Because teachers feel their presence is needed when new material is introduced, most homework doesn't involve new material, thus robbing the doer of whatever joys there might be in discovery. Although homework is an apt enough metaphor for what we do in counseling, its literal use is anathema to our purposes.

Psychological homework is no more than a detailing of what a client is committed to accomplish as a result of what occurred in a session. Counseling has meaning for clients to the extent that clients *do* things between sessions. Particularly in early stages of counseling the counselor is the one accustomed to making up lists of tasks, the one good at pre-planning, at ordering behaviors that will result in more positive living. Most clients haven't been in charge in their lives; they tend to have functioned in stimulus/response fashion, doing what comes naturally. The consequences of this willy-nilly approach to most life situations are what steered the client into counseling in the beginning. Thinking ahead, preparing for important and inevitable future events or for events a client can prod into existence is seldom a habit clients have acquired. The same may be said for most clients about efficient reviewing, analyzing, and evaluating what they have lived through in the past.

In a very real sense, then, the summarizing and critiquing of a counseling session and the explicit naming of what will happen before the next session is an important tutoring function in which the effective counselor engages. It is hardly to be taken for granted that clients will productively engage in either of the above mental activities on their own, especially when all the evidence points to the fact that they have seldom employed their minds in such a fashion. No doubt they have avoided doing so because they perceive it to be tedious work, and this imposes upon the counselor the importance of being creative about both processes—making them fun and introducing excitement wherever possible.

9. *Evaluation of what transpired between sessions.* Getting client reports, evaluating the new behaviors the client has tried, and revising goals where appropriate constitute the final step in the counseling process. It can be seen that constant recycling is inevitable where behavioral change vital to the client continues to be the center of focus. Some behaviors can be learned and incorporated into a client's total system of operation quickly, often as a result of a critical incident, but most cannot. There are too many circumstances in any client's world over which the client has no control, too many apparent barriers, too many variables. Most change is terribly difficult and exceedingly slow, and every client will only move at a speed perceived to be safe. Counselors who understand this learn not to be impatient, not to push. They learn to see the client's world through the client's eyes and emotionality, to have a feel for what is possible with each person they serve.

Added up, this nine-step process becomes an operational definition of counseling. There are obviously many skills counselors acquire to aid them in being more masterful in professional functioning at each step along the way. It has been our purpose here in discussing the steps to provide counselors with a cognitive map of the process from start to finish. Beginners might even find it helpful to write these steps down, if they have not yet committed them to memory, so that they know where they are in working with a given client at any time.[16] Hardly any counseling session, or even a succession of interviews, would show upon inspection that the steps have been followed in the order presented here. Clients continually introduce extraneous matters or reorder their counseling priorities. The point is that effective counseling is monitored by citable parameters and governed by conditions and principles; without these a counseling experience can easily become helter-skelter, wander aimlessly, and frustrate both client and counselor by lack of meaningful results and positive behavioral change.

In the introduction to this book the author alerted readers to the dangers of formula counseling. Do these steps in the process make up such a formula? If a reader so regards them, the danger of oversimplification and rigid structuralization will confine his or her counseling activity. The steps are a way of ordering an ocean of data and likelihoods. Among many definitions that others have proposed, this is but one method of organizing a definition of counseling, a way of mentally grasping and containing human behavioral diversity that may seem confusing to a neophyte. What merit this manner of categorizing and ordering has will be decided by the reader as she or he gains professional maturity through experience, acquires skills and competencies, and is better able to make valid and reliable judgments. In the final analysis what becomes "the way" for any counselor is a self-earned cognitive map that will undoubtedly differ in many ways from what has been conceptualized and presented here. (For an extended discussion of this apparent dilemma, see Chapter 4.)

Though most theories or systems of counseling tend to contain statements of what counselors do and what they are rather than what they are not, such contrast is helpful in further definition of professional role. Professional counselors are not do-gooders, for example. Nor are they in the business of saving souls. It is not their professional purpose to help clients enter the Kingdom of Heaven or to find God. Nor do they have the power to alter a client's material position in the real world, to get a client a job, to give a client money, to help a client move to another part of the country, or to adopt a client. Nor can they take over for a client, do the client's homework, stop drinking for the client, be the client's only friend or socialize with the client. Nor are they influence peddlers—"Go see Mr. Powers. Tell him I sent you and he'll take care of you." Nor can counselors prescribe medicine that will make them feel better.

The counselor's powers are strictly limited to conducting themselves according to some learned principles about helping people to change their ways of living. They are trained to do this in the very restricted context of face-to-face meetings, using only their skills in effective thinking and communicating.

There is no question about it. To counsel expertly is a tough way to earn a living.

NOTES

1. Maslow, A. H. (1971). *The farther reaches of human nature.* New York: Viking Press, pp. 40, 42.
2. Maslow, A. H. (1954). *Motivation and personality.* New York: Harper & Row, pp. 203–228.

3. Ellis, A. (1978). Critical reaction to personal mastery group counseling. *Journal for Specialists in Group Work, 3*, 161.
4. Putney, S., & Putney, G. S. (1964). *The adjusted American: Normal neuroses in the individual and society.* New York: Harper & Row.
5. Nietzsche, F. (1886). *Beyond good and evil.* London: George Allen & Unwin, p. 206.
6. Portions of the aforegoing paragraphs in this chapter first appeared in an earlier article by the author, to which the reader is referred for a full discussion of the philosophical bases for personal mastery counseling: Vriend, J. (1978). What personal mastery counseling in groups is all about: Background and rationale. *Journal for Specialists in Group Work, 3*, 104–112. Copyright 1978 by the American Association for Counseling and Development. Reprinted by permission.
7. The reader can find a summary of the history of psychology, its relationship to philosophy, and its division into subspecialties that is as cogent as that to be found anywhere in: English, H. B., & English, A. C. (1958). *A comprehensive dictionary of psychological and psychoanalytical terms.* New York: David McKay, pp. 419–426.
8. Koestler, A. (1964). *The act of creation.* New York: Macmillan.
9. Vriend, J., & Dyer, W. W. Creative labeling behavior in individual and group counseling. *Journal of Marriage and Family Counseling, 2*, 31–36. This article presents a full exposition of the personal mastery counseling position on effective labeling, including a delineation of seven criteria useful in determining when and how to do so.
10. Dyer, W. W. (1980). *The sky's the limit.* New York: Simon & Schuster, pp. 371–383.
11. Carroll, J. B. (1963). A model of school learning. *Teachers College Record, 64*, 723–733.
12. Dyer, W. W., & Vriend, J. (1975). *Counseling techniques that work.* (3rd ed.). Washington, DC: American Personnel and Guidance Association, pp. 17–18.
13. See Vital components in conducting the initial counseling interview. In Dyer, W.W., & Vriend, J. (1975). *Counseling techniques that work.* Washington, DC: American Association for Counseling and Development, pp. 29–44.
14. Dyer, W. W., & Vriend, J. A goal-setting checklist for counselors. *Personnel and Guidance Journal, 55*, pp. 469–471.
15. See Role working in group counseling. (1975). In W. W. Dyer & J. Vriend. *Counseling techniques that work*, pp. 237–247. Washington, DC: American Personnel and Guidance Association.
16. See Kottler, J. A., & Vriend, J. (1980). Initial interview checklist increases counselor effectiveness. *Canadian Counsellor, 14*, 153–155.

2

Getting a Good Grip on Emotions

I'm paying particular attention to [Carl] Rogers's work because of the great influence that his treatment of feelings has had, both within and outside of professional psychology. While his treatment of feelings has certainly increased our sensitivity to and tenderness toward each other, his treatment of feelings (the word) has, just as certainly, decreased our sensitivity to language and our capacity for intellectual rigor. I question, further, whether feelings can be treated well when feeling is treated so shoddily. Rogers's therapy depends on words; its medium is talk. What sense can this talk make when both therapist and client have so little sense of one of its main terms?

—*Peggy Rosenthal*[1]

Ⓢo simple yet productive bit of homespun research in which any counselor may engage is to ask a small gathering of people to explain what feelings are. Whether the informal survey is taken in a classroom or over the dinner table, what is usually immediately apparent is that everyone will be interested and get involved in the discussion. Everyone has feelings. We all refer to the way we feel, many of us using the term and its derivatives hundreds of times in an ordinary day. Feelings are important to us. We attend to and express the ways in which we feel. It is a condition of modern life to be "tuned in" to feelings, our own and those of others, in most areas of social intercourse. Feelings have status. We judge the value of almost everything we do by the feelings our exploits furnish. We "get high" over an exciting experience and are loath to "come down" when it is over. We dread having to live through a nasty or difficult event and are relieved when it is over. We certainly know what we are talking about when we use the word *feelings*.

But *do* we know what we mean? That we don't know will be the first finding that homespun research will yield. In most groups answers to the question tend to be mixed, ranging from the creatively bizarre to profoundly ignorant. We assume we know what we are talking about; we take feelings for granted; we have lived with them our lives long. Some people will give circular answers: "Feelings are emotions." Some people will say, "You know—anger, love, sadness—things like that." As individuals in the group feed on each other's answers, generally an uncertain agreement will be reached that feelings are something everyone possesses, and they are brought into play by external stimuli. Things and events cause people to feel good or bad. Few people have taken the time to be specific about what feelings really are, where they come from, whether or not they can be controlled. If the discussion continues and a poll is taken of what people think is true about feelings, no doubt the group will arrive at some shared beliefs such as the following:

- We have them whether we like it or not. They are a part of human nature. Human beings in particular have them, but lower species of animals have them in a lesser degree. Dogs and cats get frightened or show affection. It is doubtful that insects have them to any appreciable degree. Some converts to the fantastic idea that you should talk nicely to your plants because they, too, can feel, will insist that plants have feelings, but those who so believe will be in the minority.
- Feelings are good. People who don't feel aren't to be trusted. They are denying their feelings. They are cheating those around them by

not showing their feelings. It is important "to get feelings out," to communicate them.

- Normal people can prevent most feelings from being excessive. They can "put a lid" on them. There are social contexts in which it is OK "to let them go," or social conditions under which one is justified in giving them free rein.

- The ways in which we were raised have shaped us to be emotional creatures of one kind or another. How we show our feelings depends on early imprinting in childhood. Our characters and personalities were formed by how we were treated as children and we are more or less fated to go through life being stubborn, outgoing, martyristic, angry, affectionate, romantic, tactile, stoical, or whatever. We cannot much help the way we are. We are programmed.

- In general, feelings are more important than thoughts. One can feel sorry for intellectuals because they have no fun. They don't experience life fully. They tend to be dull and lack excitement in their lives. Thinkers are too restrained. They don't "go with their feelings." You can "think yourself silly."

- If you don't pay attention to feelings in others, you are insensitive. Being sensitive means being careful not to hurt anyone. Insensitive people are selfish. They barge ahead stepping all over anyone not caring whom they hurt in the process, just going after whatever serves their own desires.

- Feelings can "take over." They can "run amok," "get out of hand." People can giggle uncontrollably, cry hysterically without wanting to do so, lose their tempers. When feelings take over, people are possessed by them and temporarily "out of their gourds." People who unabatedly continue to be dominated by their feelings are insane, out of control.

Certainly we can add more general beliefs about feelings to this list. If we were to catalogue beliefs held about particular feelings—love, anger, fear, depression, ecstacy—we could fill a sizable book.[2] Nor does it matter that there are contradictions among beliefs about feelings. In situation X one belief holds true; in situation Y its opposite is justifiably in command. Whoever said humans must be logical? Perhaps the most commonly held belief of all is that there is no logic in feelings: "All of your logic doesn't change the way I feel!"

What must counselors know about emotions in order best to serve their clients? What are emotions? How are they formed? What intensifies them? Can they be controlled? Can negative emotions be eliminated? How do our emotions serve us? Are people aware of how they feel? Is there some virtue to "getting in touch with your feelings?" When we say that a physical condition is psychosomatic, what do we mean? Is there a theory about emotions that is useful to counselors, one that will cover all essential contingencies? In focusing on emotions, these questions and a hundred others of counseling significance may be asked.

What generally prevails in counselor training, astonishingly, is an absence of any course specifically designed to clear up confusion and ambiguity about feelings. Trainers have their own beliefs and transmit them to students, but seldom is the study of emotions a subject central to the theoretical foundations a counselor acquires. Feelings tend to be focused upon as they arise and become an issue in the conduct of counseling interviews, and here their importance is hammered home.[3] Counselors in training are enjoined to be sensitive to their clients' feelings, to recognize them, to deal with them, never to ignore them, to explore them, to help clients get in touch with them, to get them out into the open, to respect and even to honor them, not to take them lightly, to be responsive to them, to be empathic about them—the emphasis goes on.

Though the extent is difficult to determine, it may well be that the early work of Carl Rogers is almost single-handedly responsible for the emphasis the field of counseling now accords to feelings, as Peggy Rosenthal hints in the epigraph to this chapter. And if there is some validity to this implication, there is equal validity to the contention that in Rogers's work there is little focus on what feelings are, little emphasis given to any theoretical explanation of emotions. It is assumed, taken for granted, that everyone know's what feelings are. The emphasis in Rogers's work is on the individual's worth, on the client as the center of any therapeutic focus, on the counselor's acceptance of all that the client is, on the counselor being nonjudgmental and having unconditional positive regard for the client, and on the counselor being open, warm, honest, congruent, empathic, genuine.

There are many reasons for the appeal of Rogers's ideas and discoveries. The psychotherapy then in vogue and available prior to World War II was based on the medical model. The price of admission to treatment was illness, psychological dysfunctioning disturbing enough to draw attention to itself and to cause pain and grief to others. Words are important here. The one designated for treatment was a patient, not a client. The illness was diagnosed by the expert and a treatment was prescribed. If the treatment worked, all well and good. If it did not, other treatment experimentation followed. Rogers himself was trained according to this model and believed in it and practiced according to its dictates. It struck him at a certain point that it didn't work. Something was vitally amiss.

> Then came a few incidents which markedly changed my approach; I shall tell you about the one that stands out most vividly in my mind. An intelligent mother brought her very seriously misbehaving boy to the clinic. I took the history from her myself. Another psychologist tested the boy. We decided in conference that the central problem was the mother's rejection of her son. I would work with her on this problem. The other psychologist would take the boy on for play therapy. In interview after interview I tried ... to help the mother see the pattern of her rejection and its results in the boy. All to no avail. After about a dozen interviews I told her I thought we both had tried but were getting nowhere, and we should call it quits. She agreed. Then, as she was leaving the room, she turned and asked, "Do you ever take adults for counseling here?" Puzzled, I replied that sometimes we did. Whereupon she returned to the chair she had just left and began to pour out a story of the deep difficulties between herself and her husband and her great desire for some kind of help. I was bowled over. What she was telling me bore no resemblance to the neat history I had drawn from her. I scarcely knew what to do, but mostly I listened. Eventually, after many more interviews, not only did her marital relationship improve, but her son's problem behavior dropped away as she became a more real and free person (p. 36).
>
> This was a vital learning for me. I had followed *her* lead rather than mine. I had just *listened* instead of trying to nudge her toward a diagnostic understanding I had already reached. It was a far more personal relationship, and not nearly so "professional." Yet the results spoke for themselves (p. 37).
>
> I trust I have made it clear that over the years I have moved a long way from some of the beliefs with which I started: that man was essentially evil; that professionally he was best treated as an object; that help was based on expertise; that the expert could advise, manipulate, and mold the individual to produce the desired result (p. 43).[4]

The history of Carl Rogers's discoveries and how his therapeutic ideas evolved is well documented in his own writings. He unscrewed and removed the lens filter that shaded all previous conceptions of psychotherapy and zoomed in on the counseling relationship, evaluating the role of the person receiving help over that of the person delivering it. "Patients" became "clients" and all service delivery was to become "client-centered."

Although the word *relationship* had been around for a long time and had been examined by other professional groups (doctor/patient relationship, lawyer/client relationship, reporter/news source relationship, teacher/student relationship), none claimed for it the potency accorded it in the counseling profession. It was not given imperial status until Carl Rogers did a superb job of eloquently specifying what the counseling relationship ideally ought to contain, first in an address to those attending the American Personnel and Guidance Association in St. Louis in 1958 ("The Characteristics of a Helping Relationship" appeared in print in the *Personnel and Guidance Journal* of that year), and later in his book, *On Becoming a Person*,[5] where he amplified his ideas in a number of essays. Rogers concretized the abstraction *relationship*; he elaborated it, expanded it, made it carry a load of importance that had not occurred to more short-sighted thinkers. He claimed for it a centrality in therapeutic counseling outcomes and then proceeded to show why this was so by describing its attributes. His thesis was that if a given counseling relationship had certain characteristics in sufficient degree, positive outcomes would result. It was a beguiling and seductive thesis.

It had tremendous appeal for three reasons. First, each of the characteristics could be found in the counselor. They were understandable. They were virtuous. They all seemed simple. Having unconditional positive regard for a client or being real and genuine was something anyone could be, even, or especially, without training, without working too hard. One understood the necessity of so being and then strove to be such each time one faced a client. What the client's world-data were, what the problem was, what behaviors were manifested made little difference. Counselors gathered the characteristics about themselves, then went about their counseling. Whatever else happened in the counseling or in its outcome, at least there would be the plainly positive factor of the client receiving respect, understanding, thorough regard, personal attention, nonjudgmental concern, recognition of and empathic response to whatever feelings welled up, all from a person intensely striving to be helpful without being interfering or manipulative. As H. L. Mencken once observed about Calvin Coolidge, "He was never afflicted with the itch to run things." Neither were the new breed of client-centered counselors. If they actually, authentically lived through a counseling session in such a state of being as Rogers described, they could do no intended wrong. Having a knowledge of counselor saintliness, they could approach being saints and platonic lovers in every professional encounter.

Second, Rogers's thesis appealed to counselors because it so beautifully elevated the basic premise that the counselor was the instrument through which the relationship took on the ideal characteristics. The counselor's personhood was everything. He or she geared up to be in a certain way and then placed personal being at the disposal of the other. Counselors need not be fumblers in the dark, experiencing failure when their efforts seemed futile; they need not be experts about human behavior; they need not study client historical data; they need not be environmental analysts. Their primary thrust could simply become personal upgrading. They could engage in self-analysis, become better and better in authentically paying attention to others and being responsive to their feelings, understanding the other, listening harder, and reflecting back to the other whatever they understood.

The third reason Rogers's thesis had such great appeal was the concept that clients had within themselves the resources to work through their difficulties or into whatever new directions their behaviors ought to take for self-enhancement. Thus, the responsibility for self-improvement rested with the client. The counselor's responsibility was to be alive in a certain way, and if the counselor managed this, the client would then be able to recognize his or her own resources, mobolize them, and put them to use. It did not matter that the client thus could take all the credit for therapeutic change. Getting credit was not at issue. If clients felt they had done it all themselves, so much the better. Isn't that what clients ought to feel in order to be psychologically healthy? The more important factor was that counselors could absolve themselves of all responsibility for failure or success, and even if clients remained at the status quo or lost ground, they at least would have experienced a positive relationship with a noble person, a person who had given a fully surrendered self to the client for the client's sake, and who could argue against the worth of that? Besides, in those cases where clients got better, the logical conclusion that they were worse before the counseling and were better after the counseling was inescapable. If counselors could not take credit, they could be enormously satisfied with the part they played as instrumentalities. Their service, their use of their persons for the sake of the other thus established their worth and reinforced and vindicated their entire approach to their professional activities.

There is no doubt that Rogers was espousing and championing ideas whose time had come. The social climate in the nation, if not in the entire Western world, was ready for Rogers's theses. Prior to the Second World War the emphasis for the masses had been on economic and social gains, on political and class struggles to achieve an adequate standard of living and general well-being. The fights to acquire voting rights for women, child labor laws, worker rights, universal education, social security, health and safety laws, and a long list of other social and economic aims, privileges, and liberties had occupied the energies of the country. The individual qua individual, especially in the middle and lower classes, counted less than the group. America was Janus-faced: The myths of the wilderness (freedom on the frontier), government "of, by, and for the people," "anyone can grow up to be President," the "melting pot," Horatio Alger rags-to-riches stories, "a chicken in every pot and a car in every garage,"—these and a dozen other myths prevailed as one face, a dream visage. The other face was the reality of the depression. Then came World War II and its aftermath: the distrust of power in the hands of leaders who can dictate the extinction of 6 million Jews and who can invent and drop a single bomb that will destroy whole cities. Ordinary citizens decided that the authority of church and state was mortally suspect and could even become lethal in a way never heretofore imagined or acknowledged.

Plus, relative prosperity arrived during the postwar period. America's economy boomed. In most families not only did a chicken get plopped into the pot, but a garage and a car was within everyone's means. The gains were more equitably distributed. Everyone's standard of living rose. Education and leisure were readily available. Literacy and the individual's ability to think and judge and do had come of age. Heroes were discredited; one must become one's own hero. For the first time in history, it seemed, the ordinary citizen had the leisure and freedom to attend to the self instead of using all time and energy toward working for survival and economic stability. New revolts occurred—civil rights struggles, riots in the cities, campus uprisings, "women's lib," resistance to the "government's war" that nobody wanted. The "me generation" proclaimed itself important just for being alive. Feelings counted. Along with the sit-ins came the love-ins. Ordinary people threw off conformity, took to feeling good through drugs. There was now hardly any thought about the melting pot or the chicken pot—it was just pot.

Along with this general liberation of so many individuals in the coast-to-coast populace who decided that it was okay to be taken up with the self, to throw over the traces of old traditions and values, to ask new questions, to live for the *now* in a world they never made—a world of defiled environments and endangered species, a world that could and most likely would be blown up by human technology, a world controlled by a greedy, irresponsible, and power-hungry elite—along with all of this the "therapies" grew and flourished. Between the end of the Second World War and the present time, psychotherapy opened up to widespread and diverse experimentation. Most of the "approaches" and prevailing theories prominent in the field today were either nonexistent prior to that war or were the province of the elite, including the medical elite. Counseling, as distinguished from therapy, was only an embryo. Personal counseling as distinguished from guidance, particularly vocational guidance, was hardly known as a field and certainly not as a profession. As a field all of its enormous growth has occurred in the last 40 years.

When Carl Rogers came upon the scene, those who could be indentified as a part of that scene were prepared for his ideas, hungry for them. He offered a rationale for providing personal help in ways that made sense. Counseling was extended beyond the clinic and private offices of the traditionally trained psychotherapists. The "New Frontier" was an "outreach" concept. A corps of new quasi-professionals who purported to provide counseling services to everyone and anyone was developed. One no longer had to be sick to receive the benefits of counseling. Its benefits ought to be made universally available. Let us have counselors at every level, kindergarten through grade 12, in college, in the workplace, in the community, for special needs and special populations. Let us have counseling services available for everyone throughout the lifespan, right through advanced age and in preparation for death.

Implicit in this brief historical review and perspective are clues as to how feelings have been regarded over time. Attitudes toward feelings have undergone a metamorphosis, their evolution paralleling other gains in the realm of the person. Emotions, if we can personify them for the sake of argument here, were disregarded in the early half of this century and in previous times, the victims of the protestant work ethic and Victorian prudence. They were serfs, disenfranchised, buffeted about, restrained, treated as inconsequential. Their voices were muffled, suppressed, repressed. In most human affairs they were not allowed to get in the way. How people felt didn't matter. People could feel any way they liked—angry, afraid, guilty, depressed, bored, thwarted. It was expected that people would feel badly. That was their lot. They were stuck with their bad feelings. Too bad. Tough. Grin and bear it. People learned in childhood to be seen and not heard, to squelch their feelings, particularly those associated with intimacy and sex, and those associated with grievances against authority figures; children learned "to take it" like little adults, not to complain, and to wait until their turn came—usually after the age of 30—and by then it had become habitual not to give feelings any latitude.

In the decades since the 1950s, feelings have, along with other characteristics of individualism, come out of the closet. Counseling, in a large measure, exists to serve them. What prevails today is a social climate where feelings are recognized and acknowledged, where they are given expression, where in most circles their suppression is not only unwarranted but an affront to others. We live in our passions, it can be said.

Modern life is a feeling life. Happiness is feeling good, and feeling good is a democratic ideal within everyone's reach in a way that has never before been appreciated or even possible for every citizen in the land. Today the idea that we must feel good has even taken on a moral character. Since it is a goal within reach, it is our duty to reach it.

THE HYDRAULIC MODEL OF EMOTIONS

What hasn't changed is how people perceive feelings. The popular beliefs about feelings earlier alluded to in this chapter still hold sway. It is our quest here to understand emotions in such a way that, as counselors, we know what to do about them. We must view them practically so that we can be of greatest service to our clients, so that we can productively aid clients in changing their emotional behavior by changing their mental behavior. As we shall see, the definition that we shall adopt to comprehend emotional behavior and build upon in order to determine how we shall function in any interpersonal contextual sense with clients presents a complication that must be first dismissed. The definition is simply this: *Emotions are physiological reactions to thoughts.* Stated differently, *feelings are mentally caused bodily reactions.*[6]

It is when we enter the literature of academic psychology and psychiatry that the complication arises. In their efforts to model their discipline upon the methods of the hard sciences, to formulate only those hypotheses that are testable under rigorously controlled objective conditions, psychologists and medical researchers study what is going on in the body. They study physical phenomena and then attempt to ascribe cause, usually correlating bodily reactions with external events and stimuli, but often regarding physical symptomatology as though it is "free floating" and therefore externally manageable. The ascription of cause— so hard to isolate and pin down in most cases—is to them of relatively little importance, as though it will simply go away over time if undiscovered and ignored. Research of this nature has resulted in the invention of the polygraph lie-detector, the prescribing of electro-shock treatments, the use of "truth serum" (sodium pentothal injected intravenously), the lively marketing of "biofeedback" machines and technology, and the wide and questionable use of pharmaceutical treatment protocols.

Drugs to excite or calm the central nervous system, stimulants and antidepressants, have become common household words in our society. They are big business, profitable beyond the ordinary citizen's imagination. Who hasn't heard of at least three or four of these popular brand names: Dalmane, Deprol, Dexamyl, Diazepan, Elavil, Librax, Librium, Marplan, Miltown, Mellaril, Nembutal, Qualude, Reserpine, Triavil, Tofranil, Thorazine, Valium? When the "talking cure" doesn't work, manage the emotional states of clients and patients with drugs. Give them uppers or downers. Lift them from their depression with stimulants, or bring them down with sedatives and tranquilizers.

Strong or persistent emotional behavior is thus seen as a physical disease, a physical dysfunctioning that can be managed—or lived with—if the right medication is prescribed. That people can be drugged into feeling better, if not completely restored to "normal," is accepted as a kind of proof in itself that feelings are a part of our human nature over which we have little control; they can easily get out of hand in spite of our efforts to manage them ourselves. This view of emotional behavior is essentially mechanistic. It dominates academic psychology and psychiatry, and in its more popular manifestations prevails among the lay public.

For his outstanding sensible and pragmatic treatise, *The Passions*, philosopher-scholar Robert C. Solomon has analyzed the academic literature in psychology that pertains to emotions, and his reasoning draws him to what he identifies as the "Psychologist's Puzzle." "What is an emotion?" he asks. He then remarks that although it would seem reasonable to presume that psychologists had settled the question once and for all, any reading of their literature spoils such a notion. He cites David Rapaport's survey of "emotion" literature wherein the differing pedagogically-accepted theoretical delineations were regarded by Rapaport as riddled with "terminological carelessness," "loose usage" of the concept that emotions reflect a "discharge process." Rapaport decided that psychologists had "lumped together many diverse phenomena ... which should be kept carefully apart." Moreover, he found that "physiological changes occurring in emotional states have been extremely dealth with in the literature but that the problem of 'emotion felt' has been somewhat neglected."[7]

"The picture," writes Solomon, "has changed considerably since [the time of Rapaport's survey], but the 'emotion felt' ... has continued to be neglected. Understandably so, since emotion, as a predominantly subjective phenomenon, is hardly a fit subject matter for a conscientiously (if not defensively) 'objective' science." Solomon laments the emphasis in psychology on "the physiological behavioral correlates," on the "expression" of emotions, to the neglect of simultaneous attention to the subjective experiencing of "emotion felt," in Rapaport's phrase. "The obsession with the tangible, the measurable, the quantifiable, and the visible continues," says Solomon. "Here," he goes on,

> lies the psychologist's puzzle: How does one examine a preculiarly subjective phenomenon using only the tools of objective experimentation and research? How do you observe and measure this notoriously intangible dimension of human experience? . . . Today, it is simply *assumed* by most experimentalists that one cannot get objective results from subjective investigations. This view is probably mistaken, but . . . it is enough to appreciate the puzzle it poses: Can a psychologist say anything of interest about emotions?
>
> The answer, of course, ought to be yes, for it is clear that, in some sense, the phenomenon the psychologist investigates "objectively" ("What happens when a person has an emotion?") and the phenomenon that interests us subjectively ("What is it for me/us to have an emotion?") are the same. The mistake is only to think that either investigation can proceed without the other. Thus, the psychologists' inquiries are interesting—in fact, only make sense—in the context of the subjective experience of *personal* emotions. But then, too, it is clear that even subjectively my experience of my emotions cannot be severed from the "expression" of those emotions in the world, and an "objective" observer is often in a far better position to characterize and identify patterns in my expressive behavior than I may be myself (Ibid., p. 136).

Solomon's inquiry into the nature of emotions and his review of a welter of theoretical orientations in the current psychological literature and its historical antecedents leads him to find a common theme that characterizes how emotions generally are conceptualized "scientifically." He does this by positing a hydraulic model. Both Sigmund Freud and William James saw emotions as a supply or quantity of some sort that "flowed" or "gushed" or was "channeled" in a certain way by the physical system, the "juices" or "liquid" under "pressure" being variously called "psychic energy," "instinctual drive," "neurological impulses or neurons," "libidinal forces," and a cartful of other names.

> In "prescientific" psychological thinking the concepts of "force" and "energy," "animal spirits" and "bodily fluids" (bile, gall, phlegm, etc.), were permitted a holiday of poetic and metaphorical explorations, consequently structuring language and thought about the passions within an unabashed and uncritical (though admittedly dramatic and often charming) hydraulic model. It quite literally views the human psyche as a caldron of pressures demanding their release in action and expression. With the advent of scientific psychology, however, the metaphor required a tangible basis, which

James and Freud simultaneously located in the components of the central nervous system (Ibid., p. 142).

What finally obtains is a neurological conception of mind, generally described in the "language of hydraulics," which is "but another appeal to the established concepts of Newtonian physics." How else to regard the workings of our nerves, glandular secretions, hormonal activity in our physical systems? (Our blood and waste elimination systems tend to be quite literally hydraulic.) Even modern behaviorism, Solomon attests,

> is in fact a purified and streamlined version of the hydraulic model, focusing its attention exclusively on the variables determining behavior and their observable effects without bothering with the "mental way station" (in Skinner's phrase) of consciousness. It is the completion of that model, perhaps overdoing it by a step or two, and underscores the great *un*importance of consciousness in psychology by failing to reckon with it altogether.

"Objective models and theories are all too readily incorporated into subjective self-conceptions," warns Solomon. What he calls the "hydraulic model" may be "appropriate to plumbing and engineering and perhaps to neurology but not ... to a view of one's own emotions."[8]

Are the theories and findings of the experimentalists who treat feelings only as objective phenomena of no help to us in counseling? To take such a denigratory stance would be foolishly to deny ourselves of any discoveries these individuals might make. The promise that their experimentation might yield hitherto unrealized data about mind/body connections of a "breakthrough" sort could be fulfilled at any time. If so, it is entirely possible that such results would mandate revolutionary changes in how we counsel. We must keep our "weather eye" on new theories. For the present, let it be said that if we attend to the experimentalists' work we will have a heightened consciousness of all the minute ways in which emotional behaviors are physiologically manifested. As long as they continue to regard an emotion simply as "a pattern of organic response," a "formula useful in the laboratory,"[9] however, our skepticism about the practicality of their work for counseling will be warranted.

And what of the "subjectivists?" Does their point of view, that emotion ought to be regarded as subjective experience, that "emotion felt" is all that really counts, have a voice and an audience? As we have seen in our review of Carl Rogers's influence, our look at the historical climate for the acceptance of feelings in our society, and our recognition of how bountifully the various therapies have flourished in the past 40 years, there is no doubt that their view is thriving. Since the 1960s a virtual avalanche of popular psychology has slid down around us and it would seem as though the feelings industry is here to stay. Publishers are doing a lively business in self-help books, restoring emotional power to the people, at it were. There is no dearth of readily available popular resources, most of which pay scant regard to any strict definition of feelings (where they are defined at all) that would embrace a point of view or satisfy the criteria "objectivists" use for studying emotions. These subjectivists assume that we all know what feelings are. Typical is David Viscott's book, *The Language of Feelings*, and here is how he sets the stage for the drama to come in his opening paragraph:

> Our feelings are our sixth sense, the sense that interprets, arranges, directs and summarizes the other five. Feelings tell us whether what we experience is threatening, painful, regretful, sad or joyous. Feelings can be described and explained in simple and direct ways. There is nothing mystical or magical about them. Feelings make up a langue all their own. When feelings speak, we are compelled to listen—and sometimes act—even if we do not always understand why. Not to be aware of one's feelings, not to understand them or know how to use or express them is worse then being blind, deaf, or paralyzed. Not to feel is not to be alive. More than anything else feelings make us human. Feelings make us all kindred.[10]

The dichotomy between subjectivity and objectivity is a classical one that pervades many segments of our society. It is reflected in the statement, "Show me. Don't tell me." It is used to draw distinctions between science and art. It creates "camps" in psychology and philosophy. It separates mind and heart, thinkers and feelers, those who do without feeling and those who feel without doing. It is at the core of any argument about determinism versus free will.

The only resolution, the only way out that Solomon sees for himself ("my entire project, . . . after all, was to get clear about 'the passions' for myself, and share my thoughts with my readers"[11]) following his exhaustive study in his book—a Herculean achievement of rational investigation, the study of the entire landscape of the classically dichotomous "problem,"—is to harness his intellect in serving his emotions, to *reflect* on his emotional experiences and use the dictates of his intellect to help modify his emotional behavior. Here's the way he concludes *The Passions*:

> What we must do is to step out and take risks, to "live dangerously" (in Nietzsche's terms). This does not mean crusading off to foreign wars or joining any of the modern varieties of daredevil circuses; it means daring to see through our most treasured defenses and take the chance of vulnerability and intimacy, to become subjective "adventurers," intersubjective

political explorers. No exotic jungles, Quixotic missions, or glamorous foreign wars are required; just ourselves and other people.

There are no recipes for adventure, no guidebooks for exploration. But there is the need for prodding, to force us to take the first step toward such a conception of our lives. This first step is *to give up the Myth of the Passions.* [The italics are Solomon's.] We must give up the self-excusing illusion that we *suffer* our emotions, even while enjoying them, and see them as our own *creative activities.* We must give up that tragic and confused dichotomy between "Reason" and "the passions," as if only insanity and self-destructive obsessions could be "passionate," and as if only the cold-blooded calculations of unconcerned "Reason" could be rational. We must instead develop a conception of *rational passions*, cultivated conscientiously as creative means to self-realization, living our lives as works of art.[12]

As counselors, how do we help our clients to do this? Most essentially, let it be said, we will be fumbly and "botchy" in our efforts if we do not construct a well-considered and workable theory of what emotions are and what is significant about them in counseling. The next chapter contains postulates that taken together form a pragmatic theoretical set, a bedrock upon which effective counseling practice may be constructed.

NOTES

1. Rosenthal, P. (1984). *Words and values: Some leading words and where they lead us.* New York: Oxford University Press, pp. 30–31.
2. Robert Solomon has done so in a fashion eminently useful to counselors in the single area of "love." See: Solomon, R. C. (1981). *Love: emotion, myth, and metaphor.* New York: Doubleday. Romantic love being almost universally desirable in our society, the subject has spawned a long shelf of nonfiction works. If fiction were included, one could stock a large library, indeed.
3. In writing this sentence, the autor is reminded of the counselor trainer he once observed who, in castigating a counselor-student for not attending to a client's feelings in an interview, began pounding on the table with his fist to emphasize his directives and screamed into the student's face, "You've got to be *sensitive*, goddamn it. YOU'VE GOT TO BE *SENSITIVE*!!"
4. Rogers, C. (1980). *A way of being.* Boston: Houghton Mifflin.
5. Rogers, C. (1961). *On becoming a person: A therapist's view of psychotherapy.* Boston: Houghton Mifflin.
6. *Emotions* and *feelings* are used as interchangeable terms in this book, and though *affect* and *passions* tend to connote some differences for most users, they too are generally considered as synonyms; in cases where the latter are not synonymous, any additional meanings will be contextual.

7. Rapaport, D. (1971). *Emotions and memory.* New York: International Universities Press, pp. 271, 236.
8. Solomon, R. C. (1976). *The passions.* New York: Anchor Press/Doubleday. All of the quotations up to this point in the text are from pp. 134–145. Copyright 1976 by Robert C. Solomon. Reprinted by permission.
9. Young, P. T. (1941). Taken from an address to the Midwestern Psychological Association and cited by Solomon, op. cit., p. 134. The full quotation is: "An emotion is useful in the laboratory despite the fact that no one has shown how an emotional pattern can be distinguished from one which is nonemotional. A second definition has affirmed that emotion is a disturbance (disruption, upset) revealed by diffuse, excessive, aimless behavior."
10. Viscott, D. (1976). *The language of feelings.* New York: Pocket Books, p. 9.
11. Solomon, R. C. (1976). Op. cit., p. 131.
12. Ibid, pp. 430–431.

3

Twenty Postulates of an Emotions Theory for Counselors

This world is a comedy to those that think, a tragedy to those that feel.

—Horace Walpole[1]

Ⱥ theory is a set of abstract constructs about reality (what exists and events that occur), and the following set relates to both "emotions felt" and "emotions expressed." Both of these dimensions are viewed from a counseling perspective. A third dimension has to do with the two individuals in the act, the client and the counselor. Constructs pertaining to this third dimension may or may not have relevance in some other intersubjective context.

1. *An emotion is a mentally-caused physiological reaction.* The cause/effect relationship is the vital part of this definition. As we have seen, both subjective and objective views of emotion tend to ignore or minimize the role of thought in the formulation and character of emotion. To see an emotion as "a pattern of organic response," as P.T. Young has defined it in the previous chapter, without any reference to any simultaneous mental activity is to miss any opportunity for altering it. We *think* ourselves into feeling good or ill. External stimuli do not cause us to feel a certain way, to have the physical reactions we do. It is our thoughts, whether preprogrammed or generated for the occasion, that command our physical systems to go into action.

Taken for granted here is the presumption that we can change our thoughts and, therefore, our feelings. If we do not believe that we can change our thoughts, then certainly we are fated to suffer our feelings, and we will see ourselves as unfortunate or as lucky depending on capricious circumstances. Internal/external referencing takes place. If we see our fate as being externally caused, we look for external means to feel better, whether we find it in a bottle or in the positive actions toward us that others determine. We surrender our power by believing we don't possess any.

Can we change our thoughts? If any counselor doubts that we can, he or she is not in the appropriate career. The telling question is not whether we can change our thoughts, but what those thoughts are and how do we change them? It is the mind that is a mystery, not feelings. A counselor may clearly demonstrate to any client that he or she has altered thinking and therefore created feelings in response. The counselor helps that client to search recent subjective history carefully for examples. Hardly any of us go through our days without at least intermittently talking ourselves into feeling differently under some stimulus conditions. Granted that some thoughts at the seat of feelings are excruciatingly hard to change for many reasons, and the changing requires laborious, risky, frequently prolonged, and energy-draining effort. Granted that some causative thoughts are extremely difficult to identify, being suppressed or even repressed, and a counselor's talents are thus challenged beyond their limits. But this doesn't alter the fact that in our feeling states, "thinking has made us so."

2. *There is a mind/body connection.* It is worth citing what English and English have catalogued as a "problem" in their *Dictionary*:

> *Mind-body problem*: the *metaphysical* issue concerning the relation of mind, or that which is *mental*, to the body. The chief theories are: (*a*) INTERACTIONISM: mind influences body, and body mind; (*b*) PARALLELISM: mental processes and bodily processes run strictly parallel courses without influencing each other; (*c*) DOUBLE ASPECT THEORY: mind is body seen from a certain viewpoint, body is mind seen from another; (*d*) TWO (or DOUBLE) LANGUAGE THEORY: mental terms and bodily terms are two different "languages" describing the same phenomena; (*e*) ORGANISMIC RESPONSE THEORY: mental processes are a distinctive kind of response made by an organism in interaction with its environment; (*f*) EPIPHENOMENALISM: mental processes are a by-product of bodily activity and of no causal (or other?) importance; (*g*) MATERIALISM: only body is real; (*h*) IDEALISM: body and bodily processes are manifestations of mind (with many types of suggestion concerning the relation of a particular "mind" to a particular "body").
>
> If it can be granted that there is in any sense at all a distinctive set of phenomena called *mental*, there are empirical correlations to be established between these facts and the facts of physiological functioning. This is the broad area of *physiological psychology*. The mind-body problem seeks to go beyond or behind such correlation to the ultimate relationship. This inquiry is essentially metaphysical and of no greater pertinence to the science of psychology than to the science of physics, except that it uses many of the same terms. But because some of the terms are the same, the metaphysical issues are often unwittingly introduced into the scientific context of psychology. In the view of some philosophers, the whole problem is unreal, the result of starting from false assumptions.[2]

Although these words may serve to confuse some readers, they do point to some important considerations for counselors. First, the issue of what the connection between mind and body is and just how interactions take place is far from settled. One cannot simply go and read up on this issue to obtain any certitude. Second, although many mind/body theories exist, one cannot ignore the problem in counseling. If we posit a connection between mind and body, our difficulty in knowing what that connection is and how the interaction works undoubtedly resides in our relative ignorance about the mind rather than the body.

Probably no greater research frontier in human biology and psychology exists today than that of cognitive functioning, particularly research into how the brain works. Battle reports from this front are frequently reported in the communications media as well as in the professional journals; in the forefront is news about left and right brain hemispheres being in charge of different bodily functions and physical/mental/emotional behaviors.[3] Little of this research has as yet yielded reliable data for counseling practice. This does not imply, however, that counselors can afford to quit thinking about how the mind works. Beginning with a model of how his or her own mind is put together, what its parts are and how they work in harmony (or disharmony), every counselor seeking greater effectiveness must perforce become a perpetual student of what constitutes mental make-up and must operate according to some self-owned theoretical model of the mind, albeit one that is continually revised as information about its nature is partially altered by new discoveries.

Though it is not our task in our consideration of emotions here to describe a model of the mind, we must not underplay its importance. "Cognitive mapping" is vital to counseling; indeed, it is a way of judging the reality of a client's perceptions and thinking. If a client's cognitive map of reality is known to the counselor to differ from what is actually the case, the help a counselor can provide to that client seems more clear-cut. With every client the counselor is a sleuth in search of clues that reveal how a particular mind works. Ultimately it is thoughts and thought processes that must be reordered if change in a client is to come about.

3. *To have some notion of what feelings are in attendance at any given time, a counselor must have an enriched comprehension of all the "vital signs"—all the ways in which our bodies "feel."* Feelings are physical. Many are observable. Most beginners in counseling, socially habituated as they are to attend only to the most overt expressions of feeling in others, tend to note only emotional extremes, such as tears, violent movement, and gross voice changes But as counselors gain an appreciation for the role of feelings, their scope and acuity of observation increases. What clients do with their body parts advertises their feelings: facial expressions, voice changes and modulations of sounds (the full range of speech patterns—word choice, slips, omissions, inflexion, repetitions, gestures, and other vicissitudes), eye movement, limb movement, head movement, posture, hand activity—how the palm lays, what the fingers touch and pick, how they curl—and more: All these telegraph what feelings are present and waiting to be accounted for. In a counseling session, where two people are more or less stationary for long periods, the changes in bodily movement are often furtive and slight, thus demanding that an observer's antennae quiver with sensitivity. A few other

observable physical conditions, such as tears and flesh coloration, can be easily discerned, but most of what a client is feeling is unexpressed visibly.

We need not be experts in physical systems to realize, however, that through the central nervous system a wide expanse of variegated emotional activity may be taking place inside a client. Depending on what is transpiring in the mind, biological processes such as muscle tension, visceral activity, blood pressure, glandular secretions, respiratory functions, hormonal action, digestive system states, temperature changes, and neurological currents all can effect every body part, from a pore to a membrane to a capillary. Within the totality we call the body all may be at rest, in a condition of homeostasis, or it may be activated in a myriad of forms in any given portion of the whole.

How a counselor gets at what is physically happening within a client must often be via inference. Based on some hypothesis a counselor forms, the client can be checked out in any dimension ("Breathing hard?" "Stomach tight?" "Queasy?" "Mouth dry?" "Head throbbing?" "Too hot?" "Feet itchy?"). The client is the authority on self-owned feeling states and can be directed to consider what is going on at the present moment. When to introduce such invitations into the counseling process depends upon what else has transpired in a session and what is currently taking place. There is a artfulness about checking out client feelings (the specific physiological reactions—not the names—anger, sadness, exhilaration, exhaustion, we use for overall descriptions), an art and skill hard to teach but that is developed with experience. The principal emphasis here is that counselors must acquire an awareness of the range of emotional physicality that is possible in every client and must keep this awareness constantly at the ready.

4. *Feelings go on in the body all the time.* The mind/body connection is never suspended, not even in sleep. We can have heart thumping or excessive sweating as a result of a scary dream. Although our equipment may be working in such a fashion as to obscure the overt signs of expressed emotion, this does not negate the ongoing connection. The connection is not in a state of dormancy when emotional signs stronger than neutral—positive or negative signs—are missing. However benign and unnoticeable, feelings are still present. We feel something all the time.

Thus it is a mistake to conceive of humans as being devoid of feelings. Such erroneous thinking usually takes the form of projection. In a stimulus situation where I, or most people I have known, get angry, nervous, afraid, frustrated, or whatever, Wilbert does not. I then accuse Wilbert of having no feelings because I cannot imagine anyone being in the situation without becoming upset, projecting onto Wilbert my own biased view of the matter. Perhaps I see Wilbert as deprived, as being less human than I. But this is a fallacious conclusion. Wilbert, rather than I, is being more human. He is using his mind to ward off such negative emotional behavior. His thinking is healthier than mine. If I want to get rid of my own negative responses, better that I study Wilbert and learn how he does it instead of judging him delusively. What does Wilbert know that I don't? What does he tell himself when faced with the stimulus that makes his response so unlike mine?

The above illustrates an important idea in counseling, one we too frequently neglect. In every single instance of a stimulus condition seemingly guaranteed to cause emotional arousal, from a slip of the tongue to standing before a firing squad, those who think differently in the situation and thus feel differently provide models for us. Nor are these models only gifted and exceptional people somehow living on a higher plane of existence. Most of us know or have met such models, if we stop to inventory the people we know. And fiction provides us with numerous examples; it is even the principal altruistic reason why writers write; their message is usually the gift of showing us, through the characters they create, what they know about how to be different and how to think better in order to be happier. Their insights about human nature are their inspiration.

5. *External stimuli do not cause our feelings. Our feelings are engendered by what we think about the stimulus.* Though this postulate is inherent in those we have already seen, it is necessary to single it out because so many people believe the opposite. (People are tempted to say that they believe it "with all their heart," because the belief itself that feelings are caused by external stimuli bypasses the head.) Counselors can easily identify this erroneous belief in clients by attending closely to what they say. "He made me angry. She hurt me. It caused me to cry. It was their fault that I suffered. I'm always gloomy on cloudy days. I'd feel happier if my daughter, who should live right here in Cleveland now that I'm getting older, visited me more. I'm miserable because she doesn't care about me." These and other such statements regularly come from clients in explanations of their felt tribulations, frustrations, sorrows, and miseries.

Although it is obvious that someone can physically hurt me, can hit me and knock me down, what emotions I have about this are determined by my thoughts about the altercation. If I think I deserved to be hit, I might feel relieved, even grateful. If I think the attacker is being cruel and vindictive and has no justification for assaulting the innocent person that I am, I will cause myself to be angry. The relief or the anger will be expressed in my physical systems by reactions that have no bearing on the real pain throbbing in my jaw from the bruise left by the assailant's fist. If I slash my wrist with a razor, the blood will spurt out, but I may experience feelings of euphoria because I will grow faint, then unconscious, and then be transported to peaceful eternity—done with the travail of useless living. Certainly my body is thus irreparably hurt, but my feelings are flying high.

Although these are extreme examples, they make the point: There are millions of ways I can be hurt by real circumstances—losing my job, my spouse, my children, my best friend, my home, my wealth, my health, my precious youth—but none are responsible for how I feel. These undesirable, unfortuate, difficult-to-take events do not determine the state of my passions. Only I can do that. Only I can upset myself, hurt myself, anger myself, and cause my own depression by what I think about whatever is going on in my life, whether at this very moment or in general. Some people are so good at thinking themselves into misery and torment that they feel bad even when they seemingly have every good thing a human being could possible want.

The counselor's job is to help clients deal with undesirable realities, to upgrade performance, and to employ more result-producing behaviors in any situation. When nothing can be done to change circumstances, then one can learn to accept them and feel all right within them. I am punished enough by being poor; I am deprived of many potential pleasures. But if I make myself *feel* miserable over this too, then I am giving myself agonies I need not have.

6. *When we experience negative emotions, the physical hurt is real; our bodies are in pain.* What is pain? One can make a thorough search of the most detailed and complicated medical references and find no better definition than a synonym: pain is pressure. Some sort of pressure is felt. In this sense, "felt" refers to the recognition of physical dysfunction by the mind. Pain is useful to us primarily because it signals that something has gone amiss in our organic apparatus. If the body is likened to a ship, pain is a notice to the captain on the bridge that malfunctioning is occurring in the engine room or somewhere else aboard the vessel. "Captain? This is Stomach reporting in. We've got nauseating troubles down here." "Captain? Right Ankle, here. I'm definitely sprained after that last leg twist." Our bodies are superlatively designed so that most if not all the parts keep in touch with the bridge through the pain communication

channels. (No doubt, too, "they" expect the skipper to take some positive action to alleviate any apparent crisis.)

The ship analogy is inadequate, though, when we reflect on the fact that in our bodies the "bridge" can *cause* the pain (or pressure—here we go back to that old hydraulic model). Instead of a one-way direct current (DC), our systems are wired for AC, alternating current. The bridge can command that some malfunction occur in the body, can bring about the pressure, without any help from external sources. "NOW HEAR THIS! Start hurting, stomach! NOW HEAR THIS! All pores begin sweating profusely! NOW HEAR THIS! Let there be giant aching throbs behind the forehead!"

The mind/body connection that produces emotional responses is designed to protect and help us and other animals cope more favorably with the exigencies of living in a sometimes hostile environment, or so people think. Becuause the pace of our evolutionary progress has so over-accelerated due to our big brains, Arthur Koestler sees our emotional make-up as an evolutionary "left-over" that hasn't had time to drop away, a warning and power booster system that enables us to engage more expeditiously in "fight or flight" tactics when we are physically endangered.[4] Now the early warning system works against us. When our reputation, for example, not our physical person, is verbally, overtly demeaned and threatened, assaulted by some perceived enemy, our immediate emotional reaction is a "rising of gore;" emergency hormones shoot to the heart giving us greater power for fight or flight—only we cannot flee. To do so in the situation would be far more damaging than being socially reasonable; so we are stuck with our gore at full pressure. We fulminate inwardly, huff and puff, get flushed in the face, and hurt. We are in great pain because the captain on the bridge has issued the order: "OK, ADRENAL GLANDS! Fire all torpedoes, NOW!!!" And they implode within us. Too much of this and we can look forward to early heart failure or death by apoplexy.[5]

The hyperbole here is to steer home the point that emotions are physical, that negative emotions are physiologically painful, even the slightest ones. So when a client says he or she is hurting emotionally, the counselor ought to understand that such hurt is not just metaphorical. It is real. It may be slight, it may be diffused about the physical system and hard to pin down to just one organic locale, but it exists as physical pain. To the extent, also, that positive emotions are felt, the body is pleasured, as we shall discuss below. For the body there are but two such principles, for all practical counseling purposes, as Freud emphasized: pleasure and pain.

7. *All human beings have the same capacity to feel a given way and to feel so to the same degree of intensity.* There are regiments—nay, armies—of those folks who believe that we all feel alike and that anyone who says or thinks otherwise is denying this wished-for certainty, and these contrary-minded individuals would no doubt deny the presence of personal feelings in any given situation as well. This is patently not so. Hardly any of us feel the same at any given time. What *is* gloriously or devastatingly true, depending on editorial outlook, is that we all have the same *capacity* to feel a certain way. It is this capacity that is indicative of the profundity, as well as the celebrated reverence for life, in Albert Schweitzer's oft-quoted remark, "Nothing human is alien to me."

We all have the same capacity to go crazy, to buy guns and become snipers, to eat live nightcrawlers—and to be compassionate, loving, to imitate St. Francis of Assisi—but our capacity does not serve as justification for our actions. For counselors the importance of focusing on capacity has to do with the idea that changed feelings in any instance are not only possible but have been accomplished by millions. If you can control your emotions, then so can I. If you are capable of expunging anger from your repertoire of emotional reactions, there is in your success a method I can learn. If you can let yourself go and be wildly exuberant, that means there is more than mere hope for me. As long as I have been neither lobotomized nor drugged into mental oblivion (there *are* circumstantial factors that can diminish capacity), I can call upon my inner resources. I may choose not to behave in the emotional ways that you do in a particular setting, but I am limiting my range of options when I deny that I have the same equipment and can operate in the same way as you operate yours.

8. *Feelings are shadows cast by thoughts. Expressed feelings are detectable, whereas many thoughts are not. Feelings are barometers of thinking.* The same may be said of physical behaviors that appear to be devoid of any emotional component—they mirror thoughts. Most physical behaviors do evince accompanying emotion, and this emotion is, as we know, in itself physical. Thus, an interested observer will be able to judge how we feel by scrutinizing how we close a door or walk across a room. Children, without any intellectual speculation, readily ascertain how adults feel, when they mean what they say, whether a parent's mood is one of frustration, sadness, grief, or high spirits. Along with everything else, children learn to read feelings, even those that adults suppose they have squirreled away from sight. When children become adolescents (Kurt Vonnegut: "adolescence, which is children's menopause"[6]), the

source of their evidence for adult phoniness is the difference between what adults generally utter and how they act.

Feelings tell on us. They spill the beans. They say such things as:

- Carol's lying. Look at her eyes. See? She looks away. Now she's picking at her hair.
- Carl says he's pleased with the contract. But what he means is that he's resigned. Come on. Follow him out to his car and watch him bang the hood.
- Jane's smiling for show. Look at her red neck and how the tendons are bulging and you will have some idea of how frustrating it is for her to go along with this development.
- Suzi is disappointed that the gang isn't going to the restaurant of her choice. A minute ago she was lively, gay, bubbly with talk. Now look at her. She's got a long face and nothing to say. If that's not a pout what is?
- Jimmy, the kid with a hippo's appetite, hasn't taken five bites since he heard he couldn't go out until his homework was done. He just plays with his food. Look—tic-tac-toe in his mashed potatoes.

Most of us understand the language of feelings, particularly the sentences others act out for us to read. It is often harder to read our own feelings, and we end up communicating on two levels. This is partly the result of not being certain of our own thoughts. There are scads of things we haven't ruminated through to a resolution; in all kinds of areas we are bundled with conflicts, saddled with ambivalence. It is particularly in these areas that a counselor can help a client, noting the discrepancies between what the client claims and what the observable feelings reveal is going on in the client's mind. As Solomon reminds us in the previous chapter, "an 'objective' observer is often in a far better position to characterize and identify patterns in my expressive behavior than I may be myself."

As counselors we seek to become experts at reading expressed emotions to get at thoughts, some of which are buried deeply and hidden from clients themselves. We constantly check for congruence between what is verbalized and what is expressed emotionally. We are gauging, too, the importance of ideas, values, attachments, desires, prophesies, motives, plans, concerns, and a hundred other things in a client's life that will register on the barometer of feelings. Each of us, it can be said, has a feel-o-meter, and the effective counselor will become its skilled meter reader. There are times in counseling when we may choose to comfort a client, to be reassuring, to be responsive to feelings that make some demand upon us, but these times are fairly easy to heed: The emotion expressed is flagrant. What is more difficult is the consistent monitoring of the progression of a client's feelings throughout every counseling session.

9. *People are programmed to feel in certain ways in response to common stimuli.* There are some stimuli that seem to cause automatic emotional responses in us, as though we had no ability to intervene with our minds and thereby alter the response. The stimulus/response process seems to happen so instantaneously that no time for mitigating thought is left. Danger signals are like this. We drive on the crowded freeway and catch sight of a wild driver in a careening car out of the corner of our eyes, and our hearts immediately thump furiously. Or we hear a loud siren with a similar result. Can we stop the adrenalin flow before it enters our bloodstream? The answer, of course, is yes, but we probably have no good reason to do so. Such a response is a classically conditioned one in the old Pavlovian sense, developed and crystallized in childhood when we were repeatedly taught what signals meant mortal danger. We have millions, perhaps trillions, of such predictable responses programmed within us, some for pleasure where in equivalent terms we salivate to bell-ringing just like Pavlov's dogs, and some for fear: The bell signals us to get ready to avoid pain. To recondition ourselves to have different emotions in response to a given stimulus would take more time and effort than we are willing to invest in most cases, but that does not obviate our capacity to do so. There are some things we do want to alter after reaching adulthood, and although it seemingly takes forever to accomplish this, we *can* do so. The celebrated cases of brainwashing, admittedly under dire circumstances, are instances of such reconditioning.

Then, too, when we are young and impressionable we are ignorant of what is true and are prone to accept magic and the presence of ghosts and spirits who flit about, change shapes, determine events, influence terrible happenings. "Step on a crack, break your back." We are even coached in this through children's literature. Stories become real. (Today it is the television story.) We are easily frightened by much we don't understand, the possible presence of angels and devils, the power of Santa Claus, death, sickness, violence. We have registered much in our impressionable minds, and although we displace our early beliefs in occult powers with more reasonable, reality-oriented thinking in adulthood as these early beliefs fade and slip into our subconscious, they do not completely disappear. What has entered our heads stays there, however altered or covered up. How else is it that even exceptionally reasonable women and men can watch a horror movie like "The Exorcist," for example, and feel the hair on their neck bristle? One can claim in Jungian terms that this represents race-consciousness, mythic beliefs carried in our genes, the knowledge of some previous living our ancestors have undergone. But a simpler, more meaningful explanation lies in the development of our young minds as infants and children when we were fragile, impotent, and afraid of all we were exposed to in the "big people's" world. As kids we will believe nearly anything, and most of us have. We all have our buried lives, the traces of which we mostly hide and ignore, but for certain purposes at certain times we enjoy tapping into them, scaring ourselves vicariously, safely, perhaps the better to realize and enjoy our present good fortunes, perhaps to remind ourselves of the ultimate mysteries waiting for us beyond the river Styx.

If humans are anything, they are adaptable creatures. Put them in almost any environment and they will display amazing degrees of adaptability. They are gregarious, communal by nature, and will adapt quickly to the mores and acceptable behaviors of the groups they inhabit. In this sense we are all carriers of what beliefs, values, and customs we have assimiliated in the groups we have lived in and continue to occupy, not only the small circles of kith and kin, but an expanding set of groups from neighborhood to town and city to state to nation to, finally, our ethnic heritage and the entire human race. We have "group minds;" it can be said, at least, that large portions of the mental stock we carry are not the result of our own logical inductive and deductive reasoning, but the prevalent ideas and behavioral patterns we have sucked up, as if by osmosis. And we can be emotionally set off by the same stimuli that set off our kin and companions and the members of our wider circles; it is what we have learned to do by imitation and conditioning.

We can more easily undo or change a conditioned response if we change groups, if we subsist in a new social environment where such a response is not tolerated, than we can by remaining in the same old social context where changing ourselves means "going against the grain." This is what we mean when we say, "Travel is broadening." Most goals designated in counseling ask clients to go against the grain. In situations where everyone else thinks, acts, and feels one way in consort, clients must now be different. This is one of the most difficult things a counselor can ask of any client unsuited by practice to be different, especially when there is no acceptable way for the client to change the environmental status quo or to leave it.

Here it seems kindly to remind ourselves of some of the teachings of Henry David Thoreau:

Beware of all enterprises that require new clothes ... Wherever a man goes, men will pursue him and paw him with their dirty institutions, and, if they can, constrain him to belong to their desperate odd-fellow society ... The mass of men lead lives of quiet desperation ... If a man does not keep pace with his companions, perhaps it is because he hears a different drummer. Let him step to the music which he hears, however measured or far away ... Any man more right than his neighbors, constitutes a majority of one.[7]

10. *Feelings are intensified by thoughts*. Our emotional apparatus is jolted into operation by a stimulus, one we have been conditioned to fear. We are walking in the woods, let's say, and we have even given some precognition (thought on some mental level) to the fact that random dangers lurk in this environment. We have alerted ourselves. Now we hear the close-by sound of what we perceive to be a rattle. We halt, dead in our tracks, our senses glued to the underbrush from whence the sound is coming, our hearts instantly pounding, our muscles tensed. In a thrice a chipmunk jumps out of the brush and skitters across our path. We are now satisfied there is no rattlesnake and mosey on our way. The chipmunk caused the sound. If we are convinced, our emotional alarm system will subside to normal in a few seconds—10, 15, 30—taking time to run down. Nothing we subsequently think, even though the perceived danger has passed, will shorten the process. Our system must run its course.

There are those individuals whose emotional equipment would not be triggered by the sounds of a real rattler—U.S. forest rangers, perhaps, or naturalists, those who are at home in the bush, who wear the proper clothing, who know all about the habits of rattlesnakes and have no fear of them, those for whom the sound of a rattle is not an alarm stimulus but merely a call for caution. They have reconditioned themselves to be unaffected. Then there are those whose emotional systems do not return to homeostasis in typical fashion. As they continue to walk (or run wildly) through the forest, they stay frightened and may even put themselves into a state of panic by dwelling on rattlesnakes, aggravating their own emotional systems further by what they tell themselves and picture in their imaginations.

All of us go through this scenario in much the same way, consistent in response to some stimuli, fearless in the face of others, or fearful to still others, our emotional reactions determined by our prethinking and use of our minds when confronted by the stimulus. Some people are said to be phobic—claustrophobic, agoraphobic, hematophobic, coprophobic (psychiatric manuals list over 180 specific phobias; one can even be phobophobic, have a fear of fearing). A phobia is a *morbid* fear, one so ingrained that its owner goes from normal functioning to a state of panic almost at the mention of the feared stimulus. Phobias are specific fears that usually have been nurtured over a long period of time with incessant devotion, deeply entrenched fears that have a good rate of cure through psychotherapeutic desensitization treatments.

But phobias are introduced here only to exemplify and emphasize the general nature of emotional responses. We are capable of diminishing or exacerbating our emotional states. Once set off by a stimulus, how we think determines how we will respond. We all have the potential to be "possessed" by our own physiological reactions, our bodies seemingly dictating to our minds, the former being in control rather than the mental processes of will and reason. Koestler calls this "the second enemy of freedom" (the first is habit, which robotizes us).

> The second enemy of freedom is passion, or more specifically, the self-assertive, hunger-rage-fear-rape class of emotions. When they are aroused, the control of decisions is taken over by those primitive levels of the hierarchy which the Victorians called "the Beast in us," and which are in fact correlated to phylogenetically older structures in the nervous system. The loss of freedom resulting from this downward shift of controls is reflected in the legal concept of "diminished responsibility," and in the subjective feeling of acting under a compulsion: "I couldn't help it ...," "I lost my head," "I must have been out of my mind." ... Facing ... towards that unattainable core from which my decisions seem to emanate, I feel free. Facing the other way, there is the robot—or the beast.[8]

The intensity of emotional response can be likened to the arc of a pendulum. The thoughts already in the mind that are connected with a potential stimulus cause the emotional pendulum to swing into play at the point of stimulus encounter. The pendulum instantly oscillates through its customary arc. If no further mental excitation occurs, or if countering thoughts work at reduction, the pendulum reverts to its stationary state in its natural temporal interval. But if there is continuing additional mental provocation, the arc widens—possibly reaching its limits.

Here we must accent, too, that *any* stimulus can activate the emotional response in the direction of anticipated pleasure (we can become uncontrollably giggly, for example) or pain. And the stimuli can be mental, internal as well as external, or simply symbolic, invoked by the names of things rather than the things themselves. We are all programmed to react to those facets of life over which there is reason to feel strongly:

love, death, mother, money, sex, work, ostracism—whatever. The effective counselor is aware of all this and studies every client to learn which stimuli are arousers and how each client's pendulum swings once set in motion.

11. *When feelings are out of control, counseling cannot proceed.* As we have discussed in chapter 1, our emotional behavior can range from panic to mastery, and counselors are in the business of helping clients to upgrade their mental, emotional, and physical behavior in any given dimension away from panic and toward mastery. But a counselor's only time to be positively influential is during the counseling session, and the feeling state of the client at that time can adversely define the degree of counseling productivity. Therefore it is essential that the counselor become skilled at knowing how a client's emotions work.

In studying crying behavior, for instance, we will see and discern that there are specific topics, certain areas relevant to counseling focus, that cannot be broached without a client's tears flowing. For a client to bring these endemic ideas into consciousness is to cry. The very thoughts are hurtful. Crying *must* go on, if these areas are to be dealt with. The effective counselor, rather than helping the client to "shut down the waterworks," will simply reflect the reality of what is happening. "Whenever you think about your son, Wally, ending up in jail, the tears come. You can't talk about it without crying." Similarly with anger or fear. Certain foci in clients have their accompanying emotional baggage, and a client cannot make the trip through the material without the baggage going along for the ride. To ask a client to disengage from feelings is to expect the impossible. Disembodiment—emotionally detached consideration of any meaningful counseling activity—is out of the question.

In some clients, at times, anger turns into fury, crying into hysteria, fear into what is almost catatonic immobilization, and emotional panic behavior becomes starkly evident to the counselor. Under these conditions the client's mind has "taken a hike." No amount of calm reasoning will dent the client's rational faculties, and it is time to administer a different kind of help—at least until the emotional clouds dissipate. When is the client "at panic?" Counselors must learn about each client; general guidelines are seldom applicable to all cases. The observant counselor will learn the signs of excessive emotional build-up as a result of client study. Clients teach us "how they are."

Are there clients who are, as a result of or a condition of their mental and emotional make-up, incapable of benefiting from counseling? Again, just as effective counselors choose to have a theoretical model of how the mind works, so too do they choose a theoretical model of what constitutes madness in all forms and degrees. (In their excellent book, *Models of Madness, Models of Medicine*, Siegler and Osmond delineate eight different models and urge their readers to think through what they call "the model muddle."[9])

If madness means the distoriton of reality and being out of control, a counselor must decide whether either condition is intermittently present only under certain stimulus conditions or is a pervasive, ongoing, central fact of the client's existence. A counselor might be theoretically convinced, perhaps through reading such accounts as Thomas Szasz's *The Myth of Mental Illness*[10], that the psychopathic, the paranoiac, or the schizophrenic personality is a fictive designation, an erroneous labeling that serves only the labelers, but this doesn't absolve the counselor from being an irresponsible practitioner.[11] Competence becomes the criterion for ethics in this context. If a counselor encounters emotional behavior in a client that cannot be accounted for nor be professionally ministered to as a result of the counselor's training and experience, then it is time for the counselor to confer with more knowledgeable mental health specialists and to consider referring the client for expert help. One can philosophize and speculate at one's leisure on how society determines who is crazy and who is not, but not at the expense of a disturbed client.

12. *Sensations and emotions are different.* We have five marvelous senses, we say, and backing them up are elaborate physical systems of interlocking parts for gathering information about reality. This remarkable equipment seemingly works in perfect harmony, interconnected and mutually responsive to the material world outside us, serving our well-being. The senses can all come into play simultaneously, signaling to our brains whatever sight, taste, smell, feel, or sound is perceived, as when we make a loud bite into a crisp juicy apple. We generally experience the senses' operation as effortless and pleasurable. It *feels* good when they do their work.

Of course we make judgments about the nature of the world and find some things in it to be obnoxious or even toxic, and we train our senses to recoil at "bad" smells or tastes or sounds. A loud noise "hurts" our ears. A pinprick hurts. We sense pleasure and pain. We are sensate creatures, almost reflexively responsive to pleasurable and painful experiences. Many of us are slaves to our senses, hedonistically indulging them for the pleasure they provide.

But the nature and the power of our minds is such that we can forego sensual pleasures, even pervert them, teaching our minds to respond favorably to what they at first recoiled against, drinking beer, smoking, walking on high heels, wearing tight clothes, to name a few milder forms of "sense education." Our minds can determine what is pleasure and what is pain. In spite of our senses, we drive ourselves when our bodies scream out for us to quit. Here, as in most aspects of living, the mind is king. It chooses. We can be celibate or promiscuous, skinny or obese, muscular or flabby. We have the ability to cater to or deny our senses in too many ways to categorize.

When we discuss emotions, a perennial difficulty lies in the fact that these physiological reactions seem to be the same as what we experience as sensations in so many cases. Particularly is this so in the case of physical *feelings*. We can *feel* with our bodies; that is to say, we take in data about the world through our sense of touch. It *feels* good to stroke soft fur or to be lightly massaged. The same is true internally: The first effects of alcohol are pleasurable physical feelings. We talk of being good to ourselves by satisfying our bodies. A great meal, a warm bath, a soft bed, and a quiet slumber do wonders for restoring our physical systems to equilibrium after a hard day.

The chief difference between emotional feelings and sensations lies in causation. Emotions are internally caused, brought into being by mental activity, whereas sensations are externally caused, brought about by external agents. Few people find the need to make this distinction and so are confused about how to go to work at making themselves happy. Counselors, however, cannot afford to share in this confusion and still be of service to clients.

13. *Substances give us sensations that can be mistaken for emotion.* If we confuse sensations with emotions, we are candidates for substance dependency. It is a natural confusion, given the effects of various drugs upon our physical systems. The highs we get from a drug *seem* just like the emotional highs we have previously experienced without them.

We are particularly susceptible to reliance on substances if we already *believe* that our emotional behavior is caused by others, by life in general, simply because that is the way we think. If we are predominantly externally-oriented, absolving ourselves from responsibility by believing that we do not cause our own bad feelings, we will seek external remedies.[12]

14. *Most of us prize our feelings highly and gauge the worth of our living by how we feel.* With perfect accuracy we can say that *we live in our feelings*, that our passions count the most. But with equal accuracy we can also say that *we live in our bodies*, thay they count the most, for when the body doesn't function properly it controls the rest of us. And it is not any distortion of the truth to say *we live in our heads*, that the state of our consciousness is what counts most. If we habitually prize one state over the others, it seems we can choose that state and make

it true for ourselves that there is where we are most alive. Indeed, one can categorize the people one knows as predominantly "head" persons, "feeling" persons, or "body" persons. Most people emphasize one of these three life areas and concentrate the majority of their efforts in one area to the neglect of the others in their pursuit of happiness.

It is certainly possible to achieve a sense of balance, to shift emphasis continually and expend time and energy in keeping all three areas at a high level of satisfaction. We are, indeed, enjoined to do so all the time by purveyors of products and systems to keep ourselves in good mental, emotional, and physical health. There is no dearth of entrepreneurs who are specialists in each category, vying for our attention, hawking their wares, and promising us short cuts to the moon.

Every counselor, whether consciously or indirectly, learns after a time where a particular client can be located in these three dimensions, if it is necessary to make a forced choice, and most clients would be able to assign a priority to these three areas also. How important is it to do so? When one considers the pervasiveness of appeals to feelings in our culture, it would seem that a counselor does a client a disservice not to gauge in what corner of this triangle a client spends the most time.

Few clients are culture-resistant. It is not enough to decry the times and atmosphere we live in, for we must continue to live there. The task to educate a client to become a more selective consumer of cultural offerings is enormous. We are trained to *want*. We are trained to want recognition, even fame. We are trained to be vicarious, to live through others, to be spectators who resonate to the tunes others play. We are trained to seek after false big and little ends that promise good feelings. We are, indeed, conditioned and trained how to feel about practically everything in our lives. Knowing how this is so becomes a professional task for every counselor; he or she must of necessity become a culture analyst, seeing how the culture has shaped and continues to influence how a client feels.

Strangely enough, *wanting* is in and of itself a feeling state. We have desires and experience a feeling of deprivation when they are unfulfilled. The more we concentrate on our wants, the greater our present dissatisfaction. We certainly don't think it unreasonable to want, nor to think that what we want the most is to feel good. The irony is that the more we focus on our feelings the less likely we are to arrive where we would like to be. Ought we to suppress our wants, accept whatever is our lot, in order to find contentment? Then what of drive, ambition, self-improvement? As Robert Browning said a century ago, "A man's reach should exceed his grasp, or what's a heaven for?"

The apparent paradox dissolves when we apply what we know about feelings: We cause them to be whatever they are by our own thinking. In this sense it is false to say we live in our passions. Rather, we have them, like it or not, as a result of how we think. It is our thinking that must change in any single instance if we are to feel better.

15. *We choose to give ourselves particular feelings because there are immediate payoffs in so doing.* It matters not that in most instances people are mechanistically experiencing specific feelings in response to stimuli, automatons externally set in motion. If we hold that humans are stimulus-response organisms only, we shall find plenty of data to confirm this general hypothesis. If, however, we hypothesize that in each case a person has chosen to feel a particular way because of the gains so accrued and we seek out supporting data, then we will have different findings. The question becomes: "If I can think different thoughts and not feel all this anger (or guilt or sorrow or frustration or fear), why don't I? Why do I think the thoughts that always 'work me up' (or 'bring me down') so much?" The answer to the question in each instance lies in the rewards of the emotion, in how even our most negatively-perceived feeling states serve us in numerous ways.

In most cases clients don't know what their payoffs are for making themselves feel negatively, but in many cases they do. The counselor who listens well will hear clients claim:

- If I didn't worry about it, I wouldn't prepare for it.
- If I weren't angry, I'd never tell her what I think.
- If I didn't feel guilty, I would never go and visit my mother.
- If I weren't anxious, I wouldn't pay any attention to what is going on.
- My husband would think that I didn't love him if I didn't get upset over his whereabouts.
- If I had no fear, I'd be certain to do something stupid and get myself killed.

Emotions are used to justify, excuse, or promote behavior. They give us a personal or social license for conduct.

Then, too, they are defenses. We can thank Freud for making us aware of our defense mechanisms, the thousands of constellations of thought/ emotional response sets we develop as we grow. That many of these aren't necessary doesn't change the fact that we have acquired them and are constantly ruled by them. Besides, most of them *work*. They defend us against every conceivable threat. When the threatening stimulus condition is present, unless we have learned how to think and act differently and more advantageously, we require our defenses.

What we know in our hearts and our heads, if we search deeply enough, is that we choose to have negative feelings because the pain of experiencing them is easier to bear than the pain of working hard (which always means thinking hard) to do whatever it takes to be different. Strong feelings allow us to get out of doing, to avoid concentration, study, problem-solving, memorizing, reasoning, planning, and *acting* on the results of what our minds come up with. We simply take the easy way out—every chance we get. Nor do we acknowledge that this is what we are doing. We even protect ourselves from knowing (self-deception itself is a kind of defense mechanism), for to acknowledge on any level that we are the fools and victims of our own doing is too devastating. This factor is present in most resistance to counseling. It contains a special brand of internal logic: To think differently now means that I have to admit to being a no-goodnik all my life, to having thought and done all the wrong things for the wrong reasons, to admit my life has been a waste. We can lock people up in prisons for years (and we do so), yet they won't come around to admitting to themselves that they have been the cause of their own fates.[13]

It is no easy matter for a counselor to help a client to develop insight into what he or she gets out of choosing a certain expression of emotion, or the inward appreciation of it, the "emotion felt." It is, however, as has been discussed in chapter 1, a crucial step in the counseling process. Until clients realize that they can "get themselves up," the way athletes do for a rugged game or the way actors do for a difficult role or scene, that in fact they *do* get themselves up or down, clients will continue to misdirect their efforts to feel better. To acquire an understanding of *how* they have gone about thinking themselves into feeling states for the sake of the consequences these yield is a necessary step in counseling, one arrived at through recognition of emotional payoffs.[14]

16. *Others seek to contol and manipulate us through our feelings.* If we are "feeling" types, we are easily controlled. And to a greater or lesser extent, all of us are. Not only do we permit ouselves to be manipulated, we know how to manipulate others, to lay guilt trips on people, to get them angry (and thus avoid any reasonable discussion of a matter at hand), to appeal their greed, to embarrass them, to threaten their self-esteem. In our own ways we are both masters at playing on the feelings of others (at least those significant others whose Achilles' heels we know so well) and vulnerable to getting our feelings hurt. Most of the neurotic interaction in troubled marriages, the "games people play," turns on

mutual manipulation of feelings. (This is the straw that broke the camel's back and sent one woman to counseling: A chemist introduced his wife to a colleague at a professional conference, and then added, "Did you know that Joan is a chemist, too? She turns money into manure.")

Cultural mores and morals dictate that how-to books ought not to advertise too blatantly that they contain sure-fire methods for "doing in" your fellow-travelers-through-life by manipulating them, but increasingly that is the sum and substance of the message. The best-seller in this category prior to World War II, Dale Carnegie's *How to Win Friends and Influence People*, set the stereotypical pattern and style 50 years ago and has done a sprightly business ever since.

To an extent that does not seem to have changed much since David Reisman and his associates wrote *The Lonely Crowd*,[15] we live in an other-directed society and have learned to be other-directed ourselves. The first trick for counselors is to examine their own behaviors in this context. To what ends are we, as counselors, manipulated by our clients' playing on our feelings? If we are so affected (a part of what is called "counter-transference" in psychoanalytic health literature), we become not only insensitive to the very areas in which clients can most use our help, but we surrender objectivity and allow our clients to render us less useful to them. Although on the one hand we must "be with" our clients in what they are feeling, the better to understand them fully, to know what they are going through and how they function, on the other hand we must keep our feelings separate so that our "otherness" continues to be of value. Some counselors, not appreciative of the durability and resilience of human emotionality, treat their clients as though they were brittle and would break at the first nudge, as though they were eggs carried on the blade of the counselor's tableknife, subject to being splattered like Humpty-Dumpty at the first bump. Clearly such a posture on the counselor's part sends the message any client least wants to receive: "You're inadequate. You can't handle yourself. Not even in this safe, cozy environment."

17. *Reflection is necessary to get at what we were feeling and how the feeling came to be.* Reflecting on experience is the toilsome, often painful, and certainly time-consuming task that most human beings avoid. It is less difficult when we can have a willing, intelligent, and capable assistant, which is what counselors strive to be. Using our minds to replay what we have lived through, yoking all the specifics into consciousness, then analyzing them to first of all assure ourselves that we have omitted nothing, then to see how they were generated and interconnected to the external reality, to see what led up to the experience, what the

experience was, and what was racing through our minds at the time; all of this is never a task to be taken frivolously. Nor do most of us indulge in such reflection very often. We tend to roll merrily along until we run into snags and experience some dissatisfaction.

The dissatisfaction can and does build in us, particularly when we commit the same acts over and over with the same undesirable results, frequently to the point of deep depression. Such depression (or anger or guilt or fear) sits in us, a ballooning lump, perhaps maturing into an ulcer or a phobia or a drinking problem or some other phenomenon, heading us toward calamity in our unexamined living. The depression or anxiety grows, beckoning more attention to itself, in spite of our efforts to ignore it and to avoid dealing with it. Life goes on. We need our minds to live in our present moments and are loath to use them to sort out whatever might be amiss, perhaps telling ourselves there is nothing we can do about our make-up and our lot anyway. We prove this to ourselves in self-convincing ways, maybe by echoing what an outdoors sports figure has said: "It's impossible to feel depressed when you're canoeing down the white water rapids. You don't have time for it."

Bertrand Russell, perhaps apocryphally, relates this anecdote in his autobiography. In his early teens he would bother his grandmother with philosophical questions, and she would say, "What is mind? It doesn't matter. What is matter? Never mind."[16] It was a joke between them that serves to differentiate between thinkers and nonthinkers, those who seek to know and those who see little value in such knowing.

In the conduct of our lives we have no greater tool than reason if we are to be in charge of our destinies, to exercise personal control. "It stands to reason," we say. If it cannot stand up to our accurate perception and logical treatment, whatever *it* is, we surrender our freedom. This is particularly true when *it* is not just a personal "can of worms," but a sinkhole of newts, salamanders, and eels, a dark personal well of slimy, slithery, ungraspable confusions we would most like to let alone.

There is no other durable course to take through life but to reflect upon our emotional experiences and make something new out of our reflections that we can apply to further living. As Robert Solomon concluded as a result of his consummate investigation of the possibilities, this " ... means daring to see through our most treasured defenses and take the chance of vulnerability and intimacy, to become subjective 'adventurers,' intersubjective political explorers [with] just ourselves and other people."[17] In order to do this, to regenerate ourselves creatively, we "must draw back to leap," in Arthur Koestler's words.[18]

In *The Ghost in the Machine* (the metaphor symbolizes the intangible emotional component in human nature, a specter that dissolves under daylight or laboratory-light scrutiny, yet seems to account for our frequent slipping over the edge into madness, a metaphor encompassing such nebulous entities as the "id" and the "unconscious"), Koestler has told his own story of exhaustive investigation into how mind and body are inextricably interdependent. Koestler's is a pansophic mind. Not only is he able to state a principle or a theorem in a number of ways, but he is able to relate, apply, or connect it to far-reaching, seemingly self-contained, unrelated systems, disciplines, or phenomena. He explains art, science, evolution, history in "draw back to leap" ways, but his text becomes most fascinating when he discusses how living organisms of every variety draw back when they are confronted with new environmental stimuli for which no familiar response exists. He sees the psychotherapeutic encounter in particular as a process wherein a client whose train has "gone off the track" is taken back in time to that point where it was diverted from its run.

It is no doubt too simplistic to think of ourselves as being just *one* train, to regard ourselves in all-or-nothing terms, however luring the simplicity might be. Rather we are railroad magnates with many, many trains, but in each case the process of getting the cars back on track is the same. Where the wheels jumped the rails or veered us off on a spur is where we must go to look for our new learnings.

When we speak of analyzing experience to acquire new learnings and reshape emotional reactions, we must realize that counseling "how-to's" will vary from client to client depending on the mental and emotional capacity of each to absorb our ministrations. Some clients will work hard to learn quickly. Others will not. Some will respond to "Band-Aid" measures, to emotion management through techniques that do not get at the source but temporarily alleviate immobilizing emotional trauma. Prescribed drugs, hypnosis, transcendental meditation regimens, relaxation exercises, controlling feeling states by biofeedback machine indicators—all fall into this crutch category. Often there is no incentive on the part of clients to work at what amounts to a recreation of their own characteristic ways of feeling in response to the various stimuli with which they customarily contend. They want relief, and if their gratification is not immediate they will seek it elsewhere. In these cases a counselor must make difficult service-delivery choices, but he or she ought to know the difference when a symptom rather than the cause is being treated.

18. *A counselor without a coherent theory of what emotional behavior is, how it comes about, and how it can be modified will function*

at a lower level of competence than one who has assimilated such a theory and acts in congruence with it. Readers will perhaps agree that there is not enough study of human emotions in counselor training, and that generally both trainers and practitioners tend to plant themselves in one camp or the other: Either they are behaviorists seeing emotions as response mechanisms governed by external stimuli, or they count themselves as humanists who acclaim "emotions felt." The apparent dichotomy, as we have discussed in the last chapter, emotions considered and treated as objective phenomena versus emotions perceived and treated as subjective phenomena, the "Psychologist's Puzzle," as Solomon calls it, continues to confound mental health workers. There is no lack of interest in what most would agree is a salient problem with major implications for mental health practice. "The Rogers-Skinner debate of 1956 is one of the most reprinted writings in the psychological world," says Carl Rogers.[19] In this classical confrontation between a behaviorist and a humanist, the issues are clearly outlined and the far-reaching personal, scientific, social, and political consequences are addressed.

As we have seen, the matter of human emotionality is not well served by either of these two philosophical stances, for both ordinarily accept people by nature to be one way or the other; the specifics of our emotions are taken for granted and, for all practical purposes, left out. The *ways* in which we cause ourselves to feel, *how* we have come to feel the way we do, *what* it is that we commonly generate strong feelings about, and the *payoffs* we get from the emotional states we impose upon ourselves, our emotional life considered at every turn from all sides, is far too important a part of existence for counselors to regard cavalierly or to make fuzzy assumptions about and then operate as though they knew what they were doing. Emotions, along with mind and body, form the triumvirate of our aliveness in this world.

Without a logically and empirically consistent set of interrelated postulates, such as the aforegoing, a set that can be articulated first to the self, then to any client, and then to any critic, a practitioner would be hard-pressed to provide a rationale for any number of counseling interventions. What *to do* in counseling depends upon an understanding of purposes that are consistent with a view of what is possible, a view of human reality. In this sense any counselor action is a proven one that works or one chosen for try-out, a hypothesis for testing based on sound principles.

The propositions presented so far in this chapter may not be accepted by any reader as they have been formulated. Indeed, the reader's experience might dictate many alterations. Every concerned and astute person will find a great deal to agree with and a great deal to quarrel with, but, it is hoped, shall ignore none of these theorems.

19. *An early step in helping clients to become better managers of their own feelings is teaching them a coherent theory of emotional behavior using their own language and experiential data.* Most clients (there is a temptation to say all clients) come into the counseling experience without a good understanding of how their own emotions are self-generated or self-controlled. If counselors explore this issue with clients, they are sure to find a skeletal theory in the mind of each individual they serve. The assumptions that people carry about feelings in general and about each emotion in particular are often astounding in their divergence from reality. Since these beliefs govern how people feel, for a counselor not to unearth distortions and outright error in client thought is to proceed with counseling along lines that frequently lead to an array of cul-de-sacs that may even be detrimental to a client's life.

There is not always time in a counseling arrangement to help clients to clarify their thinking about such a large subject, to rethink and replace fallacious thought with a more valid formulation; thus counselors must make agonizing choices about where to concentrate their efforts. Nor can counselors simply proceed didactically, presenting their view of the matter without taking a client's habitual ways of mental functioning into account. Learning styles are seemingly as original as is each individual in make-up, history, and life-context. What a client already knows and believes cannot be overlaid with new ideas that will "take." A "transplant" or a plastic wrapper won't work. Every client's thought system has its characteristics and is governed by "go" or "no-go" operational procedures that allow for the accumulation of new experiences, new mental, emotional, and physical behaviors, and effective counselors work at figuring out what these are. We try to get "inside" our clients' heads, learning to think as they do, so that our helpful ideas will take. Our clients teach us how to teach them, and if we are poor learners our effectiveness will be minimal.

Especially must we be attentive to client communication processes, to the structure and fertility of languages, both verbal and nonverbal, our clients use. Metaphorical thought is a chief way in which we all encapsulate the universe of particulars in our lives, and how clients "fictionalize" their worlds in order to grasp and make sense of them is a vital part of the diagnostic process in counseling. This is the essential thrust of neurolinguistic programming, a latter-day development in our field making use of the analyses and discoveries of semanticists and psycholinguists that effective practitioners have always attended to on some level, albeit, perhaps, without the same degree of sophistication.

In the realm of emotions, what the effective counselor seeks to establish with any client is some commonality of agreement and outlook, a basis for congruency, so that counselor and client are not working at cross-purposes.

20. *The feelings manifested by the counselor are picked up by the client and influence the course of what transpires in the interview.* To say that clients will read how we feel when we counsel is undoubtedly to state the obvious, but it is impossible to undervalue the importance of this. All the prized words we brute about so extensively in our literature that refer to how we ought to *be* with clients—sincere, respectful, real, positively regarding, genuine, trustful, congruent, empathic, authentic—are largely descriptors of this phenomenon in counseling. Clients do not know whether or not our actions in our personal lives are consistent with what we profess, but they can readily ascertain inconsistencies between what we say and the emotional expressions we manifest in their presence.

We "give ourselves away." Our feelings tell on us if we try to put on an act. The interaction then becomes complicated, for their "proper social schooling" frequently dictates to clients that they ought not to reveal what they are thinking about this. (Out of earshot, though, they will tell their confidants.) Counselors who don't "pick up" on what the client is picking up about them, unless they specifically structure each session to get this kind of feedback, miss out on perhaps the single most important element for aiding their own professional development. Becoming the consummate counselor, in the final analysis, is dependent upon how "cybernetic" a professional is, how well the feedback learnings are absorbed.

In a valedictory statement here, after all this focusing on emotions, let it be said that we will do well to remind ourselves constantly of the preeminence of *mind* in our lives, of our intellects, our consciousness, our awareness, our capacity to understand, to control, to influence and to shape our internal and external life contexts, our ways of being. It is simply invalid, as David Viscott would have us believe, that "more than anything else feelings make us human, . . . feelings make us all kindred."[20] What differentiates homo sapiens is our ability to reason. We are *rational* beings, however irrational we often behave. To the extent that we are *more* rather than *less* rational, we will feel better. Feelings are bodily responses and states that rationality can change—if we work at doing so.

What is the injuction, "be cool," except an appeal to reason, to use one's head under stressful circumstances? We can all be cool. We have that capacity, the mental equipment, and if counselors can be said to require anything at all in their accumulation of skills and abilities, it would be the ability to help their clients use that equipment. With most clients the main difficulty lies in the fact that they have not learned how to use their minds, how to think, how to be in charge of their own minds. What they have learned is how to use their mental equipment wrongly, in illogical and self-destructive ways.

Near the end of his life Vladimir Nabokov was asked, "What distinguishes us from animals?" His immediate answer is an epigram to remember:

Being aware of being aware of being.

Nabokov then explains: "In other words, if I not only know that I *am* but also that I know that I know it, then I belong to the human species. All the rest follows—the glory of thought, poetry, a vision of the universe. In that respect, the gap between ape and man is immeasurably greater than the one between amoeba and ape."[21]

NOTES

1. Walpole, H. (1965). Letter to the Countess of Upper Ossory, August 16, 1776. In W.S. Lewis, (Ed.). *The Yale edition of Horace Walpole's correspondence* (Vol. 32, p. 315.) New Haven: Yale University Press. Original work published 1776.
2. English, H.B. & English, A.C. (1958). *A comprehensive dictionary of psychological and psychoanalytical terms.* New York: David McKay, p. 323.
3. For the couselor wishing to read further in this area, here is a short list of recently published books: Bruner, J. (1983). *In search of mind: Essays in autobiography.* New York: Harper & Row; Gardner, H. (1983). *Frames of mind: The theory of multiple intelligences.* New York: Basic Books; Hunt, M. (1982). *The universe within: A new science explores the human mind.* New York: Simon & Schuster; Smith, A. (1982). *Powers of mind.* New York: Simon & Schuster; Taylor, D.A. (1982). *Mind.* New York: Simon & Schuster; Taylor, G.R. (1979). *The natural history of the mind.* New York: E.P. Dutton.
4. Koestler, A. (1964). *The act of creation.* New York: Macmillan, p. 493.

5. In a recent case in Detroit, Michigan, the home of an elderly woman who lived alone was invaded by two burglars. They tied her to a chair and menacingly told her they would kill her in a vile manner if she screamed or struggled. She so scared herself with thoughts of this horror, that her heart couldn't handle the overload, as the post-mortem examination records showed, and she died. Later the burglars were captured and charged with murder. They were exonerated of the murder charge; the old woman had literally died of fright, the court ruled, thereby subscribing to and endorsing the theory of emotions herein set forth. The woman caused her death by her extreme thoughts.

6. Vonnegut, K. (1981). *Palm Sunday*. New York: Delacorte, p. 118.

7. The sentences quoted are all from different sections of Thoreau's *Walden*, except the last, which is from *The duty of civil disobedience*.

8. Koestler, A. (1976). *The ghost in the machine*. London: Hutchinson, p. 251.

9. Siegler, M., & Osmond, H. (1974). *Models of madness, models of medicine*. New York: Macmillan.

10. Szasz, T. (1974). *The myth of mental illness: Foundations of a theory of personal conduct*. (rev. ed.). New York: Harper & Row.

11. Ethical and legal issues related to psychological deviance and counseling competency are discussed in: Van Hoose, W.H., & Kottler, J.A. (1977). *Ethical and legal issues in counseling and psychotherapy*. San Francisco: Jossey-Bass.

12. This point is discussed at length in: Dyer, W.W., & Vriend, J. (1975). Counseling and addiction: A problem of internal versus external thinking. *Counseling techniques that work* (3rd ed., pp. 45–55). Washington DC: American Personnel and Guidance Association.

13. See Vriend, J. & Dyer, W.W. (1973). Counseling the reluctant client. *The Journal of Counseling Psychology, 20,* 240–246. Reprinted in Dyer, W.W., & Vriend, J., op. cit.

14. How can counselors get better educated about all the possible payoffs associated with anger, guilt, envy, and a long list of other "negatives" (assuming the payoffs from the "positive" emotions to be more self-evident)? The first source of education is the exploration of client case data, which is to say counselor self-education. Each client is somewhat original in this regard, though many commonalities will be discerned for all clients. There is probably no better place in the literature to look than in: Solomon, R.C. (1976). *The Passions,* op. cit. In one chapter, over 90 pages long, called, "The Emotional Register: Who's Who Among the Passions," he has judiciously and painstakingly enumerated and delineated a world of American favorites that would appear on anyone's list, boiling these down to their essential natures and showing how each results in subjective and intersubjective gains and losses.

15. Reisman, D., Glazer, N., & Denny, R. (1960). *The lonely crowd*. (abridged ed.). New Haven: Yale University Press.

16. Russell, B. (1949). *The Autobiography of Bertrand Russell: 1872–1914.* Boston: Little, Brown, p. 33.
17. Solomon, R.C. (1976). Op. cit., p. 430.
18. Koestler, A., (1976). Op. cit., p. 237.
19. Rogers, C. (1980). *A way of being.* Boston: Houghton Mifflin, p. 55. See Rogers, C. (1956). Some issues concerning the control of human behavior: A symposium with B.F. Skinner. *Science 124,* 1057–1066.
20. Viscott, D. (1976). *The language of feelings.* New York: Pocket Books, p. 9.
21. Nabokov, V. (1973). *Strong opinions.* New York: McGraw-Hill, p. 142.

Practical Counseling
Theory and Research

The models or stored theories of the world that are so useful in inference are strikingly generic and reflect man's ubiquitous tendency to categorize ... We organize experience to represent not only the particulars that have been experienced, but the classes of events of which the particulars are exemplars. We go not only from part to whole, but irresistibly from the particular to the general ... Both in achieving the economy with which human thought represents the world and in effecting swift correction for error, the categorizing tendency of intelligence is central—for it yields a structure of thought that becomes hierarchically organized with growth, forming branching structures in which it is relatively easy to search for alternatives. The blunders occur, of course, where things that must be together for action or for understanding happen to be organized in different hierarchies. It is a form of error that is as familiar in science as in everyday life ...

In the main, we do the greater part of our work by manipulating our representations or models of reality rather than by acting directly on the world itself. Thought is then vicarious action, in which the high cost of error is strikingly reduced. It is characteristic of human beings and no other species that we can carry out this vicarious action with the aid of a large number of intellectual prosthetic devices that are, so to speak, tools provided by the culture. Natural language is the prime example, but there are pictorial and diagrammatic conventions as well, theories, myths, models of reckoning and ordering.

—Jerome S. Bruner[1]

$\mathbb{C}$ an any counselor who seeks to be effective with clients fail to be a *thinker* and yet succeed? It is difficult to imagine an occupational group upon which rests a greater incumbency *to think*, to gather data, to analyze it, to order it, to relate it to known models of operation, to speculate upon its significance, to formulate hypotheses, and to test these as an ongoing aspect of its work. There is little that is cut-and-dried in counseling, little that is simple, foreordained, easily understood, for every client is a complex human being made up of differing sets of life experiences, circumstances, relationships, and conditions. To pigeonhole any client according to some predetermined typology is to dehumanize that person. When we reduce an individual to a set of concerns, problems, complaints, troubles, miseries, when we see or attempt to treat only a part of the whole person, failing to account for all that a living person is or has the potential to become, then, most surely, we permit ourselves to judge our clients as objects, to dismiss their wholeness, to ignore the fact that each is a unique wonder worthy of the most profound and vigorous employment of our every intellectual resource.

Through Hamlet, Shakespeare exclaimed, "What a piece of work is man! how noble in reason! how infinite in faculty! in form and moving how express and admirable! in action how like an angel! in apprehension how like a god!"[2] No one is excluded. Nor, 4 centuries after Shakespeare, can we scale down his assessment. What individuals of our species have wrought since Shakespeare's tenure on our shrinking planet only serves to confirm even his most excessive exaltations.

Perhaps it is one of the inevitable faults of counselors' education and training that the writers and teachers of theory and research texts in our field fail to appreciate *our* minds. We are more or less commanded and exhorted to sponge up the contents of these materials and then apply what we have learned to individual cases as we begin to counsel. It is no astonishment that we struggle and fumble so hard in our initial efforts. If theoretical constructs that we have read and heard, perhaps memorized, do not fit in with what we already know, or if clients do not respond in the ways we have been led to believe they would, we then are not only confounded and dumbfounded, but we must fight against the mental programs we have newly acquired.

Just how *are* we typically trained? First, by authority. When we enter the field as greenhorns, we assume that there is a large body of knowledge that has been assembled by our predecessors over time that is "tried and true," essential theories, substantive facts, methodologies that work, and we are not dissuaded of this assumption. There are mountains of books containing "everything you ever wanted to know about counseling but were afraid to ask." In the judgment of our trainers and mentors, though, only certain works are worthy of our concentrated attention. A half-dozen or so of all the theories of counseling and psychotherapy that have been elevated to the top of the heap by some mysterious process of popular acclaim are the ones with which we must become familiar. Or perhaps the field of theories has been narrowed down to a single "winner" that we must throughly know and exclusively use. We are inveighed upon to swallow and digest a large conglomeration of touted material that, we are assured, is necessary to our future skill and competence as counselors.

We are exposed to any number of theories and the methods devolved from these. Many particular constructs, normative truths treated as absolutes, as inviolable principles of operation, are said to be sacrosanct because they have been substantiated by extensive research done by honorable investigators who have scrupulously followed the rules of scientific methodology. When these investigators report their results, they do not lie. If their conclusions were unjustified as a result of error in their work, they would readily admit to this. There is no "cover-up" because they are ethical and professional. They present reliable knowledge and make no claims that exceed the evidential character of their findings. Research, indeed, is a holy endeavor and enterprise, and to say in our modern age that what we profess is backed by research amounts to the highest accolade, the most prestigious imprimatur upon our mental products. What research has shown to be valid is advertised as what is good and right. One does not become cavalier about research; to do so is a secular sin.

So, as fledgling practitioners indoctrinated into the fraternity of professionals, we are introduced to theories and practices backed by the authority of those seasoned and judicious builders of theories, many of whom have spent their professional lives developing their systems of operation, and by the authority of what has been garnered through research in any given aspect of our lately chosen discipline and applied science. Because we have not yet made the knowledge and methods our own, have not ingested our learnings to where they are second nature to us, we must now apply what we have learned. It is at this point, when we begin to practice with actual clients, that some of these learnings become useful. Perhaps we even marvel that they work, becoming excited especially over those that we doubted when they were first introduced. Many, however, do not work. Perhaps we misunderstood. But, no. Now it turns out that there is no "correct" way to handle every situation, every minor exchange in counseling. Our supervisors begin to equivocate. The theories didn't cover all contingencies. They were models, primarily. They were guidelines, generally prescriptive, hardly explicit. Now it is up to us to theorize about what is happening in each counseling situation. Suddenly the authority of what we have learned breaks down and we are enjoined to think for ourselves, to have a rationale for what we do that arises out of case circumstances, not one drawn from what someone else has divined and articulated for us beforehand.

And so we "win our spurs," as it were. What befalls us is not so much the discovery that the experts have been discredited as the realization that we must follow their lead; we cannot become counselors of any sizable worth and repute without ourselves becoming theorists and researchers on our own. What befalls us is the realization that few truths about counseling are fixed, stable, uniformly applicable to all clients. There is a relativity to most professional lore. An appreciation dawns in us about the paucity of reliable knowledge in our chosen field. Perhaps we are even humbled by the complexity of human nature (what is truly known is so little because the subject is so immense) and we adopt an outlook that in essence says this: To counsel means we will be life-long learners. There will be no end to learning. We can never know all there is to know about human beings in general or any given person in particular.

Is there a better way to teach counselors? Perhaps there is. Perhaps the necessity to work out our own theories from scratch would be more effective in getting us to admit that we must be hard thinkers to counsel well. For we end up, do we not, learning that *what* to think is not nearly as important as *how* to think. Our training would then take the form of learning logic, principles of deduction, the science of correct reasoning, and then of learning the scientific method, inductive reasoning, observing, proposing, hypothesizing, testing. We would then most certainly begin to study language and how it is formulated, all the ways in which communication works. From the very beginning we would be required to work out our own theories of what transpires in clients' minds, what causes client dysfunction, how positive behavioral change comes about, what interventions are helpful. If we were not allowed to dip into the reservoirs of conclusion others had formulated, what would be the result? Would we be more critical of their findings? Would we be more appreciative of what they had to say, readier and more willing to absorb their insights and guidelines?

Actually, how we are taught makes little difference once we are on our own as practitioners, if we truly arrive at the point where we *know* we must do our own thinking, that we must proceed by the unaided light of our own reasoning. We cannot be robots and help clients. There is no cookbook containing recipes for every occasion. We cannot duck our obligation to think hard and well in counseling. We must acquire and hone our abilities to theorize about what any given client presents. The emphasis in a counseling theory class is misplaced if it falls upon the memorization of existing theories. Those that have any merit, those whose excellence is accredited, immediately absorbed and understood, ought to serve more as models against which to measure one's own theories. The theories of others serve as goads to thinking. And they are reassuring in the confirmation they often supply that one's own hard-won conclusions bear a resemblance to what other serious thinkers have resolved to be true.

Counseling training programs might be faulted in their character of organization in that theory presentation is too narrow, too restricted. The fact of the matter is that humans *are* theorizers, and there are theories for everything. Each of us has a theory about almost every phase of existence. Our minds are so constructed that we theorize without even knowing that is what we continually are doing. We select units of existence, abstracting these from the real world around us. We line these up in our minds in a variety of learned or personally creative ways, ordering and reordering them to make some sense of them, a sense related to our own purposes. Then we act. The selection and ordering is necessary for action. Or, if we act first and find our action to be unacceptable in the results we have achieved, we stop and reflect, invoke the selection and ordering process again, evaluating it in the light of the unpredicted outcome data, and decide on a different course for the next similar action sequence. It is when we *don't* theorize that we are in trouble. If we fail to theorize, if we abdicate, if we are simply stimulus/response organisms, we are then controlled from without, fated, at the mercy of externals.

The undifferentiated continuum of possible human behaviors is, for all practical purposes, infinite. Certainly human beings throughout their run of history and in all places and cultures have met similar life circumstances and tasks by applying their theories and then passing on their conclusions about how best to act. The accumulated wisdom of the species is there for us to draw upon, in books, in every imaginable record, even in our cliches and idioms. What are proverbs, axioms, aphorisms, treasured sayings, except short and easily remembered secrets about how to act in every instance? Each of us has a store of these in our minds. Their piling up, it may be said, is what the process of growing up is all about. The mature have common sense, most of it learned the hard way, through trial and error, which is the most concise label we have for the scientific method, for inductive reasoning (another name we use is reality-testing, and we do this in the school of hard knocks).

It is in this sense that theory classes for counselors are too narrow in focus and content. Although it is true enough that there have to be parameters, limits to what is included in a counselor training program, the danger is that graduates believe they have been exposed to all the accumulated lore that matters to counselors. Nothing could be further from the truth. The theory province of counseling and psychotherapy is a mere drop in the ocean of wisdom, so much as to be almost discountable to the pundits and sages in our highly civilized society, to the scholars, to the intelligentsia. Do the brightest minds of our time turn to our field for enlightenment? If not, why not? Where do they turn? Certainly they gravitate to literature, the humanities, the social sciences, philosophy, to every aspect of the arts and sciences. If we talk about becoming wiser and not simply about making money and gaining power and fame (though one can argue that there is a correlation), then the entire world of human knowledge is open to investigation. Indeed, for counselors interested in broadening and deepening their thinking capacity, the richest mother lodes of learning lie outside the narrow areas of theory to which they have been introduced in their training.

WHAT IS A THEORY?

Why is this thus? What is the reason of this thusness?

—Artemus Ward[3]

A case could be made for the idea that most people are perplexed by the very word *theory*. It scares them. When they are called upon to reveal a theory about something or other, they must stop and think. In their minds they must assemble what they have considered to be the facts of the matter and show how these substantiate why they have chosen to act in a certain way. They are called upon to answer *why* they behave in the ways they do. They must furnish excuses. They must defend themselves. They must justify their actions. They must empty the contents of their minds for critical review by often hostile judges. They must explain themselves. And that is all a theory is—an explanation!

A theory is a set of propositions about reality, a series of statements that seem to explain real world events. Take any event and make a list of reasons why such an event occurs and—presto!—you have a theory. Eavesdrop on any conversation, perhaps two people's intense discussion at a nearby restaurant table, and the building blocks of a theory emerge— why Herschel acted the way he did at a cocktail party, why Sam won't quit his job, why the liberal candidate will lose the election, why the one conversationalist cannot do what the other wants ... on and on and on. It makes no difference whether these statements are true or false, valid or invalid, testable, incredibly bizarre, emphatically insisted upon or tentatively laid out. For their owners, they count. They matter as explanations for behavior, for action, whether entertained only in the mind or offered up to another person or a group.

A theory is an explanation of facts. A fact is a real event, something that happened, supposedly something objective, something verifiable. Data are facts. Evidence is composed of facts. How we account for these facts will determine the shape our theories take.

Most events, particularly human events, cannot be accounted for by a single reason, though we would prefer to narrow any explanation down to one reason, to reduce everything down to the lowest common denominator, and we work at doing this. We like simplicity not only for its purity, its essentiality, its elegance, its unity, characteristics much vaunted in the arts, but because then we can avoid thinking so hard and get on with more pleasurable or more practical ways of using our time and energies. But—alas!—few questions about the facts are dismissable by one-reason answers. When it comes to explanations about human behavior, the questions that trouble our understanding usually require answers composed of a list of reasons. We ask the questions and want the answers so that we can make predictions and plan our own future operations, so that we can behave efficiently and effectively.

Apparently, then, asking the "right" question is important. How we formulate a question will determine how we go about gathering the facts and what explanations will serve as satisfactory cancellations of the question. The terms incorporated in a good question will be unambiguous, clear, befitting. A good question will allow for an acceptable answer, or else it merely confuses an issue or remains rhetorical. In counseling we thus learn the characteristics of effective questions and eliminate those that produce low or no yield. "Why" questions tend to fall into this latter category. "Why do you keep on eating so much?" asks the counselor. "I don't know. That's what I've been trying to figure out. That's why I'm here," says the client.

Because most human behaviors are the outcome of a long personal history, former conditioning, environmental conditions, and the complex make-up of a given mind and its various ways of thinking—these among some central factors—a set of reasons must be clustered together to account for whatever behavior is manifested by any individual or group of individuals acting in consort. These reasons are propositions, proposed statements, assumptions or presumptions, that seem to explain the behavior. They are theorems, theory units.

Theory building has been developed into a philosophical science and many descriptive books exist for anyone wishing to develop sophistication in this science. Suffice it here to say that the average counseling practitioner requires only a clear-cut way of proceeding with each client in the formulation of questions and the pursuance of answers that are keys to unlocking client difficulties. Sound principles of theory building must be learned, but the development of theoretical systems can be left to devotees obsessed more with system building itself than with workaday counseling effectiveness.

About systems it may be said, here with an eye to economy, that they come garbed only in two dimensions: closed and open. An open system allows for new additions, for the entrance of more theorems or for the replacement of any given theorem with one of greater validity. A closed system, on the other hand, is a finished product and purports to have within its confines a theorem to explain every eventuality. Most "isms" are closed systems: communism, Freudianism, behaviorism, Catholicism. Folks are attracted to closed theoretical systems because within each is an explanation for every contingency, the orthodox answer to any possible question.

Most of us find we cannot accept all the tenets of a closed system, so when we are asked to what theoretical school we belong, we reply that we are eclectics. This, we have learned, is an answer that is generally accepted, far more so than professed ignorance because it seems to satisfy inquirers and gets us off the hook. The question is a hook: "What is your counseling orientation?" No one wants you to go on and on with a long dissertation about all the explanations you have accumulated in your educational and experiential travels about why this or that behavior— all the common behaviors you can name—tend to occur. The question is asked because the inquirer wants to pigeonhole you, which you don't like and so you answer, "I tend to be an eclectic." You have thus succeeded in saying nothing in response to a question that is "pretty dumb," which is to say ill-formulated, if it is to elicit anything meaningful. Among counselors and other mental health workers the term eclectic is a cliche code word, not unlike the babble of a brook, for all the meaning it conveys. To say you are an eclectic and imply that your mind is a hodgepodge of disconnected fragments, a swirl of flotsam floating around in a mental stew, is hardly a responsible position to take. Through popularization *eclectic* has lost its value as a useful word to the science of theory building, a case of Gresham's law, "bad money drives out good," applied to theoretical positioning in counseling. Better to drop its usage than to misrepresent what is really being stated, unless one means and can back up what English and English attribute to this tightly specialized term:

> ECLECTICISIM: *n*. in theoretical system building, the selection and orderly combination of compatible features from diverse sources, sometimes from otherwise incompatible theories and systems; the effort to find valid elements in all doctrines or theories and to combine them into a harmonious whole. The resulting system is open to constant revision even in its major outlines.
>
> A general temper of mind seems to determine the degree to which a systematizer seeks for the maximum of rational order and over-all consistency (with resulting temporary loss in inclusiveness and explanatory power), or for the maximum of understanding of particular issues (with some loss in the tightness of organization). For the latter approach, ECLECTICISM is an established term: for the former no good name is current, but FORMALISM perhaps describes its chief attribute. Formalism leads to the advocacy of competing schools and theories; eclecticism, though often called a school, is essentially the denial of schools.[4]

Any question about counseling "approach" or "orientation" can easily be redirected if the occasion for its appearance is clarified. The question usually emerges because its asker wants to understand the thinking behind some counseling action or some line of reasoning. The asker seeks to categorize: "Are you client-centered, behavioral, gestalt, rational-emotive, or what?" Rather than respond with "eclectic," on such occasions the respondent can identify the specific action and provide a rationale for its use.

The connection between theory and practice seems obvious to most people; it simply means acting thoughtfully rather than capriciously in willy-nilly fashion. The connection between theory and research is different. Here the implication is that we must test our beliefs, that we must substantiate our suppositions, ground our flights of speculative reason in a bed of reality. The implication is that there is truth to be discovered that, once learned, will take the form of laws, solid immutable knowledge. A theorem is an unproven statement about reality, an unproven law. A theorem is a thesis and it is best stated as a hypothesis (*hypo* meaning less than), a likelihood. Thus, we advance our theses, stating them as hypotheses that we subsequently test. A thesis that passes all our tests can then be given the supreme status of a law. We go through our lives acquiring as many of these laws, these truths about reality, as we possibly can, as each will help us more accurately to predict events and more surely to guide us in our choice of actions. Each adds precious coin to our bank account of knowledge, and knowledge, we know, gives us power.

The problem comes when we realize that there are few theses about human behavior, if any, that can be elevated to the status of laws, few that pass all tests. "The only sure thing in this life," we joke, "is death and taxes." Where and what, then, is truth? And it is precisely at this point in our quest that we learn about statistics, the laws of probability. Statistical tests have the power to tell us the *degree* of validity and reliability of our theses. Through a study of statistics we learn that truth is relative. Theses can be more or less true. They can be normatively true. Statements about reality can be true most of the time, fit a majority of cases, and through statistical means we can determine which theses fit into categories of usually true or usually false.

To apply our statistical tests we must generate hypotheses that have certain characteristics. We must state them so that they are testable, our terms being clear, and the observable facts unmistakably delineated. A good hypothesis will be adequate in scope, covering all the facts, leaving out none that count. We want our explanation to cover as many facts in the case as possible, not only a limited few. Our hypotheses must have depth if they are to get a high vote of excellence. This is to say that our hypotheses will possess the explanatory power we claim for them, that they will be adequate to our purposes. Finally, we want hypotheses to be parsimonious, to contain the fewest possible terms, to be as economically stated as we can make them. The principal of parsimony, or stinginess, is called Occam's razor. It was William of Occam, a medieval English philosopher, who is credited with saying that we must shave away to the bare skin all the hair we can, both in the number of explanations we make to encompass a set of facts and the number of words (or symbols) we use to enclose any given explanation.

If we proceed to "formal" research of our theories and our sets of postulates that seem to explain what we observe in reality, we have our work cut out for us. We must learn the principles of good research design and complicated statistical methods and procedures, and then generate testable hypotheses that satisfy the requirements just discussed. Most of us do not do this, unless, of course, we are required to do so as a part of the demands made upon us in the attainment of a graduate degree.

But in these school-required efforts we are amateurish beginners in a highly specialized area. What is imprinted upon us is the significance of such research, that it is a rigorous science, that we ought to respect the workers who engage in it, that we ought to respect their products. We learn that formal research in time-consuming, hard to do well, often exceedingly expensive, and that it usually involves the efforts of many highly trained people who are devoted to advancing the frontier of knowledge in the field. Most of us who take the practitioner's path do not see ourselves as researchers because the concept of a researcher has been elevated to a status too remote for us.

In the mental health field, though, hardly anyone is neutral about research. Some people it "turns off," others it "turns on." To some it means organization and strict rules, design, carefully followed scientific methods, statistics, mathematical skills, working with computers, structured thinking, a kind of confinement. Others welcome such structure and feel at home with it, enjoying following carefully laid out protocols. In our society research has become canonized, or so Jacques Barzun sees it. We live in a world where there is, he says,

> an epidemic cult of research. If someone today tells another in passing that he is "doing research," the one addressed will almost invariably exclaim: "How wonderful!" or at least "How interesting!" Then, possibly, he or she will ask what the research is about. This attitude is so usual as to seem inevitable, but fifty, even thirty years ago, the idea that doing research is inherently wonderful or interesting was not a commonplace, nor would the question "Research in(to) what?" have come as an afterthought or been overlooked altogether. The change is due to the recent canonization of the name research, which by becoming familiar has bred a universal faith in the supreme value of the results. In any profession nothing can be more important than research. To suggest that practice, or teaching, or reflection might be preferred is blasphemy.[5]

One must get experience under one's belt, apply in practice what one has sponged up in formal training, including all those theorems of others that have been handed down as proven by research, to begin to realize that there are no certitudes, no laws, no explanations, that consistently account for what happens in counseling, no methods or procedures that consistently work. In the final analysis all the truths are normative, all the explanations are relative, with the possible exception of death and taxes.

So where does a practitioner turn? Does this mean that ideals of counselor effectiveness and competence can be abandoned? Hardly a satisfactory conclusion. What it means is that our harvest must be the gathering of normative truths, and that we must be our own good theorizers and researchers, our research being the testing of postulates (whether self-constructed or collected from others) with each client as we go about our counseling business. In filling up our mental storage bins, we are no different, we might say, from people in general who get wiser as they grow older because they have accumulated their own storehouse of relative workable truths.

If these normative truths are to be at the ready, subject to immediate recall and applicability, it is best that they have the characteristics to which we earlier alluded. In addition, it helps if their formulation in language incorporates rhyme and meter, alliteration, sharp imagery, or other figures of speech. We see this in proverbs. They have become the wisdom of the people, so to speak, because they fit the facts most parsimoniously and elegantly. Among these few examples, it is hard to take Occam's razor and shave away any bristle without cutting up their usefulness:

Two wrongs don't make a right.
Haste makes waste.
Example is better than precept.
Love begets love.
A rolling stone gathers no moss.
Drink is the curse of the working class.
Work is the curse of the drinking class.
Old habits die hard.
Familiarity breeds contempt.
Forewarned, forearmed.
Doubt nothing, know nothing.
The poor lack destiny control.
Lost time is never found again.
Waste not, want not.
All's well that ends well.

As practitioners seeking greater competence we reap our normative truths wherever we find them. We test most of them in our own laboratories, at our work-stations of professional activity. We read professional books and journals in our field to gain what insights we can, seeing the professional literature as a likely resource for potentially useful insights because we expect that the reporters are concerned with the same theoretical and practical problems that we face. We become tough critics as we mature as counselors, though. We become adept at scanning and learn to dismiss most of what we read as having little value for our own practice. Now and then, however, we are gratified with an ample reward for our efforts.

Consider this delineation of a theory put forth by Norman Kagan:

> The concept of interpersonal psychological distance seems to be a useful construct . . . The concept is developed as follows: People need each other. One of people's most basic interpersonal drives is for some optimum level and frequency of sensory stimulation. People are the best, the most complete potential source of sensory stimulation for other people.
>
> But people learn to fear each other. Just as people can be the most potent source of satisfaction for each other, people can also be the most potent source of horror for each other. Because one's earliest, most impressionable experiences are as a very small being in a large person's world, vague feelings of fear and helplessness with each other persist in some people all of the time and in all people some of the time . . .
>
> People are unable to give up attempts to achieve interpersonal intimacy despite their fears of such contact. People appear to both approach and retreat from direct, simple intimacy with others. The approach-avoidance syndrome appears to be a cyclical process—intimacy followed by relative isolation followed by new bids for intimacy. (This back and forth "waltzing" is especially observable in insecure relationships.) The movement toward-and-away-from people appears to establish a specific range of psychologically "safe" distances unique for each individual. People "settle in" at a psychological distance at which they are more or less intimate with each other and yet able to feel safe from the dangers which they vaguely sense in the situation . . .
>
> The greater the fear one has of intimacy, the greater the distance one establishes and the more rigidly the individual holds to that position.
>
> The further the distance one establishes, the greater the likelihood that substitutes for human contact will be sought, sometimes successfully but most often, unsuccessfully.
>
> The fears people have of each other become translated into an interpersonal mythology and expectation, a self-fulfilling prophecy in which people make their nightmares happen.
>
> More fully functioning people appear to be more capable of extreme intimacy and more extended aloneness than others. They appear to be able to sustain long periods of intimate involvement (but are not compulsively compelled to) and they are equally capable of comfortably sustaining aloneness without immediate panic. So interpersonal flexibility seems to be a characteristic of the more fully-functioning people.[6]

How potentially useful Norman Kagan's theoretical constructs seem to be when so stated! A counselor who hasn't seen psychological distancing as an important variable in more masterful living wants immediately, after reading these words, to apply these ideas to ongoing cases, to help clients to assess the quality of their relationships with significant others according to these insights. Hypotheses befitting certain clients leap to mind and the testing of these in the counseling, one imagines, will surely promote progress. Or so it would seem. One can easily generate excitement over such ideas.

Perhaps the most exciting ideas of all are those conceived as a result of much practice. The author, for example, has long thought about what seems to be an equation applicable to certain aspects of behavior, what he calls the anticipation/disappointment equation. Simply stated this means that the time spent anticipating an event will be equivalent to the time spent being disappointed when the event fails to take place. To anticipate is to foretaste, to focus upon and savor in the mind what delicious goodies lie ahead, thus making oneself feel good. The more one anticipates some future event seen as extremely pleasurable, the more assuredly one will fell let down and cheated when the desirable happening doesn't take place, or when what happens is totally different (and lesser) than what one imagined. Here it is stated in its most "razored" form:

Disappointment degree and time = anticipation degree and time.

Corollaries come to mind. Does "worry time" equal "relief time," when what is dreaded doesn't occur? The ways in which we create emotional pain and pleasure in ourselves have time and intensity dimensions, and this equation is a useful reminder of these. The conclusion one draws from this, of course, is to live in the present without spending time foretasting or foredreading the future, to live according to a "no-expectation system," dealing with hardship as best one can when it arrives, and not "dying a thousand deaths" first, and fully enjoying whatever delightful experience one has when it arrives, and not before it does.

No doubt the reader can see how this equation has useful applicability in counseling. Would it make any difference to a practitioner if the author is able to state that the equation has been repeatedly tested in laboratory experiments with thousands of subjects of different ages and backgrounds in all representative geographical areas of the United States and Canada? And that the findings showed that it is normatively valid, that prolonged anticipation results in prolonged depression of days, weeks, even months? Would the reader be more convinced of its serviceability if a whole book citing countless research designs were to exist, each design thoroughly described down to the minutest detail, thus allowing for other researchers to replicate each of the many studies? If none of the research proved the equation's validity and reliability, there would be no point to publishing such a book. If the research irrefutably confirmed, indeed, that such an equation tends to describe a reality, would its value be any greater to a counselor encountering and evaluating its appropriateness for his or her own uses?

What we have been discussing in this chapter is the nature and importance of theorizing in the work we do, seeing how essential is clear and cogent thinking. In the process we have sought to put formal research into a realistic and practical perspective and to highlight the importance of informal research, that which every effective counselor does all the time with every client in her or his efforts to arrive at the delivery of counseling service that will work. What has been emphasized is that our most useful knowledge tends always to be normative, relative rather than absolute. "The chances are," we might say, impressed by the laws of probability, "that we will never be free of mistakes."

Take is an ancient English word having hundreds of useful meanings. One of these is *to do*. We take a walk, take shelter, take a chance. Sometimes we *take amiss*, the origin of the word *mistake*. A mistake is a take that missed, a take that never took. In our professional development toward consummate effectiveness we will take many of these. If we do not, we can hardly take credit for being research-minded, for being scientific, for being professional in our practice. In research there is no esoteric mystique, but mistakes abound.

NOTES

1. Bruner, J. (1973). *The relevance of education.* New York: Norton, pp. 5–7.
2. Shakespeare, W. *Hamlet*, Act II, Sc. 2, Lines 315–319.
3. Browne, C. F. (1898). *The complete works of Artemus Ward* (rev. ed.). New York: G. W. Dillingham, p. 373.
4. English, H. B., & English, A. C. (1958). *A comprehensive dictionary of psychological and psychoanalytic terms.* New York: David McKay, p. 168.
5. Barzun, J. (1964). *Science: The glorious entertainment.* New York: Harper, p. 120.
6. Kagan, N. (1978). Presidential address, Division 17. *The Counseling Psychologist,* 7, 7.

5

The Case for Regular Client-Centered Audiotaping in Counseling

Objective investigations of psychotherapy do not have a long history. Up to 1940 there had been a few attempts to record therapeutic interviews electronically, but no research use had been made of such material. There had been no serious attempts to utilize the methods of science to measure the changes which were thought to occur in therapy. So we are speaking of a field which is still, relatively speaking, in its swaddling clothes. But a beginning has been made.

Sometime in 1940 a group of us at Ohio State University successfully recorded a complete therapeutic interview. Our satisfaction was great, but it quickly faded. As we listened to this material, so formless, so complex, we almost despaired of fulfilling our purpose of using it as the data for research investigations. It seemed almost impossible to reduce it to elements which could be handled objectively.

Yet progress was made. Enthusiasm and skill on the part of graduate students made up for lack of funds and suitable equipment. The raw data of therapy was transformed by ingenious and creative thinking into crude categories of therapist techniques and equally crude categories of client responses.

—Carl R. Rogers[1]

lectronics. For most people that word symbolizes the present age. There is a fearsome quality about it. Humans controlled by machines. Push-button diplomacy. There are the experts who build, own, and control the use of electronic equipment, the technicians, the programming engineers, the telecommunications media people, and—then there are the rest of us. Electronics. So technical. So demanding of specialized knowledge. It started out with signal-sending, the telegraph. Soon it was sound, the telephone and sounds recorded on a disc. Alexander Graham Bell invented the telephone in 1876; a year later Thomas Alva Edison invented the phonograph. By the 1920s both the telephone and the Victrola were common household items. By the 1930s a radio was added; by the end of the 1950s it was television. Today it is audio- and videotapes, the computer and floppy discs. We can be bombarded by visual and sound images at will. It is the electronic age.

"What do you do to combat loneliness?" a talk-show host asks his three guests.

"I turn on the television," says the first. "You know, 'chewing gum for the mind,' as Fred Allen called it, ha ha."

"I put on a tape and turn the music up really loud," says the second.

"I call up my friends," says the third.

Electronics. The highway police detect a speeder with state-of-the-art electronic radar gear, call the license number into headquarters, and approach the apprehended vehicle already armed with the driver's record of past transgressions. Financial and many other records of practically every citizen are stored in computer memory banks and are instantaneously retrievable. We are a nation of consumers of media offerings. Electronics. There are those who scorn the electronic age and think the world would have been better off if humankind only had recourse to printed matter, which requires some effort on the reader's part, but this is unrealistic. Americans love their gadgets, anything to make living easier and fuller of conveniences. Electronics. Automation. More and more technology applied to everyday life. Bugging. Beepers. Computers, televisions, telephones, and radios everywhere. The world has changed. It will never be as it once was. The new national consciousness is an electronic consciousness. Don't even think about the next war, the electronic war. Vietnam was the television war. What will the next one be? Turn on the TV, chewing gum for the mind, and get on with your personal business. Electronics. The phenomenon is shaping our future, perhaps the telethetic boom of our last act.

If counselors consider the relationships that their clients have had with communications media in their personal history and how these electronic devices have served as companions and mind-molders, and if they assess the current relative dependency of their clients upon communications outlets, counselors will be exploring an area that ought not to be neglected in diagnostics. How much time in a day or a week does John or Jane spend listening and watching, in being a passive consumer of random information and of "sounds signifying nothing"? Just *what* is taken in, what is it that John or Jane absorbs from the tube? What remains in the mind? What use is made of the electronic equipment? What are the competitive sources of ideational input? To what extent are electronic devices substitutes for other activities?

With so many ordinary citizens now acquiring personal computers, there is a new entry bidding for electronic escapism. "Computers appeal to people who find their personal lives unmanageable," says Lasch, "often to people afraid of being overwhelmed by uncontrollable emotions ... Playing video games and solving problems on a home computer help to disassociate thought from feeling ... The computer provides a lifelike response that can nevertheless be predicted and controlled ... Exertion of control over a machine often leads to the further step of identification with the machine—to a new conception of the self as a machine in its own right."[2]

As technological progress in the electronics industry spurts ahead, there won't be a reduction of gadgetry in the American home. On the contrary, as the newest audio and visual communications items become less expensive and more readily available to every segment of the population, their pervasiveness, even their ubiquity, is all but assured. Studies of the relationship of persons to machines that are people-substitutes are bringing in early returns that have the futurologists speculating on major evolutionary changes in human nature as well as in social environments and the very fabric of society.

How does the practice of counseling fit into this picture? Counseling depends on communication. Verbal face-to-face communication is the medium in which counselors work, and any adjunct technology that can serve as a tool in promoting greater counseling effectiveness is worth looking into. Of all the possibilities currently at hand, the least expensive and most commonplace is the audiotape recorder. We have already arrived at that stage in the development of our society where almost every household has a radio, a television set, a telephone, a camera, a record-player, and, now, a tape recorder. Indeed, most homes have multiples of these things. There are few clients who do not have access to audiotape playback equipment. Nor, it can be safely said, is there an electronics communications tool with which counselors are more familiar.

We cannot turn back the clock, but we can "get in step." This is what Carl Rogers and his coworkers did in the early 1940s. They had made exciting discoveries that led them into a fresh way of looking at the therapeutic interview. A thousand questions entered their inquiring minds. They needed to study what happened between counselor and client, to reflect at leisure upon the details of interaction, to engage in content analysis. They wanted transcripts of the sessions, not merely the shorthand notes that a court recorder might make, but the sounds themselves, the inflections, the "hems and haws," the breathing, the periods of silence. For this they turned to the phonograph. It was clumsy, but it was all they had. The equipment was cumbersome and expensive, the process laborious, and the result was frequently only barely audible, but they persisted.

Here is how Rogers describes this pioneering effort:

It has been possible to install equipment which permits of the electric recording of counseling interviews on phonograph records, thus preserving an absolutely accurate account of every word spoken in the interview, and also the inflections and tone of voice ... The equipment consists of a concealed non-directional microphone in the clinic interviewing room, which is connected to a double turntable recording machine in another room. This permits continuous recording of the interview on blank phonograph discs ... We have made considerable use of these records playing them back for one or a group of counselors.[3]

From analyses of these recordings positive research gains resulted, as Rogers and his associates attempted to delineate variables in effective client-centered counseling and to postulate theorems. But the really significant and lasting advantages were those for counselor development and training. Here is Rogers, after a full and prosperous career, now a septuagenarian, reflecting back on the leap forward that recordings permitted:

Then came my transition to a full-time postion at Ohio State University, where, with the help of students, I was at last able to scrounge equipment for recording my and my students' interviews. I cannot exaggerate the excitement of our learnings as we clustered about the machine that enabled us to listen to ourselves, playing over and over some puzzling point at which the interview clearly went wrong, or those moments in which the client moved significantly forward. (I still regard this as the one best way of learning to improve oneself as a therapist.) Among many lessons from these recordings, we came to realize that listening to feelings and "reflecting" them was a vastly complex process. We discovered that we could pinpoint which response of the therapist caused a fruitful flow of significant expression to become superficial and unprofitable. Likewise, we were able to spot the remark that turned a client's dull and desultory talk into a focused self-exploration.

In such a context of learning, it became quite natural to lay more stress upon the content of the therapist's response than upon the empathic quality of the listening. To this extent, we became heavily conscious of the techniques that the counselor or therapist was using. We became expert in analyzing, in very minute detail, the ebb and flow of the process in each interview, and we gained a great deal from this microscopic study.[4]

In his retrospective review of 46 years in the profession, Rogers saw the three principal sources of his learnings to have been clients first, then his association with younger colleagues, and third his scholarly readings. In his poignant summarization of these learning matrices, interview transcripts still loom large:

The gold mine of data that resides in interviews ... staggers me. There is, first of all, the gut-level experience, which absorbs the statements, the feelings, and the gestures, providing its own complex type of learning, difficult to put into words. Then there is the listening to the interchanges in the tape recording. Here are the orderly sequences that were missed in the flow of the experience. Here, too, are the nuances of inflection, the half-formed sentences, the pauses, and the sighs, which were also partially missed. Then, if a transcript is laboriously produced, I have a microscope in which I can see, as I termed them in one paper, "the molecules of personality change." I know of no other way of combining the deepest experiential learning with the most highly abstract cognitive and theoretical learnings than the three steps I have mentioned: living the experience on a total basis, rehearing it on an experiential-cognitive basis, and studying it once more for every intellectual clue. As I said earlier, this type of interview is perhaps the most valuable and transparent window into the strange inner world of persons and relationships. I feel that if I subtracted from my work the learnings I have gained from deep relationships with clients and group participants, I would be nothing.[5]

So much is history. Rogers and his associates may not have been the earliest to employ electronic recordings extensively to increase their understandings of the dynamics of the counseling process, but they were certainly precursors of what is now accepted practice in counselor training. As the benefits of analyses of actual counselor performance became appreciated, and as recording technology advanced from disc to wire, then to reel-to-reel taping, and finally to easily portable and relatively inexpensive cassette taping, the practice of making and analyzing audio (and in many cases, video) transcripts of student sessions in counselor training has become all but universal.

Effective practitioners today, having been exposed to the benefits of interview analysis for upgrading their performance during their formal training, continue to transcribe their sessions and to emulate Rogers, even if only occasionally, to improve their skills or to better figure out what is going on in interviews with particular clients where progress seems to have become stagnant. Some practitioners tape all their sessions and these tapes constitute their client records. Tapes of sessions are frequently used in case conferences, in establishing a criterion for admission to advanced degree programs, in agency hiring and promotion purposes, or even in establishing certification and licensing acceptability. Rare is the working counselor who has had no exposure to taping and listening to the nuances of his or her counseling sessions in critical review with a supervisor. Just as the stethoscope is the symbolic artifact we associate with physicians, the tape recorder could be similarly associated with counselors, so familiar are we with this electronic aid.

The enthusiasm to which Carl Rogers testifies can readily be identified with and acknowledged by counselors who are engaged in attentively listening to and analyzing their own performances on tape. Who among those now practicing does not recall the excitement such learnings generated? It was here where theoretical principles of operation broke down or were confirmed, where decisions to function differently were made, where the idea became flesh, alive, concrete. One could grab hold of specific variables and begin to make a positive difference in service delivery. The gains were immediate. And this raises an obvious question, the kind any innocent child might ask: If Rogers and his associates were so enthusiastic over their own learnings about how they functioned in the counseling interview through the critical scrutiny of transcripts, why were they not as enthusiastic about engaging the client in the same kind of process? Strangely, these builders of a theoretical model of counseling, one which emphasized client-centering, a model that shifted the control of interview structure from the counselor to the client, did not consider the idea of putting session transcripts into client hands. One could say the client-centeredness stopped before it went halfway.

No doubt hundreds have asked the same obvious question. No doubt, too, some practitioners have discovered that providing their clients with a cassette tape of each session does in fact accelerate the pace of client learnings and growth, substantially augmenting the treatment process while decreasing the length. But counseling literature is oddly bereft of reports about such practice. One surmises that it is not a regular or even common procedure, and then wonders why not. Controlled research could easily be designed to confirm that the practice is beneficial to clients, at least to those who are willing to take the time to analyze the taped record of their last counseling session prior to their next appointment with their counselor.

A SUMMARY OF BENEFITS

Before we consider why counselors do not regularly tape their sessions and present the cassette to their clients, let us look at the benefits for doing so:

1. The client can later retrieve much of what tends to be lost in a counseling session. Clients are frequently so absorbed in themselves, emotionally distraught, exerting psychic energy in defense of their image or in justification of past behavior, or mentally transfixed upon how they will recount their own data, that much of what the counselor imparts does not register with them. At a quieter time when they are removed from the immediate dynamics of the interplay between themselves and the counselor, they can focus upon what actually was said. Many report that they then hear for the first time what their counselor was really saying.

2. Counseling sessions frequently contain counselor instructions or agreements that particular tasks will be worked upon between sessions: psychological homework. Clients often tend to fail to accomplish such mutually arrived-at goals because they forget them, either in part or number. Their memories are easily refreshed if they have a transcript.

3. Clients become aware of their own denials and defenses, if they can "stand outside of themselves" and hear just how they go about changing the subject, overtalking, interrupting, rambling, saying what they don't really mean, blaming others, or engaging in any number of such tactics.

4. Clients become conscious, even self-conscious, of their image, their personality, how they present themselves to others, how others see them, when they can pull back and "get outside of themselves" when they are alone listening to their tape. There are many clients who have made tapes before and listened to these, but the purpose of taping usually was for sending messages or taking notes the way one uses a Dictaphone. In these recordings one shapes what one has to say, is consciously "on stage," and undesirable habitual or characteristic behaviors are either squelched at the start or edited out. When clients hear themselves interacting in counseling sessions they ask their counselor, "Is *this* how I come across

to you? Is that what I'm really like?" The result is often a decision to work at changing themselves, to establish new or additional goals.

5. Awareness of characteristic speech patterns, of language use, of ineffective or low-level communication skills is frequently what comes home to clients when they are exposed to their own natural flow of self-expression. Again, a desire or decision to change or broaden the counseling focus to include altered communication styles occurs as a result.

6. When clients hear the transcripts of sessions they are more prone to evaluate critically how the counseling time was expended and to confront their counselor, thus taking more responsibility for determining counseling content. When it becomes obvious to them that what they had wanted to work on in a session got deflected or postponed, perhaps because the counselor did all the talking and introduced a game plan to which the client did not accede, they feel more emboldened to object in the next go-around. Or they are able to see that much unhelpful repetition is taking place in the counseling, or that the counselor is indulging in self-disclosure that leaves them unmoved, or any manner of additional behaviors that their counselor might manifest without apparent suitability. Counselors who encourage their clients to monitor and evaluate the productivity of what the counselor does usually don't appreciate how difficult this analytical task is, particularly when the client sees the counselor as somewhat omniscient, or at least as an authority figure. Most clients need instruction about how to proceed in more effective interview structuring, and tapes provide them with more tangible means for doing so.

7. The value of reinforcement is easily underplayed. When clients listen to their interviews, key concepts, counselor support statements, the presence of self-defeating behaviors and the ardor to work on these, declarations of intent—indeed, all that transpired during each session is reinforced through repetition.

8. By listening to their tapes, clients evidence to themselves and to their counselors that they are committed to the counseling process, committed to active self-regeneration.

9. Misunderstandings and misrepresentations are more easily identified by clients who have session transcripts to review. Frequently, too, clients have insights about what was fuzzy, what was encircled but never pinned down. With transcripts, they are better able to clarify and define concerns and difficulties.

10. Frequently clients will bring in tapes of former sessions and want to replay portions with their counselor present to clarify or illustrate

some significant revelation or interaction. With the actual record in hand, this review can be more specific and focused.

11. When clients have physical control of their encapsulated sessions, they can choose to listen to a tape in whole or part with another person, say a spouse or family member, if such is deemed productive to the counseling. The results of revealing to some significant third party what occurred in a particular session are seldom predictable, but in each case the occasion tends to serve as a catalyst for meaningful dialogue about matters of importance in a client's personal relationship.

12. Tapes of sessions contain evidence of client growth. Working on the reduction of specific self-defeating client behaviors, ineffective speech mechanisms, negative emotionality, the prevalence of irrational thinking, and an assortment of other possibilities is where counseling focus is often directed. Analysis of tapes will show clients whether progress is being made. Then, too, it is not uncommon for clients, particularly when the counseling has continued for any length of time, to declare, "I'm no different than when I first came here. I don't think the counseling is helping me." There is a big difference, in such a case, between the counselor saying, "You're very different. You no longer do "X" and "Y." Now you do plenty of "R" and "Q," and confronting a client with the truth of this through a comparison of early and recent taped sessions.

13. Both the counselor and the client know that the client can use session recordings in any number of ways, some of which might be damaging to the client and some of which might distort how the counselor's performance is perceived. This is to say that any client could breach confidentiality by playing a tape or a portion of it before anyone extraneous to the counseling and cause undesirable consequences. By giving clients control of tapes, however, counselors make two strong—even incontrovertible—statements of cohesive value to any counselor/client bond: (1) "I fully trust you," and (2) "I will act in such a professional fashion, as your counselor, that I am unafraid of 'outsider' reactions to what we do in our sessions."

● ● ● ● ●

This short catalogue of the benefits of regularly producing tapes of counseling sessions that clients will possess and manage hardly summates all possible gains. Counselors who customarily indulge in the practice will no doubt think of additions. It is needless to protract the list, however. The case for client-centered taping is compelling. Most clients are grateful and praise the practice. It would be simple enough to include pages of testimonials from clients, but their remarks would soon become redundant. Here is just one:

> One tool which [my counselor] employed, which I found of great benefit, was that he taped our sessions on cassete and asked me to listen to them later in the week. Though he never gave a specific reason for this, I listened to the tapes, which sounded [as though he were] talking with "some other guy." Since one does not hear one's recorded voice as he hears it in his ear, I found myself listening to the tapes as if it were two other people, and this "objectivity" enabled me to spot things in my speech and behavior which I was unaware of as I spoke. The defense mechanisms which I heard in the tape, such as my stalling, topic avoidance, humorous remarks, and hostilities, were very revealing to me.[6]

We have so far considered the advantages. What are the disadvantages of presenting clients with tapes of their sessions? Probably any counselor who has entertained the likelihood would be able to construct a list much longer than what is presented above. But the items on such a list would share in common, more than likely, counselor self-defensiveness and self-protection themes. "What if X or Y heard this tape? I could end up getting shot! Or what if my client's wife's lawyer heard these tapes? I could end up in a court case. I could be sued for malpractice." Certainly the procedure imposes restrictions on counselor behavior if the counselor fears that the tapes will be used errantly, that imagined hostile judges will disapprove of how a counselor performs. Any counselor who is unsure of his or her professionalism would decide against the practice, and any number of rationalizations can be put forth to justify such a stance. "It's not necessary. It's too much work. The client's privacy needs protection." Most counselors are threatened by the loss of control over case material.

Given the publicity that surrounded the theft of Daniel Ellsberg's tapes of sessions with his psychiatrist, or, more notoriously, the publicity that incensed the nation when Richard M. Nixon's taping imbroglios and embranglements were exposed, especially his cover-ups, it is no wonder that "lesser mortals" are taping-shy. But is there a better way for counselors to become authentically accountable for what they do? It is difficult to conceive of a practice that would speak louder in behalf of an effective counselor's professional ethics.

Regular taping certainly requires little extra effort. Clients can bring their own recorders to sessions or use the counselor's machine. Here is Counselor Smith introducing the idea to a new client:

> It is a regular practice of mine to make cassette tapes of counseling sessions, and these tapes will become your property. In this way nothing

will be lost of what we say to one another. You can go over our sessions by yourself and review everything between sessions. Each time we will make a tape and you can take it with you.

Some clients save all their tapes, but you can decide if this is what you want to do. I would recommend that you save some of those we make early on in the counseling because you'll then be able to measure later progress and growth against these. It's always helpful for us to have some confirmation that we are indeed making progress.

I want to stress that these are *your* sessions, and there is no reason for anyone else even to know that the tapes exist. If you want to let someone else hear a session or part of one, let's discuss that in counseling. It may or it may not be a good idea to do so.

I'll provide the blank tape for today's session. When you come for your next appointment, you can give me a blank tape to replace it and also bring another blank tape for that session. Each time you come bring a blank tape with you, a 60-minute one.

Do you want to go ahead with this practice? Maybe you would like to discuss it first.

Even if Smith's offer is rejected, the client has been introduced to the idea and it can be reconsidered later in the counseling.

• • • • •

Finally, this chapter is the appropriate place to include guidelines for "counseling by tape," a practice the author developed through necessity. Often clients move to another geographical locale and cannot continue the counseling in person, and counseling by telephone is considered too expensive. Does counseling by tape work? In the author's experience, it did. But not without some client preparation.

The author was granted a sabbatical leave and he chose to live 2,500 miles away from home base during that year, after which he would return. At the time he had a private case load of some two dozen clients. Though he attempted to refer all of his clients to colleagues, only a few were willing to continue the counseling with someone new. Because all clients were accustomed to listening to tapes of their sessions, they readily agreed to being counseled by tape. Once the practice was instituted, however, it became clear that the clients needed some guidance in making tapes that would be productive for the counseling to continue. The following guidelines served the purpose.

How did the practice turn out? Surprisingly some clients (perhaps half) gained more from the counseling-by-tape than they had from face-to-face counseling. How could this be accounted for? The author guesses that it was because each had to work harder to select and order counseling material in his absence than each had done before. The practice demanded greater client commitment, more self-activity, than was required when the counselor could be counted on to initiate meaningful counseling focus. Clients accepted more responsibility for taking charge and making a difference in their own lives.

The author's method of listening and responding to a client's tape involved the use of two pocket recorders, one to play the tape and one to create a tape for the client. Thus, he would listen to a portion of the client's tape and immediately respond to that portion as though the client were present, sometimes including bits of the client's statements within the tape he was recording, listening and responding repeatedly. At the end of the counselor-made tape, the author would summarize, perhaps ask questions, basically helping the client to organize and proceed with the next tape encounter.

COUNSELING SESSIONS BY CASSETTE TAPE: GUIDELINES FOR CLIENTS[7]

Some Background About Counseling

The heart of successful counseling is positive client behavioral change. This means that the client behaves in new ways that are self-promoting. Old behavior that persists, but doesn't add to a person's feeling better or help the person to advance his/her status in the world, continues because the person hasn't learned or hasn't integrated new or different behaviors that work better in those same situations where the old behavior is manifested. The old behavior also results in some payoffs that are hard to give up, even though these rewards are negative. For example, if I make myself angry over the way someone else behaves, I get these payoffs:

1. I don't need to be responsible for the way I feel or for shaping events. I say to myself that what has happened is the other person's fault. I blame the other.
2. Because I believe the other person has made me this way, I have a license to lash out at the other person, to hurt that person in return for being hurt. I may even need to be upset in order to say what I would like to say or do what I would like to do to this other person because I fear that person or because that individual is unimpressed by my customary agreeable way of interacting and

tends to run roughshod over me. By being angry, I get false courage. It gets my motor working.

3. I couldn't help it. I'm just reacting. Because I believe that the other person is responsible, I don't need to think about how to take care of myself when the other person acts in the way she/he acted. (If the other person would act differently, I would be OK.)

4. I don't need to do the hard work of changing, of learning new ways to think, feel, and act.

Changing behavior first of all means changing the way I think, changing my mental behavior. My emotional behavior, the way I feel at any given moment, comes from the thoughts I have. And what I do, my actions, results from what I *think* as well. So, the name of the counseling game is: acquiring new, more effective thinking, and practicing this until it becomes natural to me, until I own it. And thinking is the hardest work humans can do. Especially the kind of thinking that produces a new computer program in the head. Following the old program can hardly be called thinking. It is what will happen if I don't do the hard work of rewriting it. Once I have decided on a new program, I must practice making it stick. Practice is frequently painful because I am not good at it (because I haven't done it before), and my first efforts are bound to be awkward and will not work as well as I would like them to. There is a great temptation to give up, to tell myself I can't ever learn this new way of living in my head.

If a counselor is to be of assistance to a client, this professional needs to know what is going on in the client's head and in the client's life, what the client is dealing with day by day. Helping a client to think in new, more effective ways in any given instance is what the counselor is trained to do, but in order to accomplish this the counselor needs to know what is going on.

Some Remarks About Taping

In a session where the client and the counselor are physically together the counselor can "read" the client, see how the client feels and acts. The counselor, skilled in reading emotions, can pick up on what is happening in the client and pick out from the client's personal data those elements that are disturbing to a client. Also, the counselor can help the client to discriminate, to bring up what is important. The counselor elicits from the client that which is important for client growth. There's an immediacy in this process that is missing in sessions conducted by tape, where there is a time lag. So, in taped sessions where the counselor must react to client reports and other verbalizations after some time has passed, there needs to be an understanding that immediacy is not possible. This may be the hardest new learning surrounding taped sessions. Patience is always difficult to acquire (though extremely valuable to effective living).

Another aspect of taping that is difficult for anyone unaccustomed to doing it has to do with feeling embarrassed or inadequate about the quality of one's production. We all have been conditioned to think we must put our best foot forward. In counseling this is nonsense, as it is in most parts of our lives. The counselor doesn't judge a client's worth. The client has total worth, total acceptance, and doesn't have to earn this. It is a given.

You may not like your production for any one of a hundred reasons ("I don't like the sound of my voice. I talk funny. I come off as a dumb person. I ramble. I say 'and uh' too much. My thoughts are confused."). But how can you expect to be good at this new behavior if you have not done much of it? Again, you get good at anything by practicing, so don't have unreasonable expectations for yourself. Besides, your counselor doesn't give a thought to how you are performing, or compare you to someone else or to some predetermined standard. He/she is not grading you. If getting better at taping is a goal for you, then the counseling can focus on this, too. More important than how you tape is *what* you include, so that the counselor's reaction can be the most meaningful in helping you to advance yourself in your world, the "heart" of counseling referred to above.

When and Where To Make a Tape

You will find a method and style of taping that suits you. Experiment. Scheduling helps, if you stick to it. Perhaps you will make notes, have these in front of you after enough have accumulated, then schedule a time period of an hour or so for yourself in some place where you have privacy and won't be interrupted, and complete a tape at one sitting. Perhaps you will put 10 minutes of your thoughts on tape every day, just before you retire for the night, until the tape is completed. Perhaps you will make the tape recorder accessible for spontaneous entries at unscheduled times, placing important material on the tape when you feel a need. If privacy is difficult for you to attain, it may be that you will drive somewhere, park, and do all of you taping in the car. If you are in your car every day and travel a good distance to and from work, you may elect to tape as you make your rounds.

Be sure to date your entries and give the circumstance under which you are making each one ("I'm talking to you now at 12:30 in the afternoon, on Wednesday, April 7. I have saved 15 minutes of my lunch hour to tell you some things. I'm sitting at my desk, in my office, with the door closed, but I may be interrupted at any time."). This helps your counselor to understand where you are in your world at the exact time you are expressing yourself. Such information is frequently very important to the counseling.

Should you listen to what you have said? Not if you are bothered by the *way* you say things, but otherwise, yes, definitely. You may want to change what you have said to make it more accurate, or, in hearing your own statements, you may realize you have left out some important material, which you can then add. Just as putting your thoughts on tape in the first place will be a helpful release for you, so too will listening to yourself help you to become more involved in the counseling process.

You will find, after a time, that taping is fun. You are creating—shaping your own audio production.

What to Put on Your Tape

The choice is yours, of course. It's your session and you can determine what the focus of the session will be. In his or her response, the counselor may give you helpful suggestions for the focus of future sessions, but these will only be suggestions, for you to heed or not according to your own judgment. You are the authority in your world. You will make the decisions.

Here are some guidelines for session content:

1. Report your activities since your last session so that your counselor can know what has been going on in your world, particularly those related to why you came for counseling in the first place and the thematic concerns that have become central to the counseling.
2. Discuss the times you have felt bad in the interval. When were you feeling any negative emotion (depressed, angry, bored, lonely, jealous, worried, afraid, and so on)? When did these bad feelings occur? What stimulated them? What did you do? What were you thinking while you were feeling this way?
3. Discuss you physical well-being and activities related to health: sleeping, eating, exercise, medication, drinking, even your "regularity." If you have had any physical symptoms related to emotional distress, what were these and when did they occur?

4. Report progress or lack of it in the dimensions that have been the focus of the counseling. If there were blocks, what were they? Evaluate how you are doing.
5. Bring up any troublesome new material.
6. Discuss your relationships with important others in your world, how you are faring, how you are handling yourself in your interactions.
7. Identify your goals, those things you are working on, the new ways of thinking and behaving that you are endeavoring to incorporate into your repertoire. Then give a report on goal-achievement, how you are doing with each. Do this each time you make a tape.
8. When you are feeling down or upset, during the height of that feeling, when it is the most intense, right at that moment put your thoughts and emotion on tape, if you can. Let it all hang out. It will help you to talk about it and your counselor can get a "reading" of what you feel by the way in which your express yourself.
9. Bring up anything you see as a problem.
10. Report your victories. What have you accomplished that pleases you?
11. Report your pleasures. Have you been loving yourself, rewarding yourself, giving yourself good times?
12. Ask questions. There is a large teaching element in counseling. Pick your counselor's brain.
13. Discuss your longer-range plans. What will you accomplish in the next 2 weeks, the next month? Where will you be 6 months from now? Make predictions. Lay out your strategies for where you want to go.

Final Thoughts

Above is a "baker's dozen" of helpful hints to get you over the hurdle of making your first tape. Save room at the end to discuss the difficulties you encountered in making the tape itself. Then your counselor can respond to these and give specific suggestions for improving your tape-making behavior so that the counseling will continue to increase in productivity, so that you can become a more effective user of your counselor's expertise. Effective communication is vital to effective counseling, and you are learning another way of communicating. Getting better and better at communicating is a built-in goal for all counseling, and, more important, for all effective living.

Be yourself when you tape. Don't try to censor. Laugh when you feel like it. Hem and haw. It's OK. Say whatever comes into your head, just as you would if you were in the same room with your counselor. Make it fun, whenever you can. The struggle to become more effective as a person is tough enough, and the more fun, play, and humor you can bring into the process, the more you will want to engage in it.

If you want a tape you have produced returned to you, you must indicate this. Otherwise your tape will get erased (taped over) by your counselor.

Finally, don't feel compelled to fill up an hour's tape. If you get bogged down, or if it takes more time than you have to devote to it, send on whatever you produce and discuss why you couldn't finish it.

NOTES

1. Rogers, C. (1961). *On becoming a person: A therapist's view of psychotherapy*. Boston: Houghton Mifflin, p. 247.
2. Lasch, C. (1984, August 13, 20). A chip of fools. *The New Republic*, pp. 26–27.
3. Rogers, C. (1942). The use of electrically recorded interviews in improving psychotherapeutic techniques. *American Journal of Orthopsychiatry, 12*, 419.
4. Rogers, C. (1980). *A way of being*. Boston: Houghton Mifflin, p. 138.
5. Ibid., p. 62.
6. The excerpt is from a client's letter invited for use in peer review for licensing requirements. Thanks are due to Bruce N. Peltier, PhD, a counseling psychologist who practices in San Francisco, California, for permission to publish this portion.
7. Readers are free to reproduce these guidelines without sending for written permission but are cautioned to give publisher and author credit when making copies of this copyrighted material for professional use with clients.

Vocational Counseling: Pie in the Sky Brought to the Table

Then the Emperor walked along in the procession under the gorgeous canopy, and everybody in the streets and at the windows exclaimed, "How beautiful the Emperor's new clothes are! What a splendid train! And they fit to perfection!" Nobody would let it appear that he could see nothing, for then he would not be fit for his post, or else he was a fool.

None of the Emperor's clothes had been so successful before.

"But he has nothing on," said a little child.

"Oh, listen to the innocent," said its father; and one person whispered to the other what the child had said. "He has nothing on, a child says he has nothing on!"

The Emperor writhed, for he knew it was true, but he thought "the procession must go on now." So he held himself stiffer than ever, and the chamberlains held up the invisible train.

—Hans Christian Andersen[1]

He has no vocation to labor, and, although he strenuously preached it for a time, and made some efforts to practice it, he soon found he had no genius for it, and that it was a cruel waste of his time. It depressed his spirits even to tears.

—Ralph Waldo Emerson speaking of Amos Bronson Alcott, sire of Louisa Mae.[2]

⫿t is time to take an honest, clear-eyed look at vocational counseling, to consider this important part of what every counselor inevitably gets caught up in if she or he deals with a client, almost *any* client, for a protracted period. We must free ourselves of that bias and cant inherent in most counselor training programs, in the endless amount of literature in the field, and in what prevails in the culture itself. Vocational counseling is difficult to do effectively.

Rampant confusion exists because a plethora of terms and descriptions muddy the waters: career counseling, career education, vocational guidance, educational counseling (for the sake of career choice), occupational counseling, job counseling—or training or placement— preparation for the world of work (the list can be added to, broadened or refined), with many advocates delineating multiple practices to justify differences in labeling, and basing whatever they advocate on a set of assumptions located in a particular career development or occupational choice theory.

More confusion exists because of the tools and aids that have been generated for vocational counselors over time, many being "big business," whether they be books, pamphlets, film strips, video tapes, computer software, occupational information indexes, and such "multi-media," or whether they be diagnostic tools, tests, and inventories. *Any* test, not just occupational interest inventories, is "fair" to get a client pigeonholed into a job slot, be it the *Rorschach* ink-blot, a standardized paper and pencil test of mental maturity, an individually administered intelligence test (the *Stanford-Binet* or the *Wechsler*), a personality test, a self-esteem test, a manual dexterity test, a job-knowledge test, a job-performance test, a scholastic achievement test, a differential aptitude test—whatever! Once the route of diagnostics and assessment of client "potential" and vocational "interests" and "aptitudes" is taken, a battery of tests is usually thought of, since no *one* measuring instrument has been found that can adequately do the total task. There's "gold in them thar hills!" Every counseling professional organization's mailing list becomes the leased property of the purveyors of materials, and junk mail advertising all the latest or the best adjunct stuff in the career field comes in a steady stream to all of us who are members.

Still more confusion results from what everyone in the land thinks about work. The world of work is a part of every day's news. Employment and unemployment, business and industry, the success or failure of educational institutions based on how well they prepare their charges to enter the labor market, the crises in the cities, the new technology, the changing nature of work and the work force, the clashes between labor and management, the state of the economy, gross national product, for-

111

eign trade, inflation, the poor—all pertain to work and workers. Every citizen is appraised by a work role. If one is not a success in one's work, one flunks life.

In this chapter we will look at all of this and sort out how to perform realistically, as practically as possible, in the confusing area of vocational counseling. But first let us get acquainted with the trials and tribulations of Oscar.

OSCAR'S STORY[3]

Once upon a time, born to Oval and Peter Krossways, Oscar arrived on planet Earth. At the hospital Oval's sister, Hortense, commented on his appearance.

"He'll be a leader, just like his father. He's darker, but he has a strong chin and his head is shaped just like Peter's."

Oval never forgot that remark.

When he was three and a half, at a family picnic, his paternal grandmother put the QUESTION to him. "What do you want to be when you grow up, Oscar?"

"A big dog, just like Rusty." Oscar thought that was very funny. He laughed and rolled over in the grass.

"Be serious," said his grandmother.

Oscar sat up, looked directly in her eyes, and smiled politely. He knew how to be serious. Grandmother gave him presents.

"I want to be a big man." He threw his hands over his well-shaped head. "Just like Daddy."

Grandmother was pleased. She hugged him to her ample bosom.

When he was in the first grade Mrs. Hightaller asked her pupils to name all the jobs they could think of. Everyone who could think of one made a donation. Mrs. Hightaller (whom the children referred to as "Mrs. High-baller" outside of class) wrote them on the blackboard (which was really the green board).

After gathering twenty-six names of jobs from the children, and restraining herself from adding any donations of her own to the list but feeling pleased that she knew more than they did, she said, "Now, I want you to pick one from the list on the blackboard and draw a picture of a person doing that job."

Oscar drew a picture of a mailman coming up the path to his house. He finished before everyone else, so as an afterthought, he added in his dog, Rusty, biting the mailman on the neck, especially showing what big sawlike teeth Rusty had. Later, Mrs. Hightaller questioned Oscar.

"How come you colored everything black except Rusty, Oscar?"

"Because that's my favorite color."

"But you colored Rusty red."

"That's because I only had two Crayolas."

"How come you show Rusty biting the mailman?"

"Well, you see, that's what he really wants to do, so I thought I'd let him do it for once."

In the teachers' lounge after lunch, Mrs. Hightaller summarized the story of how Oscar ("you know, the little squirmy kid who always runs everywhere") had colored the dog red and everything else black. She added a tag-line.

"He's got black pride!"

Her voice cracked and she started to howl. Everyone laughed heartily. It was important for teachers to laugh at things; it got them through their days. Mr. Killroy, the only male teacher in the school laughed till he cried, but he could be excused: he had weak eyes. He drank.

In the third grade Ms. Printpratt (whom the children referred as "Miz PP" outside of class) introduced a social studies unit on world history and Oscar learned about the great discoverers. Since he was a good reader, he took books out of the public library and boned up on them. He learned all about Columbus, Sir Francis Drake, Balboa, Gulliver, Marco Polo, Admiral Perry, Robinson Crusoe, Lewis and Clark, even Stanley and Livingstone. Thereafter, whenever adults socked him with the QUESTION, he would say that he wanted to be an explorer. The adults, with predictably boring regularity, would explain to him why "explorer" was a flatulent choice, not practical, and since he was male that he would need to make a better one, one in which he could make a good living and *be* somebody. Then he would answer that he just wanted to grow up and be happy. The adults would trail off the conversation with a remark such as, "Well, you have plenty of time. You're young, yet."

Once around Halloween, when he was locked in his bedroom for setting a dried cornfield on fire in the neighborhood, and he had gotten tired of practicing weird faces in front of his mirror, he thought, "Why do I have to grow up to *be* somebody? I already *am* somebody." He had gone to the family reunion picnic the day before and practically every adult there had asked him the QUESTION.

Oscar never forgot that thought.

In the eighth grade along with all of his classmates, Oscar was administered the "Kuder Preference Record-Vocational." He enjoyed punching out the little holes. Later his counselor, Mrs. Ernestine-Joselle Pock, called him into her office to discuss the results of his performance and what they meant. Ernestine-Joselle had wanted to be a fashion designer until she met Harry Pock at a campus homecoming dance; then she switched her major to education because she thought she would like the hours a teacher kept and the summers off. After four years of teaching she decided the work was taxing, so she got a master's degree in counseling and finally, after much intradistrict wangling and politicking, had been assigned to the counseling office where she distinguished herself by being a well-dressed model for the girls. On special weekends she loved to go shopping for clothes and disco-dancing in Toronto and Chicago. Harry, who could afford it, was now a dentist and preferred playing golf, but Dr. Pock gave in, once a month on the average, to Ernestine-Joselle's wishes.

Mrs. Pock (whom her counselees called "Mrs. Doctor Spock" outside of school) began by explaining the reason for his visit.

"I have to make out your program for next year to send over to the high school, Oscar, and it's a good time for you to start thinking about your future. Have you given some thought to your career, what field you'd like to go into?"

"I'm not sure. Either law or engineering, I guess." Being bright, Oscar had learned some of the "right" answers to the QUESTION and could recognize it regardless of what dress it wore. "It's impractical to be a big-game hunter," he kidded. He had discovered Hemingway after his English teacher, Mr. Furlong (whom the students called "Mr. Not-Furlong" outside of class), had assigned *The Old Man and the Sea*. Also, he had dipped into a book called *Your Future in Exotic Occupations*[4] and discovered that big-game hunter wasn't even listed.

Mrs. Pock smiled but ignored the hunter reference. "I think you could make it in either law or engineering, according to your scores on the 'Kuder'." When the face on Oscar's well-shaped head showed puzzlement, she went on to explain that ... "the 'Kuder' was the vocational preference test you took in Mr. Furlong's class, the one with the holes. You scored very high on the 'Persuasive, Outdoor, and Scientific' scales. I suppose your high score on the 'Outdoor' goes along with your big-game interest." Mrs. Pock smiled pleasantly and rearranged her bottom parts, tugging at her tight-fitting skirt. "Since your mental maturity and achievement test scores are high, too, what this means, Oscar, is that it will be OK for me to program you into algebra 1, Spanish 1, and the advanced English class next fall. Do you have any questions?"

Oscar allowed as how he didn't and Mrs. Pock said, "Good," and bade him to send in Griselda, who was waiting patiently outside her office.

In the early part of his high school senior year Oscar had to have an interview with his counselor, Mr. Todd, to discuss his college applications. He was prepared for the session. It had been all settled at home. Peter Krossways was the manager and half-owner of a small lumber yard and was stern about Oscar's not counting on going to work for him.

"You get into a profession. That's the bottom line, son. Otherwise I'm not giving you a penny for college. You get an edu*ca*tion!"

Peter had often suffered feelings of social inferiority as a result of his lack of formal education and the big calluses on his rough hands. Oval Krossways simply absorbed and backed Peter's point; for her, too, life frequently had been full of hard jolts of the kind which were prominent for Peter. The settlement Oscar had won in the family discussions about his future was the privilege of attending a college in the West, even though that would be much more expensive that a state school.

Mr. Todd (whom the students referred to as "Mr. Toad" outside of the counseling office, when they referred to him at all: he was seldom discussed because he was seldom thought about) could usually be discovered at his desk. He was five feet five inches tall, weighed two hundred and sixty-nine pounds, and he found it taxing to get up from his chair.

"Let's see," Mr. Todd began, "you've listed five universities in California and Oregon, and that your parents will bear the full financial burden of your education. ...... Hmmmm ..... Your S.A.T.'s and G.P.A.'s are exceptional .... you should have no trouble there. But I see you're not involved in school activities, no clubs, sports, school government, music ..... You just come here for classes, is that right?"

"Yes, sir. I've always had jobs after school."

"Oh? What kind of jobs?"

"Working for my dad in his lumber yard, caddying, landscaping, you know. Right now I work in a fish store."

"So that's what that odor is," Mr. Todd kidded. Oscar didn't smile. He also refrained from responding that all he noticed was Mr. Todd's body odor. "Ahem! .... It's close in here. You'd think they would give counselors larger offices. Well, you're a worker. We can say that, can't we. Your 'Kuder' results show you as being high on the 'Persuasive, Mechanical, Computational, Scientific, and Outdoor' scales. You could go in almost any direction, I'd say. The 'Kuder' was that test where you punched out the holes." Oscar nodded. "You've given some thought to vocational objectives, what you'll study in college?"

"Yes, sir. Either pre-law or pre-med. I've only selected places where there is both a law and a med school."

"You seem in good shape to me. Here are applications for each of your target schools. Can you have these back to me in a week? ... Good. I wish every one of my counselees were as easy as you. Send in that heavy-set girl on the end, Griselda. She's been waiting a long time."

When Oscar was in his junior year at the University of Oregon, Peter and Oval received what they later saw as a letter containing ominous portents. By this time Oscar had discovered alcohol, sex, pot, orgies, and some other activities he mysteriously alluded to as his "debaucheries." He had been home only once, at the midyear break, an experience he decided not to repeat. The first summer he worked for the U.S. Forest Service fighting blister rust in Idaho; the second summer he worked in a cafeteria at Crater Lake National Park. The letter in question contained this paragraph:

I've made a number of visits to the University Counseling Center and taken a battery of tests, you know . . . ink blots, intelligence, vocational, even a "values" test. I couldn't make up my mind about a major. After a lot of b.s. went down (excuse the expression, Mom), I decided that I'm such a generalist, I ought to major in philosophy. You'll be happy to know, however, that I'm still going to minor in the physical sciences which will keep me being eligible for med school.

Sometime during the spring of that year Oscar hitchhiked around Mexico. When he returned to Eugene, he found that he just couldn't "get into" his classes. His parents learned this from a postcard they received in July. "I'm living in a commune, now," was the end of the brief message. There was no return address. For a number of years thereafter little contact occurred between the Krossways, elder and younger, only an announcement from the University of Oregon that Oscar was no longer matriculating, accompanied by a debit statement for tuition, residence, lab, bookstore, and library (for overdue and lost books) fees, and a rare postcard sans a return address from Oscar himself. At least he wasn't dead, they knew, but these were taxing years for Oscar's parents, especially for Oval who invented stories for her friends, hating herself for doing so but seemingly unable to stop, since her friends doted so much on the achievements of their children.

When Oscar was twenty-eight, his parents let him live with them as long as he agreed to go to work and save up the necessary money it took him to be on his own. The "story" had gradually come out: he had "renounced" ordinary materialistic goals and living, had visions, had joined a religious group and become a "Jesus freak," had fathered a son, gotten married, tried selling used cars for his father-in-law, had gotten divorced, had bummed around Canada, had learned how to live in the woods and spear fish, had practiced Zen, had spent three days in jail on a disorderly conduct charge, and had generally spent a great deal of time being "spaced out," as he put it. The one thing that pleased Oval was that he stayed firm and lean, that he had not become "flabby" the way Peter had.

As fate would have it, the years after Oscar returned appeared to his parents to be more taxing, yet. Oval often found herself wishing he had stayed away. There were many family fights; Peter was becoming thin-skinned, cantankerous, withdrawn. Oscar tried a number of jobs, but none of them "stuck." At one point Peter gave in to Oval's pleadings and took him into the family business, but that only lasted two weeks before Oscar sullenly quit. Nor did it seem that Oscar would ever find a "nice girl" and have a "lasting relationship." Finally, it seemed as though he was going to settle down and make something of himself: he landed a position as the manager of a fish counter for a large foodstore chain, saw a "future" in it if he could complete his college degree and become a buyer in the central office. His bar behavior tapered off and he started night school courses in business administration.

When he was thirty-three, both of his parents died in the same year, his father first, from blood poisoning, and his mother later in the year after a tragic bout with double pneumonia. Oscar quit school and his job, sold his inherited interest in the lumber yard to his father's partner, sold the family house, moved into a furnished room, and stayed swacked for six months. He met Christine Westerly, who was older and worked in a Chinese laundry, during this mind-quieting time. Later he moved in with her and she devoted herself to caring for him. She believed that he would "find himself," eventually, with her nurturing.

One evening, about the time Christine was contemplating "throwing in the towel," since he wasn't responding much to her ministration, Oscar announced that he had purchased an almost new truck and semi-trailer, an eighteen-wheeler, with what was left of his dwindling inheritance. In one of his haunts he had encountered an independent trucker, Duke Wheeler (whose C-B handle was "Wheeler Dealer"), had gone on some runs with him, had learned how to operate the vehicle and what he needed to know in order to "be in business." Within a year he had emancipated Christine from the Chinese laundry and married her, had gotten the necessary licenses, had made hauls to fifteen states, had accumulated some capital, and had a solid plan for starting a fleet. His C-B handle was "OK Porkpie" and he loved it. He had adopted the habit of wearing a black porkpie hat which had become his emblem; other truckers never failed to recognize him. It turned out that meeting Duke, who had exhausted his wanderlust with the help of his ever-baby-bearing-wife, proved to be Oscar's salvation. Within five more years he had acquired a fleet of six trucks, a house in one of the better suburbs, a camper, a gun collection, and the mounted head of an Alaskan brown bear which he hung over the fireplace in his den.

A number of years later, several long decades, in fact, the practicum supervisor at the state university addressed the twelve counselors in training.

"I'm not going to assign this next client to just anyone," she said. "A Mr. Krossways is sitting in the waiting room. He's seventy-two years old. Erica referred him to our center, so anyone but Erica can volunteer to work with him. Who'd like to be his counselor?"

No one spoke up.

"OK, then, why don't we choose the oldest person here to be his counselor. How old are you, Tom?"

"Forty-two."

"Is anyone older than Tom? . . . . . OK, then, why don't you take him, Tom."

"Tom, he told me he'd pre*fer* a man," said Erica.

In the cubicle Tom came right to the point. "Why are you here, Mr. Krossways?"

"Well, my neighbor, Erica Doable . . . Do you know her?" Tom nodded.

"Well, she has to hustle up some people for some course she's taking and I'm doing her a favor."

"And besides that, Mr. Krossways. Now that you're here, what do you want to discuss?"

"Erica told me you'd probably want me to talk about my problems. Well, you might say that the two *big* problems facing me right now are making out my will and figuring out what to do after I sell my company. I own a small trucking firm. I don't see any point in making out my will, since I'm healthy as an ox and my wife Christine ... Chris ... Chris Krossways, ha, ha, ha ... uhm ... People used to joke about that a lot but not any more. She doesn't get out much. Pretty much bed-ridden. It's her back and her heart. I don't think she'd going to last long. Anyhow, my lawyer tells me I'm a damned fool if I don't make out a will before the sale."

"You don't know what you're going to do after you sell your company?" asked Tom.

"No, I don't," said Oscar. "That concerns me a lot these days ... Oh, by the way. You interested in buying the mounted head of a large Alaskan brown bear? I ask everyone these days. No harm in trying, I always say."

"No, I'm afraid not. You were saying that figuring out what to do after selling your company is a problem for you."

"Yeah. Never gave it any thought till recently. Just assumed I'd keep on doing what I was doing till my damned health ran out. But I'm due for a change. It's not much fun any more, so I'd like to do something else. With Chris gone, I don't think I'd like to stay around here any more. Probably go out West."

"I see. So you're interested in some other line of work."

"Yeah, you might say that. I'm at the crossways, you might say. Ha, ha."

"I see. Well, for a start we could give you a vocational interest inventory. A lot of people find that it helps them to narrow down their decision. Let's see, now. We have the 'Kuder,' the 'D.V.D.S.,' the 'Strong-Campbell,' the ..."

"What was that second one?" asked Oscar.

Tom smiled. "Oh, the 'D.V.D.S'? That's the *Dakota Variable-Decision Survey*.[5] You think you'd like that one?"

"Does it have little holes that you punch out?" asked Oscar.

● ● ● ● ●

Oscar's story illustrates some anomalies about work in the life of just about everyone. On the one hand children are encouraged to be happy, taught that they live to learn and grow, that they have unlimited opportunity to be themselves, to develop into whatever they want to be. On the other hand they are taught that they don't count, at least not until they become adult workers, that work is their fate, and that certain kinds of work are better than others. Implied is the notion that they could become adults, end up in certain lines of work, and still not count. Along with the preparation for getting into work that counts is the childhood and youthful preparation for getting into a "relationship" that counts. If both preparations are successful, the adult will have a job that has acknowledged and visible status and provides a generous income for material well-being in a consumer society. A mate with similar values will augment the good life, presumably that of nest-building in the suburbs. There is a class structure implied here; all ought to strive to be "upwardly mobile"; as well as being the end, work and marriage provide the means.

This scenario is traditional, the American Dream reduced to its lowest common denominator. It has grown out of the history of the country. Formerly for the bulk of Americans work meant survival, having the necessities of life and little more. A good job meant not having to beg or take charity, to steal, or to be subject to economic exploitation and slavery. One could hold up one's head and have respect; one could provide for one's family and acquire a few of the luxuries, clothes, appliances, a car, perhaps even a plot of real estate. Education wasn't the answer; that was for the next generation. Getting a good job meant labor that paid well (doing for a living what one would *like* to do wasn't a factor), and getting a job where your health wasn't impaired and where you didn't get dirty every day. Getting a good job meant working hard to advance in the company, or migrating, or unionizing to fight for gains that all workers could share.

But the next generation is here, and even the next one after that. America has become a land where the suburbs predominate, where affluence has a wide base, *The Affluent Society* that John Kenneth Galbraith described for us as far back as 1958.[6] There are of course those who still live in *The Other America*[7] that Michael Harrington depicted 4 years later, those who have been left behind, perhaps even sorely discriminated against, but if pressed they too will tend to acknowledge that the Dream is real and that they are striving to participate in it. General education has become all but universal, and it has an interesting character regardless of quality: It stresses the three "Rs" but it is also designed to communicate the American Dream in its full glory. Curricula provide an array of options in the arts and sciences, in the practical arts and applied sciences, in the humanities (with large doses of history and social studies to transmit the American Dream and create good citizens), in personal hygiene, health, and exercise—including a smorgasbord of different sports. General education is designed to give all the people's children *exposure* to whatever possibilities there are. Augmenting formal general education for instilling the American Dream is general television education where the young learn consumerism, where the variety and excitement of adult life is modeled, where it is covertly but implicitly suggested that, to repeat Andy Warhol's now famous line, "The day will come when everyone will become famous for fifteen minutes."

The current version of the American Dream is that you, the average person, can have your cake and eat it too. You can become a happy individual—get into a good line of work—and live life according to Freud's pleasure principle to boot. For the first time in history you can identify yourself other than as a worker. Particularly if your parents and their parents have made enough gains, particularly if by standing on their heads *you have it made* at birth into the broad—if not yet ubiquitous— middle class, you can now think about *me* with some sense of realism. You have "life, liberty," and can take off in "pursuit of happiness," as promised in the Declaration of Independence, as Oscar did, all the while having those parental gains to fall back upon.

However tongue in cheek Oscar's story is in the telling, it is not an unrealistic one. It is, in fact, based on a combination of circumstances revealed by clients the author has actually encountered, including a man in his seventies seeking further happiness and coming for vocational counseling, acknowledging and expecting that a trained practitioner could help him in the process.

We live in new times with a new national consciousness, "Consciousness III," as Charles Reich calls it in *The Greening of America*, a book that so well defined how Americans saw themselves in 1970 that it continued on the best-seller list for months. Says Reich:

> Consciousness III is an attempt to gain transcendence. This becomes apparent when we compare Consciousness I and II. They both represent the underlying form of consciousness appropriate to the age of industrial development and the market economy, beginning in the eighteenth century. Both subordinate man's nature to his role in the economic system; Consciousness I on the basis of economic individualism, II on the basis of participation in organization. Both approve the domination of environment by technology. Both subordinate man to the state, Consciousness I by the theory of the unseen hand, II by the doctrine of the public interest. Both see man as basically antagonistic to his fellow man; neither has any theory of a human community except in terms of consent to law, government, and force. Both deny the individual's responsibility for the actions of society. Both define thought in terms of the premises of science. Consciousness II differs from I mainly in that II is adjusted to the realities of a larger scale of organization, economic planning, and a greater degree of political administration.
>
> The new consciousness is utterly different. It seeks restoration of the nonmaterial elements of man's existence, the elements like the natural envi-

ronment and the spiritual that were passed by in the rush of material development. It seeks to transcend science and technology, to restore them to their proper place as tools of man rather than as the determinants of man's existence. It is by no means anti-technological, it does not want to break machines, but it does not want machines to run men. . . . .

Each of the characteristics of Consciousness III that we have described is a specific illustration of an underlying logic. . . . . Reasoning that starts from self is necessary because the prior consciousness forgot self in an obsessive fixation upon organizations and the state. The self and its sources in nature are real; machines alone cannot create real values. The preservation of the self against the state is not "anti-social," it is of great and vital importance to the human community. Protection of nature and man from the machine is logical because of the power of the machine to dominate nature. . . . A personal moral code that transcends law is necessary where law had ceased to express a balanced set of values. A flexible and personal approach to career is necessary because technology itself is rapidly changing and because technology will dictate to man unless he preserves the power to choose his own work. . . . .

. . . We can now see the true significance of the central fact about Consciousness III—its assertion of the power to *choose* a way of life. The people who came to this country chose a life-style; it was for that freedom of choice that they left their native countries. But when the machine took over, men lost the power of choice, and their lives were molded to fit the domination of the machine. . . . The power of choice, the power to transcend, is exactly what has been missing in American for so long. That is why a new life-style is capable of dismantling the Corporate State, when both liberal reform and radical tactics are powerless. The elements of that life may vary and change; the supreme act is the act of choice. For the choice of a life-style is an act of transcendence of the machine, an act of independence, a declaration of independence. We are entering a new age of man.[8]

There were numerous reactions from the culture-diagnosticians to Reich's visionary formulations, of course, and one is perhaps worth mentioning. Sociologists Peter and Brigette Berger saw what Reich described not as the "greening" but as the "blueing" (for blue-collar worker) of America:

. . . As to the putatively green revolution, we think that the following will be the most probable result: It will accelerate social mobility in America, giving new opportunities for upward movement of lower-middle-class and working class people, and in the process will change the ethnic and religious composition of the higher classes. Put differently: far from "greening" America, the alleged cultural revolution will serve to strengthen the vitality of the technological society against which it is directed, and will further the interests of precisely those social strata that are least touched by its currently celebrated transformations of consciousness.

... The revolution is taking place, or minimally has its center, in a sub-culture of upper-middle class youth.... Youth, as we know it today, is a product of technological and economic forces intimately tied to the dynamics of modern industrialism, as is the educational system within which the bulk of contemporary youth is concentrated for ever-longer periods of life.... The cultural revolution has defined itself in diametric opposition to some of the basic values of bourgeois society. ... These same values are now perceived as "repression" and "hypocrisy," and the very promises of technological society are rejected as illusionary or downright immoral. A hedonistic ethic is proclaimed in opposition to the "Protestant" one, designed to "liberate" the individual from the bourgeois inhibitions in all areas of life, from sexuality through aesthetic experience to the manner in which careers are planned. Achievement is perceived as futility and "alienation," its ethos as "uptight" and, in the final analysis, inimical to life.[9]

Reich is neither the first nor the latest social historian to create a profile of the national character or consciousness. Defining who we are and how we think is an ongoing passtime of our intelligentsia. By 1926 Vernon Louis Parrington had completed his monumental and now classical study, *Main Currents in American Thought*,[10] a work that inspired Henry Steele Commager's, *The American Mind*,[11] published in 1950. Both of these works provide essential background understandings of how the national consciousness developed prior to World War II, a mid-century cataclysmic endurance test that forever jarred and bruised the world's face from one unconquerable and indestructable to one that could self-destruct, a war that seems to Americans alive today as the last "just" war. Following this, in 1957, Max Lerner published his massive overview, *America As a Civilization*,[12] a work that could never have been as thorough without the help of hundreds of eminent scholars from the most prestigious universities around the country. On the heels of this post-war assessment of culture and its formative effects on personality came David Reisman's work, *The Lonely Crowd*,[13] which divided Americans into "inner-directed/outer-directed" types and sketched out the hopeful vision for the autonomous person in the decades to come.

All these works, and cautiously serious studies that followed, help the counselor to have some grasp of the big picture, to provide a framework and put into a context just where the mind of each person alive today sits in relationship to a fast-paced radically transmuting modern culture. The factors that these authors introduce are impingements on everyone's consciousness, formative elements that influence how we develop and live, how we think about our social institutions or the state, how work fits in, how we shape our individual destinies within our national destiny or the destiny of all civilization worldwide. This is another way of saying that although counselors may not do the concerted in-depth thinking that enables them to write books, they ought to read widely and have a "sociological imagination," to use C. Wright Mills' expressive term.[14] Given the events since atomic bombs destroyed Hiroshima and Nagasaki, for example, who believes that our species is immortal? That it can survive another millennium? Such a consciousness certainly doesn't look much to posterity, but tends to operate on a "get it while you can" philosophy, for tomorrow—not just we—but the whole world can blow up. Dooms-day mentality inspires both dread and futility, and contributes to the meaninglessness of work.

But to introduce this picture and refer to cultural background literature in relation to vocational counseling is even more for the sake of saying that most vocational development theories and the practices that prevail in our society for assisting the young to choose careers are narrow, suspect, largely mythological, and do not take important verities into account. All the theories were formulated on assumptions in a world that preceded Consciousness III. They are outmoded and outdated, if ever they were reflective of a reality to begin with. Their credibility suffers on two counts: (1) They are based more on the ideal than the real; and (2) They tend to be oriented for the sake of the "establishment." It is not our purpose here to discuss how effective career development pro-jects ought to be constituted in the schools or over the life-span, or how parents might be most helpful in guidance of their offspring, but to center on what a counselor does with a client who brings work-related consid-erations into the counseling session. And what client considerations are totally disassociated with work?

Vocational development and occupational choice theories have grown out of the assumption that there is a best kind of work for each individual to do, that for every shape of person there is a correspondingly shaped hole, that square pegs ought to seek square holes, that a square peg in a round hole won't find job satisfaction. In no way is this assumption even remotely valid, as we shall see. Another assumption underlying the theories (to the author's mind the best place to look for a shorthand, condensed but cogent, summarization of these theories is still Robert Hoppock's book[15]) is that everyone who comes into the world goes through developmental stages that where broad freedom of occupational choice exists, when in actuality this ideal is likely for only the upper 10%, at best the upper quarter, of the nation's youth, and it is questionable even with this segment who have all the physical, mental, social, and economic advantages at birth. The average citizen has very limited choice, and those in the lower quarter will be lucky if they find work that pays enough to live at today's upper limit of what economists refer to as the standard-of-living poverty line. Work and its benefits are as inequitably distributed as ever in America, and given all prognostications for the future, where service jobs multiply as manual labor decreases, where the yawning gap between skilled and unskilled labor continues to widen, the theories of vocational development and occupational choice seem more removed from reality than ever.

The second critical objection to both the theories and practices, what teachers, counselors, and others engage in for the sake of guiding round people into round holes, is that what the "establishment" wants is what is broadcast as "right" or as what matters. What the establishment wants, the establishment gets. And it makes little difference how one conceives of the establishment, whether one sees it as "the interlocking directorate" of business and industry, the "military-industrial complex," as Dwight Eisenhower called it, "the Corporate State," as Reich refers to it above, the "powerbrokers" or *The Power Elite*, as C. Wright Mills titled one of his books,[16] or the "straight society" for which the beats left us an assortment of names: Jack Kerouac: "American P.T.A. fiddlefaddle busy body schemes"; Allen Ginsberg: "the syndrome of shutdown"; Ken Kesey: "the Combine."[17] The establishment calls the shots. Counselors and other guidance personnel tend to fall in line as unpaid extensions of a cultural and economic system that has its own best interests at heart, namely, a continuation of the status quo as it pertains to power and profits. Vocational counseling and career advisement personnel therefore unwittingly end up being spokespersons for management, not labor. The establishment, it might be said, has a "sweetheart arrangement" with counselors in institutional settings where they work with clients to help them conform to the dictates of the marketplace, all such effort being presented, of course, as being for the clients' own welfare. Seldom, at least not above-board, are there any kickbacks, though recruiters from large companies and corporations still come to campuses in droves in search of the best draft choices in the annual crop of graduating talent, their presence invited and welcomed.

Certainly management wants workers to be happy, to be contented, willing, cooperative. But management wants *production*, first and foremost, and this means having workers who are well-trained, intelligent, hard-driving, energetic, efficient, those who get the job done whether they enjoy their work or not. An ongoing campaign for the nation's talent prevails in every sector of the labor market. Recruitment for this upper-level pool of the nation's finest is aggressively carried on with the result that *everyone* in the society *knows* that education, test scores, and work track records make a difference in who advances and who is left behind, who gets the good jobs and who must settle for leftovers. What is the history of testing except an involved and constantly refined method of winnowing out the undesirables and finding those with the "right stuff?" What is the grading system, if it is not a similar winnowing method? Students are not detained at lower levels until they learn the required material; they are socially promoted, and whether they have learned or not is documented. Schools are more liberal than business and industry in tolerating the presence of late bloomers or those who are trying to find themselves, but eventually those who do not perform up to minimal standards will be excluded there too. What is the *Occupational Outlook Handbook* except a Department of Labor effort to help the nation meet projected labor force needs?

Those coming up who *have* excellent grades and test scores and who meet other entrance criteria can compete for the best slots, the biggest round holes, the warm, fuzzy, womby, generously endowed work. Members of this cream of the crop, though, aren't as likely to be among the clients one vocationally counsels. And just as Oscar with his advantageous start in life might have become a doctor, a lawyer, or an engineer had he persevered, neither is there a guarantee that the "creamettes" will not turn sour; being YAVIS types,[18] however, they stand a better chance of being recycled through professional intervention.

As we have seen in an earlier chapter, all that a theory amounts to is a set of propositions (what we *propose* is true) about real events. A proposition is made stronger, more valid, if testable hypotheses can be generated from it. If a theoretical proposition withstands all tests, it becomes a law. A law is a statement about reality that is true every time without exception, and the value of laws lies in their use for predicting events. When it comes to human behavior, there are *no* theoretical propositions that become laws (excluding those that apply to our physical systems), if we eliminate the obvious ones, such as the fact that we all eventually die. At best, a theoretical proposition about human behavior fits a majority of cases most of the time. We act on such propositions, nevertheless, whether we call them presumptions, assumptions, opinions, or truths. We all have them, too, however fuzzily formed they are, however illogical, however inadequate when applied to reality and asked to serve as predictors. By analyzing behavior after the fact—let us say that of a counselor performing with a client and making decisions about how to proceed—we can infer what the counselor thought, what theoretical construct, what idea about reality was in the counselor's mind. But the effective counselor will not have to infer; that individual will be aware of the theoretical concepts upon which he or she is basing counseling decisions and performance. Also, the effective counselor constantly modifies these propositions when the ideas don't work in practice.

When we focus on the propositions that compose the foundation of vocational (or career) development and occupational choice theories, there are not many that are very useful in vocational counseling. (Nor, it can be said in all fairness, are they *intended* to be. Their function is to explain a given reality, not to determine or abet counseling practice.) To illustrate this contention, let us look at just one, perhaps the most celebrated and touted: Donald E. Super's postulate that career choice more or less involves "implementation of the self-concepts," explained at length in *Career Development: Self-Concept Theory*,[19] and in a hundred other career and vocational guidance books, only some of which Professor Super himself has authored. His self-concept theory has spawned a virtual industry of books and articles, paper-pencil tests and inventories, vocational development programs and practices, computer programs, funded research projects, instructional units for the preparation of counselors, and training and management modifications in various work environments. The pervasion of self-concept theory into the consciousness of everyone who has anything whatsoever to do with career education, career guidance, or counseling is complete. The field is completely saturated.

Yet, the idea of the self doesn't make much practical sense, except as a substitute for "I/me," or ego, or mind, or character, or identity, or soul—all such labels being nebulous. If my "self" is the sum of all my choices and experiences in life, as Jean-Paul Sartre defines individual essence, then it is ever-changing, never static. Moreover, as countless sociological studies have shown, work roles are what cause changes in people, not what people acquire in order to fit in smoothly. If some cops become "fascistic," it is as a result of their work experiences and milieu (well profiled in John Hersey's book, *The Algiers Motel Incident*[20]); they don't start out that way. They don't have a fascistic self-concept, dormant and waiting for actualization, any more than do you or I. That work breeds certain "types" we all know, even to the point of hiding what we do for a living to avoid stereotypical judgments that limit us. Self might more accurately be used to describe role, as in worker-role or lover-role or touch-football-playing-role—a worker-self, a lover-self, a touch-football-playing-self, each person having many selves. In an amusing essay called "The Selves," Lewis Thomas uses the idea of multiple personalities to illustrate the absurdity of there being merely a single self.

"There are psychiatric patients," he begins,

who are said to be incapacitated by having more than one self. One of these, an attractive, intelligent young woman in distress, turned up on a television talk show a while back, sponsored to reveal her selves and their disputes. She possessed, she said, or was possessed by, no fewer than eight other separate women, all different, with different names, arguing and elbowing their way into control of the enterprise, causing unending confusion and embarrassment. She (they) wished to be rid of all of them (her), except of course herself (themselves).

People like this are called hysterics by the professionals, or maybe schizophrenics, and there is, I am told, nothing much that can be done. Having more than one self is supposed to be deeply pathological in itself, and there is no known way to evict trespassers.

I am not sure that the number of different selves is in itself all that pathological; I hope not. Eight strikes me personally as a reasonably small and easily manageable number. It is the simultaneity of their appearance that is the real problem, and I should think psychiatry would do better by simply persuading them to queue up and wait their turn, as happens in the normal rest of us. . . .

Actually, it would embarrass me to be told that more than a single self is a kind of disease. I've had, in my time, more than I could possibly count or keep track of.[21]

Thomas then proceeds to gossip about his personal family of selves.

It must be said in Super's behalf that in a later published statement he issued a caveat wherein he repudiated any simplistic notion of what self-concept theory might mean:

Despite the hope that I hold for a phenomenological approach, I am reluctant to be identified. . . .as a self-concept theorist. This is because, as normally understood, this term seems to leave out of consideration the objective situational and personal variables which . . . I have taken very much into account.

If, then, my approach must be labelled, let it be as differential-developmental-social-phenomenological psychology. For it is only as we make use of all of these fields and also of aspects of sociological and economic theory that we will eventually construct a theory of vocational development that deals adequately with the complex processes by which people progress through the sequence of positions constituting a career.[22]

Overwhelmed, the student seeking vital understanding and in need of some clarity might feel moved to say, "Huh? . . . What were those last two thoughts, professor? They're probably super, but why don't you run 'em by us again."

As a final brush stroke about self it is worth noting what Jerome Bruner says in his autobiographical book, *In Search of Mind*, after a productive career as a psychological researcher wherein his interests goaded him to investigate any promising path leading to just how the mind works, how it ticks and what makes it tick. Self-concepts never seemed very promising:

> "Self" is not, oddly enough, a self-evident idea. Earnest efforts to define it, to date its beginnings in an infant's life (a favorite sport of psychoanalysts), or to set its limits—all these usually end either in muddle or in philosophical priggishness. Indeed, even the vintage of "self" words in our language— self-respect, self-aggrandizement, self-centered—is surprisingly late, mostly after the sixteenth century. . . . The birth of words may not mean much, but it does suggest at least that before their arrival, the ideas to which they refer were probably not in wide or explicit circulation. The only point I would want to make about the concept of Self is that it should not be taken for granted with respect to either its nature or its origins.[23]

If the self-concept theory of vocational development is riddled with holes on the one hand and is surfeited with periphrases on the other, what about the other theories? Well . . . let the reader be the judge. When they throw out or retain very few of the theoretical propositions found in every theory about people and work, however, doesn't mean that in their efforts to help clients counselors can effectively operate in a vacuum. Obviate all the theoretical constructs of others, but counselor and client together must still ground their focus on some shared perception of what is true and real and what is myth and fallacy.

What follows is a list of assumptions the author holds that bear on vocational counseling. They may hardly be considered anything more than normative truths, which is to say they fit or describe a sample factor of reality about two-thirds of the time (two standard deviations to the right and left of a hard-to-locate mean). Nor, taken altogether, do they amount to a theory. Nor are they ordered in such a way as to build up to anything. They are simply an operating base of ideas in vocational counseling that have proven to be practical, accumulated one by one as they were plucked from the long vine of experience.

NORMATIVE TRUTHS ABOUT PEOPLE AND WORK

1. *Anyone can and will do anything if the price is right.* There are people who will do the dirtiest, the unsafest, the most backbreaking and

obnoxious jobs. If the price is right, people will go through punishing preparation periods learning how to do that in which they have no interest whatsoever. Given enough time and perseverance, most people can learn anything. "What price are you willing to pay?" is a question that accompanies any declaration of a goal. "How much money will it take to get you to do it?" is another. People will work at what they dislike to avoid more negative consequences.

2. *Talent is largely a myth.* The myth regarding its existence is perpetuated about achievers by those who don't want to do all the hard work required to accomplish what the talented achieve. Achievers like to speak of their talent, of their gifts, for the talented are given an almost reverential status in society. Thomas Alva Edison's famous remark, "Genius is one percent inspiration and ninety-nine percent perspiration," applies equally to talent. There are natural differences among people but these can be measured in fractions of inches, and the differences that are advantageous to their owners—acuity of vision or hearing, the basketball player's height, manual dexterity or hand-eye coordination—must be developed through endless effort.

3. *Artists and their ilk don't seek vocational guidance.* There are people who have decided what they want to do and work at it all the time. They are internally controlled. They are driven. Put up obstacles and barriers, they will still do it. Some are simply ambitious—for whatever reason, even neurotic programming of one kind or another. Some are artists. Whatever drives the artist or the inordinately ambitious is difficult to identify and define. But assuming the secret were discovered to be tangible, a rare substance that could be gathered and bottled and put into syringes, injections of this precious liquid into the bloodstreams of those without ambition or the desire to create would only prove the immunity of most people. The diseases of ambition and artistic drive aren't contagious.

4. *We tire of whatever it is that we have learned to do once we have mastered it.* In particular we tire of jobs that are repetitive. Because we have brains, we require new stimulation for growth, food for the mind. Boredom is a vicious enemy that undermines stationary well-being. Deleterious effects of stagnation compose the soundest argument for a career-ladder or job-switching. A colleague states: "Five years ought to be the maximum for anyone in any one job slot. After that all challenges have been met, all creativity has had its run, curiosity dies, energies wane, productivity falls, and the first ashes of burn-out appear like insidious dandruff."

5. *A goodly number of people hate all work and make no serious effort to become competent at anything they undertake.* Such people under some circumstances can be *made* to work, and under other circumstances they can be *fooled* into working. It is a mistake to assume that work is natural to everyone. Perhaps it is true that one person's work is another's play, but life isn't long enough for all people to try everything to discover which is which. Says Mark Twain at the end of the second chapter where Tom Sawyer dupes a string of buddies into doing his fence whitewashing work for him: "Tom had discovered a great law of human action without knowing it—namely, that in order to make a man or a boy covet a thing, it is only necessary to make the thing difficult to attain. If he had been a great and wise philosopher, like the writer of this book, he would now have comprehended that Work consists of whatever a body is obliged to do, and Play consists of whatever a body is not obliged to do."

6. *We are sure of what we don't like to do.* Most people don't know what they want or what they will enjoy, but they are *certain* about what they dislike and will go through creative shenanigans to avoid it. Vocational interest items are the most believable when they pinpoint negatives, and negatives are usually the result of experience. We must try a thing to know it has no appeal. Most folks are better at hating than loving, better at fault-finding than accepting, better at cautious progression than full-bore driving, and become more tentative, fussier, more carping as they age and accumulate a bigger horde of those things they know they dislike. We avoid the nasty and what is self-determined as oppressive or undesirable. We tend to choose "freedom from" rather than "freedom to."

7. *Most people do not have more than a narrow band of alternative choices among occupational categories at any given life juncture.* When we are young, wherever we live and grow up determines what our occupational choices are. If we are to choose opportunities that lie elsewhere, our connections to home-base must be broken, and this is an unlikely happening if our financial and other resources are limited. As we grow older, our obligations increase and put further restrictions in front of opportunities to switch vocational objectives. Also, as we mature, our work experience limits us to certain areas of specialization if we are to climb a career ladder. Most people are reluctant to surrender gains and take large vocational risks.

8. *Unforeseen and unplanned-for conditions cloud bright vocational promises.* The best jobs require the longest preparation, but there is no end-of-the-training period guarantee that one will even then

enjoy one's work or be able to settle into it. "Today, it is estimated that there are 125,000 Ph.D.'s without a post."[24] Competition may become too fierce. One may quickly tire of what one does or develop a craving to do something one has not heretofore dreamed of. The likelihood that one will, in Rainer Maria Rilke's opinion, find bitterness in her or his chosen thing is no doubt as great, if not greater, than a diet of continued satisfaction.

9. *Most people can do hundreds of jobs equally well and be equally happy or unhappy in all of them.* That everyone is so constituted and developed as to be a perfect or even a good match with a particular occupation, or even a set of occupations, is a ridiculous, dreamy assumption having little basis in reality. This is easily seen when we look at military service personnel who return to civilian life and then do radically different work, or at politicians who are drawn from all manner of former work to assume never-before-undertaken tasks that are commonplace to the new office. Checking out people with long job histories, we see the variety in work lives. Artists, actors, writers, and others for decades frequently earn their living performing well at jobs having no relation to their more passionately desired career aims.

10. *Vocational maturity in adults usually means scores of false starts.* Because most people don't know what they want to do, they must get experience under their belts to be sure of their calling. Probably there are more people who are never sure than those who are sure. Many people live their entire work lives and go to their graves never finding out what they wanted to be when they grew up. The proportion of folks who work to live by far exceeds the complement who live to work.

11. *Enjoyable, productive, engaging work is becoming more of a privilege than a right or a duty.* Indeed, so is less desirable work. The work of the nation must be done but the need for unskilled labor is decreasing, whether this be due to cheaper labor competing successfully in foreign markets or the advance of technology. Those jobs that are exciting and fun, well-rewarded, and have status are in short supply, and many qualified takers vie for them. Many people have learned how to survive without working, and as society becomes more affluent their numbers will increase.

12. *Many workers cause their own job dissatisfaction by making invidious comparisons.* Comparing oneself to others in almost any dimension is self-defeating, but is a culturally ingrained pasttime common to most people.

13. *Work has many meanings for each individual.* Since the invention of the printing press, the number of discourses on the meaning

of work has steadily grown. Each person has thought about what work means from childhood on, and these thoughts undergo constant revision as life progresses and new developmental tasks are faced. What one gets and wants from work (or lack of work) is a perennial subject. How one's work limits and defines one's personhood is a daily consideration that seldom remains static for long. Work and gender roles are inseparable. Most people who are out of work are in big trouble—not so much because of the loss of income (they scale down their living style and adjust)—but because they haven't been trained or conditioned to get enjoyment from life outside of their work. For this reason many people experience private emptiness, get no satisfaction from, and flunk *retirement*.

● ● ● ● ●

What we have just considered are a baker's dozen of normative truths about work, but they hardly form a beginning nucleus for any counselor to contemplate. Indeed, as long as one counsels it is productive if not essential to develop a broader and deeper understanding of the primordial position of work in the life of every client. Work is always a part of the past, present, and future context of every concern a client has. There are workaholics. There are those who lack any worthwhile work or who, like mothers and housewives, must fight to receive recognition for their labors. There are those who are seemingly incapable of any sustained work. There are those who overwork. As Peter Kropotkin tells us: "Overwork is repulsive to human nature—not work. Overwork for supplying the few with luxury—not work for the well-being of all. Work, labor, is a physiological necessity, a necessity of spending bodily energy, a necessity which is health and life itself."[25] In the best of all possible worlds, one's work is one's pleasure.

There is no easy shortcut to becoming an effective vocational counselor. But here are a few guidelines:

1. Determine the nature of the proposed counseling. Is the central focus to be job placement, exploration of opportunities for job change, upgrading satisfaction on the job, getting satisfaction outside of work, managing finances, or what?
2. Determine to whom (beyond the client) the outcome of vocational counseling makes a difference. Clients are pressured on all sides about their work concerns by significant—and not so significant—others. Frequently the client's relationship to work is not the primary cause of difficulty.

3. Determine the client's ability or lack of ability to change. What evidence supports any such such assessment? Is it realistically feasible for this client to entertain the idea of geographical relocation?

4. Discover every client's full work history, including how this person worked in school, what work a client has done for which the client has not been remunerated, what the client does and has done around the house, on vacations, for the sake of others. Investigate worker characteristics and habits, punctuality, task-completion, persistence, taking directions, self-starter skills, performance standards—the desirable and undesirable traits employers generally look for.

5. Check out all health considerations, physical limitations, handicaps, medications, work periods that were interrupted for health reasons.

6. Don't spend much time dealing with interests. To do so is to dawdle in the interstices. To reinforce the notion that work ought to coincide with interests and desires for certain kinds of fulfillment is to provide clients with justification for feeling dissatisfied when their wants are not available on the job. There are a few jobs that fill all conditions a client would place on what he or she expects to get from work. Such questions as these often lead to blind alleys or frustration: "What subjects did you like—or were you good at—in school? Do you prefer to work alone or with others? Do you prefer to work with things, people, or ideas? Do you like to work with your mind or your hands, indoors or outdoors? Are you a leader or a follower?" Compromises must be made on any job. Most people will object vociferously to a job wherein a hated condition is present and so inform the counselor. Counselor exploration in this dimension isn't necessary: all pertinent negatives will emerge.

7. Determine how well the client wears or has worn job labels that do or have identified the client as a particular kind of worker. Check out how others perceive the client in his or her work role and how such perceptions set in the client's mind. Is this client making self-incriminating or otherwise harmful status comparisons? What counts with this client, the job title or the work activity? The primary incentive for many who get advanced graduate degrees is to be seen as intelligent and worthwhile enough to complete such a program, an obvious case of title and status hunger.

8. Check out all values the client holds about work, particularly highly moralistic values.
9. Check out the relative realism of a client's job knowledge. An important part of the counseling homework may become field-testing or field-research ventures.
10. Appraise the client's relative sanity about work concerns, insanity being characterized by either or both reality distortion and compulsive, uncontrollable behavior. Fantasy about work ought to be clearly identified as such and not accepted as reality. The young and inexperienced are prone to fantasizing.
11. Do counseling work for the client, not for the "system" or for others in the client's life. It may be that such counseling benefits others, but any client behavioral change must be for the client's sake first, if it is to be lasting. Particularly when parents or spouses or other interested parties are paying for the counseling does this issue become touchy.
12. Assess how much destiny control clients have and help them to have a greater measure of it wherever possible. One of the findings of the Coleman Report, which covered 600,000 students and 60,000 teachers in 4,000 schools in all 50 states and the District of Columbia, was that children from minority groups enter school scoring behind whites in achievement and fall further back until by the 12th grade they are as much as three to five grades behind. If vast and costly research enterprises such as this, done at taxpayer expense, are to have any relevance for counseling practice, then it is exceedingly important that we do not forget that the report found achievement in school to have a stronger relationship to destiny control than *all other school factors taken together*.[26] Clients are discouraged by the perceived lack of ability to control their fate.
13. Conditioned by pervasive ideas in the culture, frequently the most difficult clients are the ones who assume and fervently believe that counseling will help them to find out what job or career they would be good at—or best suited for. Such clients want to be tested. They know that vocational tests of various kinds exist. They have faith in the results and the results they expect are a sort of external guarantee that they will make the right moves. If possible such clients can be referred to a vocational testing center or expert, there to receive whatever guidance such appraisal instrumentation and personnel might supply, while simultaneously receiving counseling. A vocational guidance person and a personal

counselor operating in tandem offer a more workable solution to the problem such clients present, especially when a counselor is ill-equipped to provide the testing and unable to dissuade a client of unwarranted biases related to the efficacy of testing. Many clients are sorely misled when test results of all kinds are inadequately or wrongly interpreted.

If there is any supposition that a final word can be written in a chapter devoted to the subject of vocational counseling, it would be this: However much the field harbors counselors who are self-declared or so designated by university degrees to be specialists in career/job/occupational/vocational counseling, concerns about the relationship between people and work cannot be outside the purview of *any* counselor who sees effectiveness in all counseling aspects as a mandate for maximum professional development.

NOTES

1. Anderson, H. C. (1955). The emperor's new clothes. In E. V. Lucas & H. B. Paull (Trans.) *Andersen's fairy tales* (p. 204). New York: Grossett & Dunlop (Original work published 1861).
2. Emerson, R. W. (1926). In B. Perry (Ed.). *The heart of Emerson's journals* (p. 176). Boston: Houghton-Mifflin (Original work published 1842).
3. Vriend, J. (1979). Originally published under the title: Two promises and a lick: On career choice. *Michigan Personnel and Guidance Journal, 10,*(2). Reprinted by permission.
4. Evers, D. R., & Feingold, S. N. (1972). *Your future in exotic occupations.* New York: Richard Rosen Press.
5. Fictitious.
6. Galbraith, J. K. (1958). *The affluent society.* Boston: Houghton Mifflin.
7. Harrington, M. (1962). *The other America: Poverty in the United States.* New York: Macmillan.
8. Reich, C. A. (1970). *The greening of America.* New York: Random House (Bantam Books ed.), pp. 382–385.
9. Berger, P. L., & Berger, B. (1970, April 3). The blueing of America. *The New Republic*, pp. 20–21.
10. Parrington, V. L. (1927). *Main currents in American thought: An interpretation of American literature from the beginnings to 1920.* New York: Harcourt, Brace.
11. Commager, H. S. (1950). *The American mind: An interpretation of American thought and character since the 1880's.* New Haven: Yale University Press.

12. Lerner, M. (1957). *America as a civilization: The basic frame* (Vol. 1). *America as a civilization: Culture and personality* (Vol. 2). New York: Simon & Schuster.
13. Reisman, D., Glazer, N., & Denny, R. (1950). *The lonely crowd: A study of the changing American character.* New Haven: Yale University Press.
14. Mills, C. W. (1959). *The sociological imagination.* New York: Oxford University Press.
15. Hoppock, R. (1976). *Occupational information: Where to get it and how to use it in career education, career counseling, and career development.* (4th ed.). New York: McGraw-Hill, pp. 68–89.
16. Mills, C. W. (1956). *The power elite.* New York: Oxford University Press.
17. These labels and more are quoted in: Plummer, W. (1981). *The holy goof: A biography of Neal Cassady.* Englewood Cliffs, NJ: Prentice-Hall.
18. YAVIS = Young, Attractive, Verbal, Intelligent, and relatively Successful. The "YAVIS syndrome" was first noted by Schofield, W. (1964). *Psychotherapy: The purchase of friendship.* Englewood Cliffs, NJ: Prentice-Hall. Schofield was speaking of those individuals psychotherapists prefer to serve, if one judges by the proportionate number of these patients seen by those psychotherapists who can afford to limit their practices. Screening out (referring) the real "crazies" is important for the therapists' own mental health; working with non-YAVIS types is too self-punishing. YAVIS patients tend to be only minimally psychologically impaired and tend to see psychotherapy as a means of growth. They are "relatively successful" because they can afford to pay for the experience.
19. Super, D. E., Starishevsky, R., Martin, N., & Jordaan, J. P. (1963). *Career development: Self-concept theory.* Princeton, NJ: College Entrance Examination Board.
20. Hersey, J. (1968). *The Algiers Motel incident.* New York: Knopf.
21. Thomas, L. (1979). *The Medusa and the snail: More notes of a biology watcher.* New York: Viking Press, pp. 41–42.
22. Quoted by Hoppock, op. cit., p. 78, from Whiteley, J. M. & Resnikoff, A. (Eds.). (1972). *Perspectives on vocational development.* Washington, DC: American Association for Counseling and Development.
23. Bruner, J. (1983). *In search of mind: Essays in autobiography.* New York: Harper & Row, p. 226.
24. Barzun, J. (1981, November 5). The wasteland of American education. *New York Review of Books,* p. 35.
25. Kropotkin, P. A. (1970). In M. A. Miller (Ed.), *Selected writings of anarchism and revolution.* Cambridge, MA: M.I.T. Press, p. 242.
26. Coleman, J. S., et al. (1966). *Equality of educational opportunity.* Washington, DC: U.S. Government Printing Office.

7

Helpful Counseling Handouts

To begin with, this anthology is for the thinker, and not for the feeler, primarily for the extrovert thinker. Needless to say, it runs over into some of his introverted and intuitive margins.

The editors laid down certain rules: ... Nothing purely inspirational, nothing sentimental. And yet nothing cynical. Nobility of thought keeps on the crown of the road, out of the gutters. Nothing that is not worth re-reading. Some things that can be chewed over almost indefinitely. Pieces that are tough enough, juicy enough to chew ... The form in which the piece is written to make no odds. Treatise, textbook, letter, novel, speech, verse, anything is given equal welcome...

There is no attempt at complete exposition. The extracts provide pegs, stout and well driven in, on which you can hang your own further thoughts.

—Charles P. Curtis, Jr. and Ferris Greenslet[1]

When clients are able to profit from reading, from the interplay of ideas, when they have engaged in erroneous thinking and have suffered in life as a result of their own flawed operational philosophy, and when the counseling is not of the short-term crisis sort but instead is protracted over a generous time span, then the character of the sessions can sometimes assume the form if not the format of a tutorial. The counselor enters the thought-system of the client, evaluates its tenets for harmony to the client's life situations, and attempts to assist the client in rethinking action principles. Counseling becomes a head-to-head teaching/learning experience.

For it follows that whenever the generic goal of counseling has been attained, which is to say whenever positive behavioral change has occurred, the client has *learned* something as a result of the interventions. *How* that learning has fitted into place varies considerably according to the make-up of the client and the life circumstances presented, how a client is capable of functioning, how the client learns, as well as how the counselor has functioned, what interventions were used, what techniques and skills were employed.

In the tutorial model the tutor's job is to stimulate the student's intellectual growth through dialogue. The tutor, whom we might envision as an Oxford University don, is well informed, has long ago acquired the matured learnings the student seeks, knows how the content fits into a broader context, is thoroughly soaked in the relevant literature, and has the weathered acumen of the scholarly pundit. The don might proceed by the Socratic method, puncturing every student offering with astutely focused interrogations that cause the student to engage in substantive defenses of whatever is being submitted for judgment, or, if she or he cannot, then to require another spell at "the drawing board," the purpose being to expose false reasoning and elicit truth or what may more frugally resemble truth. The process is dialectical, which, according to Colin Wilson, "means simply that matter is in a continual process of change and development due to the clash of opposites."[2] It is the student's job to do the outside reading, the pertinent literature search, to become informed, then to formulate theses supported by what is found. It is a time-honored method employed in higher education, usually but not exclusively relegated to study in the humanities.

Certainly, in most descriptions of the counseling process, the tutorial model is not so clearly demarcated as such, but the elements can be worked in when the relationship reaches a level where a client is willing and able to profit from leads to various outside readings, does them, finds them to be of personal relevance, and reacts favorably to what they contain. Most clients won't take the time to swallow whole books and disgorge their contents in the sessions, but they will deal with smaller, more concentrated pieces of writing that have value for counseling progress. The trick is in the counselor's knowing the client well enough so that there is relative certainty that the sort of material the counselor has chosen will grab, hold, and impress the client's mind.

For this purpose the author has long ago formed the extremely productive practice of collecting one-, two-, or three-page, and sometimes even longer, written summations of significant material. Often these are poignant excerpts from his own readings, snipped-out prose pieces containing cogently and beautifully expressed ideas that have influenced him in his own strivings for personal mastery. Sometimes they are a collection of quotations arranged on one page under a heading that gets at their essence: "The Meaning of Love," "Dealing With Anger," "Teaching Others How to Treat You," or "Mastering Courage," to name a few in his files. Or they may be a short chrestomathy of his own sayings that have a direct tie-in to common client difficulties. Or they may be short essays the author has purloined the time to write, perhaps as a result of what a particular client has introduced, or because he wanted to gather together all of his thoughts in a given life area, once and for all, and present them as trenchantly as possible.

Below, four such essays are featured. The first three are of the author's own creation and the fourth is a birthday letter he received from his eldest daughter. They are chosen for presentation here as models that readers may imitate with productions of their own, but they could just as easily be reproduced as handouts for clients to be used as the author has used them. Each has stood the test of time. Client after client has been influenced by them, has dealt with the ideas they contain in counseling sessions, and has fondly treasured them, having received positive reinforcement for newly acquired ways of thinking through rereadings. In each case, whenever a client has taken the time to absorb its contents, the resulting "tutorial dialectics" in the counseling session have helped remarkably to move the client along toward personal goals. Not all clients have "bought" and subsequently "owned" the ideas they contain, but even then greater clarification of the client's thinking has resulted.

1. LIVING IN YOUR PRESENT MOMENTS[3]

What could be more vital to any human being than a comprehensive understanding of the profound meaning of being alive only in the present moment? The present moment and present place are the only context in which you or any living thing can be alive. It seems so simple. It is a given. It is all you have ever experienced. It hardly seems worth focusing on. But, if you do not, if you have not done so, a vague uneasiness haunts you at times when you ponder your priorities, the value of your present actions and involvements. Being alive in this way or that is your perpetual charge. Each person has this charge and how it is continuously dispelled is a concomitant of consciousness.

Your whole life is one long series of present moments, which began without your say-so, before which you were nothing. Your drawn-out skein of present moments will be permanently interrupted by death, after which you will be as you were in some unrememberable point in time before your life began: nothing. Your particular life was a gift, or if you choose to see it that way, a sentence. Either you were liberated from nothingness and given the job of living or you were condemned, doomed to live for a time, forced to endure the pain of existence. You can take either point of view and fill your present moments accordingly, even painting your present moments one coloration one time and the opposite coloration another, generating an alternating current to electrify your present moments as you see fit.

Death is a useful concept, if you make it so. And that is all it is, a concept. You have an idea of your death, not an experiencing of it. You carry the idea in you and allow it to infect your thinking about much of your living. It scares you. What can be more frightening, more terrifying? You will die. You know you will die. It is inexorable. Although thoughts of heaven or reincarnation are a warm, comforting blanket to clutch when the specter, the terror of death, which is your own concept of your own extinction, stalks the dark labyrinthine corridors of your mind, they amount to little: the specks a flea might leave behind. Life after death for you? Believe it, if you will. There is no evidence in the history of the world to support it.

How then can you make your concept of your own death useful? First, by not fearing it. It is inevitable. By spending present moments, where all your living is done, occupied with thoughts about the awfulness of your own demise, you succeed in surrendering to the destruction—while you are alive—that is implicit in the concept. You are less alive at such moments, consumed by fear that in no way forestalls death or mitigates it in any way; death stays the same, while you are less than you might be. Second, and more important, you can see your death for what it is: your return to nothingness. To be dead is to be nothing; to be alive is everything. To live means to harness all your energies and resources, to have available to you every option, always within a reality context of time and place, the particular time and particular place of your present moment of living. To be nothing is death and to the extent that you are more than nothing you are a more effective living being. To the extent that you diminish your own possibility for living more fully in any of your present moments, you are experiencing death, you are savoring a void.

You have reality limitations in your efforts to be more alive, and you know this and accept the limitations. Thus, a third of your present moments are given over to sleeping, a time when you are nothing, a time when you are experiencing death. During sleep you have a consciousness of being alive. Although you know that sleep charges your energy batteries and enables you to continue to live, you can hardly grant moments thus spent the same worth as moments you spend in full consciousness. When you are fatigued, you crave sleep only so you can be alive differently, more alive, in the future; you dislike being half alive, hampered, diminished. Being alive means being aware and taking action, and you can be more alive (have a greater quantity of present moments of living) if you sleep less, sleep only enough to charge your batteries. You can impregnate each present moment with more life and less death by being aware and taking action, action that is not reliving. For example, should you use any series of your present moments to rethink old thoughts and hurt yourself with guilt feelings, which change no part of your personal history and help no one, should this be a repeated consumption of present moments in regular or intermittent intervals, you are capitulating to death, to being none of the ways you could otherwise be in those moments. You have tripped out, disappeared from the reality context in which you are and gone on a junket, taken a stroll with a gruesome companion, that cellar-dweller in your head, Big D. Know what living is by studying what it is not.

Living is learning. Living is growth. Living is environmental involvement. Living is making full use of all your faculties. Living is choosing. Living is being in charge. When any of these are missing, wholly or fractionally, in a present moment of your life, you are less alive. All are missing in sleep. To sleepwalk through your life or any part of it is a horror to avoid. Be not frightened by death at some distant rendezvous point in your future time. Rather, scare the pulp out of your innards by how you are dying now, by the way you kill or half-murder so many of your nonrecoverable present moments in each day.

There are some pragmatic concepts in the philosophy of existentialism that can light your way to living more fully in your present moments.

Disencumbered from the esoteric jargon in which philosophers enscase their most precious jewels, these concepts regard essence, freedom, responsibility, engagement, and the human condition.

The concept of essence, yours and that of every other human being who ever lived or will live, refers to that which makes you what you are, without which you would not be you, a powerful, a potent concept, superloaded with good stuff, the best stuff. Thus, you are the sum of all your past living and your essence changes as you add more living. Your existence preceded your essence. You choose your essence, not your existence. You select your essence, piece by piece, moment to moment. Your essence is what you live through. You invent it, create it, determine it by your choices. You, now, are the sum of what choices you have made before this moment. To talk about you is to talk about the living you have done to this moment.

The concept of freedom refers to those choices you make, all of the time. You are free to make any choice within the reality of your life. You can make dumb choices. You can make wise ones. You can choose to let others decide what will happen to you. But you are the chooser, make no mistake about it. And you choose in every present moment of your life. You are free to choose, and your absolute freedom is limited only by the number of choices you consider in a given present moment. If you consider fewer alternatives in any given situation, you narrow your freedom accordingly.

The concept of responsibility flows from your freedom. Because you are a chooser, which is inherent in your nature, only you are responsible. You can blame no other. When you choose to blame another, you are less alive. You surrender your freedom, and Big D. wins again. There is agony in accepting responsibility for dumb choices, and so there is an enormous temptation to avoid doing so. You see it everywhere in the people around you: denying responsibility is a part of the national culture. The weak have institutionalized the practice.

The concept of engagement refers to being taken up with and involved in the environment, being in meaningful contact, a part of whatever reality context in which you find yourself. It means being engaged, as fully as the circumstances allow. Present moment contextual reality circumstances have much in them, and to be engaged, to be more fully alive, implies values, chosing engagement on the basis of criteria. You are human and a part of all humanity, and you accord yourself the highest, the apex value, supreme importance. Fail to do so and Big D. stalks your present moments again. Second to you is any other human being you choose. Being meaningfully engaged with other humans is where the fullest living resides, after you have learned how to be fully engaged in your own living within yourself. Using your mind, emotions, and physical self to the hilt, involving all these in what surrounds you, registering what is happening to you as it is happening, being aware, choosing the best of all your present moment options, and acting with full commitment: Such is what engagement means. You can engage in swimming, cleaning the wax from your ears, grinding a rock, planning a menu, eating a raw toad, making sweaty love, boozily exchanging viewpoints with cocktail partiers—your billions of options can overwhelm you—but how you engage yourself distinguishes the extent to which your present moment is packed with more or less life, more or less death. Remorse, resentment, self-protection, ambivalence, guilt, approval-seeking, distrust, and a cargo of other names describe the characteristics of tender hearted, testy, reactive, cautious engagement. Exercise your freedom. Add to your essence. Grow. Live. Involve yourself. Be in your reality, neither a sleepwalker nor a fearful witness of it. Neither fear nor deny your responsibility.

The concept of the human condition stems from your own humanity. Deny, if you will, that anything human is alien to you, and, in such denial, you will have curtailed your own freedom once more. Your natural home is in the human community, however seemingly base or lofty it may at times appear to be, and the human condition of your life has been heightened by an untold number of the parts of the collective wisdom of the human race. That pool of wisdom has nourished you, however much you choose to disavow recognition and claim it as your birthright. Your very thoughts are composed of language units handed down to you. To live in isolation, to be unconcerned about your own human condition and that of others in the receding circles of life around you is to cut down your opportunities for greater present-moment living, for adding to your essence.

Whether you like it or not, whether you do it more or less fully, you only live in the here and now. You have no other choice. You have an undifferentiated continuum of possible choices to draw on. What you can turn the present moment into, how and where you can be in any present moment, depends entirely on you. The number of places you can be in a given present moment is one, only one, but in a lifetime there can be trillions. Go. Let death be in more of your present moments than life, but do not claim you are innocent. You are in control. You are free to choose. You are responsible for your choices. If you do not know how to be more alive in any present moment, your essence can be enlarged by learning. You can choose to learn: You can commit yourself to so doing. And your best school is other human beings. Some of them have already learned what you know not. Get engaged in the human community. Ask yourself: "Am I more dead than alive at this moment?" Keep on asking. And answer every "Yes" with another question: "What can I do about it? Right now?" If your answer to the second question is "Nothing," then you are in love with death, with *being* nothing. You are asleep. Throw icy water on yourself and ask your second question again. Or hit your toe with a hammer. Or brush your teeth. Or find a person to rub against. Or plant a tree. Or eat a bucket of sand. Does nothing matter? Only you can make any present moment matter. As each moment is buried, what epitaph you carve on each is your own business, a personal commentary on the business of being intensely alive and human.

Do you have any more important business? Right now?

2. CONTROLLING YOUR MIND

If you are caught up on thoughts about past events and relationships, the mulling over of which is bugging you, causing negative and hard-to-handle emotional reactions in you, the way out is to divert your mind by absorbing enterprises. You need to understand how your mind works. Being conscious means that something will occupy the central focus of your mind at all times, but you can gain control over what inhabits it at any time. Your mind, when it is not focused inward, watching the movie scripts of your past living, your bungling and sorrowful times, must process the here-and-now situation, the present moment data, in order to guide the total action of your being.

The more engrossing, challenging, difficult are present moment demands, the more engaged with the immediate your mind must become in order to care for you, to see you through all contingencies surely and safely. Or, in a given stretch of present moments, your mind can be put to problem-solving, being oblivious to environmental stimuli and serving you in task completion. The more important the payoff in the completion of the task, the more willingly and steadfastly the mind will remain on the job, whether this involves such heavy mental work as your writing an important document of some kind, doing your income tax, planning or packing for a trip or a party, or any of the tasks you undertake to complete in your paid employment or personal world.

Focusing on future events in order to prepare for them and give them birth in the form most pleasurable and advantageous to you is another form of mental activity not unlike other problem-solving mental action.

Although such may require your sifting through your brainbag for useful data from the past to guide you to greater accuracy in structuring future events, you do this in a goal-directed way and prevent yourself from getting sucked into the miasma of old stuff that has no good in it, stuff that is the garbage pile of what you have already lived through and will never live through again, the trash heap left over from the now dead-time in you, the graveyard of your world till now. Your personal past is inexorably gone, and you will not see its like again. That human beings are so wired together that they remember what they have lived through is helpful for growth and development, for learning, for a host of here-and-now uses, but where memories do not serve their owner, they ought to be allowed to remain dormant, unsummoned, asleep. When they awaken and start climbing into consciousness, they ought to be sternly dealt with. Few, if any, matter.

And this includes positive memories, the good times. If you prefer to dwell on the sweet memories, to fondle the better parts of your recalled past life, you probably are not rich in present-moment satisfactions, and the welling up of good memories ought to be the stimulus kick in the head that tells you this and gets you moving, gets you to do something more productive, gets you into more effective grappling with the circumstances of what is happening now, at the moment. Escapism is negative. And the good old days were never any better than what is possible to bring into being currently. Because you are so much more than you were a year ago, 10 years ago, regardless of your chronological age, you can wring more from any present living than you might have done in the past.

3. STARING DOWN FAILURE

Failure is the world's greatest teacher. How you or anyone else in the world learned anything at all meant doing it, finding out by trial and error and retrial until success occurred. Fearing failure and then avoiding any action can result in womblike comfort, but this is always at the price of zero growth. Folks who fail and find this bad, who fault themselves and fan their fears of failing again in the future, who use their experience to quit a certain endeavor, these folks flail themselves with self-deprecation and reinforce feelings of worthlessness. Instead of relishing the knowledge that can be creamed off abortive attempts, instead of using the data that can be garnered from these efforts as treasured coin to be spent in self-improvement, such timid operators feel doomed over their self-ineptitude, assess themselves as being restricted and limited by their own inability, and become avoiders who spend their energies in building rationalizations, in constructing self-defenses to trot out before others when their hanging back is questioned. This is a picture in which you have no desire to sketch yourself.

Actually, failure is a myth. It does not exist. Failure is only an editorial stance, the opinion of a critic. What is true about any human behavior is that it had a certain nature and certain effects, it was a performance that was executed at a certain level of effectiveness. Attaching a label of failure is to project a label onto behavior, an unnecessary, unproductive, patently dull way of looking at the world, a negative, denigrating practice indulged in by enemies. Although our culture is overwhelmingly crowded with the fiction of failure, where critics ready to judge the acts of others as miserable failures are as prevalent as the trees that make up the forest, that nonetheless does not make the existence of failure a reality.

The clear-minded thinker views all behavior as neutral, but caused and purposive, and to the relative extent that the purpose was accomplished, it was effective or ineffective. With increased practice one can become skilled at anything, even at criticizing and finding creative means to dub the behaviors of others as dismal flops. You know this, but you tend to forget it. After all, you say to yourself as you straighten your features into a look of scientific objectivity, we do not think of animals as failing. They simply behave. No one thinks of the howling or barking dog as having a failing performance.

4. TREASURE CHEST

Dear Dad,

You once told me that I had a Treasure Chest. Mine alone. No one could ever take it away. Do you remember telling me that? I marveled at those words, as only a child of six could, hearing them come from the person I admired most on the whole planet. You spoke of the Treasure Chest at one of our famous father-daughter talks.

At these sessions I was privileged to have your special thoughts and feelings that my sisters were too young to understand. Feeling very mature and favored, I drank in—in gulps—all the serious ideas you imparted to callow me.

It was at one of these talks that you gave me the realization that my mind was a Treasure Chest. I could gather treasures wherever I went, you explained. From those I met, from what I read, from nature, I could glean precious stones. My Chest would never fill up, you assured me. It would never burst from overloading. Wonderful. Magical. These ideas gleamed in my young mind.

Since that day I have been putting treasures into my Chest, and Dad, you were right on all counts. The gems I have stored are still there. It hasn't filled up, has oceans of room, and the best thing is that it is portable. I can alight anywhere and examine the riches that I have been amassing now for more than 30 years.

Another thing you told me was how really valuable my Chest was, that when I got to be as old as you my body would begin to deteriorate, to become less reliable, that it would slowly wear out, but that my Treasure Chest would never do so. It would be just as good at the end of my life as it was at the beginning, in fact it would be even better, much better, because I would have put so much in it. The more I put in it, the richer I would be. I did not understand that too well as a young girl, but now that my body is not what it used to be, I understand fully. It keeps me treasure-hunting more than ever. I play a little game with myself these days: I am not allowed to go to sleep on a given day if I have not put some treasures into my Chest.

Since the early fifties, when you gave me the keys, the Treasure Chest has lost its childhood aura of magic. Instead, it has become one of my most concrete realities. I now realize that owning a Treasure Chest is not my gift alone. Anyone can have one. But one must recognize its value and meaning, otherwise it will be barren.

A man I dated for a while praised the investment value of a swimming pool over a trip to Europe. As my plane took off from London and I realized that I had drained the funds he would have used for a pool, a smile floated to my lips. For I knew that my travels were going into the Treasure Chest—much more durable, portable, and a thousand times more precious than a pool.

Beyond being portable and durable, my Chest is also shareable. I don't lose a jewel when I give it away. I can give away anything I choose and I have not really separated it from me: I only give away the double. The original remains. Of course, there are some jewels—those most dear to me—that I keep in a separate compartment. I only make doubles of these for friends who would truly appreciate them. Offering the treasures— the dear beads of my intimate thoughts, or the gold of ideas I can share generally—is a way I show love. I have always believed that giving one's time is the greatest gift of love. This most likely had its birth in the values you gave me with the Chest.

In short, the Chest instilled the idea that a person's words have the value of precious stones and console and nourish more than tangible blessings. Keeping a journal became a natural extension of my Chest. There are stored words of beauty from Tagore, Einstein, Chardin, and the contents of the rare "father-daughter" talks I have had with God. My contentment has come through the wealth of the mind and the spirit.

Dad, I am writing this just to let you know what a great gift you gave me. In an intimate way you gave what was most precious—the thoughts of your heart. Under the spell of the all-absorbing conversations with your eldest daughter, you planted an idea that has inspired much of my growing. Though circumstances separated me from you while I was still young, the Treasure Chest and a part of you remained. I thank you and ask you—through your capacity as a writer—to extend the idea to others, so they might gain the joy of consciously gathering jewels of knowledge and experience to store in their own Treasure Chests. I don't think I ever thanked you before, but I do so now. Please accept my thanks as your birthday present. Put this in your Treasure Chest. I hope you will.

Love,

Diana

The above specimens hardly exhaust the genre when one thinks about handouts. They could take the form of behavioral-goal steps applicable to specific client requirements, directions on how to get from here to there. They could be scheduling or budgetary or dietary models. They could be summations of vital information pertinent to a client concern that surfaces often and requires specific data for amelioration; lists of particular referral sources fall into this category, as do points of law. They could be stories to illustrate a way of handling a frustrating or puzzling aspect of living. They could be short tests to be taken between sessions. The point of handouts is that they extend the counseling beyond those comparatively short and usually expensive times when counselor and client can physically meet. They are a counseling resource to be exploited and prized for the manner in which they can increase counselor effectiveness.

NOTES

1. Curtis, C. P., Jr., & Greenslet, F. (Eds.). (1962). *The practical cogitator, or: The thinker's anthology* (3rd ed., rev. by J. H. Finley, Jr.). Boston: Houghton

Part II

Group Counseling

The process of counseling now goes plural to its own advantage. How much more behavior clients emit in a group! How much more they reveal! How many more resources counselors have at beck and call to help them do their job! Powers and passions are heightened. Communication is enriched. Variety of interaction escalates. The interplay of many minds at work lifts the counseling game into another league. Communal fun is a new potential. Risking within the counseling process takes on a new meaning. New powers, new passions, new challenges, new calls on competence and expertise present themselves to the counselor who would sit amongst a circle of clients and serve them all, each and every one.

8

Group Counseling: What It Is and What It Isn't

RICHARD EVANS: . . . Aside from group therapy as such, variations of group-encounter techniques such as sensitivity training, an outgrowth of the group dynamics orientation, have taken on new importance. . . . The whole personal growth movement has moved into what we call the encounter group. Dramatic variations, such as nudity among participants, touching, massaging, spiritual and various other transcendental dimensions are becoming a part of group encounters. . . . Suddenly the message is: "Yes. Use every technique of communication, tactual, visual or what have you." How do you see yourself in regard to this whole movement?

CARL ROGERS: . . . It's a field in which I'm very much involved . . . In many ways it can, and, in some respects, has gone completely wild, and I regret that. In its more solid aspects, it's one of the most significant social inventions of this century because it is a way of eliminating alienation and loneliness, of getting people into better communication with one another, of helping them develop fresh insights into themselves, and helping them get feedback from others so that they perceive how they are received by others. . . . In my own work with encounter groups, I have very much the same theory and philosophy that I've been talking about. As a group facilitator, I would try to hold much the same attitudes that I was describing as effective in individual psychotherapy . . .

EVANS: What are some of the fears that you have about this movement? ...

ROGERS: ... I don't really object, basically, to people trying various approaches—Zen, mysticism, even nude groups if they want to. The social effect that will have, though, is going to be very bad because the general public may get turned off ...

EVANS: ... You're really saying, then, that some of these experimental approaches may have some value, but the extremist views could damage the encounter-group movement seriously?

ROGERS: That's right. It could damage the whole picture of encounter groups in the public eye.[1]

The Association for Specialists in Group Work (ASGW), Division XI of the American Association for Counseling and Development, published a special issue in May 1985 of its quarterly *Journal for Specialists in Group Work* devoted to the subject, "Critical Issues in Group Work: Now and 2001." The author was an invited contributor to that issue. What he saw as the most critical issue of all, the professional desirability of sorting group counseling out from other variants of therapeutic group activity, required an historical perspective. What follows, with slight alterations, is his contribution:

In Joseph Heller's novel, *Something Happened*, the character who tells the story says at one point, "It's an idea whose time is gone." Can we say the same of group work?

Certainly it has its history, its genesis at the turn of last century in the investigations of sociologists, in their focus upon humans as social beings and how social institutions affect the lives of everyone in a society, how group life determines and modifies growth and development, particularly the primary small group of the family. Then came almost half a century of lively interest, experimentation, and research in the promising new field of group dynamics, producing a high yield of normative constructs that more or less accounted for how people behave in small groups, particularly in task groups where roles, leader styles, decision-making processes, division of labor, and communication variables were examined. Sociological and psychological research centering on small group processes and structures flourished, especially in academia. As the findings accumulated there were practical questions.[2] What did they all mean? Are they useful for social engineering?

Then came the landmark summer of 1947. In Bethel, Maine, the National Training Laboratory (NTL) in Group Development, part of the National Education Association, held its first laboratory session. T-groups ("T" for training) and the "laboratory method" were born.[3] Seeking innovations in re-education and using the small group as their laboratory, experimentors from many disciplines and professions from universities and community settings throughout North America gathered to learn how people function in the context of a small group, first using themselves as subjects. The group was a lab where the behavior of the participants counted for more than any effort leading to specific collective outcomes, to any group goals. The lab was a safe place to explore individual behavior and feelings, to become sensitive to one's own inner workings, characteristic behaviors, and the reactions of others to oneself as a person apart from social roles.

Under the auspices of the NTL, which continued each summer at Bethel and soon became an autonomous entity, the T-group movement grew. In the next 15 years T-groups sprang up on campuses around the land and became widely known enough to impinge on the national consciousness. It was a fresh concept with enormous appeal. Here was a whole new way of working on oneself to become more sensitive, to grow, to activate one's potential. Soon "sensitivity training" was faddish. It spilled over into the general culture and everyone in the vanguard, it seemed, got into the act. The nation was hearing of the "human potential movement," of the exciting developments going on in California, especially at the Esalen Institute at Big Sur and at La Jolla where Carl Rogers and others established a Center for Studies of the Person, two communities where experimentation was not subject to the structures and constraints imposed by more traditional institutions. Soon came marathon groups and encountering. In groups convened for the purpose, one encountered not only others, but the stifled self as well.[4] *Encounter* was to become the generic term for these group experiences. It was the time for openness, getting in touch with feelings, expanding human awareness.

It was the 1960s, the time of social ferment, of counter-culture reverberations. On the one hand the nation was undergoing social convulsions with protests and riots on the campuses and in the cities, civil rights groups struggling to erase all the years of discrimination and "second-class citizenship," the "me generation" kicking over traces, taking LSD and smoking pot, engaging in radical politics, denouncing the conflict in Vietnam; on the other hand purveyors of the personal consciousness expansion were selling *Joy*, as William Schutz entitled his popularly successful second book.[5] Four years later he would write *Here Comes Everybody*.[6] At the turn of the decade the encounter group movement was having its heyday. In its promise of individual happiness it stood in opposition to paternal governmental values that were crumbling before the nation's eyes at the Watergate hearings on national television.

Out of the 1960s came a new consciousness, "Consciousness III," as Charles Reich called it in the mirror he held up to the nation in his best-seller, *The Greening of America*.[7] It was characterized by liberalization, concern for the self—"the absolute worth of every human being—every self,"[8] the importance of commitment to community and personal relationships, and the rejection of comparative merit, subservience, and authority. This new consciousness, supported by the "group movement," was winning converts and being validated by national events. For the first time in history a president resigned and an unpopular war ended in ignominy.

But of importance to any assessment of the evolution of the group movement are other events that tended to counter the liberalization of consciousness. The nation was shocked by the Charles Manson killings, a "family" or group affair, by Patty Hearst's apparent loyalty to her abductors, by the terrorist group killings at Munich at the 1972 Olympics, and by the mass suicide of 912 members of Jim Jones's People's Temple in Guyana. Although these groups were political or religious "cults," they aroused and exacerbated latent fears about groups and the extent to which permissiveness can go. There were dangers ascribed to group activity, dangers in the new freedoms, and there were critics aplenty.[9]

The 1960s and 1970s were tumultuous decades in America, filled with adventure, sexual awakenings, shifting manners and morals, political upheaval, attention to formerly disenfranchised segments of the population—decades of strain and strife. For professionals in education and mental health they were times of experimentation and excited interest in group procedures. Advocates, many of them recipients of group-experience benefits, felt that group work held vast promise for new ways of helping people, for involving more people in therapeutic processes. Training programs began to include a course on group dynamics and how participants could make positive behavioral changes in a group experience, usually providing professional neophytes the opportunity to participate as members of such a group. On the campuses where committee work was common, there were now rap, brainstorming, and consciousness-raising groups. More and more textbooks were published. By 1974 ASGW was formed and its membership escalated to 3,000 by the end of the decade, where it seems to have leveled off. The acceptance of group work by the established professional associations in the country had quietly consolidated. Group procedures had moved from the periphery of mental health training and treatment closer to the center, from controversial maverick status to a position indicating endorsement if not orthodoxy.

At the close of the 1970s in a special issue of its official publication, NTL asked the question, "What's happened to small group research?" Two of the contributors noted that the percent of articles on small groups in the journal had fallen from 53% in 1964 to 8% between 1977 and 1979.[10] Why the falloff? Research progress, it seemed, was mired in cross-purposes and confusion.

The editor of the special issue, Martin Lakin, noted in his prefatory comments that "the small group area lay between psychology and sociology. Alternately focus was on the person and on the group. ... It is important to be reminded that *social*, not therapeutic purposes marked initial efforts to study small groups.[11] In the beginning the focus was on social pressures, democratic ideals, power structures, competition and cooperation issues; then came a shift of focus to mental health, personal awareness, growth, and personal security. Summing up what the special issue contributors had to say, Lakin noted that "no coherent theory of small group process has yet been developed. Concepts of the researchers as well as those of practitioners remain slippery and imprecise. The key problems remain: those of identifying the really central processes and of specifying how groups influence participants as well as how participants influence them."[12]

Small-group research, apart from confusions about group purposes and conceptual imprecisions, presents seemingly insoluble methodological problems, and in every case fails to account for the influence of particular personalities of leaders and members upon outcomes. Unless the structure of a group experience is so highly controlled as to disallow idiosyncratic personal behavior, most studies are impossible to replicate. In spite of this the acceptance of group work in the social sciences has moved apace with the growth of the various therapeutic theories and practices, based more on advocacy by strong personalities serving as models of "right" thinking about group work than agreed-upon formulations arising from research efforts. In the group-work field today we have adherents for an array of procedures to be used for different populations under special circumstances, adherents for less structured versus more structured group experiences, adherents for each of the many countervailing, unresolved, philosophical issues that beset the field.

Publishers serving professional education in the human services now regularly include group-work books on their lists, and the divergent issues in the field are addressed. What group adherents share is their belief in the value of educational and therapeutic group experiences. The dust has settled after 2 decades of tumult and broad latitude in experimentation, and now a corps of group workers has been absorbed into the professional mainstream, a corps that is aware of but eschews extremes (nude hydrotherapy groups, "primal scream" or "rolfing" groups, "est" and other such "private sector" practices). This corps is professionally responsible, sensitive to public fears, and it is willing to band together in support of group work while mindful of difficulties and internecine differences. This, in essence, is what ASGW represents in the counseling and human development field in 1985.

This retrospective look at the group movement, it would seem, contains the chief elements for a perspective on the next 15 years. Humans have always known there is strength in collective action to accomplish tasks or to achieve political goals, and in this century the dynamics of group structure and participation have been studied to great avail in honing logistics and strategies, in training leaders, in creating organizational change. Less certain is what has been learned about the group experience as a therapeutic matrix. An apparent rift exists between two functionally divergent models, a historical legacy. Lines of distinction between the two models are not clearly drawn. Permutations of theory and practice from both models are mixed in training programs and are evident in the delivery of services through group methods in the professional marketplace.

Can we rely on a model (B) which presupposes that every therapeutic group develops its own norms and content, inevitably goes through stages, and will have its positive effects upon participants helped only by a facilitator who participates in "player/coach" fashion, a leader who rudders the process but doesn't determine its nature, the process itself being what causes (or allows for) therapeutic change in members? Essentially this is the encounter group model. The counseling group model (A), on the other hand, presupposes a trained professional who determines and takes responsibility for the structure of the experience, a leader who teaches group members by example what constitutes effective therapeutic behavior in the group, one who bases each intervention on a rationale emanating from a theory of counseling.

Model B has its limitations, some of which are ethical. It is appropriate to volunteering adults who are notified that they must take responsibility for whatever happens to them in a group, less appropriate for special populations, for the young, for those assigned to a group experience. Model A, in its variations for special populations, requires leader expertise and responsibility, a considerable amount of training and experience. What are the basic competencies required? What preparation is necessary to produce qualified group counselors? What minimal professional background and skills ought to be required of an individual who is credentialed as a group counselor? The confusions that exists today and permeate preparation programs and credentialing considerations are descendants of the unresolved differences between Models A and B.

In the next 15 years the issue cannot continue to languish unattended. Its resolution does not depend upon further research. Rather, resolution will come about through the dedication of responsible advocates of group work to develop training programs within degree-granting institutions and through their professional organizations. The obstacles are formidable, but given the hard-earned acceptance of group work as a therapeutic modality in the traditional bastions of counselor education, they are less formidable than they once were. The principal obstacle is funding. To train a group counselor adequately, he or she must first be a competent counselor. Following this, adequate training for such an individual to become qualified in group counseling mandates that many hundreds of supervised hours be logged by the trainee with assorted groups where the focus is counseling and not simply encountering. The problems of program development, staffing, supervision, gaining access to various populations, drawing out the length of the training period, and more can all be translated into a problem of where the funds for any proposed design will come.

Can the status quo, the muddling of models A and B, continue to obtain for the next 15 years? After we have come all this way, one would hope not. If in the year 2001, however, strongly entrenched training programs based on model A are not in existence, it will be reasonable to assume that group work is an idea whose time is gone.[13]

So end the author's perceptions of this most critical issue. What the article had no space to include was an assessment of the road down which group counseling has traveled as reflected by the literature in the field. Here we see a curious development. Although theories of individual counseling acknowledged to be front-runners, those generally studied in counselor training programs, are almost exclusively the products of theoretical system-builders who identify themselves and their ideas with psychotherapy, who answer first to the title of psychologist, the same is uncharacteristic of thinkers who have authored books on group counseling.

It is perhaps both unfair and inaccurate to say that prevailing theories of individual counseling are but adaptations, interpolations, and extrapolations of psychotherapy theories. Nevertheless, it is hard to make a case for there being a theory of counseling that is exclusive of the tenets found in therapy theories, one grounded in philosophical and hypothetical assumptions emanating only from the discipline of counseling. As one goes backwards to beginnings, perhaps to Freud and "the talking cure," one sees that counseling is a latter-day development compared to psychotherapy. What constitutes the corpus of counseling theory has been more of an external than an internal development. Psychotherapy is a more established phenomenon and has more prestige, and counselors have sought authorization for what they do based on those theoretical formulations that have gained acceptance and prominence in the public and professional mind. Some professional associations corollary to the mainstream of counseling have even changed their titles during the 1970s to identify with the more prestigious appellation of "therapy" as opposed to "counseling." Thus, the American Association of Sex Educators, Counselors, and Therapists was originally entitled the American Association of Sex Educators and Counselors; and the American Association for Marriage and Family Counselors has now become the American Association for Marriage and Family Therapy.

Counseling, as opposed to therapy, has grown out of a different matrix, one that had normal developmental concerns for *all* people, not just those of the psychologically pathological or maladjusted, at its focal center. Counseling was at first chiefly vocational, taken up with the problems of occupational choice, work being common to all, and then with educational concerns, helping all the people's children to get the most from their schooling. Just as free schooling for all became more universal in this century, so too did the offering of supplementary guidance and counseling services. As the century wore on and the value of personal helping services in these realms was acknowledged, more and more special segments of the population were seen as likely beneficiaries of assistance through counseling. Nor has this thrust abated. Counseling services over the life span being available to all—with some counselors developing into specialists with particular expertise in given developmental areas or in areas peculiar to the needs of certain subpopulation groups—would seem to be a predictable hallmark of the arriving 21st century.

Given the installation of counselors into so many social settings, it is only natural that they should turn to every existing human behavioral discipline in search of what is known and what works. They are neither vultures nor birds of prey. They are simply hungry for practical knowledge. Nor is it true that psychotherapy and counseling are opposed, as was stated above. There is no clean line of demarcation between therapy and counseling, unless it be that therapists only work with the severely troubled or disturbed and that counselors work with everyone, including those who might be regarded as mentally ill but who cannot afford the services of a therapist. For many counselors, much of what is found in psychotherapy theories is irrelevant or requires adaptation. Counselors make additions to existing psychotherapy theories and modify them to suit their own requirements for serving clients. It would seem that psychotherapists, if one reads their writings, hardly ever look to the literature generated in the counseling field for clarification or amendment of their ideas, whereas the opposite is true of those who write about counseling. The latter look everywhere and democratically garner their ideas from whatever source is accessible. Most if not all of the educational and training texts for counselors being trained tend to be abstractions and compilations of vast surveys of a broad range of related literature.

The "counseling movement," if we can so signify it, grew out of the "guidance movement," a phenomenon in the field of education. At one time education of the young was fairly restricted in North America to school subjects, to the acquisition of specific bodies of knowledge and skill training in the three "Rs," reading, 'riting, and 'rithmetic. The curriculum opened up with John Dewey's philosophy: Preparation for a life was conceived as broader and more various than what was more narrowly conceptualized as the traditional curricula, and efforts were made, notably among those rallying behind the need for "progressive education," to turn the classroom into a miniature model of the community at large. Apace with this development the concept of "moral education" was reflected in the establishment of "guidance" lessons, generally taught by "homeroom" teachers but evolving later as the specialty of certain faculty members who had some preparatory training for the task. If it were decided by those in the power structure or by social pressure groups that something was deemed worth passing on to the young, then the schools were the place to do it, because all the people's children went to school. Traditional scholastic or vocational education (trade schools) began to incorporate more and more electives, more ancillary services. The idea that teachers teach people, not subject matter, resulted in "humanization" of the curriculum, arriving finally at the concept of "psychological education."[14] Guidance was becoming a subject in its own right.

Advocates for the expanded role of guidance in the nation's schools were thinking big. Writes Norman Sprinthall in 1971, "I would like to . . . contribute toward opening up a new inquiry into the directing constructs, the psychological and educational assumptions, and the overarching framework from which school guidance practice can be derived. Further, it is my aim to bring within the scope of this discussion the concept of optimum human development as the primary objective of guidance and of all education."[15] In his well-argued treatise, *Guidance for Human Growth*, he proposed to "keep the student in the spotlight yet give guidance a major institutional function paralleling and complementing the teaching function."[16]

In all of this there was the practical notion of getting the job done. Certain students were troubled enough or psychologically disturbed enough that they could not learn well in school, through no fault of their own except to be misbegotten into a familial context that mitigated against their chances for normal healthy growth and development. There was no lack of societal as well as professional recognition that this was so, and thus expert intervention was required beyond what the classroom teacher could provide. Guidance workers became counselors; counselors provided personal help with psychological problems; counseling became an accepted offering among regular guidance services. So, too, did group counseling slowly win a place in the schools, especially inasmuch as a school guidance counselor could serve many more clients by meeting them in groups. With high case loads, one way to be more accountable and get the job done is to increase client contacts through group procedures.

The value of the move to spread group counseling out among different population groups in the society, recognized early on by many counselor educators, continues today. It is no accident that so many have made themselves experts in group work in general and group counseling in particular. The first 10 presidents of ASGW were counselor educators of this character, each an author of books or articles on group counseling, their professional identification being not with therapy or group therapy, but with counseling, particularly *group counseling*.[17] We can now confidently say, with the backing of professional history, with the *defining* and *characterizing* of *what it is* by a core of dedicated hard-thinking professional advocates, that group counseling has come into its own as a separate entity, one having its own identity amid the confusing welter of mental health treatments and services, among the large mosaic of psychological theories and practices for both individuals and groups.

Now let us turn from the general to the particular. The following montage of glimpses into three lived-through aspects of group life is introduced here to provide a reality context. What the counselor(s) did in each instance is revealed, but any reader could ask, "How would I have handled the situation? What guidelines would I have followed?" The instances were chosen to illustrate three different aspects of group counseling. In the first there is a "happening" that is extraneous to the group but impinges upon it. In the second something has "happened" to the counselor with which he must contend. In the third something "happens" to a group member.

THREE GROUP COUNSELING SKETCHES[18]

I

It is midsummer. It is hot, even muggy, in the cavernous meeting room of the old Atlantic City hotel. The room is high-ceilinged, echoey. Largebladed fans common to the era before air-conditioning hang from the ceiling on long black poles and rotate lethargically. Floor-to-ceiling windows span one long side of the rectangular room, the drapes open, mid-afternoon light spilling in; on the opposite side floor-to-ceiling mirrors cover the entire length of wall broken only by the massive entrance doors open to welcome more air.

Over 100 people sit in concentric circles on folding chairs around a demonstration counseling group of 12 members and the co-counselors. Most of the observers are fanning themselves with their workshop programs, straining to hear all that goes on in the "fishbowl" group, uncommonly cooperative under the conditions, being careful not to scrape their feet or move their chairs, avoiding sidetalk. The counseling group has been in session for an hour, one-half of its scheduled time. The interpersonal interaction has grown meaningful to several of the members. The level of counseling help has gotten vital and profound. The in-group participants are 90% oblivious to the horde of friendly and interested observers, absorbed with and focusing on the concerns of May, Joe, and Miranda who have plunged personal revelations about their current life situations and struggles, who are sensing that they can receive authentic help from this experience, inviting it.

Suddenly, from who knows where, a sparrow flies through the open doors and circles the room, perching briefly on a chandelier, then exploring for a way out, again circling the room.

One of the counselors says, "A bird has just entered this room. Normally this would be an unusual and interesting distraction, and any one of us might be tempted to break our concentration and attend to the bird. But we didn't come all the way to Atlantic City to watch a bird, did we? It has been hard for each of you to shut out all the observers, to forget them and work hard at making this experience worth your while. But everyone seems to have managed that. Now, let's also try to ignore the bird, to work at using this time in the way we agreed to do. Is there anyone who feels that she or he cannot do that?"

Some discussion ensues about whose responsibility it is to take care of the bird. All decide it is someone else's. After a few minutes the group grows intensely absorbed in the counseling process. The bird is ignored. The observers, too, take their cue from this. The bird, for the next half hour, grows more confused. It flies against the large window panes, falls to the floor, stunned, several times. Next it smashes into the mirrors reflecting the outdoors from the windows. It falters in flight, once perching on the head of an observer. Finally it rests, bewildered, under a chair. When the fishbowl ends, someone captures it easily and releases it into the outer world of Atlantic City.

II

It is the final meeting of a counseling group that has gone through 12 sessions. The co-counselors have conferred after the last session and have planned to end the group with an evaluation and feedback exercise, one that includes reinforcement of postgroup goals and future plans for each client-member. They work well together. They have co-led many groups, for thousands of clock hours. Philosophically and strategically in tune, they complement each other in interventionistic style. It is an early morning meeting.

The previous evening one of the counselors received a telephone message from one of his grown daughters that her older sister had cut her throat with an electric knife. She had given herself a tracheotomy. She is hospitalized, under sedation. "She talks with a horrible burble, Dad!" This is the third and most serious attempt she has made to eliminate her own life. She lives across the continent. Dad feels helpless, disturbed, depressed.

In the morning he arrives at the counseling room early and writes on the blackboard:

> This is the way the group ends,
> This is the way the group ends,
> This is the way the group ends,
> Its throat gets cut with an electric knife.

His co-counselor arrives, reads the message and asks, "Don't you think that's a bit strong?" Dad shares his story. "Are you going to be OK? Do you want me to take over the group?" asks his partner? "No. I'll be OK. Just be sensitive to what I'm carrying in my breast, and confront me if I fade from the business at hand."

Members arrive, buzz back and forth over the stark image, and the group begins with a focus on the jolting affects of separation, the abruptness and finality of closure. The image, as catalyst, works. It has potency. "Dad," in his professional role, has not denied his personal reality nor his feelings. He integrates what is internally heavy into his counseling service actions. There is no self-disclosure to the members. After the group, he and his partner process his internal as well as the group's dynamics.

III

The counseling group has been meeting for nine sessions out of a scheduled dozen. Everyone has become known, disclosed private matters, used the group time to focus on personal concerns, set goals, and work on these between the weekly meetings, everyone except Junellen. Junellen has not uttered a word. She has never smiled, though there is lively conviviality and humor in the group, much laughter, session after session. The group is cohesive. All the members have a sense of belonging. They have become a family, except for Junellen, who is the outsider. The others begin to resent her.

Earlier, sorties to include Junellen were nonverbally rebuffed. She would look down at her lap when any attention came her way. The counselor's few attempts to include her had made no difference.

After the third session the counselor met with her privately and she confided that she just couldn't bring herself to participate; she wanted to drop out. Hearing her story, learning of her lifelong fear of being in small groups, the heavy details of her personal struggle, the counselor agreed to meet with her between sessions to discuss her thoughts and feelings—what she had experienced during the group sessions—and vowed to support her against the group in her silence or whatever stance she wanted to take. He was convinced that the group experience was more important for her than for any other participant. It was the laboratory she needed to work through her lifelong anxiety/avoidance pattern of behavior. It was a shaky hypothesis. Perhaps, if he were in error, she would become more traumatized. It was a therapeutic risk and his professional judgment was called into full question. What he banked on was his willingness to give her his close attention in the group, to monitor her behavior and internal psychological set. Should the members gang up on her, he would protect her and "take them on." In the private meetings he repeatedly encouraged her to share her fears and her background with the group. He had the faith in the other members that she lacked.

During the ninth session it happened. Members talked to each other about her, discussed the fact that unless she made some effort to say something to them, to give some explanation for her standoffishness, they would want her to leave. Many, if not every one of the 13 other members, directly confronted her. The counselor said nothing, held back, but watched her closely. He sat next to her, as was his wont, to give her physical comfort. Tears came. She found it hard to breathe. The counselor touched her arm, rested his hand there, and asked, "Junellen, do you want me to answer them?" Long pause. Heavy sighs. "No . . . I will." Then she talked.

"I like all of you. But I can't help myself that I'm not like you." More tears. Wads of tissue paper emerge from her purse. "I . . . want to talk . . . . Oh, it's so hard!" Finally she got going. It poured out. What was happening to her, in her life, had nothing to do with them. She went on to say how important to her was each piece of private information she had garnered from particular members. Once the dam had broken and her story gushed out, the members were first contrite, then sympathetic, then realistically helpful. The ninth session ended with two-thirds of the members going for coffee afterward to relate to her, to welcome her and solidify her entry into the fold.

Up until now in this chapter we have been abstract, albeit unfolding the story of the rise of group counseling as a cultural phenomenon and as one service among many in the range of psychological services that have developed in this century. And this is for the sake of locating ourselves in a professional context, for consciously positioning ourselves as group counseling practitioners, for knowing what we are and what we are not. When we enter the group field and look about to find our bearings, the early realization strikes us that a Babel of voices crying out for our attention is the prevailing condition. Within the confusion, somehow, we must find ourselves. Where lies truth? Where lies practicality? Where lies professional direction? We must ask ourselves: With whom do we propose to be allied? We must ask ourselves: How do we propose to function?

A concrete example of group life helps us to come down from the abstract heights, but it neither absolves us nor frees us from establishing principles of operation for ourselves. We must constantly make sense of experience. Seizing it, reflecting upon it, analyzing it is necessary to our learning, or else we behave the same in a similar case, the same being "according to a preprogrammed response," or we fail to act, shifting responsibility for action to others. Because in each case a generous spectrum of options is always open, it behooves us to have a sound operational philosophy, some principles to guide us that we have abstracted from reality—indeed, from the many realities we have lived through or borrowed from others and vicariously tried on for size.

What we can see in the three illustrative cases is that a leader operating from a group encounter orientation might easily have sailed on a different tack. Presuming, in the first case, the leader took no responsibility for determining how the group ought to deal with the bird, and bird lovers in the group were able to persuade the other members that the sparrow's welfare was a higher value than any one of the group member's concerns, the session might have ended then and there, while bird capturing amid general tumult became the business at hand. In the second case, the encounter group enthusiast, who saw his role as including the sharing of what churned within him, would no doubt have used the group to help himself deal with his powerful feelings. In the third case he might have let the group do its thing where Junellen's fate was at stake, taking no special responsibility for her deep-seated apprehensions in relating to others, particularly in a group context, with who knows what consequences resulting? Perhaps he, too, would have confronted her head-on.

It is perhaps idle to speculate on what might have happened were the counselor(s) to have been of a different counseling orientation than what is laid out in this book and in *Counseling Techniques That Work*, or what might have happened if an encounter group framework governed the proceedings. In any and every instance of looking at a slice of life in an ongoing group, one can see how the script might vary depending on whether the encounter group model or a group counseling model were used.

We have been reviewing how group counseling has evolved to the present day. It is now worth noting that the Council for Accreditation of Counseling and Related Educational Programs, an official arm of the American Association for Counseling and Development (AACD), has approved the following standards at their official meeting during AACD's 1984 Convention in Houston, Texas.[19] These standards were developed by the Association for Specialists in Group Work and apply directly to group counseling, not to group encounter, and not to group psychotherapy. The standards speak to the issue of what knowledge and skills are significant to professional practice. They are the distilled product of the minds of many experienced practitioners who have reached agreement on what group counseling is and what it is not.

PROFESSIONAL STANDARDS FOR TRAINING OF GROUP COUNSELORS

Preamble

Whereas counselors may be able to function effectively with individual clients, they are also required to possess specialized knowledge and skills that render them effective in group counseling. The Association for Specialists in Group Work supports the preparation of group practitioners as part of and in addition to counselor education.

The Professional Standards for Group Counseling represents the minimum core of group leader (cognitive and applied) competencies that have been identified by the Association for Specialists in Group Work.

DEFINITION

Group Counseling

Consists of the interpersonal processes and activities focused on conscious thoughts and behavior performed by individuals who have the professional credentials to work with and counsel groups of individuals regarding career, educational, personal, social and developmentally related concerns, issues, tasks, or problems.

Designated Group Counseling Areas

In order to work as a professional in group counseling, an individual must meet and demonstrate minimum competencies in the generic core of group counselor standards. These are applicable to all training programs regardless of level of work or specialty area. In addition to the generic core competencies, (and in order to practice in a specific area of expertise) the individual will be required to meet one or more specialty area standards (school counseling and guidance, student personnel services in higher education, or community/mental health agency counseling).

Group Counselor Knowledge Competencies

The qualified group leader has demonstrated specialized knowledge in the following aspects of group work:

- Be able to state for at least three major theoretical approaches to group counseling the distinguishing characteristics of each and the commonalities shared by all.
- Basic principles of group dynamics and the therapeutic ingredients of groups.
- Personal characteristics of group leaders that have an impact on members' knowledge of personal strengths, weaknesses, biases, values and their impact on others.
- Specific ethical problems and considerations unique to group counseling.
- Body of research on group counseling in one's specialty area (school counseling, college student personnel or community/mental health agency).
- Major modes of group work, differentiation among the modes and the appropriate instances in which each is used (such as group guidance, group counseling, group therapy, human relations, etc.).
- Process components involved in typical stages of a group's development (i.e., characteristics of group interaction and counselor roles).
- Major facilitative and debilitative roles group members may take.
- Advantages and disadvantages of group counseling and the circumstances for which it is indicated or contraindicated.

Group Counselor Skill Competencies

The qualified group counselor has shown the following abilities:

- To screen and assess readiness levels of prospective clients.
- To deliver a clear, concise, and complete definition of group counseling.
- To recognize self-defeating behaviors of group members.
- To describe and conduct a personally selected group counseling model appropriate to the age and clientele of the group leader's specialty area or areas.
- To accurately identify nonverbal behavior among group members.
- To exhibit appropriate pacing skills involved in stages of a group's development.

- To identify and intervene effectively at critical moments in the group process.
- To appropriately work with disruptive group members.
- To make use of the major strategies, techniques and procedures of group counseling.
- To provide and use procedures to assist transfer and support of changes by group members in the natural environment.
- To use adjunct group structures such as psychological homework (i.e., self-monitoring, contracting).
- To use basic group leader interventions such as process comments, empathetic responses, self-disclosure, confrontations, etc.
- To facilitate therapeutic conditions and forces in group counseling.
- To work cooperatively and effectively with a co-leader.
- To open and close sessions and terminate the group process.
- To provide follow-up procedures to assist maintenance and support of group members.

Can we accept these standards literally? Any reader knowledgeable about group counseling would undoubtedly want to quarrel with their language and content, to rewrite some, exclude some, perhaps add others. This is a group's product, which is to say that individual contributors conceded and compromised to reach consensus. The statements are the planks of a party's platform. Then, too, there is the question of who will decide if a certain individual has met the standards and is now eligible to practice? And *how* will such judges make their decision? The standards serve as benchmarks against which to measure oneself. In the end it becomes the individual practitioner's responsibility to internalize standards, and with justification to be conscious of where his or her own standards diverge in any interpretation of a professional association's minimal norms of qualification for practice.

It is worth reiterating that a group counselor is first a counselor. This is to say that he or she functions in group sessions out of some coherent theoretical and operational philosophy of counseling. Nor is this less true of any worker in groups that are convened to help individual members grow in some differently conceptualized therapeutic way. As Carl Rogers, a self-styled encounter group advocate, says in the quotation that begins this chapter, "In my own work with encounter groups, I have very much the same theory and philosophy that I've been talking about. As a group facilitator I would try to hold much the same attitudes that I was describing as effective in individual psychotherapy."[20]

Personal mastery counseling in groups first of all presupposes that the counselor knows what individual counseling is all about and is able to perform it.[21] The special circumstances of counseling in a group do not obviate the expertise required of the counselor when only one client is present. It is assumed that a group is not an entity having a life of its own. Indeed, the group as such does not exist; only the individual members exist, and each of these is there to receive counseling. Human beings cannot be added together for any purpose without each surrendering his or her individuality. Thus the personal mastery group counselor is not interested in the totality, only in helping each individual member. The counselor has multiple clients simultaneously. She or he counsels and orchestrates the counseling that comes from the members. Each of these helpful participants and witnesses is there to learn, to get self-enhancement from the experience.

Because the counselor has a number of clients to work with at the same time, the difficulties of counseling are multiplied. There is more behavior to absorb, understand, and remember. There is a greater variety of behavior emitted. There are special helping resources in members to be assessed and called into play. In the event of counselor passivity, certain behavioral phenomena are likely to occur that are antithetical to productive behavioral development. The group counselor will be challenged more, perhaps angrily by all the group members in concert, and the counselor's functioning under such stress calls for a higher level of mastery than what he or she is likely to require for effectiveness in a one-to-one session. There are lessons to know even before the group gets launched so that group composition is determined according to principles, which, when followed, augur for the greatest degree of counseling good to the greatest number. After one has become a trained and effective dyadic counselor, one can then begin to learn all there is to know about providing the same service to individuals in a group setting.

How does personal mastery group counseling differ from other forms of group work? First, it is like group psychotherapy in that the counselor is the avowed expert in the group, the trained deliverer of counseling services who takes responsibility for what goes on in the group. It is unlike group psychotherapy in that no group member is presumed to be sick, abnormal, or inadequate. Each group member is considered to be normal, which is to say that she or he is a person who can benefit from the experience. This is anyone.

The concept of normality requires special explication here. The personal mastery counselor deems the statistical concept behind the "normal curve" as having little or no serviceable meaning. Group members are human beings, all of whom have human behaviors, some of which are grossly self-defeating, but most of which work for the individual who owns them. To call anyone abnormal is to compare a unique human being with another unique being, to take a part and call it a whole, to label a person for the sake of dismissal. What makes more sense than the concept of normality is the concept of insanity, which the personal mastery counselor defines operationally. *That person is behaving insanely who loses conscious control or distorts reality to a greater or lesser degree.* It is the counselor's job to be able to diagnose when such behavior is being manifested, to judge when such is detrimental to a client or others in a particular here-and-now context, and to be able to intervene and provide effective assistance when such behavior exceeds limits of acceptable self-management or interpersonal functioning. (Each of us, by the way, according to insanity so understood, are helplessly insane when we are asleep, for example, and we are on our way to getting there when we consume any alcoholic beverage, experiencing greater distortions of reality and greater loss of control with each glass we pour into ourselves. So too have we lived through the dimunition of our control and accurate reality perception when we have upset ourselves sufficiently in the past. We know what insanity is because we have experienced it, however mild its degree.) If a person were out of control and distorted reality all the time, obviously that person would not be a likely candidate for a counseling group, and to the extent that the person manifested more rather than less of such behavior in a group setting, the counselor's expertise would have to be more considerable. And the principle is progressive when more of such individuals inhabit a group and manifest grosser forms of such behavior. That there are such individuals is what will keep the specially trained—psychiatrists, psychoanalysts, and other psychotherapists—in business for a long, long time.

The category of group work called "encounter" (a term that seems to have won out over "sensitivity," "human relations training," "growth," or "T"-groups, though these appellations have not completely disappeared from the scene and others in the same genre exist or crop up intermittently) differs from personal mastery group counseling in several ways. Although both seek to provide a safe human laboratory where members can try on new self-enhancing behaviors, although both are convened to assist individuals in self-development, in an encounter group the emphasis is on a fairly well outlined group process and not on a counseling process for which the leader takes responsibility. The encounter group leader tends to disavow expertise and likes to be called the group facilitator. He or she facilitates the group process, and it is the process, rather than the facilitator, that accounts for the changes the members experience. The facilitator's role is one of a more experienced member, a player/coach, so to speak. Encounter group leaders tend not to do individual counseling. They also tend to use the group "to get in touch with their own feelings," thus saying to members, "I'm no different than you are. Don't look to me for direction on how to run your life." Group counselors, on the other hand, would not think of using the group to work on their own concerns. They take responsibility for what happens to any individual member of a group they head, and they will extend their services to participants on an individual basis outside of the group, if such is called for. It is a condition they establish before a group is even begun and they consider it unethical not to render themselves available in this way.

The designator, "marathon," although usually associated with encounter groups, really indicates that a group continues for a long time at a given session. Marathon counseling groups can go on just as easily as marathon encounter groups. By lengthening the time interval, the experience becomes intensified because it is a strain for human beings to struggle after personal behavioral change goals uninterrupted for any protracted period. If rest or sleep is denied and a session goes once or twice around the clock, defenses break down and emotions flare up. If sleep deprivation continues long enough, schizophrenic behaviors emerge. Knowing this, the competent personal mastery counselor provides rest periods and limits marathon sessions to a normal 8-hour work day. That desirable new behaviors are likely to occur in a marathon group as a result of strain, pressure, or defense lowering may be true, but the likelihood that they will be lasting for individuals in their own worlds outside the group is slim, without the support system that a group provides. And the ultimate goal of personal mastery counseling, the one that counts for each client, is always that positive behavioral change will be evidenced and lasting outside the group.

There are other special categories of group work, such as T.A. (transactional analysis) groups, gestalt groups, values clarification groups, but most of these are highly defined in terms of structure, theory, and particularized purposes, and they are not likely to be confused with counseling groups. Suffice it to say that personal mastery group counselors know what they are about, and because they know, they do not denigrate nor eschew other group work experiences. Rather, they are inveterate students of all of these, seeking to discover useful learnings that they can adapt to their own practices. Any experimentation that continues to go on in the field of small therapeutic groups may yield new and welcomed learnings. What is currently known about how people can be best helped to change in groups may well be but a scratch on the surface of what will one day be known. What group counselors know for certain is that the group is an especially potent place in which to do counseling. For most clients, positive behavioral change occurs more quickly there.

NOTES

1. Evans, R. I. (1975). *Carl Rogers: The man and his ideas*. New York: E. P. Dutton, pp. 32–33.
2. For a now classical summary of these ideas, see: Hare, P. A., Borgatta, E. F., & Bales, R. F. (Eds.). (1967). *Small groups: Studies in social interaction* (rev. ed.). New York: Knopf.
3. The story is told in another classic in the group field: Bradford, L. P., Gibb, J. R., & Benne, K. D. (Eds.). (1964). *T-group theory and laboratory method: Innovation in re-education*. New York: Wiley.
4. O'Banion, T., & O'Connell, A. (1970). *The shared journey: An introduction to encounter*. Englewood Cliffs, NJ: Prentice-Hall; Hamachek, D. E. (1971). *Encounters with the self*. New York: Holt, Rinehart, & Winston; Bebout, J. (1973). A study of group encounter in higher education. *Educational Technology, 13,*(2), 63–67; Maliver, B. L. (1973). *The encounter game*. New York: Stein & Day.
5. Schutz, W. C. (1967). *Joy: Expanding human awareness*. New York: Grove Press.
6. Schutz, W. C. (1971). *Here comes everybody*. San Francisco: Viking Press.
7. Reich, C. A. (1970). *The greening of America*. New York: Random House.
8. Ibid., p. 242.
9. Rowe, W., & Winborn, B. B. (1973). What people fear about group work: An analysis of 36 selected critical articles. *Educational Technology, 13,*(1), 53–57. See also: Janis, I. L. (1972). *Victims of groupthink: A psychological study of foreign-policy decisions and fiascoes*. Boston: Houghton Mifflin.
10. Goodstein, L. D., & Dovico, M. (1979). The decline and fall of the small group. *The Journal of Applied Behavioral Science, 15,* 320–328.
11. Lakin, M. (1979). What's happened to small group research? Introduction. *The Journal of Applied Behavioral Science, 15,* 266.
12. Ibid., Epilogue, p. 426.
13. Vriend, J. (1985). We've come a long way, group. *Journal for Specialists in Group Work, 10,* (2). Copyright 1985 by the American Association for Counseling and Development. Reprinted by permission.
14. See Mosher, R. L., & Sprinthall, N. A. (1970). Psychological education in the secondary schools. *American Psychologist, 25,* 911–924.
15. Sprinthall, N. A. (1971). *Guidance for human growth*. New York: Van Norstrand Reinhold, p. v.

16. Ibid., p. vi.
17. The Association for Specialists in Group Work was chartered as Division XI of the American Association for Counseling and Development in 1973. Its first 10 presidents, listed chronologically as follows through 1984, were: George M. Gazda, Jack A. Duncan, Clarence A. Mahler, Merle M. Ohlsen, John Vriend, H. Allan Dye, Walter M. Lifton, James Gumaer, Rex Stockton, and Marguerite R. Carroll.
18. Vriend, J., & Kottler, J. A. Group work as a synergistic modality. In Kottler, J. A. (1983). *Pragmatic group leadership* (pp. 2–5). Monterey, CA: Brooks/ Cole. Copyright 1983 by Brooks/Cole. Reprinted (with slight modifications) by permission.
19. American Association for Counseling and Development. (October 18, 1984). CACREP issues group worker guidelines. *Guidepost*, p. 5. Copyright 1982 by the American Association for Counseling and Development. Reprinted by permission.
20. Rogers, C. (1970). *Carl Rogers on encounter groups.* New York: Harper & Row, pp. 32–33.
21. Beginning here and continuing through the end of this chapter, material is included that first appeared in slightly different form in: Vriend, J. (1978). What personal mastery in groups is all about: Background and rationale. *Journal for Specialists in Group Work, 3,*(3), 104–112. Copyright 1978 by the American Association for Counseling and Development. Reprinted by permission.

The One and The Many

Fifty years ago, when I was a boy of fifteen and helping to inhabit a Missourian village on the banks of the Mississippi, I had a friend whose society was very dear to me because I was forbidden by my mother to partake of it. He was a gay and impudent and satirical and delightful young black man ... who daily preached sermons ... with me for sole audience. He imitated the pulpit style of several clergymen of the village, and did it well, and with fine passion and energy. To me he was a wonder....

One of his texts was this:

"You tell me whar a man gits his corn-pone, en I'll tell you what his 'pinions is."

I can never forget it. It was deeply impressed upon me ... The black philosopher's idea was that a man is not independent, and cannot afford views which might interfere with his bread and butter. If he would prosper, he must train with the majority; in matters of large moment, like politics and religion, he must think and feel with the bulk of his neighbors, or suffer damage in his social standing and in his business prosperities. He must restrict himself to corn-pone opinions—at least on the surface. He must get his opinions from other people; he must reason out none for himself; he must have no first-hand views.

I think Jerry was right in the main, but I think he did not go far enough...

It was his idea that a man conforms to the majority view of his locality by calculation and intention.

This happens, but I think it is not the rule...

Broadly speaking, there are none but corn-pone opinions. And broadly speaking, corn-pone stands for self-approval of other people. The result is conformity. Sometimes conformity has a sordid business interest—the bread-and-butter interest—but not in most cases, I think. I think that in the majority of cases it is unconscious and not calculated; that it is born of the human being's natural yearning to stand well with his fellows and have their inspiring approval and praise—a yearning which is commonly so strong and so insistent that it cannot be effectually resisted, and must have its way.

—Mark Twain[1]

We are always coming up with the emphatic facts of history in our private experience and verifying them here. All history becomes subjective; in other words there is properly no history; only biography. Every mind must know the whole lesson for itself—must go over the whole ground. What it does not see, what it does not live, it will not know.

—Ralph Waldo Emerson[2]

The paradoxical concept of the "one and the many," singularity and plurality, the unit and the collectivity, the individual and the group, has daily effects and affects upon us all, both trivial and profound. We do not live an hour without being confused in our own thoughts about when we ought to stand alone or to include ourselves in the opinion of a group. Some of us have not, perhaps cannot, see ourselves as unique individuals, different and apart from all others who have ever lived, in any aspect of our existence whatsoever. To think of ourselves as original in any way is to invite haunting horrors into our minds, nightmarish specters, for we want to belong and be accepted by the human communities of our choice and fear being the ridiculed, the outcast, the disowned, the exile, the discounted, the loner, the abandoned. To have our own minds, those thinking machines, shaped by our own design and desires and filled only with what we have privately created seems to many a description of madness. Having minds of our own may even be totally impossible.

What would that human being be like who was raised alone, who grew and developed to adulthood without any human contact? This question, absorbing to all of us who know of no other life than growing up in a human social context, is what feeds an ancient and perennial myth of wild primitivism; it provides the theme and plot for many an imaginative movie or book. It arouses our fascination for *Tarzan and the Apes*, our interest in werewolves, in feral children raised by other animals, going all the way back to the pagan belief that Romulus, son of Mars and founder and first king of Rome, and his twin brother, Remus, left as infants to die in the Tiber River, were suckled by a she-wolf.

The reversal of the question is equally fascinating. This is to say, can we take a child, one whose early contact with humans has been minimal or exceedingly primitive by modern standards, and raise this uncivilized being to fit into our society? There is such a true story, not of a child but of a gentle middle-aged man who grew to adulthood in a culture almost as primitive as that of the stone age, the last of his disappeared people, the Yana Indians of northern central California. The story is told in *Ishi in Two Worlds: A Biography of the Last Wild Indian in North America*.[3]

> Ishi was, literally, a Stone Age man, the last of a "lost" tribe, when, only half a century ago, he stumbled into twentieth-century California. Undoubtedly Ishi anticipated death as a result of his arrival in an enemy world, but almost miraculously he came to the hands of T. T. Waterman and Alfred L. Krober, anthropologists who were among the few men in the country equipped to understand his dilemma and his personality ... The "discovery" of Ishi,

"the last wild Indian," was well advertised in the newspapers in 1911, and in the next five years thousands of visitors watched him chip arrowheads, shape bows, and make fire by his age-old techniques in the halls of the modern museum where he so oddly made his home.[4]

We have our own dreams of innocence, of being at one with nature, of the noble savage, of the bountifulness and tranquility and smell of the Garden of Eden. We remember the freedom and innocence of childhood and liken the state to what it must have been for Indians and other nomadic peoples untroubled by the rat-race into which we have transformed life for ourselves. We read the anthropologists' reports of idyllic communities of far away and long ago—Margaret Mead's *Coming of Age in Samoa*, for example,[5] and feel an envious ache. "The serenity and satisfaction of infancy and the more primitive stages of man alike, existing before the cumulative repressions of societal sacrifice, the fullness of a presocial and more organic functioning (in . . . memories and dreams . . . at least)," says Maxwell Geismar in his discussion of *The Adventures of Huckleberry Finn*, are "all . . . shattered by . . . the dregs of civilization."[6]

Culture-bound as we are, how can we create ourselves, be ourselves? There are more and more of us, and we seemingly crowd together more and more, impinge upon each other more and more. "The enemy is us." The inexorable march of civilization seems to be a herding of more and more of us into larger and larger groups, not only in football stadiums, in traffic rush hours, in schools and stores, at Disneyland, in the large metropolitan areas, but in our own living rooms through vicarious living via the tube. The earth shrinks and the psychological and social space is what is surely the first to go. The very density of our numbers is choking off our air of individuality. We can identify with Ishi's fear, when at one point his protectors took him to the beach in San Francisco to show him the ocean. He hardly noticed the ocean. What shocked and scared him was all the bathers. So many people grouped together! His natural xenophobia was elevated to a state of panic. Soon, though, this stark fear began to subside, for "the friendly crowd was beginning to fragment for him," says his biographer, "to individuate, to lose some of its robot terror."[7]

"To individuate." So important for this noble savage, so important for the noble savage within the breast of each of us. To be an individual, a one among the many, is hardly a modern problem, but the escalating odds against it are overwhelmingly difficult to surmount. How to come to terms with the concept of the one and the many is a lifelong enterprise for every individual conscience. How to contend with the idea of being "my brother's keeper" or "being kept by my brother?" How to participate in the human community, in all of the peopled circles we inhabit, and retain our sense of ourselves; how to be in personal charge of our lives?

Do we even understand that most of the time we are not in charge? Do we know how we are being personally diminished by our membership in groups? Are we so conditioned that we don't care? Do we have the courage to fight for individuality? Is it worthwhile to be different from our brothers and sisters? If so, how?

A PARADOX: ME VERSUS WE

In this chapter we shall take a diversified look at the concept of the one and the many, seeing how it has infiltrated and determined so much of our mental life and how it has, therefore, governed our social relations, how we customarily think, feel, and act. This concept is at the root of reason. It is present in all the products of our minds. It determines how we absorb, conceptualize, and integrate our worlds. It preempts the two methods we use to arrive at principles of operation, for we seek to reduce the many to one so that we may apprehend and comprehend reality, and we seek to relate the one to the many so that we may grasp its significance and place it in a context. We seek to order the chaos of experience through classification of similarities and differences. The one and the many, whether or not we have ever pondered over the intellectual and cultural problems with which it confronts us, is at the heart of our existence. And in group counseling it is blatantly present. It is nakedly there, a phenomenon, an invisible force in continuous operation, though it is seldom perceived and even more rarely acknowledged. Now and then an individual has some dim realization of its power and resists either the pressure of the group toward conformity or the pressure to stand defiantly alone in some regard, but by and large the presence of the difficulty is blithely ignored.

Just how the paradoxical concept of the one and the many falls "smack-dab in the middle" of counseling in groups can be described simply enough. It has to do with ends and means. The end of counseling, the desired outcome, is behavioral change. This idea proposes that a client change her or his mental behavior and corresponding emotional and physical behavior from whatever it was into something more self-serving, something more self-enhancing. When a person uses a counselor in the process, the counselor's cooperation and agreement are sought. The counselor represents "the other," not the one, is even symbolic of "all others." But in a group these vaguely understood others come to life.

There they are, in the flesh, in a real sense the enlargement or multipli-cation of the counselor, the counselor subdivided into alive units, each with an opinion and a voice, and the counselor's task becomes that of bringing these opinions and voices to bear on the one according to some counseling orientation. This is to say that the counselor's job is to or-chestrate what goes on in the group so that the happenings are produc-tive, so that for any member of the group the individual behavioral change goals are reached whenever and wherever possible. This is the end. The means are group means. The message would seem to be: The way you can metamorphose into a happier, more in-charge individual is to become like us. Here lies the paradox.

How does this paradox pervade every aspect of our lives? First, it has to do with how we grasp the *essence* of things, that which makes a thing whatever it is, the "goatness" of a goat, the "treeness" of a tree. The concept of essences goes back at least as far as Plato. Any reading of Plato will show that he saw us as coming into the world with our ideas pre-formed. Thoughts about the world and its objects are not what we in-vented; we are born with our ideas, with a knowledge of essences, even with a knowledge of such abstractions as goodness, beauty, and justice. Our knowledge of justice, for example, is "a first principle which intui-tively we later know again. Further, we can make inferences about the ethical nature of human acts because we know the idea, justice, to start with," philosopher Arthur Brown points out in his discussion of human morality. He goes on to say,

> Insofar as it is a type of moral absolutism, Platonic *Idea*lism is similar to religious and secular traditionalism. It is different in that its sanctions are rooted not in divine or historical authority, but rather in intuition. Although intuition as a way of knowing is often rejected by empiricists who would require evidence of a different order, it is the case that some contemporary psychologists, linguists, and scientists do accept the view that certain struc-tures embedded in the human organism limit or direct thought and action. The leading figure in moral education, for instance, Lawrence Kohlberg of Harvard, is a Platonist.[8]

Aristotle and the empiricists, unlike Platonists, hold that we acquire our ideas by abstracting from the many what the essence of anything is. Thus, we must see many goats to have the idea of goatness. The same holds for the idea of humanness. But we are still dealing here with central essence, that essence peculiar to all units of the same class. What the essence of one person is, the essence of Richard M. Nixon as differentiated from that of Ronald Reagan or from that of anyone else (we know and expect that physical appearances are different—not "of the essence"), is an abstraction problem of a different order. Jean-Paul Sartre helps our understanding in this case by proposing that our existence precedes our essence. We choose our essence, says Sartre, piece by piece over time: We create ourselves by our choices, for the essence of each of us is the sum of our experiences. We *are* what we have lived through.

This is not the place to argue for any resolution of how the one and the many are intermingled, how each interdicts the other when the concept of essence is invoked. Rather, it is our purpose to introduce the overall primacy of how the concept of the one and the many permeates all thought and human action. Emerson, in his reading of Plato, is struck by just such an appreciation:

> If speculation tends thus to a terrific unity, in which all things are ab-sorbed, action tends directly backwards to diversity. The first is the course or gravitation of mind; the second is the power of nature. Nature is the manifold. The unity absorbs, and melts or reduces. Nature opens and creates. These two principles reappear and interpenetrate all things, all thought; the one, the many. One is being; the other, intellect: one is necessity; the other, freedom: one, rest; the other motion: one, power; the other, distribution: one, strength; the other, pleasure: one, consciousness; the other, definition: one, genius; the other, talent: one, earnestness; the other, knowledge: one, possession; the other, trade: one, caste; the other, culture: one, king; the other, democracy: and, if we dare carry these generalizations a step higher, and name the last tendency of both, we might say, that the end of one is escape from organization—pure science; and the end of the other is the highest instrumentality, or use of means, or executive deity.[9]

Now let us turn to a second area in which the concept of the one and the many captures and shapes our thinking, this time in the very words we use to formulate thought. It is inherent in grammar, in the parts of speech, particularly in the case of nouns. A noun is a naming word. The word *goat* is the name we give to all such animals. They share the name in common. If we give a particular goat a particular name, let's say, "Alfred" (or "Alfreda," if female), in grammar we call that name a proper noun, as opposed to a common noun. Alfred is only proper to one goat out of all the goats that be. We do not go around naming and so conferring dignity upon every item in the universe, only to those that are important enough for us to individuate. We designate importance through the use of proper nouns. Alfred is important or he would just stay a goat, one indistinguishable to us from the many goats in the world.

It follows that to demean a person, to lessen any person in importance, we need only to divest that individual of his or her proper name and delegate the one back to just being a face in the crowd, a part of the mob, bestowing on that person an ordinary "goatness" not exceptional enough to name.

We have collective names, too, nouns that designate a collection of units: mob, herd, group, bunch, gaggle, school, troop. This is so we can capture the many into one. We can confuse and complicate matters by treating such a collection as a one, and often we do. In law, for example, a corporation is treated as a person, all the stockholders absorbed into one person who is granted certain legal rights and privileges.

In our minds we know all things in this world by the names we give them. Things are represented by names in the recreated world of our minds. This even includes abstract nouns, the names we give to ideas, to those items that can exist only in our mental worlds. Words are symbols, thought-units we use to signify what is in both the real world and the world we carry around in our heads, our minds. We combine these units in ways that make sense for us, and we give names to these sense-making units, all abstract nouns. We seldom even stop to think that we are only dealing with mind-products, with mentalizations, and this is where many of our troubles originate. There is no corresponding reality for duty, justice, goodness, love, beauty, or a million other ideas to which we give such names. They exist only by the definition we accord them. They exist only in our minds.

The common nouns that name ideas are confounding to most people, and yet they do not know that they are confounded by them. They are words that name ideas, and all of us hold these names in common. This is to say we "agree" that these abstract words are names for that which must surely exist, yet we are talking only of mental fabrications, of ideals, not of things in the real world symbolized by concrete nouns, those common nouns we use to name concrete objects that have a real referent. We fail to be impressed in our schooling from kindergarten through college by the sheer overweening quantity of abstract nouns that we employ in our thoughts and communications, by how much we rely on common knowledge that is essentially abstract. Humans hold abstractions in common through the very words they use. Most books, including this one, employ abstract terms in numbers far exceeding their counterpart of concrete terms, and some books rely exclusively on abstractions. Just in this paragraph, for example, the following abstract (common) nouns appear:

abstraction	names
communications	nouns
counterpart	number
example	paragraph
fabrication	quantity
ideas	referrent
ideals	terms
knowledge	words

You cannot go out into the world and find an idea, a fabrication, a referrent, a term, or an example and kick it, paint it red, or tell a dog to go fetch it.

In 1946 Wendell Johnson published a book he called: *People in Quandaries: The Semantics of Personal Adjustment*, which might fruitfully become required reading for all counselors. "It is neither an index to human nature nor an accident of chance," he writes, "that most, if not all, so-called maladjusted persons in our society may be viewed as frustrated and distraught idealists ... The ideals of the maladjusted are high in the sense that they are vague. Being vague, they are difficult to recognize; being difficult to recognize, they appear to be elusive."[10] This leads to

the basic design of our common maladjustment. We may call it the *IFD* disease: from idealism to frustration to demoralization. Probably no one of us entirely escapes it. It is of epidemic proportions. Certainly anyone occupied professionally with personal problems of men and women—and of children—comes to recognize it as a sort of standard base upon which are erected all manner of specific difficulties and semantic ailments ... In my experience, no other ailment is so common among university students, for example, as what I have termed the IFD disease. It is, moreover, a condition out of which there tend to develop the various types of severe "mental" and nervous disorders, the neuroses and psychoses that fill our "mental" hospitals with such a lush growth of delusion and incompetence ... There remains to be considered one other symptom of what we regard as personality maladjustment ... A practicing psychiatrist, Dr. Coyne Campbell, expressed it so pointedly and so simply that it will serve our purpose well to recall his main statements ... Patients who were brought to him because they had been judged to be seriously maladjusted or even "insane," showed one chief symptom: *They were unable to tell him clearly what was the matter*. They simply could not put into words the difficulties with which they were beset. Surely no one who has made it his business to help people in trouble has failed to observe their relative inarticulateness.[11]

This view leads us to a third aspect of the one and the many. Just as we hold words that signify the infinite diversity of the world in common, each of us incorporating these into our thinking processes in relatively similar fashion, so too do we hold *sense* in common. We are fond of saying that so-and-so either has or doesn't have common sense. Or we speak of "conventional wisdom," a phrase John Kenneth Galbraith introduced into modern parlance.[12] Somehow or another we prize common sense. It seems a cultural legacy, everyday wisdom passed on by the generations. Yet this sense that we hold in common, particularly if it is the only sense we have, can be inimical to living in self-enhancing ways.

Common sense is frequently "herd" sense, destructive to the individual. Says Arthur Koestler, "Any single individual who would today assert that he has made a pact with the Devil and had intercourse with succubi, would promptly be sent to a mental home. Yet not too long ago belief in such things was a matter of course—and approved by 'common sense' in the original meaning of the term, *i.e.*, consensus."[13] He goes on to quote *The Concise Oxford Dictionary*: "*Philosophy of commonsense*; accepting primary beliefs of mankind as ultimate criterion of truth."

It may be stated with approximate reliability that many of us, if not most of us, have "group minds." Our individual minds are inhabited by the many. We have few or no thoughts of our own, only those we have sponged up from others, from whatever has been currently floating about and exchanged in the groups we have inhabited. We lack *un*common sense. Such knowledge as we possess is composed chiefly of hand-me-downs, cliche-thinking, not what we have arrived at as a result of our own reasoning. It is understandable enough that we want outside corroboration and so turn to what others think. We do not want to fall into solipsism, a shaky reliance only on ourselves in our beliefs, where the individual mind is the ultimate criterion of truth, the theory that nothing exists or is real outside of the self. If we do not have strong minds, we fail to trust them.

The dangers of being group-minded are real, too, ultimately leading to George Orwell's *1984*, provided we all join the herd. Bertrand Russell asks:

> Why do we believe what we do? In former times, philosophers would have said it was because God had implanted in us a natural light by which we knew the truth. In the early nineteenth century they might have said it was because we had weighed the evidence and found a preponderance on one side. But if you ask a modern advertiser or political propagandist he will give you a more scientific and more depressing answer. A large proportion of our beliefs are based on habit, conceit, self-interest, or frequent iteration. The advertiser relies mainly on the last of these, but if he is clever he combines it skillfully with the other three. It is hoped that, by studying the

psychology of belief, those who control propaganda will in time be able to make anybody believe anything. Then the totalitarian State will become invincible.[14]

In our pursuance of a full appreciation for the pervasiveness of the one and the many in our lives, we now come to the crux of the matter. We could go on and on, too, seeing how we settle for "averages" as a way to grasp the many in so much of our thinking, where we buy into statistics as a reflection of reality, and yet no individual case ever fits the average. (The ridiculousness of such thinking is made plain in such a statement as this: "The average family in the United States now has 1.867 children.") We could go on to discuss fads, to analyze popularity, or to look at why original work in the arts so quickly is imitated, why the demand for copies is so great. But there is no need. What the one and the many comes down to, ultimately, is what Jean-Paul Sartre has called "existential despair." We are imprisoned within ourselves, within our individual consciousnesses, and we seek to transcend this state. Some seek vertical transcendence, the appeal of religion, unification with God. Others, perhaps most of us, are actively pursuing horizontal transcendence, a melding with other human beings. Some chase after both vertical and horizontal transcendence. We are alone, separate, conscious of our separateness, and we want to belong.

We want to belong to the human race in a more tangible sense, to feel integrated within it, or to some portion of it, even if only to one other member of it—the way we belonged in the womb—and by absorbing the many into our minds, we get some contrived sense of belonging. We are aware that we will die and often feel as though we have experienced our entire lives pinned down within our own minds, as though we have been unconnected. We respond to the sentiment of "Reach out—and touch someone." Aloneness, being unconnected to the many, being only the one, as was alluded to in the opening paragraph to this chapter—is a haunting horror, and dwelling on the condition can lead to madness. So we subconsciously welcome group-mindedness. "Immersion in the group mind," says Koestler, "is a kind of poor man's self-transcendence."[15] And from there it is only a mini-step from being group-minded to having only a group mind.

It is always important for counselors to respond to this phenomenon in our lives, to understand it in themselves and in others, to hear it when it crops out in a client. And in groups it crops out often—in many forms. Here are three different clients speaking out, voices that rose up in three different actual group sessions:

Georgia answers a question about marriage.

"I'm not married now. I was married for 15 years."

She pauses. She sits, hands folded in her lap, and stares down at her feet.

"Looking back, it was a time that just went by. I had no hand in shaping it, making it into anything. I was programmed. Programmed to be married. Programmed to have the kids. Programmed to socialize with other married couples. Programmed to deal with my parents, with my husband's family. Programmed, programmed, programmed. Except to get married, I can't even remember what I wanted to be when I grew up. It was my husband who left me. I didn't leave him. I just got older ... and heavier ... and less interesting to him. And I did everything for him. For the kids, too. I was always pleasing other people. Now here I am. Alone. I feel like I'm 13 years old and my life is just beginning. Except I'm 36."

Tears come. They spill down her cheeks.

"I can't stand my parents, now. I hate it when they call. I've started to hate my kids. I'm actually jealous of them. Can you believe that? I'm 36 and I'm farther behind than they are ... What's happened to me?"

● ● ● ● ●

Ken soliloquizes on television-watching.

"I spend too many hours in front of the tube. It's crazy. I'm addicted. I can't stop myself. What makes it so crazy is that I'm watching '*them*!' They're not watching me. If the people in the tube watched me, what would they see? I don't do anything. I just sit there. They have no reason to watch me. My life is dribbling away, sitting there. Just sitting there. My mind is taken up with *their* lives, not with my own. I can't stand it at times. Sometimes I even talk out loud—don't nobody laugh!—to the people on the screen. No one can hear me, but I talk. How crazy can you get!

"I live through people I don't even know and don't even care about. Actually, they're not even real. The stuff is all *made up*. They've sucked me up ... swallowed me. I have no life. I've disappeared. During the day I find myself wondering what is going to be on the tube tonight. Thinking about it! Can you imagine that? Who am I? Nobody. I don't know what's happened to me. I've had more life in this group in the last month for a few hours each week than I've had in all of last year of thousands of hours of tube-watching."

● ● ● ● ●

Tess speaks of a retirement she doesn't want. She is vibrant and youthful in her late 50s. She has been talking about her husband's retirement coming up this year.

"Ted has always had his sights fixed on retirement at the lake property. It's what his father did. His lifelong ambition has been the same. It's inevitable."

Tess will go along with this. The property is remote, fairly isolated. She tries to work up some enthusiasm.

"Ted's been adding a room, a big room. It will have a long beam across it. I'll hang lanterns from it. The room needs light. When all the children and grandchildren come to visit we'll spend a lot of time in that room."

She grows reflective.

"The young don't realize how quickly the time passes, how important the moments are."

Alas, Tess is speaking about herself and has vague misting longings streaking through her thought-passages behind this utterance, though ostensibly it is a commentary on her children and their choices and activities. It is Ted who wants to retire at the lake and it is Tess who goes along. She talks of what Ted wants. What Tess wants is rather a mystery. Inconstant dreams rattle in her, vaguely formed, prods on the underside of her consciousness, not intensely screaming as they once did, but murmuring only, muttering in their restless slumber. Tess may be liberated from the retirement, if Ted were to die early, but one hardly feels she would do much then to alter her life. She will continue with grandmothering, with being connected. She has suffered in her life from overconnectedness, though she would see this as the source of her life's joy and not understand how she has suffered; she would not understand that the person she might have been was systematically put to sleep, only to dream. And today, if her dreams are no longer nightmares, they also no longer make much difference. They are rumbles against death, quietly muffled thunder, far away. It is too late to change, too late to go against Ted's plans for retirement.

"The young don't understand how quickly the time passes."

An old ache for a lost self.

For each of us other people are the problems in our lives; we are seldom problems unto ourselves. If everyone in the world could understand this and act upon it, there would be no mental illness. But most of us choose not to be alone and therefore feel we must take others, or at least one other with whom we choose to be very close, into account. Now we have a problem. If we lack the skills to influence the other into understanding and accepting us and what we do, if we lack the skills to create the kind of space we require for personal freedom, we are then thwarted, diminished, thumped, stumped, and perhaps finally dumped, engaged in pleasing behaviors or defending behaviors to the exclusion of simply living according to our own wishes and dictates. We sacrifice aloneness for a togetherness, and find the togetherness wanting in some regard.

The concept of the one and the many has everything to do with our mental lives, with the shape of our minds, with *what* we think and *how* we think, with the ways we define ourselves, experience ourselves. We live in our minds, first, foremost, and always. Although we have powerful instincts pushing us toward a blending identification with the group, directing us even toward total group submersion, we also desire to have our own essence out of all the particular human essences that there are. We want to be Alfreds and Alfredas, not just goats. Practically every great thinker our species has ever produced has been superbly aware of autonomy versus belonging, of the paradox of the one and the many, perhaps mostly because an abundance of thinking leads to greater separateness, to being the isolate by virtue of producing so much *un*common sense. Here is Emerson once more, this time saying what can be done to reconcile the one and the many dilemma:

> What I must do is all that concerns me, not what the people think. This rule, equally arduous in actual and in intellectual life, may serve for the whole distinction between greatness and meanness. It is the harder because you will always find those who think they know what is your duty better than you know it. It is easy in the world to live after the world's opinion; it is easy in solitude to live after our own; but the great man is he who in the midst of the crowd keeps with perfect sweetness the independence of solitude.[16]

THE COUNSELOR'S RESPONSIBILITY

So how to translate the paradox of the one and the many in its varied forms into action in a counseling group? No technique is involved. Not unless it is the overriding one of keeping a comprehensive and roundly sculpted knowledge and understanding of its primacy in our lives well to the forefront of our minds as we go about our business of counseling in a group. There is, of course, the consequential regard for precision in the use of "we," but this is hardly a technique. It is more of a guideline to rope some of our looser verbal behavior. When a member says a "we" statement and can only mean "*I* think this is so," a counselor intervention is called for. Any "we" or "the group" uttering ought to refer to unanimity without any holdouts. A counselor can say, "We will end the group session at four o'clock sharp today," only because the counselor will see to it and has the responsibility as well as the power to make that happen. When a "we" is appropriate and valid, it can be used. Otherwise it is more in conformance with reality to address individuals by their given names; then the pronouns to use are singular: "you" or "I."

The counselor who has a perpetual awareness of the far-reaching implications of the one and the many will help clients to clarify and order their thinking about themselves, their choices, their behaviors in their lives. Being an original thinker, having self-made principles, rules for personal conduct, ideas about the self and the world and all the zillions of individual units it contains, does not mean that a person has any thoughts that no one else has ever had. There are few original thoughts that are not fictive. Whatever you or I think has been thought by someone else. That is a safe premise to go on. We may be sure that we have a thought that no one else has ever discovered only to bump into the same idea sooner or later in someone else, if we live long enough and encounter the thinking of enough others, whether in person or through television, movies, or the printed word.

What *is* original with us is the total constellation of thoughts we have sucked up in our travels through life. We all pick up different ideas and combine them differently within ourselves. Everyone is unique in that no two people have had the same collection of experiences in life, the same combination of learnings, including the same acquired baggage of errors, wishes, misinformation, contradictions, and private beliefs in totems, ridiculous theories, and outright falsities. And these collections can be fortified by the determination of anyone to *own* the learnings. Being the architect of one's personhood and make-up means being in charge: "I think what I think for my own reasons, based on my own logic, my own field-testing of my ideas. It matters not that others harbor any number of the same thoughts. I simply see them as having good sense, too. When we agree, that does not make us partners or allies. If for some specific end I band together with others who hold the same ideas, I realize that I do so to accomplish a purpose I cannot attain as easily alone."

If a person thinks only certain ideas because these foster acceptability to a group, or to some "other" who is seen as the authority or as having ominous power, that individual is subject to confusion, lack of direction, and a docket of additional difficulties. In the absence of the authority or group to support, ratify, confirm, or validate the ideas, the espouser is then alone—adrift at sea. If we do not own our thoughts and must appeal to others for whatever power or security they provide us, we are dependent and restricted in our living. Having proprietorship of our thoughts means having the resources of our own minds as the last court of appeal.

These observations do not pertain to those thoughts that constitute truth, insofar as we know what truth is. What we perceive to be true, both absolutely and relatively, we base on some kind of evidence. Data exist to support what we believe. This includes immutable laws, those in the physical sciences, as well as facts of existence. It includes normative principles: an outcome reliably can be expected most of the time, half of the time, some of the time, or on rare occasions—the way a tornado shows up.

The crucial area wherein individual versus group thought makes a difference to all of us is in the opinions we hold, particularly those that govern our conduct. Acting imitatively, blindly following in the footsteps of others, may be fine in many life circumstances, even fruitful and self-enhancing, saving of time and energy. There are those life areas where we even reward others to do our thinking for us. We pay our physicians, dentists, barbers, auto mechanics, accountants, and other consultants, and follow their directions in good faith. We choose leaders and models. But are we willing to take our chances, in those life areas that really matter to us, based on the justification that "40 million French citizens can't be wrong"? If history tells us anything, it cries out that whole nations *can* be wrong, wrong for us, wrong by any reasonable standard. Mob psychology is to be feared. It scared the framers of our Constitution. The group has power in numbers, and many a wrongheaded group hellbent on having its way has caused the slavery of individual dissenters. Numbers and might have nothing to do with what is right, with what is true, reasonable, or worthwhile.

It is through conformity that we lose our freedom. If Hitler's Germany taught us nothing else we ought never to blot from our consciousness the lesson of how millions of ordinary citizens going along with the malevolent game plan of a charismatic but demonic and tyrannical crackpot can lead to the most seemingly unimaginable hell. Freedom is preserved only by the efforts of those who do the hard work of thinking for themselves. And many, far too many individuals consider that work so hard that they seek to escape. In his analysis of Nazi Germany and how an entire nation could fall under the mesmerism of a fanatical leader, Erich Fromm has delineated this phenomenon in a book he has appropriately titled, *Escape From Freedom*.[17] It may be said that we must be fearful of those who have no thoughts of their own earned by the hard work of a life of reason, those whose minds are turned by every breeze. It is not enough to say that they surrender their own freedom; by their numbers they threaten and place ours in jeopardy. The multiplication of such nonthinkers, the endless proliferation of mindlessness lined up behind a despotic leader, becomes a force not easily deposed. In counseling groups we can help nonthinkers to understand that they act as weathervanes, iron roosters atop inconsequential and empty barns, and can be blown away by any big storm of strong opinion. The whittling away of personal freedom begins in small groups, family groups, social groups, work groups, play groups, small enclaves, acting like fertile cells that can subdivide and proliferate like amoebas. Nor is a counseling group any exception: All the conditions and dynamics for the reinforcement of mindlessness or wrongheadedness are present. No counseling group is immune from the possibility of erroneous thinking that is spread through contagion.

What is most important in group counseling is that the counselor be neither a weathervane thinker nor passive about the pervasiveness of erroneous ideas, whether beguiling or toxic, and not challenge members who too easily and too quickly buy into a certain rationale for change simply because of the pressure of others. Members frequently line up in agreement that a certain person in the group ought to go a particular way, think a particular way, for reasons seemingly healthy or benign, seemingly sound, but basically patently unsound. The pressing faction in the group may be unconscious of their own hidden agenda—a pet bias held in common, a desire to get on to new and more lively group business, an unstated conviction that the one being urged to change is a nebbish or a wimp and needs pushing. The danger lies not in the counselor's lack of awareness of the underlying dynamics in such a case, but in the counselor's joining the faction or permitting its sway. A client so bombarded by the strength of opinion voiced by a bloc of members, who then makes new moves in his or her own world outside the group based upon them, not owning the ideas but simply wanting the approval of group peers for following through on their line of thinking, is in a state of danger for which the counselor must take some responsibility.

All the blessings of various kinds of help are available in counseling groups, but so too are all the dangers present, albeit in less than macroscopic ways. Group pressure is a force that can be beneficial. It might help to dislodge and jar loose some stones of self-defeating thinking heretofore masoned into a rock wall within a particular member's mind. On the one hand this force backs and enables a counselor to penetrate a seemingly fixed and undesirable position within a client's mind. For the first time in their lives, many clients will be confronted and look at, examine, and rethink their ideas in a counseling group simply because so many strangers without any apparent vested interest will straightforwardly question them and find their ideas idiotic or insupportable. On the other hand the force can itself be inimical to positive behavioral change. It is continually up to the effective counselor to gauge the difference.

In the final analysis, as counselors we must know that the beauty of the one is real. There are only individual minds. The beauty of the many is illusory. Though we hold language and thoughts in common with others, we are still the deciders of whatever thoughts belong to us. We choose to act based on what we think. If we abdicate and don't think, we become robots or clones and surrender control. We may seek a lifetime of emotional and physical pleasure to the detriment of our mind development because we have not been stopped short and forced to think, but in the long run we pay heavily when we do. In the final analysis, counselors seek to help each and every client become a better thinker, to see with the mind. "In the land of the blind, the one-eyed man is king."

Using and developing the mind, yes. But it remains the quintessential act of the mind to classify, to take ones of a similar nature and distribute them into groups that may then be treated as newly formed "ones" in their own right. Just as there is no group life as such, only the life of individuals within the group, so too there is no history of nations, institutions, or families, only the individual lives of members within them; the collectivity in each case is a mental convenience, a way for the mind to think. How else do we make sense of all the diversity? Our minds serve us best when we make sense of our worlds and our experiences. And there is no doubt that this is hard work, difficult under all circumstances and conditions, but even harder when in later years we lack the physical energy of youth, and harder still for those who have formed no habits of thought, dealing satisfactorily with the one and the many over time, making sense of experience all along the route, those who have chosen the pleasures of the body and the continuous goal of living more passionately at the expense and sacrifice of developing mentally.

Here are some related thoughts from Gilbert Highet:

> During our life on this earth, the body gradually dies; even the emotions become duller; but the mind in most of us continues to live, and even grows more lively and active, enjoys itself more, works and plays with more expansion and delight, makes better discoveries and deeper investigations— all this within a body which was once an arrogant and irrational master, but with age becomes a surly but half-obedient servant. The long-range aim of our lives is therefore to enjoy our physical being as long as possible; but, knowing that this enjoyment will last only a short period, say three or four hundred months, to build up the longer-lasting and more reliable enjoyment of the mind. . .
>
> Many people have played themselves to death. Many people have eaten and drunk themselves to death. Nobody has ever thought himself to death. Thought is the only human activity which does not generate large quantities of harmful acids and alkalis. The chief danger confronting us is not age, or weariness. It is laziness, sloth, routine, stupidity, forcing their way in like wind through the shutters, seeping into the cellar like swamp water. Young

people always think that they have all the hard temptations to face. But other temptations, less ardent but more persistent, will assail them later: the soft, sweet, cozy, temptation of *laissez-faire*, the Sunday-morning-snooze temptation of casualness, the long-weekend temptation of triviality and temporariness. Many a brilliant mind, many a rich and powerful personality has fought its way through all the dangers, only to fall victim to the comforts. Both dangers and comforts are good for us; both can also be bad for us. Let us meet them both and beat them both.[18]

Beware of the many. Beware of the many in every disguise it might wear. Such a consciousness is hardly teachable or even salable to every counselor who undertakes the responsibility of leading a group, but if it were possible, your author, at least, would favor loading syringes full of such inoculum and injecting same into the bloodstream and therefore the brain of every candidate. "The lonely mind of one man is the only creative organ in the world," said John Steinbeck, "and any force which interferes with its free function is the Enemy."[19]

A QUESTION OF ETHICS

Ethics: n, the study of the ideal in human character and conduct.

—*A Comprehensive Dictionary of Psychological and Psychoanalytical Terms*[20]

Ethic: n:, 1. the discipline dealing with what is good and bad with moral duty and obligation 2. *a*: a set of moral principles or values *b*.: a theory or system of moral values *c*: the principles of conduct governing an individual or a group.

—*Webster's New Collegiate Dictionary*[21]

We can hardly say adieu to the subject of the one and the many without giving recognition to the phenomenon of ethics in group counseling, which is a classical case of the application of so many of the ideas we have been discussing in this chapter. We have seen in the previous chapter how group counseling has evolved over time and become a regular and accepted professional service. As such it is a treatment over which professional counseling bodies have sought to exercise some control, both in training and professional practice circles. As the Association for Specialists in Group Work developed, as group counseling advocates got together to discuss their specialty, as they consolidated and grew in number, they became more and more conscious of a need to produce a code of ethics to which members would subscribe, thus separating themselves as a conscientious and responsible group of professionals apart from any freewheeling mavericks in the field. As group counseling in its nature involves serving many clients simultaneously, it follows that the potential exists for more things to go awry. Group counseling is exciting because numbers allow for more different things to happen in a group, because more activity can be called into play, and therefore more counseling creativity is possible, but for the same reason the risks are increased that a counselor operating unethically could cause undesirable outcomes.

To introduce the idea of ethics in most arenas of human affairs is to reinvoke memories of sunday school for many, if not the majority of us. We are eager and high-spirited, wanting to get on with the business of performance, and when the "rules of right conduct" are imposed upon us we see them as a damper. Ethics tend to be restrictive, and therefore, to most of us, boring. Once again we are to be told what we *can't do*. We are impatient with ethics. Ethical considerations are downers. We think that if anything can be boring, then ethics of any kind vie for first place in the list of possibilities, being boring per se. It has been the author's experience that members of a professional group, when subjected to a report from an ethics committee, fidget, yawn vigorously, endeavor not to fall asleep, ask few questions, can hardly summon the good taste and decorum required to wait out the report before going on to more interesting and stimulating business. To most people ethics are dull, the product of watchdog types, overseers who don't trust individuals to act responsibly, and ethics tend to deflate individuality and personal freedom.

Taken as a branch of philosophy, ethics is that subject of study concerned with the morality of human behavior, with right and wrong, good and evil, duty and obligation, rules of proper or prudent conduct. From birth onward we have been subjected to rules. We are born into a "ruled" world where we are told by others in every circle of human activity what the rules are, and that we do right by obeying them. When we disobey them, we do wrong and we are bad, evil. Always, it seems, there have been two ways to go, the right way and the wrong way. We are discouraged from thinking that there are many ways that simply have different consequences. Just two ways? Well, that is not accurate, either: There is just *one way*, the right way, and any other way is wrong. So, in order to be good, we must do what we do in the *right* way, and avoid any other way at all costs.

Now, this imposes great difficulties on growing humans, a whole style of learning. Rather than figuring out the best way to do something, the learner has to run around and find out what the rules are, what is the right way to do anything. Frequently the rules are handed out, but many times they are not. When they are not, and the learner chooses to behave in a certain way that is not the right way, then consequences occur, usually punishment. The purpose of punishment is often to teach the right way. This continues as one grows up, and most of us find it boring to have to learn and obey all the rules in order to be good. We do it, however, regardless of how tiresome this is or how restrictive of our individuality. We more or less accept it as a fact of life in the human community. Some of us, though, refuse to be so bored and we ignore the right way in favor of any old way that is handy, any way that seems to work for us. We deviate. And deviants, as everybody knows, are *bad* people. Nogoodniks. Some need to be locked up. Others simply bear watching. And then there are those for whom some hope exists, those who will respond to teaching.

Rules, we are told, are for our own protection. They are made and ought to be followed so that each person will be protected from the bad behavior of others. Rules, it seems, are intended for all those times (and there are literally billions) when humans are around each other. It is possible to have rules for one's own behavior when one is not in the company of anyone else, and some of us, if not all of us, mainly because we are so conditioned by rules, make up rules that we then follow in order to be good people in our own eyes—when to brush our teeth or eat a piece of cake, what shoe to put on first, what route to take to the grocery store, what to say when we pick up the phone, when and how to swab the kitchen floor—whatever. We may call them habits, but we have our reasons for picking them. For many of our behaviors we have forgotten the reasons, and we simply go on behaving in the same old way because it feels right to do so. And for countless of us, too, that old familiar "right feeling" is about the best emotion we can hope for in many an uneventful, mopey day.

It seems very reasonable to us that rules for right and wrong conduct exist and are followed by most people, and we include ourselves when we think of the "common good." We subscribe to the "social contract." In some very important ways rules are the glue that holds us together. Without rules, how could we ever live in big cities, for example, so *many* of us bumping into each other all the time?

Now, what about ethics for group counselors, for the professionals who work with clients in small groups? First, such rules of right conduct are for the protection of the members of such groups, not for the leaders: It is up to the leaders to protect the members, to act responsibly. Second, ethics become the concern of the members of a professional group for their own self-protection, based on the idea that the welfare of the professional association as a whole is threatened every time some member acts wrongly and is found out. The public in general see the professional organization a certain way, it is hoped in a favorable light, and if members act irresponsibly, the professional group is discredited. The professional group's *raison d'être* is to provide services to the public, and if it were to be thoroughly discredited, it could not remain in existence. Its very livelihood is thus at stake.

Ethics, then, connote a jury of peers looking in on the professional behaviors of its members and judging, criticizing, perhaps even chastising and punishing deviants and wrong-doers by banishment or disaffiliation. So if one wants identification with one's professional association, if one desires to be a member "in good standing," it behooves one to know and follow the rules of right conduct. Ethics urge members to be professionally self-governing in peer-approved ways. The member can ask, at any given juncture, "Would a jury of my peers endorse this action?" and make decisions based on an imagined response of "yes" or "no."

Ethics, so conceived, are helpful to professionals. Self-governance is always difficult, as there are always so many decisions to make, especially when one's work involves people. People are always complex and seldom act in predictable ways, and when they are all mixed together in the unfamiliar context of a small counseling group, their unpredictability escalates. This is exciting. But we don't want excitement to get out of hand, and ethics help us to contain it.

Perhaps the whole question of ethics and boredom can be easily resolved if one looks more closely at the nature of boredom. "Boredom, I knew," said Colin Wilson in a perspicacious moment, "meant not having enough to do with life's energies."[22] Wilson's observation is useful in removing the root cause of boredom from the object and placing it in the subject. Thus, nothing in the world is boring per se. One becomes bored by thinking thoughts about what is in the world, assigning responsibility for being trapped or shackled by what is outside of oneself in the exercising of one's energies. Understanding this, one never need be bored again. By anything. And least of all by friendly, useful ethics. One might even go so far as to say that it is quite unethical to think or utter that ethics are boring, especially in professional company. If one is of a mind, one can think *good* thoughts, the *right* thoughts, and so banish boredom from all association with ethics.

Given such prethinking, we would be remiss if we did not turn to the ethics of group counseling. Let us now conclude this chapter with a presentation of the ethics that have been established by the Association for Specialists in Group Work.

ETHICAL GUIDELINES FOR GROUP LEADERS (1980 Revision)[23]

Preamble

One characteristic of any professional group is the possession of a body of knowledge and skills and mutually acceptable ethical standards for putting them into practice. Ethical standards consist of those principles which have been formally and publicly acknowledged by the membership of a profession to serve as guidelines governing professional conduct, discharge of duties, and resolution of moral dilemmas. In this document, the Association for Specialists in Group Work has identified the standards of integrity and leadership among its members.

The Association for Specialists in Group Work recognizes the basic commitment of its members to the Ethical Standards of its parent organization, the American Association for Counseling and Development, and nothing in this document shall be construed to supplant that code. These standards are intended to complement the AACD standards in the area of group work by clarifying the nature of ethical responsibility of the counselor in the group setting and by stimulating a greater concern for competent group leadership.

The following ethical guidelines have been organized under three categories: the leader's responsibility for providing information about group work to clients, the group leader's responsibility for providing group counseling services to clients, and the group leader's responsibility for safeguarding the standards of ethical practice.

A. RESPONSIBILITY FOR PROVIDING INFORMATION ABOUT GROUP WORK AND GROUP SERVICES:

A-1. Group leaders shall fully inform group members, in advance and preferably in writing, of the goals in the group,

199

qualifications of the leader, and procedures to be employed.

A-2. The group leader shall conduct a pre-group interview with each prospective member for purposes of screening, orientation, and, in so far as possible, shall select group members whose needs and goals are compatible with the established goals of the group; who will not impede the group process; and whose well-being will not be jeopardized by the group experience.

A-3. Group leaders shall protect members by defining clearly what confidentiality means, why it is important, and the difficulties involved in enforcement.

A-4. Group leaders shall explain, as realistically as possible, exactly what services can and cannot be provided within the particular group structure offered.

A-5. Group leaders shall provide prospective clients with specific information about any specialized or experimental activities in which they may be expected to participate.

A-6. Group leaders shall stress the personal risks involved in any group, especially regarding potential life-changes, and help group members explore their readiness to face these risks.

A-7. Group leaders shall inform members that participation is voluntary and that they may exit from the group at any time.

A-8. Group leaders shall inform members about recording of sessions and how tapes will be used.

B. RESPONSIBILITY FOR PROVIDING GROUP SERVICES TO CLIENTS:

B-1. Group leaders shall protect member rights against physical threats, intimidation, coercion, and undue peer pressure insofar as is reasonably possible.

B-2. Group leaders shall refrain from imposing their own agendas, needs, and values on group members.

B-3. Group leaders shall ensure to the extent that it is reasonably possible that each member has the opportunity to utilize group resources and interact within the group by minimizing barriers such as rambling and monopolizing time.

B-4. Group leaders shall make every reasonable effort to treat each member individually and equally.

B-5. Group leaders shall abstain from inappropriate personal relationships with members throughout the duration of the group and any subsequent professional involvement.

B-6. Group leaders shall help promote independence of members from the group in the most efficient period of time.

B-7. Group members shall not attempt any technique unless thoroughly trained in its use or under supervision by an expert familiar with the intervention.

B-8. Group leaders shall not condone the use of alcohol or drugs directly prior to or during group sessions.

B-9. Group leaders shall make every effort to assist clients in developing their personal goals.

B-10. Group leaders shall provide between-session consultation to group members and follow-up after termination of the group, as needed or requested.

C. RESPONSIBILITY FOR SAFEGUARDING ETHICAL PRACTICE:

C-1. Group leaders shall display these standards or make them available to group members.

C-2. Group leaders have the right to expect ethical behavior from colleagues and are obligated to rectify or disclose incompetent, unethical behavior demonstrated by a colleague by taking the following actions:

(*a*) To confront the individual with the apparent violation of ethical guidelines for the purposes of protecting the safety of any clients and to help the group leader correct any inappropriate behaviors.

(*b*) Such a complaint should be made in writing including the specific facts *and dates* of the alleged violation and all relevant supporting data. The complaint should be forwarded to:

The Ethics Committee,
℅ The President
Association for Specialists in Group Work
5999 Stevenson Avenue
Alexandria, Virginia 22304

The envelope must be marked "CONFIDENTIAL" in order to assure confidentiality for both the accuser(s) and the alleged violator(s). Upon receipt, the President shall (a) check on membership status of the charged member(s), (b) confer with legal counsel, and (c) send the case with all pertinent documents to the chairperson of the ASGW Ethics Committee within ten (10) working days after the receipt of the complaint.

(*c*) If it is determined by the Ethics and Professional Standards Committee that the alleged breach of ethical conduct constitutes a violation of the "Ethical Guidelines," then an investigation will be started within ten (10) days by at least one member of the Committee plus two additional ASGW members in the locality of the alleged violation. The investigating committee chairperson shall: (a) acknowledge receipt of the complaint, (b) review the complaint and supporting data, (c) send a letter of acknowledgement to the member(s) of the complaint regarding alleged violations along with a request for a response and relevant information related to the complaint and (d) inform members of the Ethics Committee by letter of the case and present a plan of action for investigation.

(*d*) All information, correspondence, and activities of the Ethics Committee will remain confidential. It shall be determined that no person serving as an investigator on a case have any disqualifying relationship with the alleged violator(s).

(*e*) The charged party(ies) will have not more than 30 days in which to answer the charges in writing. The charged party(ies) will have free access to all cited evidence from which to make a defense, including the right to legal counsel and a formal hearing before the ASGW Ethics Committee.

(*f*) Based upon the investigation of the Committee and any designated local ASGW members one of the following recommendations may be made to the Executive Board for appropriate action:

1. Advise that the charges be dropped.
2. Reprimand and admonishment against repetition of the charged conduct.

3. Notify the charged member(s) of his/her right to a formal hearing before the ASGW Ethics Committee, and request a response be made to the Ethics Chairperson as to his/her decision on the matter. Such hearing would be conducted in accordance with the AACD Policy and Procedures for Processing Complaints of Ethical Violations, "Procedures for Hearings," and would be scheduled for a time coinciding with the annual AACD convention. Conditions for such hearing shall also be in accordance with the AACD Policy and Procedures document, "Options Available to the Ethics Committee, item 3."

4. Suspension of membership for a specified period from ASGW.

5. Dismissal from membership in ASGW.

In any reflection upon these "Ethical Guidelines" two summary thoughts are important for group counselors: (1) These are the imperfect product of a group of professionals who have reached agreement through compromise. In places their wording is vague ("insofar as possible," "as realistically as possible") and ill-defined (what *are* "inappropriate personal relationships," for example?). But they are a first attempt to arrive at professional self-governance, and a group counselor aspiring to professionalism would be seriously remiss not to be mindful of what his or her peers consider ethical and unethical conduct. (2) Wherever a professional group counselor disagrees with these guidelines, let him or her so advise the Ethics Committee of ASGW. It often takes decades and the input of many minds to produce a workable document that all can live with and that will stand the test of time.

NOTES

1. Clemens, S. L. (1973). *Europe and Elsewhere*. In M. Geismar, *Mark Twain and the three R's: Race, religion, revolution—and related matters.* (pp. 214–217). Indianapolis: Bobbs-Merrill (Original work published 1923)

2. Emerson, R. W. (1940). History. Essays: First Series. In B. Atkinson (Ed.), *The complete essays and other writings of Ralph Waldo Emerson.* (p. 127). New York: Random House (Modern Library ed.) (Original work published 1841)

3. Kroeber, T. (1967). *Ishi in two worlds: A biography of the last wild Indian in North America.* Berkeley, CA: University of California Press.
4. Ibid. From: Foreword by L. Gannett, p. vii.
5. Mead, M. (1928). *Coming of age in Samoa.* New York: Morrow.
6. Geismar, M. (1970). *Mark Twain: An American prophet.* Boston: Houghton Mifflin, p. 97.
7. Kroeber, T. (1967). Op. cit., p. 138.
8. Brown, A. (March, 1982). Can there be morality without God? A Bargman Memorial Lecture given at the Shaarey Zedek Synogogue, Southfield, MI. Detroit: Wayne State University (Mimeo.), p. 4.
9. Emerson, R. W. (1940). Plato; or, the philosopher. Representative Men. In B. Atkinson (Ed.), *The complete essays and other writings of Ralph Waldo Emerson* (p. 477). New York: Random House [Modern Library ed.] (Original work published 1850)
10. Johnson, W. (1946). *People in quandaries: The semantics of personal adjustment.* New York: Harper & Brothers, p. 4.
11. Ibid., pp. 14–15.
12. Galbraith, J. K. (1981). *A life in our times: Memoirs.* Boston: Houghton Mifflin, p. 339.
13. Koestler, A. (1967). *The ghost in the machine.* New York: Macmillan, p. 303.
14. Russell, B. (1948). *Human knowledge: Its scope and limits.* New York: Simon & Schuster, p. 52.
15. Koestler, A. (1967). Op. cit., p. 284.
16. Emerson, R. W. (1940). Self-reliance. Essays: First Series. In B. Atkinson (Ed.), *The complete essays and other writings of Ralph Waldo Emerson.* (p. 477). New York: Random House [Modern Library ed.] (Original work published 1841)
17. Fromm, E. (1941). *Escape from freedom.* New York: Holt, Rinehart, & Winston.
18. Highet, G. (1976). *The immortal profession: The joys of teaching and learning.* New York: Weybright & Talley, pp. 17–19.
19. Bruccoli, M. J. (Ed.) (1978). *Selected letters of John O'Hara.* New York: Random House, p. 226. The quotation could serve as John Steinbeck's epitaph; it crops up repeatedly in his letters. Bruccoli mentions it because Steinbeck had painstakingly carved the inscription into the wooden lid of a handmade cigarette box he sent to his contemporary, John O'Hara.
20. English, H. B., & English, A. C. (1966). *A comprehensive dictionary of psychological and psychoanalytical terms.* New York: David McKay, p. 189.
21. *Webster's new collegiate dictionary.* (1976). Springfield, MA: G. & C. Merriam, p. 392.
22. Wilson, C. (1957). *Religion and the rebel.* Boston: Houghton Mifflin, p. 167.
23. Copyright 1980 by the American Association for Counseling and Development. Reprinted by permission.

10

More Group Counseling Techniques, Strategies, and Structures for the Practitioner

Variety's the very spice of life
That gives it all its flavour.

—*William Cowper*[1]

The chapter in *Counseling Techniques That Work* that presented techniques, strategies, and structures for the practicing group counselor proved to be, by all accounts, one of the most useful.[2] It is easy to see why this is so. These techniques enable a counselor to change the menu, to dish up experiences in different ways to stimulate an appetite for counseling and growth, to set a table where group clients don't continually sit down to the same old meal nor to leftovers.

Some group counselors don't vary their format. They fall into routine ways of opening and conducting their groups, seldom deviating from the set pattern, perhaps being unwilling and inflexible about doing so, thus putting upon the members a responsibility to like it or lump it. Some group counselors convey the notion that the sessions are very serious business where there is not room for levity, where laughter may even be looked upon as a threat to their professional stance, almost as though the group will get out of hand if members enjoy themselves and have fun. How many members drop out of groups because what transpires can be foretold, claiming the experience was boring or too heavy? Is it any wonder that many counselors seek new constructs for their groups, to introduce variety and to liven up the atmosphere? People are stimulated by change, demoralized or turned off by routine. Learning increases when human beings are more active, more involved, when they enjoy what they are doing, when they are given different ways to view a scene, a relationship, a condition, or made aware how their behavioral patterns are self-defeating.

With any given client in the group a counselor can seldom predict what events or interventions will bring about positive behavioral change. Counseling frequently gets stuck. Impasses are common. When the group counselor has a long repertoire of techniques, strategies, exercises, and structures on which to draw, he or she can be more creative and challenging and simultaneously provide a lively and pleasurable group climate. Members won't come to sessions expecting the same kinds of bewhiskered discussions if any one of various possibilities might take place.

Sometimes the only gain a member can claim after a group counseling experience is this: "I learned that there are a lot of people who are just like me. I thought I was the only one who had such problems, and it's a comfort to know I'm not alone." One then imagines a group counselor who, having gotten Joan to expound enough on her troubling circumstances, sees the need to go around the group soliciting members to relate similar thoughts and feelings, how they handle or mishandle their own affairs in a similar situation. The counselor then ceaselessly repeats this same pattern as though there is no other way to structure the sessions. The aim of counseling is not to confirm that misery loves company. We can all learn as much from the six o'clock news.

> How can I help this client to change her thinking, feeling, and doing behaviors in this situation? Does she know what her payoffs are for continuing to make herself miserable? Is she really trapped? What hand has she had in building her own trap? What structure might I invoke here to help her see an alternate way of thinking about it?

One presumes that this is the way the effective group counselor's mind is working. When the last question wiggles its way into the counselor's mind, a counselor who is familiar with an array of group structures that serve different ends, there is less likelihood that efforts to help will get bogged down. Unlike what is true of individual counseling, where there are just a counselor and a client present to work through a difficulty, the group provides multiple resources for a smorgasbord of interventions.

So once again, this chapter presents additional techniques and structures for a counselor to employ at different times in the life of a group. Some are more elaborate than others. Some are discussions of factors that can be altered to upgrade a certain aspect of group counseling, some are how-to responses to questions about procedures or format that group counselors have asked. But in each case the rationale behind the use of the structure is indicated.

BEGINNING A GROUP: CRITERIA

Let us assume that a counselor has effectively followed all the steps in selecting members, setting up the group meeting, and delivering the necessary opening statements about counselor and member roles, confidentiality, gains to be expected from the upcoming participation, has defined counseling and procedural concerns (all of which are already detailed elsewhere[3]), and is now ready for the action to begin. There are any number of different structures a counselor could choose. Probably the least effective of all, though many counselors falsely feel they must have a low profile in the group and consequently so begin the proceedings, is the counselor's sitting back, waiting for members to take the initiative. Such a beginning usually gets the process off on the wrong foot. Members cannot be expected to know how to proceed and what moves are appropriate to the process, so they fumble and grope, testing as they go along, becoming frustrated, resistant, perhaps even sullen.

Some members decide not to participate and remain a mystery in their quietude. Others babble on about anything at all insomuch as talking excessively is their customary first choice for discharging their anxiety in tense situations. Members tend to resent a captain who goes through all the preparatory steps of crew selection, outfitting the ship, launching it, giving the crew instructions, and when the voyage is about to begin, when the ship pulls away from the dock and skippering is most needed, abandons the helm.

What opening structure is preferred? The decision need not be complicated if three important criteria are kept in mind. Although any number of results are desirable and attainable, these are the essential purposes a productive initial group session must serve:

1. Every member talks.

Talking is a way for the client to show off the self: "This is what I'm like. I use this kind of vocabulary. I act in this way when I send messages. My voice sounds like this." Our ways of talking make a myriad of subtle points about us that have nothing to do with the content and meaning of our statements. We perform when we talk. We advertise ourselves. We know that others will gauge our personality, our smarts, our likability by what we say and the way we say it. We are on trial, and we know it. Every group has members who have a low opinion of their ability to communicate, who are tentative, unsure of themselves, apologetic, just as there are those who are confident and don't even consider this initial encounter to be risky. There are those who will use humor to hide behind and those who will ramble and overexplain. When everyone has talked, each person can locate himself or herself with regard to all the others and make decisions related to personal comfort or discomfort, decisions about the relative safety of the experience.

When all talk, tension is reduced. Social beginnings are nervous times for human beings. Hosts know "deicers" are helpful. Television audiences must be put through warm-up exercises. Members are more at ease after each has talked because they have interpersonal data to go on that are more than a simple gestalt of what the other appears to be, what our physical selves communicate about us. Even with relatively little talk taking place, we feel we *know* the other, at least enough to judge our own feelings of attraction or repulsion. Talking also represents commitment to the process: The talker has got his or her "feet wet." Talking is the first point of involvement for each member, an act of joining.

2. Counseling data are elicited.

As they talk group members reveal what they are like. Although this has paramount importance for the members in getting acquainted, the counselor is more interested in studying each person with questions in mind about where to go to work, how to counsel each client. Counselor interventions, therefore, take the form of drawing out data that will have counseling pertinence. It is as though each client is in an initial counseling session and the counselor is exploring to gather insights into what is behind those flashing eyes, how the client's mind works, what is disturbing or troubling in the client's life, what resources the client has; doing, in short, much the same thing effective counselors do in initial one-on-one sessions, but less obviously, in a more random and unstructured way. From the moment each person begins to talk the counselor is adding to what will become a bank of data about each individual in the group, a bank account to be drawn upon in counseling each person as the life of the group unfolds. Beyond this, the counselor is seeking to assess the resources members have for helping others, a data collection effort unnecessary in one-on-one counseling.

3. Some counseling takes place.

If members can leave the first session with a demonstration of how counseling works, what the process is like, they will be able to address questions or reservations about their fate in this group more satisfactorily than any amount of talking *about* it could serve. There is so much to accomplish in the first group session that time variables and constraints do not always permit a counselor to lead a client through all the steps of the counseling process. But to the extent that effective counseling is modeled in the very first meeting of the group, the session will be more rather than less productive. In an effort to achieve this end, therefore, the counselor might choose a minor and relatively uncomplicated area for counseling with a client who displays a high readiness to become involved and go to work.

BEGINNING A GROUP: SUBDIVIDING

Subgrouping is done for many purposes and is a strategy never far from center focus in the effective group counselor's mind. Providing clear directions and perhaps some necessary modeling, and then sending the members off in dyads or triads to accomplish a certain counseling task, is a structure that breaks up the routine and can be instituted at any time in the life of the group. Its uses are limited only by the counselor's lack of resourcefulness and creativity. For beginning a group, it constitutes one of the standard effective openings.

As a beginning group procedure, this rationale pertains: Most strangers find it hard to relate to one another, but relating to one other person, or to two others, is less difficult than simultaneously endeavoring to relate to 10 or more. It is an imposing proposition to introduce oneself to a group of unknown individuals with whom one is supposedly programmed to become fairly open and intimate. For some, the prospect is terrifying. "What will they think of me? What shall I say? What should I reveal? What should I keep hidden?" Such self-questioning normally accompanies the informal initiation.

Once the opening "pitch" detailing how the group will function has been delivered and it is now time for the members to introduce themselves, the counselor can proceed in the following fashion:

> OK, let's get started. In a few minutes I'm going to ask each of you to interview another member of the group, to learn what that person is like, not what he or she does for a living, or if the person is married or single, or a parent, or what education the person has had. No, what we are interested in is this: who is this human being? How is this person different from all others? What is she or he like? What are her or his characteristics and qualities, what traits and attributes does he or she have? What will I like or dislike about this person if we were going to spend any time together? We don't care about roles. People get into roles and we expect them to act a certain way. What we want to know is what they are like, really like, when there is no call upon them to act a certain way. Does everyone understand? ... Fine. OK, I'm going to assign you a partner. You and your partner can leave the room and go wherever you like and interview each other. Each one take 15 minutes to investigate what his or her partner is like and we'll all return to the group in one-half hour. Because we have an equal number of men and women in this group, let's have cross-sex partners. Mary, why don't you be first. Choose a male member of the group. OK. Now Tom, it's your turn. OK. Now Ruth, pick someone. OK ... (and so on till all are picked). When we come back, each of you will introduce your partner to the rest of the group.

When the counseling group is reconvened and the introductions commence, each client feels as though one other person, at least, is not a stranger and can be relied upon for support. If the group is subdivided into triads for the interviewing exercise, each member has the back-up of two others. In a very large group, say one of 16 clients, the exercise can be modified so that it is progressive: first pairs go off for a determined interval, then designated fours, then eights. Then, when the full group convenes, each member feels as though he or she already is acquainted with half the group, and it is hardly possible to help strangers get any more comfortable than that. In planning this strategy, ample time is needed. To keep the show going according to plan, the counselor becomes a roving consultant and timekeeper who visits all the subgroups and helps them not to get bogged down. When the full group is reconstituted, all members ought to have an introducer, with no omissions because time expired in some phase of the exercise.

COUNTING OFF

In the subgrouping instructions exemplified above, the counselor called upon members to select partners. This is one variation of placing individuals into subgroups: members do the selecting. Calling for volunteers or having members choose each other is not always the best subgrouping or task-assignment design. In a group where some members already know each other, a design that prevents them from being in the same subgroup is preferred. A second design, seemingly accomplishing random assignment, is "counting off," though there are more random procedures. A third method is where the counselor simply assigns clients to a subgroup. This last is frequently the most appropriate, but calls for prethought on the counselor's part; it calls for a rationale having to do with counseling expectations, the probable benefits that might accrue from two particular members being more or less compelled to interact. Were the subgrouping to be done for the sake of accomplishing a "committee" kind of task, the rationale for subgroup composition would be related to how well members can work with certain other members.

Counting off is frequently the easiest and most expedient way of proceeding. In the above example the counselor might say:

> Because we have six men and six women in this group, let's have cross-sex partners. Will the men count off . . . one, two, three, and so on, starting on my left with you, Tom, and proceeding clockwise . . . OK, now the women, starting with you, Mary. OK, do the ones, twos, threes—all know who they are with? All right. Will the six pairs now go off to their own place and return in one-half hour.

"Their own place," it is presumed, has already been specified in the counselor's instructions.

Another mode of randomly assigning individuals is by having them write their names on a slip of paper and draw a partner's name. Still another way is for the counselor to think of a number from one to a thousand and have members write down their guess of the number. When all have done so, those whose estimates are numerically closest to each other become partners. Other methods of randomizing will occur to a counselor who decides upon doing so ahead of time, perhaps bringing in a deck of cards, some dice, even differently colored poker chips or marbles to draw out of a container.

It cannot be emphasized too strongly, however, that the method of assigning be predetermined and that the instructions be clear. Fuzziness and ambiguity cause waste of time and frequently either undermine or get the whole activity off to a rocky start.

TO CIRCLE OR NOT TO CIRCLE?

Counseling in groups usually takes the form of the members sitting around in a circle of chairs and, although it is difficult to conceive of a physical arrangement that improves on this, resistance to its commonness may arise in some members, perhaps even in the counselor. Certainly other layouts are possible: a diamond, a rectangle, an oval, a crescent, but none has the simple perfection of the circle. In a circle everyone faces everyone else. A circle around a table diminishes the amount of nonverbal body behavior available for observation and affords too much protection for those who want to hide what their telltale feet are doing. A group lounging or sprawled around a room on sundry stuffed furniture, pillows, or the rug encourages too much comfort and gives the impression that counseling is not work but simply a more focused social gathering. A good counseling room need not be austere, but too much of a down-home familiarity dilutes the let's-get-down-to-business atmosphere. Good lighting and acoustics are preferable; interruptions from telephones and drop-ins are not.

A colleague likes to tell this circle story. Seems he had given several hours of in-service instruction to a class of aspiring substance abuse counselors, most of whom were recovering heroin addicts, many of whom had served jail terms. Now it was time to form the class into a counseling group for the first of a series of planned sessions, their participatory experience as clients being a part of the in-service training design. The required number of chairs were rearranged into a circle and the members and counselor all seated themselves. All except Duke. His seat remained empty. The counselor looked around and saw that Duke, a large muscular man of ominous, scowling countenance, was scrunched into a chair in the far corner of the room.

"Well, let's get started," said one of the members.

"We will. As soon as we are all seated in the circle," the counselor said.

The group sat. Sidetalk, small talk, and some general twitching ensued.

"Come on . . . Let's start without him," another member said. "He's just contrary. He ain't going to come. If he does, he'll do it on his own time."

"We'll start as soon as we're all here," said the counselor, loudly enough for Duke to get the message.

Exasperated, a member shouted over to Duke. "Hey, man. Get in the group. You're holding up the show."

"I ain't *sitting* in that circle," announced Duke.

The counselor now addressed Duke. "You're having a tough time making a decision, are you?"

"Hell, no," said Duke. "I've *decided*. I'm not getting in that circle."

"Well," said the counselor, "perhaps you can share your reason with us."

There was a long pause. No one said anything, but all eyes were on Duke. Finally he said, "Look man. I spent 9 years in 14 different prisons around this country. In every one of them I was assigned to a therapy group. If I had a dollar for every hour I spent sitting around in a circle talking about what's wrong with me and the other cons, I'd be rich. I can't stand to sit in one more circle now that I'm on the outside."

The counselor understood. He'd feel that way, too, if he were Duke. If you looked at it from Duke's vantage point, the circle represented confinement, loss of his freedom.

"I see what you mean, Duke," he said. He looked at the floor awhile, thinking about this impasse. He didn't want to start without Duke. Finally, he looked back at Duke and said, entreatingly, "All those circles, huh? . . . How about we make this circle into a *square*? Could you join us then?"

Duke hesitated before he agreed. "I guess so. Sure." He got up then and slowly ambled over as the members laughed and rearranged their chairs.

When all quieted down, someone said, "Duke, you're something *else!*"

Duke smiled. "No way you could've got me in that circle."

The colleague reports that was the one and only time he ever led a square counseling group.

ALTERING THE SEATING CHART

People will, for the most part, habitually seat themselves in the same place at a gathering that is recurrent, in a classroom, a staff meeting, a committee room. They stake out a claim, so to say. But advantages accrue to that person who breaks this pattern and deliberately chooses a different place to sit each time, perhaps to get better acquainted with each member of the group in turn, or even to erase expectations that others might form about her or him. Where individuals are situated in a counseling group yields data about them, as they don't always interact the same way when they sit in different spots, next to or across from the co sandwiched between members of the opposite sex, and so on.

The counselor can call attention to this, have the members think the advantages of being able to function effectively regardless of in the group, and set up a schedule for changing seats. At every a different member can be in charge of assigning everyone to p Each member thus gets a chance to tell the counselor and all th where to sit and takes responsibility for doing so, an opportu each member to be responsible for manipulating others in a where too few such opportunities exist. Then when the group begins, the designer of the new seating chart can announce rationale was behind the considered choices in the rearrange mix. The gambit is not quite "musical chairs," but it does st sedimentary nature of plopping into place.

CHAIR IN THE CIRCLE

Long a familiar gestalt exercise is the "hot seat," a chair placed in the center of the circle upon which sits one member of a group while the others fire away questions the occupant must answer. In this context the person on the hot seat is "taking a risk," for any question may be asked, queries about the person's sex life, strong emotions such as fear, hate, and guilt, family relationships, unfulfilled passions, fantasies, questions having to do with honest and perhaps touchy feelings toward the counselor and the other members, and more.

Who in the group is the most attractive to you? Who is the least attractive? Tell us about your first sexual experience. What are your fetishes? Do you love your parents? Which one of your children do you favor? Have you ever thought of killing yourself? Reveal the circumstances. Have you ever committed a crime? Many? Tell us about your most lawless act. What does the counselor do that irritates you? What act in your life are you most ashamed of? During the last group session you stifled yourself when you addressed Norman. Tell us now what you couldn't bring yourself to say then.

The questions can lead to intimate revelations. If the person "cops out," refuses to answer, this frequently reveals as much or more about the risk-taking capacities of the individual as do some of the answers. The other players in this game are enjoined to make the seat as "hot" as their imaginations will permit, the better questions being the ones causing the most stirring and squirming, hemming and hawing. There are times in the life of the group when a counselor may introduce this exercise with dramatic effects. Taking a risk in the controlled context of the group stimulates and is a prelude to more consequential risk-taking in the client's real world. Just as a nonassertive individual who continually suffers because he or she does not stand up to others and is helped in the group to practice assertiveness, the hot seat can serve as a strategy for productive risk-taking. Following such an experience, when self-learnings have been analyzed, appropriate risk-taking goals in the lives of some or all of the members can be targeted in the interval between group sessions.

The chair in the middle, however, has other uses. Just leaving the circle's circumference and occupying the chair is a worthwhile accomplishment for some individuals. Whosoever sits in the chair is on stage, front and center, the focus of all attention. The occupant is isolated in a sense, detached from others now in an outer ring, put afloat. So encircled, one feels at risk. Images of the lonely trapper potentially vulnerable to attack by encircling hungry wolves are not too far-fetched for the imaginative mind. Given the tension that such positioning in the group creates, the alert counselor will be sensitive, wary, responsive, supportive.

The chair in the middle can be employed to heighten affect during a first session. Within a 3-minute time frame members are asked to introduce themselves without reference to the roles they enact in their lives, answering the question, "What kind of a person am I?" Only they do it from the center chair.

CHAIR OUTSIDE THE CIRCLE

When one considers the possible physical arrangements in a counseling group and decides to experiment, much juggling can occur. The center of the circle can become the arena wherein two or more chairs are placed for the enactment of psychodramatic scenes. Or all members may be asked to turn their chairs around and face away from the center of the circle so that they do not look at each other when they talk. Because members are thus less distracted, this arrangement is useful when the counselor introduces any exercise requiring the use of the imagination. Or at any given time members can switch seats, if this would benefit the counseling action. Two members sitting side by side, for example, who are engaged in a prolonged exchange, might be asked to take positions diametrically opposed from each other, such "squaring off" enabling them to involve the others in the group more directly.

There are those times in a session when a member has been the center of attention for a protracted period and counseling progress seems stalled. Facts and information have been elicited, but the client is not "taking in" whatever important feedback is being tendered by the counselor or the members, perhaps because the client's "gore is up," the emotionality being too overweening, or because the client's need to be defensive excludes any possibility of helpful intervention. The counselor perceives this to be the case and says something like the following:

> Look, Oswald, I'm going to stop what we're doing here. You've gone on and on about your situation and have told us everything we need to know. You've been repeating yourself and objecting to whatever suggestions you receive from anyone. Plus, you're obviously very worked up. Your voice has been getting louder, your speech more rapid, you're wriggling around a lot. You seem pretty agitated. Perhaps it would be helpful now if we gave you a reprieve, a chance to calm down. I'm going to ask you to move your chair back out of the circle and turn it around so that you face away from all of us. We'll close you out of the circle. Then what we're going to do is go over what you have told us and figure out ways to be of help to you. Don't look around and don't respond to anything anyone says. When we're finished, we'll invite you back in. That's when you can tell us if you heard anything you think would work for you in this situation. You'll then get a chance to react. OK?

When the client is situated outside the circle, the counselor leads the review and evaluation of what has transpired, involving all members in the counseling process. What has been going on in Oswald, as each member perceives it? How might Oswald be helped? Has Oswald heard what George said? Did it sink in? What is Oswald getting out of being so defensive? When Oswald is outside the group, it is important that members talk *about* him and not *to* him, and that the counselor winnows from this concentration on Oswald's case what is irrelevant to counseling.

Two things are bound to result that would not happen if the client continued to remain in the group: He will *hear* what is being said and he will become calmer. The focus is not on his person at this point, only upon his data, so he has no need to expend his psychic energies in defending himself. Because it is *his* data, he will intensely want to hear all what is verbalized about him.

When Oswald is invited back into the ring and responds to what he has heard, a new perspective is almost inevitable. This temporary removal of a client from the group is a powerful tool in the hands of an effective counselor. But a counselor could go even further with this same idea, if professional judgment supported doing so, by asking a client to leave the room until recalled, presuming there were some advantage in Oswald's *not* hearing what was said in his absence. In such a case the counselor could instruct him as follows:

> Look, Oswald, I'm going to stop what we're doing here. You've gotten yourself worked up and you're repeating yourself a lot, even showing us that in your own mind there is a lot of confusion. I suspect you haven't thought these issues through in any detail and it is hard for you to do so with everyone firing away at you. I'm going to ask you to step out into the hall for a spell. While you're out there, think through exactly how you want to present this situation to us, what you think we might do to help you, what you want from us. Also, think about what George and Althea had to tell you and decide what difference that made to you. I'll have someone check on you in 5 minutes or so to see if you're ready to come back. OK?

In the client's absence, the group can review and evaluate his material, or go on to fresh business.

A WALK AROUND THE CIRCLE

This exercise is a variation of having someone sit outside the group ring or leave the room. A client is asked to walk around the circle in a strolling fashion, casually, perhaps looking at the floor or straight ahead, but not at the members of the group. As the client walks, he or she talks aloud, free-associating about whatever was deemed important. It helps in this exercise to dim the light, if this is possible. The counselor introduces the exercise thus:

> Look, Oswald, I'm going to stop what we're doing here and ask you to do something. You've told us about how difficult it has been to deal with your father, what the situation is like at this time, how you interact with him,

what he's like. But there seems to be much that is missing. Also, when you try to respond to everyone in the group, what you are telling us is confusing. I'm going to ask you to get up from your chair and start walking around the outside of the group. Don't look at any of us, but begin talking about whatever occurs to you to say about incidents in your past, events that you remember from the time you were very young having to do with your dad and you, how you were treated, the good times and the tough ones. Bring up anything that seems to fit. Talk out loud and just keep walking around and around the circle. We won't interrupt you. If you get stuck, I'll prime the pump with a question or two to help you. OK?

The ambulatory movement helps a client to breathe more deeply, reduce tensions, and focus inward. Being removed from the necessity to interact with others in the group enables a client to free up some of the personal underlying material that has a bearing on what he or she has been trying to communicate in the group but cannot because it is blocked by emotionality. Some thoughts hurt too much to say in a dialogue, the hurt constricting or confounding their utterance.

The counselor who tries this exercise and sees how productive it is will find a number of occasions to invoke it. It is particularly effective in eliciting past history, significant biographical data associated with a given counseling focus. When the circle walk is completed, it is important for every member of the group to react to what the client has said. New perceptions and understandings are almost inevitable.

FIRST IMPRESSIONS: VARIATIONS

In *Counseling Techniques That Work* a beginning group session exercise was introduced involving the use of adjectives to record positive or negative first impressions that each member of a group has of the other members.[4] First impressions that others have of us always occur whether we agree with them or not, but seldom do we have the opportunity to know just how others perceive us when they do not have much data to go on. Our culture doesn't condone our walking up to strangers and inquiring, "What do you think of me?"

Instead of using descriptive adjectives, members may be asked to put their first impressions into a metaphorical frame. The category of animals might thus be invoked, where members are asked to declare what animal comes to mind when each of the other members are focused upon and how the resemblance makes sense. Almost any familiar category will serve the purpose: fish, birds, insects, well-known people, foods, automobiles, even diseases. Members may be asked to predict what emotional state they think is a predominant or recurring one the other tends to manifest. Presuming that the category of inanimate objects is settled upon, here are some typical kinds of offerings that might be expected:

- You remind me of a rubber band. I can see you stretching out just so far toward someone and then snapping back.
- I think you're like a big overstuffed chair. You look inviting, easy, comfortable, as though you'd be protective and one could be relaxed in your company.
- You make me think of racer's skis. I think you'd like to go as fast as the wind, that you want action, lots of room to maneuver. I think you would be hard to keep up with once you got going.

When the counselor ushers in this exercise, it stimulates members in formulating their thoughts if some examples, such as these just listed, are given. Members are encouraged to study each other closely, to take into account manner of dress, posture, behavior, all the data they have.

Nor need this only be a beginning group activity. At different times during the life of the group, members' impressions of each other can be fruitfully solicited using this technique. When people know each other better, the impressions are sharper and more appreciated. It enlivens the group proceedings, especially when they have fallen into a routine, and furnishes the opportunity for members to dust off and flash their creative talents.

PASS AROUND THE DOLL

Were a counselor to carry a baby doll of either sex into a group where both sexes were represented, pass it around, and ask members to physically relate to it, to talk about it, including how they felt about holding it, varied reactions could be anticipated. Often sex roles become the center of focus in counseling; members try to mask their characteristic ways to fitting into such roles and the relative ease or discomfort they display in handling themselves under certain role stimuli. By bringing in an object associated chiefly with one sex or the other, a worn baseball mitt, a woman's frilly hat, a pipe, a pair of pantyhose, responses are engendered that lead to revelations that move the counseling along while simultaneously sparking up the group atmosphere. In groups where focusing on sexual matters is their reason for being, passing around dildos, contraceptive devices, or similar artifacts is an effective practice.

But *any* object may be introduced and similarly passed around the group if the counselor has some insight or a rationale for doing so: a menu, a knife, tickets to a ballet, a heavy link chain, a TV schedule, a box of tissues. There are objects in all of our lives that are heavily symbolic and foster immediate and strong reactions, but practically every familiar item will provoke client connotations and associations.

A variation of this strategy is where all members choose a keepsake from pockets or purses or wallets, pass it around the group, and make it talk about its owner, its owner becoming the ventriloquist. The counselor may want to model this exercise:

> I'm a real old dried-up four-leaf clover that has been in John's wallet, pressed into this plastic cover, for the last 16 years. He has put me into eight new billfolds in that time. He always thinks, when he wears out a billfold and gets a new one, that he ought to throw me away, but he can't quite bring himself to do it. He doesn't see me as bringing him good luck. I think he keeps me because I represent the unusual, and because he's fond of the memory I invoke for him. He discovered me in a meadow high up in the Rocky Mountains of Montana . . .

. . . and so on, until all pertinent connections between owner and object are revealed, whereupon the members interact over what they have learned about each other.

THE HOURGLASS

Along with Ecclesiastes, effective counselors know there is a time for everything. They constantly work within time boundaries and so learn not only how to pace the action and themselves, but to keep track of the various levels of time. There is the amount of time remaining in a particular session. There is the amount of time left in the continuous life of the group (when groups have no set limit for demise, they are less successful[5]). There is for every client in the group an ongoing growth process having to do with his or her time of life, but more significantly for every counseling intervention, a time of readiness for moving ahead, for trying out new behaviors. If a counselor is impervious to time and finds its management difficult in a one-on-one counseling relationship, that difficulty is expanded and confounded progressively in a group by the addition of each new member. The group counselor's consciousness of time must be everpresent and is a perpetual challenge to competence.

The old clock on the wall keeps on ticking. In a valid sense, the group counselor is like the maestro of the proverbial three-ring circus.

In schools the bells ring when class periods are over and students change classes. Some professionals have secretaries to schedule and manage them; often it is the secretary's chief responsibility to interrupt the boss who spends too much time with a certain customer or activity. Hospitals have a whole phalanx of troopers to keep all the routines and schedules in smooth-running order. Who does the counselor have? In a group this question has a great answer: all the members. Getting members to take responsibility for as many time-circumscribed operations as can be related to them not only frees up the counselor to concentrate on more vital matters but it benefits the members as well. The more opportunities members have in a group to act out behaviors they are seeking to master, the better. This is certainly consistent with theory and practice leading to self-mastery. Time consciousness, thus viewed, will lead to innovative practices.

In this chapter, if not elsewhere in the book, several references are made to "going around the group" in a short time frame, 3 minutes or so allotted to each person. In an exercise where each member is called upon to perform some act, whether it be self-introduction, a feedback schedule, or a timed summarization or similar response, few members will stick to the recommended interval. A timekeeper is almost mandated. The least effective procedure, then, is for the counselor to assume such a role. Not only is the counselor unnecessarily preoccupied and handicapped with this additional charge, but it reinforces an I'm-pulling-all-the-strings-here stance that mitigates against the helper concept inherent in a well-orchestrated group. Usually some volunteer will assume the role, but it increases counseling productivity if the counselor assigns the job to a member for whom "playing the heavy" is not easy, an individual who will benefit from clock-watching and interrupting when members exceed their allotted time span. A variation, here, might be the introduction of a dinner bell for the keeper to dingdong, bell-ringing usually lending a merry note, or of a clapper or clicker.

An even more effective mode of timekeeping, though, is the use of an "hourglass," a sand or salt crystal timer such as cooks and chefs use for 3-minute eggs or baked Alaska. Purchased at gift or variety stores, the larger ones, 6 or 8 inches in height, suit the purpose admirably. As each member's turn to speak comes, he or she is given the hourglass to hold and time is up when gravity has pulled all the sands into the bottom compartment.

Members who handle the hourglass fiddle with it in various ways, emitting nonverbal behaviors that enable the counselor to gain additional insights about them. Plus, the shifting sands are observable to everyone in the group, and other members take it upon themselves to inform the holder that time is up, or to hurry, or not to fudge by slyly turning the glass over again, or whatever, totally removing the counselor from this particular brand of time consciousness. Group counselors who haven't tried using this device will fall in love with it and soon consider it standard operating equipment, perhaps adding several such acquisitions to their counseling toolbags, each of which metes out a different interval of time.

PARTY TIME

A party is a time of fun and play, gaiety and celebration. There is hardly a more inviting word in the English language than *party*. "Let's have a party!" It names a group activity. One can hardly party alone. Partying is institutionalized in our culture as an OK thing to do. There are times, New Year's Eve is one, when we feel deprived if we have no party to go to, when we feel we *should* party. Everyone should party some of the time, we feel. Partying is a just reward for life spent in more serious endeavors, even a group thanks-giving according to the Pilgrim model. Time spent in partying is often acceptable as an excuse, even, an alibi.

"The reason I didn't call you Saturday was because I was partying."

"I would have been there, but I had to go to a party."

One can, of course, party to excess, party one's life away, become a party-person if one can find enough companions, and earn the enmity of nonpartyers, thus gaining a reputation as being unreliable for other pursuits. If all work and no play makes Jack a dull boy, all play and no work makes the man Jack a poor employment risk. Partying is adult play, and most adults see life as needing the balance of work and play, usually seeing such balance as a ratio where there ought to be six parts work to one part play, if the sabbath be looked at as time-out from work.

The question of a counseling group having a party comes up frequently, usually at the end of the group's tenure. "We're through working. Now let's party." The feeling is: "Let's let our hair down and romp together, now that we all know each other so well. Let's have one last good time without having to be so serious, before we say goodbye." There are reasons why an end-group gala is an ineffective epilogue for the counseling experience (see below, in this chapter), but these do not pertain to a party scheduled earlier in the group's existence, perhaps half or three-quarters of the way along in the scheduled number of sessions. For some groups, because of external constraints or the make-up of the group, a mid-passage party may not be feasible or appropriate. In other groups, after each session members tend to go off together and socialize, frequently rehashing highlights of the evening. But if these factors are missing and if the counselor can see some counseling advantages to the members spending time together in a play-oriented way, it can be a productive exercise.

A few conditions ought sensibly to be imposed, if the happening is to enhance the main business of the group, the business of counseling.

- A strong commitment from each member to attend is important. If a member is left out, what went on at the party will thereafter be a mystery and alter that member's status in the group. A party tends to increase group cohesion by increasing familiarity and decreasing psychological distancing.
- The surroundings ought to be conducive to partying, but not in a bar or a restaurant where strangers are present, preferably in some member's home. Holding the party in the same place where the group counseling is going on is a weak choice, too, because it dilutes the "official" climate of those surroundings in the minds of some members. If the weather is clement, an outdoor affair in a nature setting or at poolside allows for many activities not possible indoors.
- The party ought to be for members only. Even the addition of one mate, friend, or family member gravely changes the mixture of relationships and violates the code of confidentiality.
- Food and beverages ought to be a part of the festivities, but what food and what drinks are something an effective counselor will have a hand in monitoring. How clients behave with regard to imbibing is a datum of counseling interest.
- To the extent possible all members take part in planning, organizing, and assigning tasks. Group solidarity is enhanced and members are enabled to make a contribution to peers in ways not possible in regular group proceedings.
- Although the decision to have a party or not, where and when to have one, would be determined within a given counseling session, the planning and arrangements can be done by clients on their own time. Group time is always precious and a conscientious counselor will guard against admitting extraneous use of it.

The chief counseling advantage to a midpoint party lies in what the counselor will learn about each client. A party presents an opportunity for people to flash customary styles of behavior in a different social setting, to show facets of themselves that otherwise remain dormant. Therefore, at the party the counselor is still at work, observing and data-collecting. This is not to say the counselor is aloof, but simply that counseling responsibilities are not forsaken. Although the counselor may take no hand in organizing the party, thus experiencing some relief from leadership functions, the counselor does not step out of role and become a group member. Another advantage is that a party atmosphere creates gaps that allow the counselor to interact with members on an individual basis. It opens up the structure so that he or she is more approachable and willing to focus on matters that may be waiting in the wings of a client's mind. There is no doubt, too, that partying together helps a group to become more cohesive, and if rampant divisiveness is present in a group, this may be the principle justification for having a party. Another advantage is that a party enables a counselor to do some behavioral modeling not as easily done in regular sessions, to demonstrate how to have fun or how to encounter or engage others in pleasurable social intercourse. Finally, a party provides the counselor with an opportunity to display other self-dimensions than those that ordinarily emerge in the group meetings.

If time and circumstances allow, holding a group session during the party time is a wise counseling decision, for it reminds all members of their commitment to the counseling process, the reason for their involvement with one another. It would be almost remiss for a counselor not to program a 2- to 3-hour counseling session, with all members seated on the grass during a picnic day in the woods, where eating and drinking, softball, sack races and other contests, dancing, perhaps a talent show, and other outdoor activities are planned.

GREEK CHORUS

Long, long ago, before Greek dramas, perhaps when humans lived in caves, it was learned that the prayer or song intoned aloud at a gathering, religious or otherwise, has a unifying affect. Families and friends still gather around the piano or record player to carol at Christmastime. Coaches get their teams to yell "fight" chants before they run out on the field. Picket line walkers holler their slogans: "DOWN with wage chiselers! UP with union labor! Solidarity forever!" Led by cheerleaders, crowds cheer the players on the field. Why not carry this phenomenon into the counseling group at selected intervals?

"Three cheers for Debbie! Hip, hip, HOORAY! Hip, hip, HOORAY! Hip, hip, HOORAY!"

It is a great reinforcer for a job well done, a task accomplished, a goal met, a risk taken. Choral approval is a way for all members of a group to reward a client. And it creates unity in a group. We are so wired together in our natures, it seems, that we want to be a part of a larger concurring assemblage. It stirs up our blood with good feelings.

A colleague customarily indoctrinates his groups with the concept that nothing is more personally difficult than changing behavior in some major fashion.[6] All of one's life one has gone about one's business responding to a specific set of stimuli with a particular range of behaviors that are predictable, whether they are called characteristics, traits, habits, customs training, or whatever. Because "that's the way I am" doesn't mean that is the way I must always be. Because they are habitual doesn't mean that such behaviors smoothly and effectively serve their owner. In the counseling group they come to light, they are examined and evaluated, they are probed and pummeled. When they are disassembled and scrutinized, when they are judged for goodness of fit, they fall short of the mark. They are found wanting. New ways of doing the same old thing are broached. Other members contribute alternate patterns that work better. Change is mandated. But, "Oh, by the whiskers and tresses of the gods, it is so hard to change! Lordy, I don't know if I can do it. It is *so hard!*"

It is at this point that my friend calls for a choral response from the group.

"How do we do it, folks?" he asks, looking around at everyone.

In unison they all sing, "WITH GREAT DIFFICULTY!"

The telltale objection flows from clients in many forms. "It won't be easy," they say. "I don't know if I can make that happen." And a list of obstacles and barriers to change will be brought up. Clients have a thousand evidential and logical reasons why they cannot change, all of which add up to the fact that change is hard. It is one-tough-son-of-a-gun. Agreed. Therefore, there is only one way to do it. My friend hears the telltale objection and invites the chorus.

"How do we do it, group?"

"WITH GREAT DIFFICULTY!"

"Yeah, yeah, I know," says the client, usually with a smile. All know. All go through the same thing. In common they share the knowledge that change is hard work. But once done, once the work is accomplished, the client bravely having tried out new behaviors between sessions and reaped the fruits of tough endeavor and reported back, *because* the work was so difficult, it is time for the choral reward.

"Three cheers for Debbie! Hip, hip, . . ."

Obviously this is not the only instance where the Greek chorus can be used. Any number of such instances arise in well-run counseling groups and there is no limit to what chorus lines an imaginative counselor can choreograph.

"What don't we do?"

"REFRAIN, EXPLAIN, COMPLAIN!"

"How do we deal with gripers and accusers?"

"WE KEEP THE BALL IN THEIR COURT!"

The chorus works. Groups enjoy it. It's fun to yell out what one has learned.

"HOW *COLD* WAS IT, JOHNNY?"

"Ha, ha. Well, let me tell you. It was *so* cold that my black cat, Mort, jumped into my freezer to get warm. It was *so* cold that . . ."

LEADERLESS GROUPS

In the life of some groups there are times when it seems to the counselor that nothing productive is going on. Members aren't accommodating to the counseling process. They seem stuck. Or resistant. Or even worse, antagonistic. Try as the counselor might, no movement seems possible. There is a logjam. The counselor cannot reckon what is happening.

At such a time the counselor might remove herself or himself from the group. It may well be that the counselor either is or is perceived to be the cause of the deadlock, and the members do not want "to take the counselor on." For whatever reason, they are unwilling to air their reservations before the counselor. Perhaps, outside of the group, members have groused aplenty, but in the group atmosphere they hold back. When the counselor is not present, they can work through whatever the difficulty seems to be.

Having made the decision to stay out of a session or a portion thereof, several arrangements are possible. These may be broached to the members in some such fashion as the following:

Something has happened in here and I'm not sure what it is. I think many of you know what the trouble is, but you aren't telling. What I am seeing is a kind of hanging back. The most active members of this group are no longer active. Lilly, you haven't said a word in the last two sessions. Laurie, you've even started to make faces. When there is counseling time available to use, no one is vying for it. Perhaps it is me. Something is going on that I ought to be doing something about, but I'm baffled. So here is what I have decided. I'm going to sit out the rest of this session and let's see how you go to work without my presence interfering.

There are several ways I can do this. First, I can sit outside the circle, observe what's going on, even take notes during the session. If it helps, I can face away from the group the whole time. Second, I can leave the room entirely. I'll come back before time runs out and spend the last fifteen minutes in the group to get the results of whatever you learn in your meeting without me. Third, you can make a tape recording while I'm gone, and I'll listen to whatever you decide to put on the tape after the session. I'm willing to go along with any consensus. What do you think. Henry, what's your reaction to what I've said? . . . Mollie, what do you think? Wilbert, . . .?

After such focusing on the possibility of the counselor's "sitting out," members frequently deal with the impasse and the counselor is enjoined to remain in the group. Nor is the counselor necessarily the cause of such an impasse. In more than one group the author has counseled, such a stalemate situation developed because some member breached the confidentiality code and the others had decided that any serious participation in the counseling process would jeopardize them.

The decision to invoke a leaderless session could be for entirely different purposes, perhaps to see who in the group would assume leadership among members who all seem equally passive. In the absence of any guidance, who will take initiative and responsibility for what occurs? Will some member behave differently when the counselor is missing? By leaving the group, the counselor alters the mixture.

RANK-ORDERING

Rank-ordering can go on at any time in a group with productive results. A series is identified and units in the series are lined up according to some standard of priority. Perhaps this has to do with data in a client's life, others who are significant, task priority rating, what to spend money on, value considerations surrounding what job to take, whether or not to get married, whether to move to another part of the country. Often counseling takes the form of helping a client to think through and sort out. But rank ordering can also be an effective strategy in a group involving the members themselves.

For example, it can be assumed that in any group of individuals a certain performance level exists for any specific behavior one might choose to name. Our levels of mastery differ for everything we do. A counselor mentally asks the question, as alert group counselors have trained themselves to do, "Who is this group is the most helpful in counseling behaviors?" Several members come to mind easily. Then the counselor focuses on: "Who in this group is the least effective, perhaps even getting in the way?" Others come to mind. In rank-ordering, the ends of a series are more readily determined than the middle. Based on the line-up in the counselor's mind, a line-up that shifts as the members reveal more about themselves over time, a counselor makes intervention decisions, calling more on the helpers than the hinderers. But members can be ranked at any time for any productive purpose. The counselor says,

> Let's stop for a while and take a look at how we are doing. Look around the group at each member and think about that person, what that individual has been working on. Now, let's decide who has been or is closest to reaching his or her goals. Line up all 11 people in your mind. Who's the farthest away from reaching any goals? When you are considering all the members, give everyone a number, including yourself.

It doesn't matter if everyone is assigned a number or not. The strategy motivates members making decisions to consume more of the counseling, or not to be at the tag end of the ranking the next time the exercise is repeated.

The caution to contemplate in using such a protocol is whether or not the group members are all functioning at a level of psychological well-being so as not to be unduly pressured or bruised by being singled out, a delicate matter of counselor observation.

Ranking abets, too, the process of summarization and review of group events. What has gone on in the group? If happenings can be identified and labeled, they can be rank-ordered. What worked the best? The least?

TELLING A JOKE

Humor represents a universal good for human beings. There is a sense in which it means "spirit." To be in or of good humor is to have good spirits. Beyond this, having a sense of humor is lauded as worthwhile. But there is even a more vaunted level of humor, consonant with effective counseling, the ability to create it at will. Assuming that the counselor's overarching goal is to help every client to be as personally masterful as possible in every life contingency and behavioral dimension, then members of a group getting better at being humorists or at reeling humor into their lives constitutes an area of appropriate group focus and content.

How does a counselor go about doing this? One method is to program clients into joke-telling. For many, those at a higher level of humor creativity, this is easy. For others it is new and a harder proposition. Members can be assigned to appear at a subsequent session prepared to tell a joke or a funny story. One-liners are discouraged. They must bring to the group a joke with a build-up and a punchline, an involved joke.

Then members relate the jokes during the following session. That's when the analysis of the teller's style occurs and members are aided in understanding humor, why something is funny, why jokes fall flat with one teller and are hilarious when someone else spouts them. Elements of drama and dialect, effective ordering of material, appropriately close attention to one's audience and a gauging of where reactors are in their heads, studied pausing, even a philosophical realization of what is funny in life: All these and more are inherent in creating humor. Members profit in all sorts of categories through this exercise, receiving feedback and receiving insights that are applicable to characteristic styles of relating to all others in their worlds. As a result of this participation, frequently a brand new path is mapped out for particular clients. Every veteran group counselor has met the client whose life is humorless, for whom nothing is fun or funny, who cannot seem to laugh without forcing it. A total lack of "a funny bone" is psychologically pathological. Such a person, difficult to work with in one-on-one counseling sessions, can be more effectively helped in a group of potential laughers.

THE LECTURETTE

There was a moment back in his novice days when the author co-led a group with a partner whose counseling orientation and style were unfamiliar to him and she said to the group, "You will have to excuse Vriend. He's given to making these little lecturettes." The remark rang in Vriend's ears. His behavior was discussed in postsession clinicking. Not that he felt upbraided or subverted by his partner: he could handle that. What intrigued him was whether or not his little speech had any value to the members, whether or not it moved the counseling along, whether it had a place in the proceedings. Rather than simply stifle such an urge to inform (his partner had judged him to be "showing off"), to share practical wisdom, he began to experiment with lecturettes, planning them, introducing them at various points in the counseling process.

Since then the author has become convinced of their import, particularly because so many members over time have absorbed and echoed their content. There is a receptivity to certain kinds of on-target information delivered at the telling moment in a group, where members are struggling to upgrade their behaviors, a receptivity-set that occurs at few other propitious moments in people's daily rounds. Group sessions are self-help events, significant intervals in the lives of members when the mind of each is open and ready for any poignant new learning. The trick, one that is difficult to teach or make into a general operational principle, is to know when the critical moment is at hand in a group.

It pays the counselor to have a full bag of such lecturettes: how emotion is self-generated, the composition of anxiety and how it serves wasteful neurotic behavior, how psychological distancing works, the meanings of "letting go" and conditions for doing so effectively—the beat goes on. As the counselor becomes more experienced and knowledgeable, the bag bulges. It is expected by members that the counselor is a "together" person and *knows* a great many secrets about more productive living, by virtue of training and professional experience.

But it is not only the counselor who can produce fruitful lecturettes: There is hardly any member who also cannot deliver a concise summary of some hard-won verity garnered along the path of life. And clients can be asked to put their nuggets together for presentation to the group in a prescribed length, let's say 3 minutes' worth. This can even become a group exercise when events have reached a plateau and a lull occurs:

> Let's take a few minutes to think of something you have learned in life, learned the *hard* way, an indelible lesson you have never forgotten and that now guides some of your action in life, a lesson you feel would benefit anyone and that you are willing to share. Then each of us will deliver our prize in a lecturette, a mini-lecture, if you will, lasting no more than 3 minutes. Mary, since you have a sweep-second hand on your watch, will you be the timer and yell "Stop" when 3 minutes are up?

Following the rendition by the last member, the counselor analyzes and evaluates the presentations based on the criterion of useful applicability to various member concerns and difficulties.

HERE COME DE JUDGE! TRYING A CASE

There are times when counseling progress with a particular client bogs down. The client is suspended in a life-situation that involves another person who is not present in the group but who is super-significant in the client's life, a lover or spouse, a parent, an offspring, a sibling, a friend, a co-worker, a boss, whoever. The outcome obvious to everyone in the group, but *not* to the client, is that the client must change his or her thinking about "the other" (because the other has a solid position in the relationship backed by a potent rationale or characterological rigidity and is unwilling to budge for the sake of the client, no matter what) in order to feel better and behave differently in the situation, or else to go on feeling trapped, hurt, and miserable. It is time for a decision. Were this case to go before a judge or jury, a resolution would occur as a result of the trial and ruling by the bench, one the client would be more likely to accept after a fair hearing. Such a "mock trial" can be made to happen right in the group.

Because the "adversary" is not present, someone in the group must take that person's role. The client could choose the adversary from among the members based on a resemblance of the member to the adversary. Or someone who can closely identify with the adversary's point of view or situation can volunteer.

The stage is now set. Chairs can be rearranged to resemble a courtroom, or the action can occur in the middle of the group space to accommodate various phases of the trial. A judge or a panel of judges can be chosen by the client. The client can chose an "attorney" or several attorneys, as can the adversary. Judge or lawyer or witness roles can be assigned to all members of the group. It may even by opportune to have a court recorder or a friend of the court.

The trial now takes place according to the counselor's (and members') idea of how a trial proceeds, with opening statements from both lawyers, the calling of witnesses, the presentation of facts, the closing statements, and so on, the counselor not taking any role (except perchance to demonstrate how a role ought to be enacted), serving instead as director of the drama throughout. When all cross-examination of witnesses is concluded and both sides have presented their entire case, the judge(s) must precede the ruling with an account of the reasoning that led to the decision.

Time is a factor. There must be enough time to follow the whole trial through to a conclusion and still allow for the group to regain its composure and report to one another how they felt about the experience and what they learned. In particular it is important in posttrial follow-up that the client, whose life-script was being enacted and judged, be allowed to ventilate, to reflect, to verbalize what affect the proceedings generated, what self-learnings accrued, and what the experience meant in terms of personal decisions and future action.

Variations would include the client's taking on the adversary's role or that of the judge. The success of the whole venture depends on the counselor/director's skill in stopping the action when necessary and making adjustments in the proceedings, including the moving of the client in and out of several roles, inasmuch as it is the client's perception of his or her reality that constitutes the script. For example, if the client is not pleased with the attorney's performance, the client could act as attorney for a spell.

When this lively structure is appropriately used in a group, it is helpful, powerful, and often a freeing experience for a client, enabling that person to objectify a troublesome internal conflict and make a new start in a sour relationship that seemingly has no exit.

SCAVENGER HUNT

The essence of a "scavenger hunt," a game usually played by partygoers, is this: Two or more teams are required and each is furnished with a list of items that are odd or rare, if not outlandishly weird, that each is required to find somewhere within a given time. Though a winning team is implied and prizes may be awarded, the fun of the game is in the searching. Usually the hunt results in strange and exciting adventures. Indeed, the list-makers, whether the teams construct them for each other during a huddle wherein members call upon their best Machiavellian or diabolical talents or whether the party host has done the task, get their jollies beforehand *imagining* what great scrapes the scavengers will get into.

Playing this same game in a group can be a fun-filled and productive experience for members. The responsibility of the counselor is to make it a productive, counseling-related activity. First, there is the question of how to compose the teams. Depending on the purposes or what has already transpired in the life of the group, members might be assigned to particular teams. Men might square off against the women, if sexist issues are flagrant in the group. Appointed captains might choose their own teammates. Second, there is the question of what goes on the list. A counselor might have made up lists ahead of time. Or the teams, once formed, could produce lists to exchange. But essential to effective list-making are guidelines a counselor imposes. Such guidelines would limit the *domain* of the hunt to what is in the heads of the opposing team members, or to what had already gone on in the group.

Here are five example items that a team might be asked to find:

1. Ten good reasons why Shirley should continue to stay married (provided either by Shirley or the whole team).
2. Three reasons each for Tom, Dick, and Harry explaining what they were feeling when episode "Q" occurred in the fourth group session.
3. What each member of the opposing team is famous for among significant others in her or his life.
4. How many times Fred, Nancy, Jeff, and Marie have cried (or giggled to the point of tears) in the last year, and over what?
5. Five drawings of Morris by team members showing how they think his wife sees him.

Teams need to subgroup to plan their strategies, and then the game takes place right in the group, or if it facilitates the action, the teams can mill about the room. The counselor functions as a roving observer and consultant, as well as timekeeper, reconvening the group for reports, analyses, and evaluation.

Variations: (1) The action takes place between group sessions, team members pairing up or subgrouping to gather items on the list. Team X, for example, could construct a list that would have the members of team Y go out for goals they had declared in the group: having a summit meeting with mother, a confrontation with a friend, a visit to a school to investigate educational programs, a job interview, three encounters with a new member of the opposite sex, or whatever. (2) One member of the group at a time races the clock to find as many items on his or her list as possible, say within 5 minutes. Each member of the group then provides a written list-item for that hunter, disguised but containing one or more clues, an item that would name what would be constructive for the item-maker to bring out and work on in the group. Thus, George might think it would be to his advantage if he worked on his procrastination behavior in the group, so his item reads: "If I eliminate this, I'll be a happier person." The hunter can be restricted to three guesses in this variation. What this variation has going for it, as a useful group counseling exercise, is that George's idea of what he wants to work on comes out in the end, even if the hunter doesn't uncover it.

CLOSING THE GROUP

The final session of a counseling group, if well conducted, includes two crucial elements. First, some kind of evaluation occurs in which each member is given the time to verbalize what he or she has gotten from the counseling experience. What changes were manifested in the mind and in the life of this member? What group events were critical? What interventions made a difference, caused learning? Who were the particular members contributing a certain growth? How did they do it? Central in this evaluation process is the counselor's effectiveness. This is the appropriate time for the counselor to receive feedback on his or her performance; feedback is necessary if the counselor is to go on learning and developing as a group counselor.

Nor is it only the members who engage in giving feedback. They all want and are entitled to the thoughtfully considered and honest evaluation that the counselor is able to furnish, not how they performed as an entity, as a team, but how the counselor perceives each individual as a client working on his or her concerns, on the progress each has made, on the impediments to further growth, on the contributions members have made to the growth of other members. Too often counselors neglect to give summary evaluations to group members, even though it is their regular practice to do so in a final interview when counseling an individual. If the group counselor is conscientiously professional, homework is called for. What is to be delivered to each member in the final session will have been thought through beforehand.

Second, there are declarations from all members on what they are going to work on in their lives now that the group is about to vanish and the support and assistance they have received will no longer be available. They verbalize their goals. It is the last opportunity they have to receive critically honest impressions and assessments by accepting and concerned peers of what they intend to do. The very fact that they "testify," that they voice their goals in the group, increases the likelihood that they will follow through on their good intentions. When we haven't announced our plans to others, it is far easier to allow them to stay dormant, to renege or to repudiate them and excuse ourselves. By announcing our intentions we create an expectation set for others, one we would like to honor, should we ever again encounter any of them.

Because of the cohesion that has flowered during the life of the group, because the members have come to value one another, to feel as though they *belong* in this group, ending the experience is difficult. Letting go is always hard, harder on some than on others, but always hard. One feels a sense of loss. There is even an affectional ratio: The more I like/ love these people and the time we spend together, the more I don't want to give up the ongoing meetings. In the general culture of our society, rituals have been developed because endings are commonly so traumatic, as is observable when we consider the function of graduations, the prevalence of bachelor parties prior to marriage, or most final of all, the extravagances of funeral ceremonies. Some recognition of this phenomenon is appropriate in the final session, perhaps a short lecturette by the counselor on effective "saying-goodbye behavior," or on handling "let-downs."

NO PARTY

What many group members want to do is have a party during or after the final session. Given the send-off and goodbye celebrations that prevail in the culture, a party seems a conventional and pleasant way to polish off what has been a productive association of people who have shared intimacies and worked diligently and helpfully together. But the counseling group is unlike a task group, where all pull together to accomplish a mutual goal, where something has been built as a result of common effort and there is an achievement to celebrate. In the counseling group each member has gone his or her own way; the gains are individual ones.

Experienced group counselors learn, after participating in enough such end-group parties, that some of the gains are subverted, particularly if intoxicating beverages are a part of the gathering. Folks now sidle up to each other with personal inquiries and revelations that were inappropriate for group sessions. Efforts to become closer take place that increase the letdown and affectional difficulties in saying goodbye. Frequently, even, a member can be heard to admit, "You know what I said I was going to do back in our last session? Hell, I'm not going to do that. It sounded good at the time, but I know I won't change." By such postgroup admissions, clients let themselves off the hook. Then, too, it is not uncommon for some people to become needlessly cold, if not hostile. They seek to expand the psychological distance, as though they must push others away and deny the affection they have felt, as though some kind of "strangerhood" must be reinstituted so they can take their leave without any loss or hurt.

If there is to be any partying, let it happen earlier in the life of the group (see above).

FOLLOW-UP SESSIONS

During the final meeting of the group the counselor can suggest that a follow-up session take place, "3 or 6 months or a year from now." If all the members of a group concede to such a session, then it is important to get commitments from them and to appoint a subgroup that will be in charge of contacting members and making arrangements. An actual date can be set in the group, but alternative dates must be designated, too, for there are always those who cannot foretell their own calendars with any certainty.

Commitment to a follow-up session increases the likelihood that members will work on and achieve their declared postgroup goals. Members will want to report that they have attained their aims. It is also wise for the counselor to get these specific goals in writing, perhaps appointing a client to serve as secretary for this purpose during the final session, so that during the future meeting these *are* the identified goals that are truly followed up. Given any great lapse of time, it is difficult to recall exactly what each member had been working on. It will come as no surprise to some readers that many counseling groups have reunion and "booster shot" sessions on a regular semiannual or annual basis, often with individual members providing support for one another during the intervals. If this kind of postcounseling rapport can be installed, it is certainly a mark of how meaningful and productive the group counseling was in the first place. Additionally, this kind of ongoing intermittent contact gives counselors the often-desired-but-seldom-granted opportunity to learn what interactions and interventions in the life of the group made a lasting behaviorial difference in the growth of their clients, providing insight into what worked and what did not.

CLOSING THE GROUP: THE MOST LIKELY TO . . .

During the final session each group member is asked to list the names of all the members (including self) and declare in writing after each name what positive development each member is most likely to bring about. Thus, Anita is the group member most likely to meet her major goal first. Jenny is the most likely to eliminate procrastination behavior. George is most likely to bring his weight down to where he wants it to be. And so on. When all or most have completed the task, members declare what they have written about Anita and support their contentions with their evidence and logic. Then they do the same for Jenny, George, and the others. Inasmuch as this exercise is done without consultation, when several members hit upon the same "most likely to," it has a powerful and boosting affect on any given member. But even when there is no agreement, clients find the feedback useful. After analysis there is usually aggregate affirmation approaching consensus that a particular "most likely to" *is* the most likely.

CLOSING THE GROUP: GRADUATION CEREMONY

One group counselor whom the author knows, who owns his own university graduation gown, hood, and cap, dons this regalia for the last meeting of groups he counsels and conducts a graduation ceremony at the end of the session. Ahead of time he makes up miniature "diplomas," rolls them and ties them with a ribbon. Then he calls up each member, presents the diploma along with a short speech about the member's progress in the group, formally shakes hands, bows to the member with a flourish, and goes on to the next one. His groups love it.

More and more it is becoming the practice for developers and conductors of in-service training workshops to present attenders with official-looking certificates acknowledging their participation. Surely we all appreciate receiving something a tad more tangible than a cancelled check to show we have been willing and dutiful learners, something we can show around or hang on a wall. Why not do the same for those who have gone through a group counseling experience?

A variation of this closing ceremony: Subgroups of members prepare various parts of the graduation service. A valedictorian may be chosen, songs may be composed and sung, photos taken, speeches prepared—the bill of fare can be left to the imagination and creativity of the "steering" committees. Nor need mementos be restricted to certificates or diplomas. T-shirts, buttons, caps, armbands, ribbons, and other paraphernalia are equally in order.

Every assortment of possibilities of what might be accomplished in a given life context must end somewhere, and the presentation of techniques, strategies, and structures of application under particular conditions in a counseling group ends here. For each group counseling practitioner whose ongoing professional development is a personal commitment, it is presumed that these suggested activities add to a battery of assorted resources the counselor has been accumulating all along. For the beginner or the neophyte in the field, however, that person who is unsure of his or her own ability to translate or to project thought into action, this question inevitably arises: What if the counselor chooses an exercise to impose on the group and it doesn't work? Frequently counselors attempt to incorporate a certain design and find that what looked good on the drawing board fizzled in the real situation. A few guiding questions governing the selection, installation, and evaluation of any group exercise try-out are worth considering here.

- Was I flexible in my planning? Did I account for contingency developments? Did I stick to my plan, trying to ram it into being when it obviously wasn't working? It is all right to abandon a plan at any time. Members have no expectation that every action introduced in a group will work smoothly.
- Were my expectations for myself too high? Do I think I can use a structure for the first time and seem to be its master? Every action improves with practice.
- Did I choose to invoke this structure without sufficient justification, perhaps just because I wanted to liven up the group, just because I thought the exercise would be fun to do, or just because I wanted to see how it actually works out in reality? Every structure has its appropriate uses in the counseling process—the primary concern in a counseling group, its reason for being. Getting more clever at "gamesmanship" is for the sake of counseling ends.
- Did I really understand how to implement this exercise? How well did I digest all the steps beforehand? Certainly there was a discrepancy between my vision of how it would work and what actually happened. Perhaps my instructions weren't clear. Perhaps my modeling of the activity lacked concreteness.
- Some structures can be used in any group, but others require a sufficient number of members if they are to work well. Was my group large enough to pull off this exercise adequately?

What can be said with assurance is that the use of any technique, exercise, or structure cannot be improved upon until it is tried. The conscientious practitioner will evaluate every experimental attempt to uncover its flaws and weaknesses, whether it worked or didn't. In this process of evaluation it is crucial to receive the input of those who participated in the experience, the members themselves. For the counselor to decide against the embodiment of an exercise because he or she might "bomb" is to sell the members short. Clients appreciate a counselor's openness, willingness to engage in helpful strategies, in the new and different, and they are perceptive of such attributes as lack of initiative or defensiveness. If the counselor's own skin is being saved, clients know it. When group counselors unbeguilingly contend with the ups and downs of group action in good spirit, with éclat, demonstrating the courage of their convictions and a game readiness to tackle the consequences, they serve as models of exemplary behavior and confirm their credibility as leaders.

NOTES

1. Cowper, W. (1785). *The task and other poems.* This quotation is from: *Book II: The timepiece,* lines 606–607.
2. Dyer, W. W., & Vriend, J. (1975). *Counseling techniques that work.* (3rd ed.) Washington, DC: American Personnel and Guidance Association. Chapter 10, pp. 177–198.
3. Dyer, W. W., & Vriend, J. (1980). *Group counseling for personal mastery.* New York: Simon & Schuster. See Chapter 7: Your first group counseling session, pp. 183–201.
4. Dyer, W. W., & Vriend, J. (1975). Op. cit., pp. 180–181.
5. Running an open-ended group always presents problems, the biggest being the phenomenon of losing members. When new members are introduced to an ongoing group, particularly one that has been in operation for many weeks or months, the members don't take kindly to the intrusion; they don't see the need for bringing the interloper up-to-date and they feel put-upon for having to adjust the relational mix in the group, for having to go through the process of learning what the newcomer is like, and no amount of explaining on the part of the counselor adequately justifies the act. Nor does the added member ever quite feel as though he or she belongs; the newcomer's equal status in the group is almost impossible to earn, resulting in that person's always feeling like an outsider. If a group diminishes in size to the point where its continuance becomes a farce, it is far better to disband the group and have a fresh start with some old and some new personnel, making it clear that this is a *new* group with a new contract for the number of sessions it will continue. But even when the group size remains stable, after 10 or 15 sessions a new limit-setting contract can be negotiated. Such renegotiation of time-limits ideally ought to include additional modification, what members would like to see more of and less of, an evaluative reconsideration of purposes and goals.
6. Belated acknowledgement and thanks for this revelation are due to J. Jon Geis, a practicing psychologist in Manhattan, New York City.

11

A Fully Equipped Computer-Assisted Group Counseling Research and Training Lab[1]

If this is the vision of the future—if this is the direction in which we want to move—the next thing we must consider is how we propose to get there, and what obstacles lie in our path. For such a vision is never self-fulfilling. We cannot stand idly by and expect our dreams to come true under their own power. The future is not a gift: it is an achievement.

—Robert F. Kennedy[2]

⎰magine having unlimited funds to construct a group counseling research and training facility. With today's technology, what could be built? Watching television—professional football games, with isolated camera feedback, with instant replay, stop-action, slow motion, split-screen techniques, or the roving reporter at the political convention with his communication tether to the principal commentator in the scanning booth, or seeing the communications back-up personnel and equipment at "Houston Central" during an Apollo moon trip—any sophisticated citizen can figure out some ways to adapt such razzle-dazzle technology to a few schemes of his own. Harnessing the computer is a little more difficult, but, with an elementary understanding of its capacity, it is not to be eschewed by the aggressive group counseling daydreamer.

ASSUMPTIONS

For the sake of the model to be presented, however, it is important that we waylay the supposition that we are merely daydreaming, that the model represents merely a futuristic conception, something that may or may not arbitrarily metamorphose into being in the year 2001. We therefore need to reemphasize that we are dealing with *today's technology*. The model itself can be built as early as tomorrow. Also, we assume the following:

1. There is a need for such a facility, a super-endowed experimental laboratory for pushing at frontiers in both the advanced training of group counselors and in group counseling research. An analogous laboratory in the medical field is the fully equipped operating room used for surgical research and as a theater for the training of surgeons, or, to name another analogy, the now-famous laboratory that Masters and Johnson were able to construct for their human sexual response studies.

2. The proper place for such a laboratory to come into existence would be a training institution to which a steady flow of counseling psychologists and counselors would journey to receive intensified, in-depth, advanced knowledge, skill, and competence building in group counseling, on both a short- and long-term basis. Such an institution could even be independent of a university, supported by an agency such as the Ford Foundation or the National Institutes of Mental Health, having group counseling research, development, and advanced training as their paramount reasons for being. Let us assume an as-yet fictitious National Foundation for Group Counseling Research, underwritten by both the federal government and private funds, motivated by the spirit of philanthropy

and the search for truth in behavioral science, the national mecca for study in the discipline.

3. Once some of the components of the model are understood, they can be instituted in existing research and training systems and laboratories. Indeed, places currently exist where some dimensions of the model already are being put into operation.

4. All of the aforegoing assumptions add up to the fact that the model, presented pictorially in Figure 1, is a wholly pragmatic portrayal of what is significantly possible in today's world, given sufficient commitment, money, and manpower.

FIGURE 1 EXPLAINED

Group Counseling Room

At the National Foundation for Group Counseling Research headquarters there are many group counseling rooms, none of which are the same, all of which have been used for different purposes, but the lab room, as it is known alike to trainers and those whom they train, is something special.

First of all, it is round and its ceiling is dome-shaped, a half-sphere, with powerfully bright recessed lighting in the superbly sound-proofed white covering. The acoustics are almost inconceivably sharp: Even the softest breathing, when silence descends on the group, becomes audible. One can almost hear the sound of an eye blinking. Although at times the furniture and arrangements have included some bizarre combinations, sprung from the minds of the co-counselors to meet certain prescriptions arising out of the interpersonal data of some members, such as is needed in role-working[3] or blackboard briefing sessions, generally speaking the room customarily contains 12 not-too-comfortable stainless steel and black leather chairs, stationed in the traditional circle, each situated on the unbelievably soft, plush white carpeting so that the mounted stationary cameras assigned to each member can do their appointed task of recording visually the member's behavior in the group session. The circular side wall of the room is made of a continuous one-way viewing mirror, presenting a rather confusing distorted-image experience for new group members; it is overstimulating at first, an implosion of slightly elongated images of fronts and backs of heads, an overstimulation one soon learns to ignore most of the time, but to relish and focus on when the action in the group flags or becomes tedious.

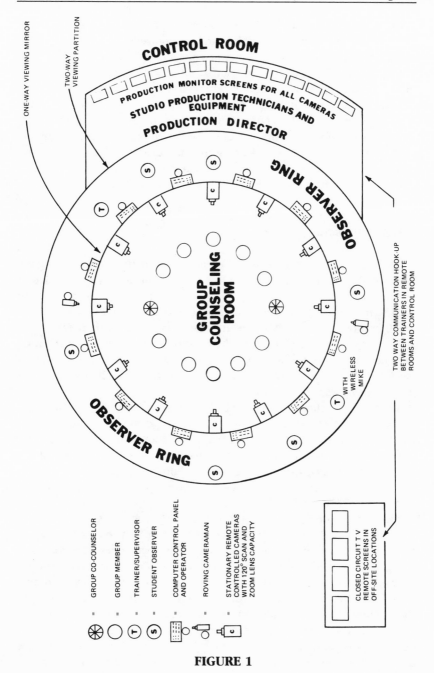

FIGURE 1

As sparsely depicted in Figure 1, the cameras are indicated in relationship to the 10 group member and co-counselor symbols, but one must imagine the chairs, the bright, white dome, the lights, the all-encasing mirror, the rug, and the fact that this cast of characters do not play out their appointed rounds removed from the rest of the world, privately ensconced in some secluded hideaway. They are observed, scrutinized, monitored, and their living in the group is televised to others, as well as made permanent in videotape and audiotape records. In the case of the co-counselors, at least, someone outside the group can even talk to them; they've been surreptitiously and appropriately "bugged" for the sake of their own skill and competence development.[4]

Group Counselor Trainers

Because training group counselors to be optimally effective is such a heavy and valued part of scheduled ongoing programs at foundation headquarters, the trainers compose an elite corps of experts among the total staff, their importance rivaling that of the research designers. (Indeed, in most cases, the trainers are research designers themselves.) In any event, they must coordinate their efforts with those of the research designers and, along with the co-counselors who might be leading a particular session, execute and orchestrate the kind of behaviors needed for ruddering experimental variables.

Although the chief involvement of the trainers during a given group session is with the co-counselors leading the group, their function far exceeds that of being a "coach" who now and then sends in some "plays," as could be inferred from a cursory consideration of the meaning of the communication hook-up between trainer and co-counselor. But this dimension of the trainer–co-counselor relationship is a significant one and not to be undervalued: A part of the extensive research being conducted at the national center is to explore this relationship. The wireless microphone carried by each trainer enables her or him to talk to the particular co-leader who is bugged to receive trainer messages. This absentee-cuing, in turn, is picked up by a second microphone worn by the trainer for the purpose of having his or her remarks to the co-counselor reproduced on selected taped records in "voice-over" fashion, according to the judgment of the production director and the technical assistants in the control room. An array of programmed absentee-cue schedules have been and are being tried out, but it has become regular practice to have this one-way communication connection between trainer and co-counselor even when it does not enter into a particular research design, for it has long ago proven its worth as a training adjunct.

Without going into all the explanatory details that would enable an interested party to understand fully the trainer role and responsibilities, it can be revealed that the trainers are fully qualified expert group counselors themselves, totally knowledgeable about known group dynamics and techniques, teachers of demonstrated excellence. It was learned long ago that one of the chief ingredients for imparting group counseling skills and competencies is the protégé or apprenticeship system adopted at the foundation. Although there are occasional reappointments for one adjustive reason or another, the usual arrangement is for each counselor to become the training responsibility of a particular trainer during his or her entire tenure in the learning program, and in posttraining follow-up as well.

As shown in Figure 1, the trainers have free mobility and can walk about at will in the observer ring, thus enabling them to interact with sundry onlookers, the roving camera operators, or computer control panel operators. Although trainers usually station themselves at opposite sides of the ring the better to read the facial and other physical behavior of their assigned counselor subjects, they frequently get together to confer on operational strategies or options that were unaccounted for in the preplanning for a given session by the two different apprenticeship pairs.

Observer Ring

The observer ring is a concentric circle around the group counseling room, a 12-foot wide passageway allowing a viewer to walk entirely around the counseling group to witness the action from any angle. As the counseling room, it is sound-proofed and air-conditioned, and one could scream or beat a drum in the observer ring and members of the counseling group would be oblivious to the noise. It can accommodate more than 200 observers with the custom-built floor tiering available for those occasions when a large audience is invited to watch a given event, such as some of the demonstrations of innovative dramatic techniques that have lately become of great interest to so many professionals and which, too, have earned the lab the in-group sobriquet of "theater." The usual number of people in the ring, however, is under 30, including, in addition to the ever-present student observers, the two trainers, the 12 computer control panel operators, and the two roving camerapersons with their portable equipment, who have learned to be expert at taking zoom and angle shots focusing in on any untoward or emotion-indicating physical behavior of group members or group leaders. The "photogs," as they have come to be known around the center, are bugged by the production director who, when aware of the need or the opportunity to do so, can direct their attention to the filming of special effects.

It is dark in the observer ring, but indirect floor lighting in key places is important for safety underfoot, the computer control panels are unobtrusively lit (different colors for different buttons), and in the 2 dozen observer seats (hydraulically adjustable to heights of 6 feet) a tiny light sufficiently illuminates a writing surface for notebook jottings. Inasmuch as all sound from the group counseling room is piped into the observer ring, the available earphones are usually unnecessary. The mirror that allows one-way viewing is between the counseling room and the observers, but not between the observers and the control room. Separating the control room from the observer ring is regular glass, which permits visual communication between the production director and the trainers or photogs.

Audio-Visual Delivery Capability

Perhaps it should be emphasized again that the National Foundation for Group Counseling Research exists primarily for training, research, and the development of useful techniques, practices, and even software products for the advancement of group counseling as an applied science, as a behavioral truth, as an effective rehabilitative treatment, as a self-enhancing service to all. Thus, the center does not exist for the sake of the lab; rather, the lab exists for the sake of the foundation and for which it stands. The distinction is important, for we must realize that not all of the research, and precious little of the training, takes place in the lab. But what *does* go on there can hardly be better accomplished anywhere else: The lab is a nerve center, the heart of all that is possible when training and research in group counseling are seriously considered.

Although it is true that most training experiences at foundation headquarters are experiential, with students participating in group counseling and other experiences as members, endlessly participating in structured social exercises, practicing as co-counselors in numerous groups, and living through a rich variety of programmed activities that tax their powers and challenge their energy reserves, students are far from the totality of their learning. In the center constant use is made of the closed-circuit TV system, and many of the scheduled programs emanate live from the lab. (An impressive number of these programs, through the television cable system and the educational channel cooperation, are transmitted to other training institutions and commercial stations across the country.) The students observe hours and hours of group counseling in the lab. They must serve as computer control panel operators, developing enormously important zeroing-in and screening out of skills and mental sets. They themselves must study all the videotape records, including the personal one made for each performance, of every group session in which they participated, whether as member (yes, each counselor in training is a committed member of an ongoing counseling group scheduled for lab appearance at regular intervals) or as co-counselor. In addition, they go through all of the important audio and video records that the foundation has developed that are pertinent to their particularized learning programs. It is these productions that have come to be so valuable to the profession, a storehouse of leader-modeling, do's and don'ts, illustrations of unusual and advanced counselor techniques and practices, common human behaviors that repeatedly crop up in group counseling, an ever-expanding library of group counseling lore, know-how, and technology.

What the lab delivers, or can deliver, audiovisually, includes the following:

1. A videotape record can be made of each individual in the group, taken by the wall-positioned remote-controlled camera, which can move as the individual moves, and which has a telescopic lens. Thus, the technician in the control room operating the camera can make it move on a vertical axis from face to hands, or swing in horizontally to catch a side view, or telescope in to show only the subject's eyes, or mouth, or neck muscles.

2. For each group session a master videotape is made. This tape is a work of art that can be improved upon through postsession editing and splicing, but seldom is, for the production directors have become extraordinarily proficient in their principal function of ongoing image selection. While the group is in session, the director decides which of the possible 14 camera images to bring into focus, including those of the roving camerapersons. In addition, the director is able to direct the photogs and control room technicians to pick up special effect shots that are seen as possible or desirable. (More than one of the directors have come to the center after a career in television, two of them having retired early from national network stations to join the foundation staff.)

3. The closed circuit TV system, in any given live programming, receives the imagery that the director determines shall go into the making

of the master videotape. Any other tape or film, of course, can be piped into the system.

4. Some experimentation in groups of less than 10 participants is currently going on with stop-action, slow-motion and instant-replay techniques being employed within the group itself. TV monitor screens are set up in the counseling group lab room as companion equipment for each group member, and group members are given control over what will appear on their personal screen, including various kinds of playback options. The varieties of controllable structures for research purposes are endless. (Much of the inspiration for these studies has come from the pioneering work on interpersonal process recall done by Norman Kagan and his associates at Michigan State University.[5]) One possible structure, for example, would be where everyone in the group focuses on, and works with, the personal group interactive data of one member who operates his or her own companion equipment in the most productive way, according to the goals to be reached in the given session.

5. Probably the most elaborate and significant function of the lab audiovisual delivery system is the "production company," as those staff members of the foundation have come to be called who are engaged in the production of group counseling training tapes, both audio- and videofilms as well as other materials.

6. Master audiotape records are made of each group session, but the lab has the capacity to make isolated voice transcripts of individual members as well. These individual transcripts, executed by technicians in the control room, are designated by the production director according to usually preplanned needs that arise out of consultation with the trainers and co-counselors. The transcripts have proven to be extremely practical for research purposes, for leader skill building, and for the achievement of desirable counseling outcomes for the client members of the group. In particular, separating out individual interaction from the matrix of action and doing content analysis studies has become a fertile resource for encouraging the attainment of individual member goals, so members are routinely programmed to go over their own audio records, in the event that a personal video record was not made, between the scheduled group counseling sessions.

Computer-Assisted Research

As can be seen in Figure 1, a dozen computer control panels and operators are situated next to the one-way viewing partition at evenly spaced intervals around the perimeter of the group counseling room.

These panels are uncomplicated keyboards of lighted punch buttons that have a single go/stop capacity: The key is pressed to start, and pressed again to stop. What happens between "start" and "stop?" The computer records that that interval of time, in relationship to where it occurred in the group session, had whatever quality was coded and assigned to the key. The code assignment changes, but the keys do not. Thus, at computer panel station no. 1, key A might be coded to represent "self-references," key B, "member-to-leader-directed responses," key C, "apparent daydreaming, tuned-out behavior," and so on.

Although much of this kind of data can be gathered from a content analysis of tape recordings, such a process is extremely time-consuming and laborious, and accuracy of diagnosing verbal behavior and assigning meaning to it is considerably more difficult than in the computer-assisted system developed at the national center.

As the particular behavioral data of a particular group member is quantified and stored in the computer's memory system, all kinds of important answerable questions can be asked. For example, over the course of the counseling meetings in a given group, has Deborah Wilson, who has been working on the personal goal of overcoming her fear and becoming more involved, actually shown an increase in later meetings of initiating and responding behavior compared to her earlier meetings?

FUTURE PROMISE

The imaginary fully-equipped group counseling training and research laboratory that has been pictured does not yet exist. There have been group counseling training labs that incorporate some of the features of the model shown,[6] but nowhere does a lab exist that has them all. In particular, no such training facility has harnessed the computer in the fashion herein illustrated. Short of programming a computer to convert language sounds of conversing humans into a printed script of the dialogue, a breakthrough that may one day happen, the use of the computer as herein described constitutes a revolutionary notion for counseling researchers.

What makes the future promise of the described model so important, however, is not the thrilling first-rate training and research it can liberate, but the fact that the process of group counseling itself contains such an enormous potential for improving the quality of human existence through supercharging personal effectiveness. Any development that increases the quality, power, validity, and reliability of that process and helps it become an ordinary everyday service to more and more people across the land ought to be voted into existence.

● ● ● ● ●

CODA

In June of 1969, your author was privileged to attend the 6-day Invitational Conference on Computer-Assisted Systems in Guidance and Education held at Harvard University and directed by David V. Tiedeman and his associates. Conference attenders were addressed by many computer experts and researchers in the behavioral sciences, including Joseph Weisenbaum of the Massachusetts Institute of Technology, the developer of "ELIZA—A Computer Program for the Study of Natural Language Communication Between Man and Machine,"[7] whose thinking, though certainly anchored in what was at that time state-of-the-art computer technology, was futuristic and excitingly visionary. Much of what he predicted has come true, especially the reduction of computer equipment costs and the consequential availability of personal computers for home use. Before another decade passes, word-processing skills, at least, certainly augur to become as universal in our society as typing skills have; and most of the current elementary school students will grow up being familiar with the computer's operation and potential, accepting computers as versatile and friendly tools and adjuncts for expanded and more enlightened choices in living.

The conference was exciting, indeed. Attenders were exposed to whatever information and learnings there were to be had about computer-assisted systems then in existence, in particular the Informational System of Vocational Decisions (ISVD), being developed by Tiedeman and his associates, and the Education and Career Exploration System (ECES) that Donald E. Super and his associates were developing. Both ISVD and ECES were forerunners for systems now in standard operation in schools and agencies across North America. Position papers were circulated bearing such titles as "Can a Machine Develop a Career?"[8] and "Can a Machine Admit an Applicant to Continuing Education?"[9] It was but a hop, skip, and jump to such question is as "Can a Machine Counsel a Client with a Personal Problem?" or "Can a Machine Lead a Counseling Group?" Vriend could hardly wait to return to Wayne State University and, in his role as contributing editor to *Educational Technology* magazine, write up what he had seen and absorbed. This he did, and his report was published in March of 1970.[10]

At the conference he made the acquaintance of David R. Cook, who was midway in the production of a book that was to incorporate all of the fresh and exciting ideas about what was causing rapid transmutations in our society and how these ideas would revolutionize guidance and counseling procedures and practices in education. He felt he could hardly omit what the conference had delivered. He asked Vriend to write a chapter for his book that would examine the whole range of possibilities that computers promised for the guidance field, including what had been learned at the conference. Like Barkis in *David Copperfield*, Vriend "was willin'."

This writing commitment thrust Vriend into total immersion of the then extant relevant literature, and further expanded his horizons about computers, making him even more wide-eyed than he had been following his Harvard visit. The chapter he wrote is called "Computer Power for Guidance and Counseling," and interested readers will find it in Cook's book, *Guidance for Education in Revolution*.[11] As a coda to the chapter, David Cook wrote this personal observation:

> I met John Vriend at a one-week conference on computer systems for guidance, a conference that literally "blew my mind." I think it "blew" John's mind also. Inherent in the computer is the possibility that technology can be made human. The computer is an extension of man's mind and therefore, by definition, a "mind expanding" tool. It is exceedingly fitting that a profession so concerned about helping human beings become more fully human should take an interest in computers. Nevertheless, as John has pointed out, the challenges are immense. But we mustn't let that scare us off. The counselor in the 70s will fail to explore the "human" use of computers at his peril. For it is possible that the machines will master us if we don't master them. And if that happens it will be our fault, not the machines'.[12]

Subsequently Vriend could not ignore the promise and vast potency that the computer held for changes in his field. Though pragmatism and practicality were always more his wont in thinking about counseling than was any visionary futuristic orientation, he had been profoundly moved by what many meanings for social transformation were imminent in the computer, and in his work and professional development he brooded considerably over how it could be harnessed to advance what was known and what was being done. It was a result of such meditations that he conceived of the group counseling lab described earlier.

Now, more than 10 years later, your author is astonished not by any anachronism in the piece, for whatever was possible then is, as a result of the accelerated changes in computer and communications media technology, exceedingly more possible now. What *is* striking is that nothing even approaching such a conception of a group counseling training and research facility has emerged into being. Taking for granted the popularity and national interest in group work during the 1960s and 1970s, back then one naturally supposed there would be familiarity, incorporation, and even the institutionalization of such advanced technology into the field by 1984.

Perhaps it never will materialize. Whether such a lab and a National Foundation for Group Counseling Research (and training) or its resemblance ever comes to pass depends entirely on national priorities, upon the collaborative willingness to fund such an enterprise (for it could in no way be launched as a local "momma/poppa" operation) of those with the financial resources and authority to make such a decision. The author still feels, however, and solicits group counseling advocates and professionals also to become imbued and identified with this idea, that it "ought to be voted into existence."

Who knows? Perhaps a U.S. Congress member, a former recipient of group counseling benefits, will grab hold of this model and plan and introduce a bill for the government to create just such a national foundation and center. Certainly many stranger things have already happened in this world.

NOTES

1. Vriend, J. (1973). A fully equipped computer-assisted group counseling research and training lab. *Educational Technology, 13,*(2), 57–60. Copyright 1973 by Educational Technology Publications. Reprinted by permission.
2. Kennedy, R. F. (1969). *Robert F. Kennedy: Promises to keep.* Kansas City, MO: Hallmark Cards, pp. 51–53.
3. Dyer, W. W., & Vriend, J. (1973). Role-working in group counseling. *Educational Technology, 13,*(2), 32–36.
4. McClure, W. J., & Vriend, J. (1976). Training counselors using an absentee-cuing system. *Canadian Counsellor, 10,*(3), 120–126.
5. Kagan, N. (1973). Can technology help us toward reliability in influencing human interaction? *Educational Technology, 13,*(2), 44–51.
6. Tarrier, R. B. (1973). New trends in technology management for training group counselors. *Educational Technology, 13,*(2), 52–56.
7. Weisenbaum, J. (1966). ELIZA—A computer program for the study of natural language communication between man and machine. *Communications of the Association for Computing Machinery, 9,* 36–45.

8. Tiedeman, D. V. (1968). Can a machine develop a career? A statement about the processes of exploration and commitment in career development. *Project Report No. 16a.* Cambridge, MA: Harvard University Graduate School of Education, Information System for Vocational Decisions (Mimeo.).

9. Tiedeman, D. V. (1968). Can a machine admit an applicant to continuing education? *Project Report No. 19.* Cambridge, MA: Harvard University Graduate School of Education, Information System for Vocational Decisions (Mimeo.).

10. Vriend, J. (1970). Report on the Harvard Invitational Conference on Computer-Assisted Systems in Guidance and Education. *Educational Technology, 10,*(3), 15–20.

11. Cook, D. R. (1971). *Guidance for education in revolution.* Boston: Allyn & Bacon.

12. Ibid., pp. 447–448.

12

Brief Answers to 20 Questions About Counseling: A Dialogue With H. Allan Dye[1]

To be, or not to be: that is the question.

—William Shakespeare

H. ALLAN DYE: To start this off, let me say that I know that Hamlet's famous line is one of your favorites. But might not a more appropriate prologue quotation for this chapter be: "When to counsel or not to counsel: that is the question?"

JOHN VRIEND: Given the terrain we are about to cover, I heartily agree. I'm even amused—nay, delighted by that twinkle in your eye. But I don't know to whom I could ascribe such a quote.

DYE: Then ascribe it to me. I say it to myself all the time. It could be put to music and become the "Group Counselor's Theme Song."

But on to business. When you first published these questions and answers in 1979, you introduced them with some of the following remarks: "The questions appear in no particular order, nor are they exhaustive of all the productive or insightful questions that could be or ought to be posed about counseling in groups. They are merely the ones that I have been asked over and over, and that make sense to me to ask. My answers are brief but not offhanded. In plain language I have tried to state the essentials of each case as I know it, as each has grown out of my experience. As a group counselor, particularly in the early phases, I sought answers to most of the same questions, and the workable answers evolved out of my own experience. Indeed, an answer not used in real settings is no answer at all, regardless of the source; it is only a hypothesis, a proposal for action."

Good enough. I would agree with you that these are basic questions, though I would like to add some to your list. But it is your list, not mine. One would presume that any veteran group counselor would disagree with any other veteran—that is to say: someone with a long arm of experience of counseling in groups—about what questions are at the heart of professional practice. As an editor of this book I have become familiar with your ideas and I find myself having a number of minor differences of opinion. But that is to be expected, from my point of view. One cannot erase individual style, which we will get to, further on.

In your opening remarks you go on to say, "I refer to no research support for my answers not because there is no research support or because my answers are untestable by behavioral science methodology. They are testable and research support exists. I simply find it unnecessary to link my answers to research in order to make them more credible, more worthy of belief. The committed counselor or beginner looking for answers will not prize a link to research authority for its own sake, and that person will award plausibility to each response I make based on its 'goodness of fit' when measured against her or his own experience."

Isn't it offhanded or at least misleading to bypass references to research so facilely?

VRIEND: Well, perhaps. There are large grey areas where there is no research support because of the difficulties in validating through research in group counseling much of what a group counselor does and how it is done. It goes back to the variable of individual style, to which you alluded, idiosyncratic behavior and personality variables. Then, too, no two groups are alike because all members are different. In each group there is a unique mix of people. It is when group counselors get stuck that a question arises, which is to say that counselors must get some experience under their belts before they can match any answer, including what a research report might yield, against what they already know and make a decision to try a different way of functioning.

Also, I thought that it was essential to keep my answers brief. A certain amount of pedantry, if not dullness, creeps in when making the effort to back every statement with multiple references. If I were addressing re-searchers, that would be expected. But I am not. I see myself as speaking to fellow practitioners.

DYE: We are not exactly in accord here, because I would treat research less lightly than you seem to do. But let us go on to the questions themselves. *Number 1: What is the best size for a group?*

VRIEND: This question is as old as counseling and therapy groups are. Beginners ask it. It is a criterion against which to test the self-proclaimed group worker. If you have experimented, you quit asking. I've counseled groups of every size up to 23. The producers of the early group counseling literature suggest sizes of 6 to 8, and the inexperienced repeat the for-mula. I don't like to counsel in a group smaller than 8 or larger than 12. The ideal range is 8 to 12.

The size question is easily resolved if one thinks about the nature of experience in groups. The principle is this: If a group is small, there is heavy pressure on all members to contribute; it is very difficult to be in an undersized group and not to talk; your freedom not to talk is impinged upon. If a group is large, over 12, there is pressure on the member not to participate. In a large classroom the questioner risks the disapprobation of the other class members who are each impatient with anyone else's personal quest or agenda. At a Billy Graham rally, who wants to stand up and take on the speaker with a personal concern? Size is a matter of importance in group counseling. If a group goes for 10 sessions, let's say for 2 hours at each session, it is obvious that some individuals will get less focus on themselves than will others. Make the number too large and the experience gets watered down for too many. Make the group too small, and some will get more time than they bargained for. Ten is a round, workable number, if all show up for each session.

If I have a group of 15, as I've had many times, I proceed as though it is a regular counseling group. Some members come forward, use the group, and others hang back. I don't judge the rightness or wrongness of this, of who uses the group focus and counseling time and who doesn't. Some will; some won't. These individuals will live with what they do or did not do. As the counselor, I simply serve. I don't pass judgment. I don't compare.

DYE: How does size affect members, and does the counselor's role vary with the group's size?

VRIEND: Early on, size affects members mainly in two ways. A larger group is more intimidating to some people—so many pairs of eyes are upon them when they speak. On the plus side, however, is the fact that they are more likely to find someone with whom they can identify if the group is larger.

The counselor's role doesn't vary with the size of a group but the counselor's work certainly does. An effective group counselor sees every member as a client, and this means doing the diagnostic work that is necessary in order to know where to be of productive counseling assistance to each member. So data-gathering increases. Then, too, the exercises that a counselor introduces would be varied according to size. An exercise, for example, that requires input from each group member might take too long if the group is too big. On the other hand, when a role-working script is invoked,[2] it is an asset for the counselor if more members are present upon whom to draw in the assignment of roles.

DYE: *Number 2: How long ought a group to run?* How much time is required for a successful group counseling experience? How many sessions are required, and how long should each session be?

VRIEND: This is a two-part question referring both to the length of each session and to the total number of sessions. The length of a session, particularly in some institutional settings, is frequently determined by constraints such as the press of other scheduled activities. In a school setting, for example, counselors must work within class periods of rather short, under an hour's, duration. Given the nature of a group counseling session—the time devoted both to starting and ending a session effectively—it seems a handicap to cut off a session in anything under an hour and a half. If this is necessary, then the frequency of sessions ought to be increased, occurring for 45 minutes three times a week instead of once a week, for instance. The ideal amount of time for a session, in my experience, is a minimum of 2 hours and a maximum of 3. This allows the counseling focus to get around to everyone who requires some group time without anyone tiring unduly. If the group meets once a week, this allows the members to practice their new behaviors, the goals set in the group, in their outside worlds between sessions; meeting more than once a week cuts down on such opportunities. The interval can be increased, though, with little loss of productivity, provided the counselor is attuned to members' energy levels and spurs on the involvement of those who tend toward lethargy.

Regarding the amount of session time, each session ought to be for an identical, fixed amount of time. Beginning group counselors, in particular, frequently let a session run overtime because what was going on "was so important." This is poppycock. It teaches some members that they needn't work within the time they have, but this goes against what happens in their outside worlds, for which they are being trained. Also, some members become disgruntled and build up hostility; within themselves they ask, "Why should I have to stay here because Gladys wants more feedback?" or some such question. They know that if the issue is important, Gladys can get back to it at the next session.

To convene a group that will run for fewer than 10 sessions, I have found, is to program learnings for the members that are much less than what they could receive. For most if not all of the individuals who seek counseling in a group or have it mandated for them, it takes time to observe and to test the process, to see how it works and how they can adapt it to their own uses. This "wait and see" behavior ought not to be interpreted by the counselor as resistance. It is simply a scientific, hypothesis-testing time—productive behavior for anyone. Ten to 15 sessions is ideal; beyond the latter number, the potency of the learnings per member diminishes. Beyond the life of the original schedule, it is effective to have one-shot follow-up sessions, perhaps lasting half a day or all day, every quarter-year or semiannually. Having established after-the-group goals for themselves, participants relish the down-the-road opportunity to report their progress in becoming more personally masterful. Follow-up sessions provide opportunities for the support that many clients welcome—a kind of "booster shot" to keep up their enthusiasm for goal achievement that is difficult for many. Then, too, the follow-up session gives the counselor important feedback against which to evaluate previous counseling performance.

DYE: *Number 3: How do you go about selecting people for a group? Is it better if members have the same or different problems? What about age, sex, race, educational/vocational level? For what reasons would you exclude someone?*

VRIEND: As a result of my experience I am willing to work without preparation with any random collection of people, particularly adults, in a counseling group, though I hardly see this as ideal. Ideally I would want to screen applicants and prepare them for the experience ahead of time. I would not be looking for factors for screening out people so much as for factors for screening them in. I would look for participants' potential for personal growth, their commitment to growing, and what resources they would bring to others in the group. I would try to get a capsule picture of where they are in their lives, what characteristic self-defeating behaviors they have, how frequently they experience any sort of negative emotions, what the quality of their relationships with significant others is, and more. Functional intelligence or communication skills I would note but not use as criteria for inclusion. I would pursue what their former counseling experience had been and what their expectations for the group experience were. Then I would prepare them for the experience in the same intake interview, first by correcting any distortions in their expectations, and second, by helping them to specify, define, and become committed to areas of their lives where changed behavior, new learnings that they could acquire in the group experience, were fervently desired.

One thing I have learned not to do, though a great deal of what I see as mythological claptrap in the groupwork literature still extols the practice, is to form a group made up of individuals with common problems. Aside from the benefits that accrue in a heterogeneous group because of the variety of mental and behavioral resources that unlike individuals are able to provide for one another, the likelihood is minimized that no one but the counselor will be able to model at mastery levels the desired new behaviors. A group of so-called "losers" tends to be of little help to one another, and the counselor in such a group requires a long arm of experience related to the problem area in order to be effective. It becomes a Sisyphean effort.

When it comes to mixing people of different backgrounds or those of variable demographic features, I see such a mixture as a plus. Certainly there is no better way or place to work on cultural and class biases than in group counseling, I have discovered. This is what theory behind desegregation is all about. I would not, however, mix children in a group where the age range is more than a couple of years; the varying maturity levels decrease counseling productivity.

The question of exclusion is a difficult one, so dependent on particular case circumstances as to be meaningless in the formulation of a principle or standard. Given selection choices, I would choose for inclusion those whom I thought could profit most from the experience. Once the counseling were underway, if there were some reason to exclude a member due to some exceedingly aberrant behavior, perhaps I would then bring the issue up in the group and involve members in the decision, having counseled such an individual privately and declared my intention, then leaving the decision up to the individual to drop out or deal with the group's reaction to the issue.

DYE: *Number 4: Don't groups go through stages?* How does a group that has met for, say, eight sessions differ from a group in its first or second meeting? Does the counselor's role or behavior change across time? If so, in what ways?

VRIEND: Much is written in the group work literature about the stages that a group goes through: the "getting to know each other" stage, the "struggling for power or leadership" stage, the "getting down to meaningful work" stage, and so on. Writers even compete for the acceptance of their own favorite labeling of the parts. And it is true that such stages will come about if there is leader passivity or no leader at all. But if the counselor is active from the start in dealing with individuals, not a collectivity that must somehow agree or compromise in order to progress, the purpose of the group is clear to everyone and there are no false starts. If there *are* stages in a counseling group (though it seems meaningless to me to note them), they are different from those of a typical encounter group. Some participants in a counseling group hang back and wait until they feel they know the other members well enough before they choose to take advantage of the counseling focus available to them, but this is seldom true of all the members. So much depends on the expertise of the counselor as well as on the relative openness and readiness of the client members that no statement about the stages makes sense, except to say, perhaps, that people are different and partake of group counseling according to their own lights. One of the beauties of a counseling group conducted by a masterful counselor is that it is a place that allows for these and other individual differences in behavior.

The chief way in which the counselor's role and behavior change across time in a group, if she or he has done a responsible job of modeling effective counseling and has helped the members to learn what constitutes productive interaction, when viewed from some theoretical perspective of how counseling works, is that counselor activity decreases markedly. The counselor then tends to orchestrate rather than determine what goes on, involving members more and more in the process of helping each other.

DYE: Members *do* act differently as they accumulate experience, and in predictable ways, though you may not want to section a group's life into "stages." Also, I think counselors try to do certain things, depending on a group's maturity, though you may not want to agree or even to discuss it.

VRIEND: I don't see where we disagree in this. As the members of a group become more acquainted with the process and feel more at home, more like a family or a special small community, more open and adventurous, the counselor can introduce more sophisticated kinds of procedures and exercises that would not be as successful early on, as neither the counselor nor the members know one another well enough to engage willingly in interaction that might be of a strongly personal or emotional nature. Some "testing of the waters" must go on.

When it comes to stages, as they are generally depicted by the writers who discourse on the nature of group counseling, what I find objectionable is any attempt to characterize and crystallize the parts of the development and evolution of the counseling group in a formal way. I think the emphasis on stages is misleading to beginning group counselors especially. In a sense it lets them off the hook as practitioners. When they analyze the history and progress of groups for which they assume responsibility, it is too facile to say that what is going on is simply a stage through which the group must pass, as we stereotypically say about children: "Oh, it's just that she's in the awkward stage. She'll grow out of it. Simply tolerate it. Be more patient."

Surely group counseling experiences have a format and character, a beginning, middle, and end. A certain form is present, not unlike a drama with acts and scenes, a prologue and epilogue. But if we look at the analogy of a play, what interests the audience is what goes on in and among the characters, how they handle the circumstances they encounter, how they change and grow. We identify with their conflict situations, how they handle themselves and their affairs. We expect that this takes place within a recognizable structure, but our interest is held by what happens to the individual characters in any drama of substance, not in the costumes, settings, plot, or other externals. If our focus is upon these externals, one might say that the playwright, producer, director, and cast have not done their job well, as dramatic critics frequently proclaim. Wouldn't you agree?

DYE: I see your point. Let's go on. *Number 5: How are group norms established?* Are norms different from rules? Are some norms useful whereas others are not?

VRIEND: Here again, as in the case of stages, norms in a counseling group are different from those in an encounter group. The group norms are in the head of the counselor and emerge as the life of the group unfolds. Norms for working hard at self-change, language variety and range, openness, behavior that makes productive use of counseling help, these and more are modeled by the counselor. Many are noted in the counselor's opening statements. Many are focused on when an event occurs in the group. For example, the effective counselor takes the time to help other members understand that there will be no call on them to follow suit after one member reveals a particularly tender and trouble-some life concern and weeps agonizingly when relating it, even though it was perfectly appropriate for that member to use the group in such a fashion. The counselor accepts every concern equally and helps each member with whatever that person chooses to work on. One person, working through the difficult decision to get a divorce, for instance, has no more status with the counselor than another person whose desire is to lose weight or eliminate servile headnodding.

The question of norms could be switched to one of rules. What rules does a counseling group abide by? There are some. Attendance, the time given to each session, commitment to confidentiality, what goes to make up counseling material (conversations, discussions of topics labeled as inappropriate), whether smoking will be permitted. But the fewer the better.

DYE: Groups differ, of course, and one way of explaining level and pace of participation and disclosure, risk-taking and so on, is by the norms established by individual members—that are *not* under the control of the leader. Are you maintaining that everything that happens in a group is a function/responsibility of the leader?

VRIEND: Function, no. Responsibility, yes. At least in a counseling group. How the group was conceived and what operational understand-ings were accepted at the "starting blocks" determines how the "race will be run." A facilitator of an encounter group would abdicate from any control as a condition of leadership and resist being held responsible for what transpires in the group, with full announcement of such a stance. The group counselor, on the other hand, is conscious that each member is a client, there to be served, there to receive counseling benefits. So she or he would be assessing the therapeutic nature of any norm against the acumen of training and experience, determining its usefulness or its detrimental effects, supporting or protecting individual members. A norm, after all, is an abstraction, a kind of summary idea of what condition or social climate factor has built up, an expectation system. Some members, perhaps in concert, could be active lobbyists in the group for what they want to have happen as an accepted stricture on group activity or as a radical departure from what the counselor would endorse as a productive direction. Under these circumstances the roadblock to progress must be dealt with. Blockages of any kind must be worked through. Any norm, including what the counselor proposes, must be accepted if it is to prevail. Clients will balk or withdraw or oppose a norm that goes against their better judgment. In this sense members control whatever might be possible for the counselor to impose in a group.

DYE: *Number 6: Are there no goals for the group as a group?* How do individual goals compare with group goals? Can the counselor help in meeting both group and individual goals?

VRIEND: A counseling group, unlike a committee, a jury, or an athletic team, exists only for the sake of the individuals who constitute it, for what each one can derive from the experience. Although the counselor works hard at providing personal growth experiences for every single member, attempting to spread the counseling focus to each person at different times during the group's life, his or her concern is not with the group as an enclave and what it is accomplishing. The behavior of individuals is not additive; no quantifying is meaningful. If the members of a group were to decide to take some action in concert, they would cease to be a counseling group and become a political body. Yes, there are no goals for a counseling group as a group.

DYE: *Number 7: What is a member's role in a counseling group?*

VRIEND: A role is a set of social expectations for how an individual must act in a particular context. Counselor expectations are that each person is in the group to work at changing old thinking, feeling, and doing behavior for more positive, self-promoting behavior. When a member deviates from such work, the counselor intervenes and helps that client to understand how to go about using the counseling provided in the group more productively. This is a teaching process. Few individuals are skilled in being clients. In the early sessions much time is spent in such teaching and modeling. Members learn effective client behavior more quickly in a group than in individual counseling because other clients model the process before their eyes. The counselor also expects that every client is capable of learning and ascribes slow learning to his or her own lack of expertise, not to any client deficiency.

DYE: *Number 8: How active should the leader be? What is her or his role?*

VRIEND: The leader is the counselor, the one who knows how to provide help, how to involve others in the counseling process in helpful ways. The leader is never passive. Even when the leader doesn't verbalize much, that is a choice based on criteria for effectiveness, on an assessment of what is going on in the group. For one reason or another, some members are more responsive to certain other members than to the counselor—their feedback is more valued, they are closer to the concern expressed, they have recently hurdled the same obstacle and are full of enthusiasm for their recent victory and explicit about the how-to details. The counselor sits back and gauges such exchanges, perhaps pulling from helpers that which would be the most telling contribution, teaching the potential helper how to help. In the earlier sessions the counselor is very active, but as members learn how to be more helpful to one another, as they learn the steps in the counseling process, the counselor can afford to be less active in maintaining the quality of what members contribute to one another, intervening to do direct counseling of any given individual only when the occasion warrants it.

The effective group counselor has a superactive mind during the group time, however, so the question of his or her activity, when it means involvement or participation, can hardly be reduced to a formula. He or she counsels a number of clients simultaneously and has a responsibility to serve each one. The counselor's head is perpetually full of questions: "Ought that concept to be reinforced for Mary, or has she absorbed it?" "Is it time to summarize?" "Is Cliff ready to accept the introduction of some specific goals?" "Should I invoke a role-working structure here?" "What about Reba? It's the third session and she has hung back from the beginning." Questions, options, decisions, study of each member, assessment, searching for structures, choosing appropriate interventions—the counselor's mind is busy during the entire life of the group. To counsel in a group is to work *hard*. I know of no mental activity that is more difficult.

DYE: Is there a relationship between counselor "style" and effectiveness?

VRIEND: Definitely. But style is so hard to define. Seemingly no two individual styles of group counselor operation are comparable. Style is the peculiar combination of traits, attributes, knowledge, training, cultural influences, linguistic habits, physical characteristics, personality factors and more—that go to make up the individual and determine idiosyncratic behavior. One could launch a cogent argument stating that strongly individualistic counseling theorists have developed their own theories to fit their styles, their ways of being and therefore their ways of counseling. Carl Rogers, Albert Ellis, and Carl Whitaker are examples, to my mind. It is difficult to imagine any of these men functioning in ways that are imitative of each other. As a deep-voiced male, 6-foot-3-inches and over 200 pounds, my very presence is imposing to some people. I have strong opinions I can defend with powerful logic. I have to be sensitive to clients who back off from me because they think I am not open to their points of view, their experience and logic, their peculiar and different operational styles. I must constantly work at transmitting the fact that I'm "approachable." This is tough work for me, because in my personal life I have developed a nearly opposite demeanor.

Exceedingly more so than in individual counseling, clients teach group counselors what it is about their style that works or doesn't. Over time one tends to develop a style of delivery in group counseling that is really the result of many clients whittling away at the rough edges.

DYE: *Number 9: What are the dangers in a counseling group?*

VRIEND: If the group has a skilled and competent counselor, dangers are minimized. Adults realize that they are at risk in a counseling group, and so proceed cautiously at the beginning, carefully choosing their level of involvement. As one goes down the maturity scale into childhood, natural caution is less evident. But just *what* is at risk is less clear to clients. Most don't want to get their feelings hurt or to hurt the feelings of others and be disapproved of, believing that such is a likelihood. Less consciously known is the idea that this might be a place where the fabric of their lives will be altered as a result of decisions they will make. This is to say that members frequently make decisive moves in their lives influenced by the support of group members, and later, when the group support is no longer available, they feel let down, incapable of doing what seemed so easy earlier on, regretting their temporary show of "false courage." Appraising a group client's capacity and ability to make serious life changes thus becomes an ongoing counselor responsibility.

The effective counselor works hard at diagnosis and learns to read the signs in an individual's behavior that indicate when an intolerance level is being reached. Then the counselor intervenes, takes responsibility for providing support, shifts the focus, or does whatever is appropriate. Without this diagnostic skill of gauging the effect of interpersonal action on a given client—how that individual is reacting to self-perceived stress—or without a repertoire of strategies to employ or significant interventions to make, there is a chance that a member might be harmed in some way. But brittle people experience much more stress in ordinary living than the stress that a counselor would allow to happen in a group session. This question of danger has no easy answer, because it depends on the competency of the counselor in any given instance.

DYE: What if someone has a psychotic episode?

VRIEND: Were a client to have what some writers call a "psychotic break," to engage in panic behavior right in the group, it would be incumbent upon the counselor to stop the proceedings and come to that person's rescue. Under such circumstances the counselor does "Red Cross" work. Being available for and providing such care is a concomitant responsibility, an ethical responsibility, in the assumption of the group counselor's role.

DYE: *Number 10: Suppose you aren't competent to handle a problem that a member brings up?* How do you know? What should be done?

VRIEND: Non-risk-taking counselors are quick to abdicate for their own safety and prematurely think, "This is over my head. Let's avoid it." The group counselor learns not to assume incompetency too quickly and explores the possibilities with the group, involving others, probing to determine if some resource for getting genuine help exists in group members. When all avenues are exhausted, it is referral time, a skill in itself. Usually this is done outside the group sessions. The counselor helps the client to be aware of specific helpful resources in the community and prepares the client to make the best use of them, and gets a commitment to follow through. But such a commitment is best made *in* the group; if the client has vowed before a number of others to seek specific help, the likelihood that the client will persist increases.

DYE: *Number 11: Do you ever kick anyone out of a group?* How do you handle members who dominate, or bully others, or seem to be disturbed?

VRIEND: Over time, there have been drop-outs, usually because members prematurely assumed they would not derive enough from the experience and it was a waste of their time. Occasionally members left out of fear that something harmful would happen, and they were unwilling to risk the possibility. From time to time I have dealt outside the group with members whose in-group behavior was grossly overt or inappropriate and detrimental to others. Some of these individuals responded favorably after a single conference; others required individual counseling coterminously with the group sessions and a great deal of special in-group support and monitoring.

There have been a few isolated occasions when I have asked a member to leave a session. These were instances where a member had been under the influence of drugs or alcohol. In each of these cases I invited the member outside of the room for a conference, once his or her condition was obvious to the entire group, and explained my position. Upon returning to the group I would simply state that so-and-so had agreed that he or she was too "high" to derive any benefit from the group experience today and if any focusing on this is necessary, we can do so when the client shows up for the next session.

Bullies and dominators seldom understand how ineffective and self-defeating their own behavior is. A group is the ideal place for them to receive help because the counselor can employ role-working structures to give them an objective picture of themselves in action. Role-reversal here works wonders. The one bullied can act out what the bully has done and the entire group can confirm the authenticity of the portrayal. Usually an overly aggressive and bullying member will admit to his or her tactics, see their undesirability, and make a declaration to work on acquiring more effective replacement behavior. Where any one member is intimidated by another, I go to the support of this person, sometimes nonverbally by simply sitting next to that person, perhaps providing coaching in "asides," suggesting responses. A group context has it all over individual counseling when it comes to helping clients modify characteristically antisocial behaviors. The counselor's resources are so much greater.

DYE: Dealing with any extreme is always a delicate proposition calling for creative intervention, isn't it? *Number 12: How do you handle prolonged silence?*

VRIEND: These days there is seldom any silence in groups I counsel, and if it occurs, it only lasts a minute or so, a restful time. All it takes for a group not to be silent is one person talking, and the counselor can choose anyone in the group and start counseling that person. Protracted periods of silence in groups occur when the leader is passive. For those who find group silence to be troublesome, a regularly recurring phenomenon in the groups they counsel, I would recommend that they take the bother to look up the article Wayne Dyer and I wrote that discusses the practical steps a counselor can choose.[3] Basically these involve using the resources available in the group, going to individual members with requests or invitations, such as: "Pete, whom do you think is most like you in this group, thinks like you or acts like you?" "Raye, 3 weeks ago we spent practically the whole session dealing with your mother/daughter situation. How is that going along now?"

DYE: *Number 13: What about strong emotions, when people get angry, enraged, or break down and cry?*

VRIEND: A counselor deals with emotions all the time, is conscious of what anyone in the group is feeling at any given moment. Emotional behavior is the key to what a person is thinking, and proficiency in reading emotions is a prime part of the counselor's expertise. The counselor understands that weak or strong emotions come from and accompany thoughts, and deeply troublesome thoughts can hardly be expressed unemotionally. The counselor understands, too, that the person manifesting the strong feelings owns them and the counselor need not, indeed, cannot experience them in like fashion. Under these circumstances, the counselor is emotionally neutral but completely accepting in a reaching-out way. Most people are not skilled in handling strong emotions in others and tend to avoid them, but handling emotions in others is part of the effective counselor's stock-in-trade. A counselor who finds this difficult has some basic growing to do. To answer this question simply, in a group strong emotions are dealt with by the counselor, neither covered up nor avoided, and they are welcomed to the extent that they provide a breakthrough when the counseling process seems blocked.

DYE: *Number 14: What do you do when the group turns on the leader?* How often does this happen and for what reasons?

VRIEND: When the group turns on the leader, usually I turn on him, too. Whenever something is going on in the group that I don't understand, I look first to my own behavior and my activity in the sequence of preceding events. If the state of affairs is such that the entire group is "attacking" me, finding fault, obviously I have been inexpert in my service delivery. Usually such a state of affairs exists, whether in the whole group or a part, because I have not shared my operational rationale. Doing so frequently dissipates the attack. But many times it doesn't, and then I learn from the experience. The group teaches me that my counseling behavior is not working. Such learnings are valuable and I welcome them.

DYE: Ganging up on the leader isn't always a response to the person or his or her skills. Some folks are basically hostile, and sometimes a group's hostility is a metaphor for something else, a particular frustration, say, that has nothing to do with the leader. Would you concur?

VRIEND: It's hard for me to think of "the group's hostility" as I only think of what is going on in each individual, even though there may seem to be consensus on some point, a unanimous agreement. The times when this has happened have usually been over the external conditions—too small a room, too hot, too noisy, too uncomfortable a setting. If the group is a part of an institution, a school, a prison, an agency, the frustration is usually over superimposed rules or administrative interference. When such is the case, I set group problem-solving into effect, though I wouldn't label this counseling. We discuss alternatives or decide to live uncomplainingly with the conditions. "What can we do about it?" becomes the focus, a rare "we" intervention I would make.

There are those individuals who either because of roles they have occupied or because it is their wont in life who vie for leadership and try to control the group. If they are any good at it, I defer to them and use their skills to advance the counseling process wherever possible. There is no point in having a contest, a shootout at the "OK Corral." To "put down" such a person is to create an enemy within the group. Further along in the group's life when all members are familiar with each other, I might review such vying behavior with this person and help him or her to evaluate its effectiveness as a habitual style of operation.

DYE: *Number 15: Are you ever afraid, intimidated, or nervous?* If so, do you share your feelings with the group?

VRIEND: Reading my own feelings when they are stronger than neutral, whether positive or negative, is something I've trained myself to do all the time I'm in the group. If my feelings can help me to be more effective, I want to use them; if they get in the way, I want to know how to eliminate or alter them, and I set developmental goals for myself to work toward. These days my own feelings seldom get in the way. I hardly ever feel intimidated, nervous, or afraid. I never feel guilty or bored. Early on in my group-counseling development this was not true. I tried sharing what I felt, but learned that this seldom made a positive difference in helping a member or members. Effective group counselors have a rationale for whatever they do, one they can trot out for inspection at any time. Self-disclosure of anything seldom works, for it brings the focus to the counselor, who is not in the group to benefit personally from it. This is not to say that self-disclosure, when used with discretion for a particular purpose, does not sometimes work. My personal guide is: If I have doubts about self-disclosing, I pass up the opportunity.

DYE: *Number 16: Does a group ever meet without the leader being there?*

VRIEND: A counselor might choose to opt out of a session in a planned way and for a purpose, yes. No one can predict how a particular constellation of individuals will function together nor can a counselor predict how he or she will function within it. In certain groups, it sometimes happens that the counselor's presence, because of the way events have evolved, acts as an inhibitor. A counselor sensitive to this might choose to be absent during a session or part of a session. Usually members open up to each other and are able to become more cohesively confrontive when the counselor returns, and whatever was in the way gets ironed out. According to the same reasoning, I might divide a group into subgroups for a time, perhaps visiting these subgroups and sitting in, perhaps not. Again, the use of such tactics is a decision based on an accurate assessment of what is going on in the group and sound counseling principles, never as a whim.

DYE: *Number 17: What about the use of group exercises, role-working, or special structures?* How is it possible to know when to use such techniques, which ones are appropriate for accomplishing which objectives?

VRIEND: I find it immeasurably broadens group counselors' competence to have at their disposal as many structures, strategies, procedures, and techniques as they can. In *Counseling Techniques That Work*, Wayne Dyer and I devoted an entire chapter to role-working and another to detailed instructions suggesting when and how to use a large number of special structures.[4] More techniques and strategies have been laid out in the previous chapter of this book. And the literature in the field is gorged with special exercises and strategies for special uses, most of them related to specific counseling purposes.[5] Once one has appreciated the advantages of having a number of structures and strategies upon which to draw, one reads to enlarge one's repertoire.

As a result of exposure to certain techniques experienced as a group member and then through training, a developing group counselor tends to use those that have been previously demonstrated. As more group counseling time is logged, when competence and confidence have increased, counselors experiment and refine exercises and strategies, learning their special uses and the conditions under which they are inappropriate or don't work.

It can be said in somewhat blanket fashion that the "same old thing" going on session after session tends to mitigate against effectiveness. We humans prize variety and change. We become bored easily when group life becomes repetitive and predictable. We prize humor and play. Generally speaking, we love games. The trick for the counselor becomes one of introducing fresh activity and fun into group sessions without decreasing the professionalism of counseling purpose.

A solid counseling philosophical and operational orientation to support whatever direction a group counselor chooses to go is a first requirement in the selection of a special group structure. Second, based on such an orientation the counselor is clear about objectives for a particular client, for some or all of the members of a group. Third, the counselor sorts through his or her repertoire and decides on a procedure.

DYE: Can you provide an example of how this goes?

VRIEND: Well, I might see that Jonas is absorbing none of the poignant and helpful feedback that group members are presenting to him. He isn't listening. He's too busy being defensive or trying to convince the group how they should view and judge him, or he might be unrealistically denying that they can offer him any useful and insightful information about himself. Whether the feedback will make a difference to Jonas, I cannot be certain, but I am certain that he is not taking it in.

What to do? I could ask him to move his chair outside the circle, to turn around and say nothing, and then have members give him the feedback as though he is not present and a tape is being made. I can have him sit quietly in the group and have each member send him a one-way message, after all of which he can react. I could place an empty chair in the middle that we all imagine is occupied by Jonas, and each of us, including Jonas, may only vocalize to the empty chair. I could ask one or more members to take turns *being* Jonas, demonstrating how he acts, reenacting the feedback efforts and how he parried these. Perhaps I would choose to invoke a role-working script wherein Jonas was assigned a double whose task would be to verbalize his feelings, surfacing the fears he has, what causes him to deny, showing what he is defending against.

Any one of these strategies may or may not work, but my objective is clear. Which I choose may depend on the make-up of the group, on temporal constraints because we will want to do postexercise evaluation, on Jonas's willingness to participate. The point is that I have a sound rationale for my invocation of a special structure. Seldom is a counselor with a large repertoire to draw on limited to only one choice.

Have I made my case?

DYE: You have to my satisfaction. As a group counselor I'm always on the lookout for fresh and productive ways to stir more life in to the group, even to keep myself from tiring of old routines. *Number 18: What about co-leading?* What are the advantages and disadvantages? What makes for a good match of co-leaders?

VRIEND: Members can derive more help in a group that is effectively co-led than in one where only one counselor leads. There are many reasons why this is so: Members can be more thoroughly observed; more behavior can be picked up on; the leaders can consult, give each other feedback, plan, work in consort or tandem, relieve each other, use two different styles simultaneously, provide contrast, support, or a model; the number of special structures used and the variety of these can be increased. These and more reasons make it a preferred mode. I should say, though, without going into all the ramifications, that co-counseling means equal status for both leaders, and that a group co-led by counselors from two different counseling orientations and theoretical backgrounds seldom works well. As a matter of fact, co-counselors from different orientations usually succeed in confusing and fractionalizing the group and diminishing productive behavioral change.

DYE: *Number 19: How do you judge whether a group session has been productive?*

VRIEND: By one criterion: the extent to which individual clients behave more effectively in their worlds outside the group. For clients to behave in new self-enhancing ways in the group is but a first step, a prelude to transferring these learnings to their personal worlds. This transference completes the counseling process. Beginners frequently report that they had a "terrifically good session because everyone participated," or for some similar reason, erroneously stroking themselves. Better that few participate and someone changes than that everyone participates and no one changes.

DYE: *Number 20: You talk about the group counselor being an expert. How does one get trained?*

VRIEND: Unfortunately there is no one place, no one training program that I know of where one can go and graduate as a masterfully competent group counselor. Certain advanced degree programs for counselors have more course offerings than others. Workshops in various group counseling orientations are continually being offered by professional organizations. There are books and articles. For the person committed to professional development as a group counselor, however, these are but a beginning, even if one availed oneself of them all. One becomes competent through practice. And the best way to begin is in apprenticeship to someone already competent, in co-leading groups with a journeyman counselor. Nor is there ever an end to being an effective group counselor, a point at which there is no more to learn. And, from my perspective, that is a positive professional derivative: Counseling in groups never becomes dull.

NOTES

1. Originally published under a different title: Vriend, J. (1979). Brief answers to 20 questions about group work. *Journal of Employment Counseling, 16,* 133–142. Copyright 1979 by the American Association for Counseling and Development. Reprinted (with major additions and revisions) by permission.
2. Dyer, W. W., & Vriend, J. (1975). *Counseling techniques that work.* (3rd ed.) Washington, DC: American Personnel and Guidance Association. See Chapter 14, Role working in group counseling, pp. 237–247.
3. Vriend, J., & Dyer, W. W. (1975). Effectively handling silence in counseling groups. *Canadian Counsellor, 9*(1), 2–8.

4. Dyer, W. W., & Vriend, J. (1975). Op. cit. See Chapters 10 and 14.
5. The reader will find the following to be of practical value, rich in descriptions of special group structures, strategies, and procedures: 1. Otto, H. (1970). *Group methods to actualize human potential, A handbook.* Beverly Hills, CA: Holistic Press; 2. Cohen, A. M., & Smith, R. D. (1976). *The critical incident in growth groups: A manual for group leaders.* La Jolla, CA: University Associates. (See the author's review of #2: Vriend, J. (1977). *The school counselor, 24,* 219–220.); 3. Kottler, J. A. (1983). *Pragmatic group leadership.* Monterey, CA: Brooks/Cole. In any further search, the place to look first is: Zimpfer, D. (1984). *Group work in the helping professions: A bibliography* (2nd. ed.). Muncie, IN: Accelerated Development.

Part III

End Game

Herein the author has introduced a list of personhood variables significant to more powerful and passionate living in general, and useful to counselors and clients in particular. Then, to end the game, he playfully chases some pesky maverick pawns before arriving at checkmate. A pawn can be powerful, too, if overlooked or neglected and then permitted to be in the right place for a telling move, perhaps just because there are so many of them on the chessboard of a counselor's life.

13

Variables For Greater Personal Mastery

There is nothing noble about being superior to some other person.
The true nobility is in being superior to your previous self.

—Hindu proverb

If you can keep your head when all about you
Are losing theirs and blaming it on you;
If you can trust yourself when all men doubt you
But make allowance for their doubting too...

If you can fill the unforgiving minute
With sixty-seconds' worth of distance run—

—Rudyard Kipling[1]

Who is personally masterful? Is there such a one? Or is the concept always a matter of degree? How do we measure degrees of personal mastery? Or degrees of freedom or restraint to *become* more personally masterful? What criteria can we use? As counselors, are we not forever evaluating where our clients stand in a certain dimension of effective behavior, effective living? And don't we compare ourselves to them, asking ourselves by what right we stand in judgment? Do we know, do we have some sense of certitude about what behavior is better for our clients, what ways of being are better for enlarging a person, or do we abdicate any responsibility for deciding? In short, do we have a fully fleshed-out vision of the good life, of the healthiest way to be most human?

So much of counseling is crisis-oriented, where a counselor is sought out to help rescue a client, to do patchwork, to do repair, to do clean-up, to provide first aid, or to help stave off the final misfortune, the splat at the end of the diving spiral. Particular professional efforts thus seemingly mandated by case circumstances are more or less clear-cut. But what of those clients who can rise above the short-term goal of conquering maladjustment, those whose life circumstances permit some choice in destiny control, the choice of enlarging or modifying one's essence in particular dimensions, those who have the will to shape their own additional development, those who seek to reconstruct their characters and personalities according to some higher model of what a human being can become? The counselor who has no theory, no set of postulates about what constitutes the higher reaches of human development must then be at a disadvantage in providing direction and help.

As counselors we can take the position that it is not up to us to decide what a client ought to work toward in reformation of the self, and many of us do. Can we also take the position that it is not up to us to shape our *own* development, to take charge of our own lives? If *we* do not, who will? The concept of being shaped by others versus molding ourselves according to our own best lights is antithetical to the basic services we provide. On some level, at least, we require knowledge and judgment about what is mentally, emotionally, and physically healthy, what is desirable when it comes to the shaping of our natures.

But individuals and collectives among our species have been struggling to define the good life, the good character, since time immemorial. We find variegated guidelines in the earliest recorded history of every culture. Philosophies, religious and secular, abound. Where to turn? In the last analysis each of us must decide what counts, where our time and energies ought to be focused. If we agree that the unexamined life is not worth living, as Socrates is reputed to have declared, where do we begin our examination? How do we distill all the possibilities for expanded living into a manageable container of essentials?

After 40 years of vaguely feeling some inchoate pressure, some nebulous but persistent inner nudging to get on with such a task, the author more or less stumbled into generating a list of personal mastery variables. The story is simple enough. The decision happened a decade or so ago when he felt he ought to establish criteria for selecting doctoral students with whom to work in his capacity as a professor in counselor education. As he became more absorbed in the exercise, he saw how being rational or scientific in the selection or retention of people in his *personal* world was also a grand idea worth implementing. Previously he had pretty much gone on intuition, trusting in some amorphous entity of attraction or repulsion that he subjectively felt in new encounters and throughout the process of getting acquainted, making any number of errors expensive in time and energy, often extending himself fruitlessly. Why not reduce the trial-and-error period? So he created a list of what he called "recruitment variables," those personal features he most appreciated in people and would desire to be present in any friend he might add to his social circle. His list was crude, at first, redolent of other people's thinking, redounding in clichés. But he kept at it, crossing out and adding, paring down his descriptive definitions, refining his list as time went by.

By applying the criteria to people already in his world, the author concluded that on a subconscious level, at least, he had been doing *some* screening. His personal world included all kinds of folks who scored high marks on any number of variables. He had and has few friends, for example, who were and are devoid of a sense of humor. Acquaintances who lacked this crucial variable did not advance to a condition of true friendship.

This list in its present form has a number of substitutions and additions, but it still incorporates some of the original criteria used for the selection of doctoral students, though these criteria are considerably revised. ("Good writer" was on the original and has been retained in a metamorphosed way, but "obsessive worker," heedfully more significant for doing doctoral work than as a friendship quality, was expendable.) When one takes all the complexity of human beings into account, one begins to understand that keeping the list open-ended is the best policy. One keeps bumping into new or overlooked desirable variables, especially if one discusses one's list with others, which is worthwhile in itself. "What do you prize in a friend?" generally starts off a valuable exchange, when asked of a deep-thinking person. So the process of adding continues.

In making such a list, there was a temptation to rank-order the variables, even to cluster them. Many are kissing cousins, members of the same family group. But the author decided that rank-ordering the variables would be difficult and serve no pragmatic purpose except as simply an exercise in idealization. He was not, after all, attempting to construct a standardized test. He found that he prized one or more variables in person X and a different set in person Y.

When one thinks of the practical application of such a list, one can see how this can be done differentially. For instance, how does it fit in the case of a lover, a friend, a business partner, a co-worker, a family member, a golfing associate, a companion on a travel tour? When one knows what a relationship will be and that one has a choice in its formulation, then one can weigh some criteria more heavily than others.

In its various revisions, including the one presented here, the author has used the list in his counseling to great advantage. Clients welcome the abstracting and ordering of so many personal mastery variables into a manageable number that can be used to evaluate the significant relationships in their lives. Inevitably, too, they apply the criteria to themselves and the list helps them to set behavioral goals that they had not thought of in their everyday comings and goings. In counseling groups, too, the author has found that when the list is introduced early on, members return to the variables time and time again during the life of the group, particular definitions becoming touchstones for some members that result in poignant decision making, often of a life-changing nature. Its potency as a counseling tool is the principal reason for including it in this book. Other counseling practitioners who have used the list have long urged its publication.

The inevitable application of the criteria to oneself also constitutes a powerful use of the list. "Am I all these things I look for in others? How do I score on these variables? Would someone I would like to know more intimately choose *me* because I have these skills and attributes, these ideas for action that are integrated into my character and being?" In this sense the list provides benchmarks for self-improvement. Anyone can place a scale of 1 to 10 next to each variable, produce a score, and plan for self-change based upon it.

Though the author's consciousness of such list-making by others back in history did not occur to him when he began, today he is well aware of their efforts, even of the primacy and seductiveness of such thinking. Ultimately such listing has to do with a vision of all that a human being can become. When Rudyard Kipling (1865–1936) wrote his poem, "If," in the early years of this century, he drew on Alexander Pope's recorded efforts (1688–1744), who drew on those of Horace (65–8 B.C.). Other old-time predecessors include Shakespeare (1564–1616) in Polonius's advice to Laertes in *Hamlet*; Lord Chesterfield (1694–1773), in his letter to his son; Nicolo Machiavelli (1469–1527) in *The Prince*; and the "Decalogue for the Practical Life" that Thomas Jefferson wrote in a letter in 1825. The ancestry can go on and on. The Boy Scout's "Oath" is such a list. As is Dale Carnegie's *How to Win Friends and Influence People*. Though stated in the negative, "The Ten Commandments" are such a list. In more recent times one is reminded of Abraham Maslow's list of characteristics of "self-actualizing people." Proverbs, the collected and repeated wisdom of ethnic groups, comprise such a list.

Parents, though few write one down, have such a list for their children. Bosses have such a list, however vaguely formulated, for selecting and promoting employees. Though not articulated and broadcast, practically everyone in the world has a list of variables against which to measure everyone else, for whatever reason. It would seem to make good sense for every citizen to have a list almost as a defense against everyone else's program for human virtue.

Behavioral science researchers are prone to think in terms of measurement, of dependent and independent variables. Does any component of a person's behavior on the following line-up lend itself to reasonably accurate measurement? Can we calibrate and quantify differences in subjects' sense of humor for instance? Probably we can—if we narrow down the concept to some single observable facet of the whole. No doubt a few dogged researchers are out there, somewhere in the world, doing it right at this moment while you are reading these words, perhaps counting laughs and smiles, distinguishing between belly-busters, thigh-slappers, giggles and titters. But does it make any sense to divide up the whole, just because whatever fully denotes a sense of humor is so hard to designate behaviorally? Hardly. Long before any behavioral researchers came upon the world scene, humans have determined in their own way who has a sense of humor and who doesn't, even assigning degrees of this variable to those under consideration.

In the collection put forth in this chapter dimensions in people are called "variables" not only because that word invokes a concept of behavior associated with each category, but because such aspects of a person do vary, both among people in degree and in the formations they assume. They are indiscrete, imprecise. In every designation of the term they are abstractions, parts of the person abstracted by the mind from that which cannot be, in any *real* capacity, subdivided. Like any abstraction, they mean whatever they mean by definition, not by virtue of their referential existence, the way a concrete noun has its actual referent—the real thing—located in the material world. They are accidental to the person, not of the substance. Their existence in anyone you meet, when you consider if that person has a particular variable in abundance or short supply, is only your perception, not a concrete reality. In every case it is a "judgment call," to borrow a phrase from the argot of refereeing; it is subjective, not objective. But so what? We fain must go through our lives being our own umpires whether it matters a farkleberry or not. Better we should like doing so, as it is better for us to be engaged in assigning criteria and judging, doing the mental work rather than being lackadaisically passive.

The serious point in abstracting has to do with defining. If you are to know what you mean when you use an abstract adjective, noun, or noun phrase, then you ought to be able to define it according to your own reasoning. You can borrow the definition of another and make it your own, or you can alter it to suit your meaning, or you can make up your own definition. In the end, though, you must integrate it into you consciousness. You must own it, or it is useless to you. And owning means that you can specify it in language, not in a rambling, roundabout, digressive manner, but in carefully chosen terms that make sense. Unless you have decided what love is, how can you call yourself a lover? Too many of us in too many significant portions of our lives put the pleasure or the burden of defining on others. Having no workable definition of "love," no categorical way of making a sound and practical judgment, we ask others to decide if we are lovers—usually if we are "adequate" or "good" lovers. We surrender birthright authority and allow ourselves to be defined, in whole or part, by "them." We wind up seeking approval, confirmation, reinforcement. And we don't know *who* or *what* we are. We fear being alone, for then we are nothing.

Now onto the variables-of-personal-mastery list itself. It is presented in two forms. First, the variables are simply named, for easy access, for use as a rating scale should the reader desire to engage in such subjective measurement of the self or any particular other person. Then follows the same list with the author's definitions, his expansion of the variables into language that identifies what he means when he uses each term. It is expected that any thoughtful reader will agree and disagree, fuss and bicker, with parts of every definition, indeed, with the list as a whole—whether a given variable ought even to be included. So much the better. The best function the list can serve, to the author's mind, is as a model. In the best of all possible worlds, such agendas would not be hidden.

VARIABLES LISTED

1. Relative honesty

2. Sensitivity to the other

3. Accepting of all reality

4. Egalitarianism

5. High functional intelligence

6. Enthusiasm

7. High energy level

8. High-level communication skills

9. Scientific mind

10. High personal standards

11. Aggressive truth-seeker

12. Psychologically independent

13. No regrets, no grudges

14. Great sense of humor

15. Ego-integrated

16. Thoughtfully rebellious

17. Has experienced life

18. Loves work

19. Sexually full-blossomed

20. Wide-eyed commitment

21. Spontaneity

22. Goal-oriented, self-directed

23. Open-minded

24. Responsible

25. Free of negative emotions

26. Lives in the present moment

27. Understands and practices loving

28. Rarely complains or apologizes

29. Welcomes the unknown

30. Avoids sentimentality

31. Plays heartily

32. Has patience

33. Knows reality and appearance are different

34. Is good at shifting

35. Sees ways around rules

36. Governs money

37. Knows what matters

38. Prizes freedom above all

Such lists would come out of hiding and help to clear away the steamy fog that shrouds so many human relationships.

VARIABLES DEFINED[2]

1. *Relative honesty.* A willingness to deal with the significant realities of the world, including me as part of same. The honesty is "relative" because "true confessions" are usually foolish, because effective pragmatism requires an understanding of the realities outside the self and the exercise of discretion. Such honesty is appropriate, not self-disclosure for its own sake. Dishonesty requires that a dress, or a suit of armor, cover the truth. A lack of defenses in normal communication is apparent in the relatively honest person thus defined, not because they are unknown or missing from the person's repertoire of behaviors, but because they are unneeded. Such honesty thus denotes personal strength: These persons "say what they mean, and mean what they say."

2. *Sensitivity to the other.* Having sensitivity to the other in one's life-space that exceeds the sensitivity to one's self in all encounters and exchanges as a matter of habit. Reading the other person. Being free of any need to protect self, a proactive outlook and behavioral style stemming from, "I'm OK. What are you all about?"

3. *Accepting of all reality.* Accepting every part of the world as it is. Not being silly, programmed, or screwed up in the head about the world not being different "for my sake" or because it "should be" and then getting whacked out of shape because it is not. Appreciating that the world would be a lesser place if diamonds and dogs, mountains and mumps, valleys and vomit, or anything else were missing.

4. *Egalitarianism.* Having a profound sense of social inequality and being on the side of social reform based on equal rights as a matter of birth. An egalitarian political mindedness. Devoid of bigotry.

5. *High functional intelligence.* Common sense and self-earned uncommon sense. Knowing what counts. Seeing what's there. Mind at the ready, tuned-in, alert. Knowing what works and what doesn't. Penetrating all sham. Taking nothing seriously, but able to establish priorities in the face of the existential meaninglessness of everything. Street smarts, moxie. Growth in mind use over time: a track record that validates a continually expanding consciousness.

6. *Enthusiasm.* Excited about living and doing. Knowing what boredom is, how self-imposed. Knowing each moment of life is a gift and

making the most of it. Self-generated activism: waiting for anything sucks. Finding ways out of the quicksand. Depending on no one, but using all personal resources for an "out." Hardly ever resigned but generating *joie de vivre*.

7. *High energy level.* Great physical stamina. This is learned, not a personality nor an inherited variable. Gets the most out of physical resources. Absence of fatigue or lassitude. "Running" is a life-style choice.

8. *High-level communication skills.* A loving understanding of what language is about. Good at sending and receiving messages on all levels. Loves to read. Knows the good stuff of the world is written down, the greatest heritage of the human species. Excited over ideas. Understands the meaning of personal vision and how it cannot be accurately transmitted without the ability to formulate it. A good or a terrific writer, and therefore a trained clear thinker. Has understood since childhood. Loves to write. Getting better at doing so has royal priority. Judges getting "better" by effective communications criteria, not by the editorial opinion of others.

9. *Scientific mind.* Knows the value of and habitually practices inductive reasoning. Thinks in scientific modes and structures. Understands probability laws, normative truths. Loves to design research projects; excited about possible outcomes.

10. *High personal standards.* Regardless of what the "other" thinks, knows what must be done to satisfy personal demands and will exceed demands of others if they are below these. Knows the difference between living up to one's own standards and neurotic perfectionism. Unemotionally self-analytical and self-critical; doesn't shoot down or up over results.

11. *Aggressive truth-seeker.* Wants to know and knows when does know by a clean set of empirical criteria, which can be articulated in any given case. Knows the difference between seeming and being. Takes truth seriously; depends on it in decision-making to the extent possible. Understands why others are not willing to work hard to attain it, the price in time and effort often being great.

12. *Psychologically independent.* Doesn't *need* any other person to fulfill self in order to feel OK. This includes lover, family, friends, all significant others. Chooses others and when to be with them. Doesn't act out of obligation.

13. *No regrets, no grudges.* Has learned that, as life goes on, regretting anything is useless. Once examined, regretting teaches that one must

live so as not to regret. This means following one's bent, taking advantage of one's opportunities. We regret what we did *not* do in life, the lesson in Robert Frost's poem, "The Road not Taken." Grudges are equally useless. Revenge, vengeance, retaliation, getting back at, holding any grudge, tasting any bile, thinking one's self the victim of another's malice, demeans the soul and gives one's outlook on life a slimy film of putrefaction. That person who regrets or begrudges is a bad-news companion, especially when that person is oneself.

14. *Great sense of humor.* Humor is nonhostile, based primarily on the ridiculousness of everything, of every human being in particular. Is skilled at creating humor, not simply an appreciator of the humor others create. Knows that nonlaughers exhibit psychological pathology and avoids such.

15. *Ego-integrated.* At home with self. Loves, appreciates, respects self; has a realistic notion of self; accepts all circumstances about self; doesn't dislike self for limitations, doesn't gloat over advantages. Doesn't see self in relation to others, doesn't compare, doesn't project self onto others.

16. *Thoughtfully rebellious.* Rebels against culture in appropriate ways, not hurting self or others thereby. Our culture is an evolutionary legacy; it is the nurturer and enemy by turns, frequently against life-fulfillment. Those who buy it whole cloth, try to adapt, swing with it, get on the bandwagon and evangelize for it are suspect, perhaps incapable as a result of conditioning of having a mind of their own. The clear-eyed understander of when, where, and how culture is sick and harmful invents contra-culture behaviors to resist its pejorative impact, is the one who stands up to culture, who has a battle record. This thoughtful, risking rebel is rare but well worth knowing.

17. *Has experienced life.* All get older and live through what they live through. Some don't grow; they relive. The ones who grow will be able to relate dispassionately what they have lived through, to say what the lessons have been, and how they are unwilling to repeat experiences that were painful, dumb, a waste. Has breadth and depth of mind based on experiencing.

18. *Loves work.* Understands what work is and what it is not. Work is purposeful self-activity, meaning given to what one does. One can work for an exchange, labor for money, or to increase one's skills and competencies, or to build, to create what never before existed. Work is pleasure in action, life activity, what one does to affect one's environment, to advance one's position in the world. All animals

have their work cut out for them, do it, and never complain. The human without the desire to work, without work to do, surrenders personhood, robs life of what possible sense it can make.

19. *Sexually full-blossomed.* Everyone has the capacity to engage in sex freely, openly, delightfully, the way kids enjoy Popsicles in midsummer. But few do. Sex is joy, and culturally sex is power. Any individual is suspect who is not in tune with sexual juices stirring within the body and connected to a mind that alternately dictates and responds to the miracle of animal nature, the pleasures of the flesh. One's animal nature can be thwarted in ways that would be astounding to a native skunk mysteriously gifted with human reason. Sex is responsible for the best in human relationships, the ancient seat of love. Those who are sexually full-blossomed know this, are unrepressed, exhibit physical joy, satisfaction with their own bodies, love to be physically responsive, can cut through all sexual sham, social repression, and bunk. Reproduction and every associated activity in all living species as seen is glorious. Only in humans does it become unnaturally petty or discredited by little minds. Sexually full-blossomed humans know this, and they refuse to be out of step with nature.

20. *Wide-eyed commitment.* Being committed is to surrender or stifle doubts, to lend one's self fully to the task, the program, the person one has intelligently accepted as worthwhile. Being wide-eyed is in contrast to being slit-eyed, blind, or fuzzy, being unsure or tentative. Commitment doled out in percentages or made with reservations is a contradiction in terms. Commitment is to do or die, risking all, giving all, backing one's action with total personal resources. When commitment stops, it is sudden, with full knowledge. What tapers off is not commitment. True friends and lovers are committed to each other. Who is not committed to the dictates of one's mind is not a thinker of conviction.

21. *Spontaneity.* Quick responders to external stimuli in creative and delightful ways, pleasurably unpredictable, even unto themselves. They prize the different, appreciate the infinite variety in life, rebel against the familiar with gay abandon, in the manner of children not yet culturally programmed. Children have spontaneity naturally, a bright light that dims with age in the average adult.

22. *Goal-oriented, self-directed.* Purposeful living characterizes those who have worked at making destiny-control their own responsibility. Some folks know what they want, how to get there. When tested

plans don't work, they have alternate ways to go. Planning always means having alternative, contingency plans.

23. *Open-minded.* Open-minded folks let it in, whatever it is. They have a readiness to let in whatever they encounter. Their scoopers are in front of them; their antennae are always searching for signals. Their posture always seems to say, "If you can lay one new thing on me that I haven't encountered, I want to know that." They have suffered back in time and learned by it, suffered from keeping something out based on their own preprogrammed (closed) minds. They have removed their blinders.

24. *Responsible.* The responsible person presents a demeanor that seems to announce to all comers: "I have taken it upon myself to shoulder these things, no matter what. Screw the world. I'll carry these burdens for my own reasons, which I refuse to explain." There are no explanations in such an announcement, no excuses, no request for gratitude, respect, approval, not even for recognition.

25. *Free of negative emotions.* Worry, guilt, anger, envy, jealousy, fear, depression, boredom, avarice, and the rest of the crowd of negative emotions are missing, not because the person has never known them, but because he or she has learned how to be rid of them. These self-induced emotionally neurotic states, feeling behaviors invoked for the sake of payoffs in specific times and places, all related to other people, have been chucked in favor of more productive ways to be alive, in favor of continually feeling neutral or more positive. Such folks make great company.

26. *Lives in the present moment.* Thinks it is foreign that anyone can be *alive* anywhere else. Understands that the mind can take one anywhere, to the past or future or never-never land. Such trips, however, are a better choice only for the sake of *preparation* (planning for a more important and inevitable here-and-now to come, a future one has decided one must live through); or for the sake of *learning* from what one has lived through (understanding the lessons to be garnered from past living); or for *releasing the mind* to wander in speculation, for creativity. This is in contrast to what those do who relive to feel guilty or to find pleasure not now present; or those who dramatize to feel scared and helpless or who dream up a mental place to be in order to escape what is now happening.

27. *Understands and practices loving.* Love is giving. Loving is action. To love is to give of the self, time and energy, labor, communication, all the good stuff one can generate. If the lover expects a return, the

action is not love but an exchange of services. Love has no strings attached. Nonlovers give only to get, or act out of duty or obligation, not choice. Lovers understand how to love one's self before all others. As the object of another's love, they expect to be second in line. "If you cannot love yourself," they reason, "why would anyone else choose to love you? If you do love yourself, you aren't desperate for another's love, even though you understand and welcome it." True lovers have a poet's soul: They love life, the world and all that is in it.

28. *Rarely complains or apologizes.* The noncomplainer knows that complaining changes nothing. Such a one does not explain or try to prove anything by verbally assaulting anyone. Is proactive, not re-active: a doer. Is into getting good news, or just news, not into listening to the bad news of others or visiting same upon them. Is rarely defensive or apologetic. Deals with others in an up-front way about what can be done now, when things go awry. Doesn't blame. Doesn't find fault: There are only causes and effects.

29. *Welcomes the unknown.* The unknown is new. Such a person is internally settled about the old and reexamines the old only when new data relate to it. Takes risks to bring the new into being. Feeds on the new. Goes after it. Prizes learning, adventure, has wanderlust.

30. *Avoids sentimentality.* Knows the difference between sense and sentimentality, between warranted natural emotion and worn-out unnatural emotion. Shuns low-level emotion for its own sake. The sentimentalist doesn't feel but is in love with *re*feeling: conjures up the old stuff to have a remembered feeling recur.

31. *Plays heartily.* Play is pleasurable activity engaged in for its own sake. When it is over, nothing remains. In play harnesses are off, cares are shed. One romps, indulges the carefree spirit, is hearty and joyous, whether alone or in company. Lusty play confirms the cyclical nature of life, fills the time between work intervals, between eating and sleeping, getting and spending, caring and striving.

32. *Has patience.* Knows that if it is important, future time can be de-voted to it, whatever it is. Has a sense of time, how everything unfolds. When time passes, the hot misty steam evaporates. The fog leaves "on little catfeet" and the landscape is clearly revealed. In the young, patience is a sign of early maturity. A sense of the meaning of history takes up residence in the patient person, particularly one's personal history. So much of the world is predictable; what is not cannot be known immediately. Impatient folks complain, fret, or act fruitlessly.

33. *Knows reality and appearances are different.* Reality is there, known by the senses. Appearances take so many forms as to flabbergast the mind. Tilted minds lose sight of reality. Seeming is never reality. Seeing that seeming is not reality requires a straight-shooter, one who hasn't forgotten the forward vision of childhood. This one knows that no one is more important than anyone else or one's self. Expects to encounter gross egocentrism in others, in snobs, in those who occupy socially esteemed roles and niches and take themselves seriously, the parade of talk show personalities, those elected to high office, but is unimpressed, unfooled, down-to-earth, and matter-of-fact about their status. Such slots will always be filled by someone, the revolving door disgorging the next self-inflated bozo who has competed to be in line.

34. *Is good at shifting.* Makes effective transitions as a matter of habit. When this chunk of living is over and done with, there is no lingering around to retaste it whether it was delicious. If it was painful or difficult, there is no dwelling on the hurt. Such a one goes on to whatever is next and becomes fully engaged. Spends little or no time in the interstices. If a task is unfinished and must be abandoned in favor of other impingements, the good shifter schedules time for that task and forgets it.

35. *Sees ways around rules.* This variable is related to rebellion against harmful cultural influences. To get around the rules implies corruptness, when viewed from the rule-maker's position. To be corrupt in this sense is to be pragmatic. The world is corrupt. Nothing is fair or just. Someone who understands this and operates out of such understanding has a clear-eyed view of rules, which are always made to govern the greatest number and only seldom are beneficial to the rule-obeyer. Because rules are restrictive to human growth, freedom of movement, individuality and well-being, and because there are always those to whom the rules do not pertain, the "corrupt" person opportunistically seeks to join that group of persons to whom the rules do not pertain without harming others or self to get there. Understands that a law is a social contract, and lives within laws; but would defy an unjust law if it mattered enough.

36. *Governs money.* Does not allow money to govern and then become upset and mean of soul. Money will buy almost anything, but if one doesn't have it, one can still survive and be as happy as the average flea or earthworm, neither of which has the capacity to think about the rate of exchange when crossing borders. The trick is to have

good survival skills and to know how to improve one's economic lot. Such a one does not allow money to interfere in significant relationships. Is neither a spendthrift nor a miser, neither foolishly generous nor stingy. Understands frugality and the monetary value of things. Pays, doesn't freeload. Lives within means.

37. *Knows what matters.* In the final reckoning no one thing or event matters more than any other. Knowing this, the "together" person also knows that establishing value involves personal decison making, a lifelong ongoing process, the values continuously shifting. To a squirrel or a bedbug, a pigeon or a crocodile, its next move matters more than knowing that a tidal wave wiped out Hawaii or that a computer was invented by humans. What matters is always relative, sits differently in every human mind. Even in the face of knowing that it doesn't really matter, decides what matters and acts as though it truly does matter.

38. *Prizes freedom above all.* Freedom means taking responsibility for one's actions, as in a free state all choices are possible. The free are autonomous: They own their choices and deal with consequences. Small minds seek freedom *from*, to get away from perceived negatives. Large minds seek freedom *to*. They pursue things, people, events, ideas, what is in the world. When imprisoned, large minds seek to escape in order to do and to be, not simply to get out of prison. Far too many folks are in love with their chains, do not even see or feel them, are frightened by freedom and responsibility that comes with choosing. If "the truth shall set you free," they hug falsehood. In the United States of America, freedom is our legacy. It is worth dying for. Those who do not define it for themselves, who do not know what it is, are self-enslaved.

NOTES

1. Kipling, R. If—. (1946) In R. L. Woods, (Ed.). *A treasury of the familiar.* New York: Macmillan, pp. 656–657.
2. This list may be photocopied and used by counseling practitioners or trainers for the professional purpose of working with clients or students without requesting permission in writing from the author or publisher, but in every case of such use author and publication credit must appear in writing on each copy. Any *publication* use of the material, however, must be through the written permission of the American Association for Counseling and Development.

14

Useful Idea Round-up

Whoopee ti yi yo, git along, little dogie,
It's your misfortune and none of my own;
Whoopee ti yi yo, git along, little dogies,
For you know Wyoming will be your new home.

—*John A. Lomax*[1]

The idea of a round-up, familiar to all Americans if not from actual experience then by virtue of their exposure to that native art form known as the cinema horse opera, is a suitable one for this final chapter. There are counseling strays and mavericks that do not easily join the herd but wander off into draws and canyons, culverts and winding river bottoms, or clamber up the rocky slopes of the mountainside. They are, nevertheless, beef on the hoof as valuable and ultimately as succulent and tasty as any already herded, and therefore worth rounding up. The straggle of strays corralled here were either overlooked during the writing of earlier chapters or of too maverick a nature to warrant inclusion elsewhere.

Exactly when and how a counselor might use the following ideas will seem obvious to some. To others a certain one of the insights will be precisely the key that clicks open a sticky lock, the missing piece that solves a persisting puzzle, the nudge that dislodges a stalled counseling case, and that intermittent feeling of satisfaction will be theirs. Here are the pragmatic kinds of observations and insights that practitioners trade when they seriously discuss with like-minded peers their professional struggles to understand, to make a difference, to increase their effectiveness. Here is solemnity and playfulness, a few let-ups in heavy concentration upon matters already too weighty, a few biases, a few satirical and iconoclastic remarks of the kind peers exchange when they feel more relaxed and appreciate being in good company. Productively precious are such "swap-meets," the source of some of the ideas to follow. Others came from readings, usually outside of what might be considered the field. Some arose from the simple but time-absorbing act of reflection and ratiocination. And still others were hard-won from the experiences clients related. The more one counsels, is committed to being of service to every client, encounters diversity and is invited to enter the private lives of clients and join in their struggles for personal mastery, the more one learns.

IS LIFE A SENTENCE OR A GIFT?

For some people, a rare subspecies, life is a gift. Life is a privilege accorded them, a wonder, a continually ongoing joyous adventure. They didn't ask to be born, but there they are and "ain't *that* just fine!" There is a world to encounter that can never be totally absorbed. Ten lifetimes would not be enough to see it all, to participate in its glories, to discover all that reality holds in store. They are neutral about what is in the world, accepting of all it has to offer. The world would be a poorer place, they know, without its shadows: death and disease, violence and suffering, the dirty, the smelly, the obscene. Nothing daunts them. There is a place for everything under the sun. They go to meet it. They welcome the unknown, the not-yet-discovered. They are happy to exist. They are in love with being alive. Adversity is something to conquer, and having met adversity, they are larger, more adaptable, wiser. They learn as they go, and they are in love with learning. Every stage of life has its wonders and benefits. They yank along into adulthood the inquisitiveness and playfulness, the fresh awe and sparkle and demeanor of the child. They keep on living instead of reliving. In their wide-eyed wonder and gratefulness they have trouble even understanding such concepts as boredom, jadedness, or burn-out. Just as it does with other animal species, revulsion escapes them. They are energized self-starters.

For others, and their numbers are in far, far greater plenitude, life is a sentence. These folks feel their existence as a burden. But it is not their fault that they are here, in this "vale of tears." They are not responsible. They did not ask to be born. They have learned how to be masterful sufferers. Every Denmark has something rotten, every cloud can brew a tornado, every victory is hollow, and germs are everywhere. They read T. S. Eliot's poem, "The Wasteland" or "The Hollowmen," and they cry, "Yes, yes. That is how it *is*! How profound! We live in a wasteland. That person who is joyous is a fool. People will do you in. They will hurt you every time you give them a chance. The meaning of life is torture, at the best it is a temporary reprieve." They spend their time preparing themselves for HELL or many little hells. They make HELL happen for themselves in order that they can become inured, numb to pain. They were put on earth to suffer. They are the butt of a cosmic joke they neither understand nor question. They spend their energies protecting themselves, avoiding the new and different. They seek comfort, security, a shelter against the evil world. They are doing *hard time*.

Can everyone you meet be assigned to one of these two camps? Those in the first, if they are pure specimens, hardly ever show up for counseling. Those in the second camp come in droves. But most people aren't pure. They are a composite. For them, 10% or 20 or 30% percent of the time, life is a gift. They have highs and lows when they feel one way or the other. Perhaps 30% of the time life is a sentence. In between they feel numb.

It is the job of the counselor to help every client see that life can be a gift, to increase the amount of time it is so felt. *How* a counselor does this will vary enormously according to the particular makeup of any given client. Counselors with a short supply of strategies, techniques, abilities, those who are low on creativity, on resourcefulness, on adaptability, those whose diagnostic skills yield insufficient knowledge about how a given client is wired together, in short, those who lack competence in a given counseling relationship will be less successful.

But one thing is certain. It follows as the night the day. If it is the *counselor* who sees life as a sentence, something to be endured rather than to be met headlong with enthusiasm, who sees life not as riches to be spent but as a howling blizzard to be fortified against, who has no other vision than this, no other life-understanding than this, a person who has not experienced the gift of life or who is incapable of sustaining such a vision, then his or her client can hardly be expected to change. The client's pendulum won't swing. It will stay stuck.

FIRST-ORDER MORAL IMPERATIVE

> *Don't let yourself be victimized by the age you live in. It's not the times that will bring us down, any more than it's society. When you put the blame on society, then you end up turning to society for the solution... There's a tendency today to absolve individuals of moral responsibility and treat them as victims of social circumstance. You buy that, you pay with your soul. It's not men who limit women, it's not straights who limit gays, it's not whites who limit blacks. What limits people is lack of character. What limits people is that they don't have the fucking nerve or imagination to star in their own movie, let alone direct it. Yuk.*

> *—Tom Robbins*[2]

If there is a single moral imperative on planet Earth that applies equally and indiscriminately to all living things from microbes to giant redwood trees, from field mice to pachyderms, it is that each individual of a species must care for itself before it cares for others of its own kind, a *life* principle. This is even true of mothers, where the instinct to do for another beyond the self has the greatest potency: Unless mother sparrow or mother polar bear survives in relatively good shape, her offspring are doomed. Once launched into independent living, though, these same offspring must make do on their own. The job of parenting, all of nature teaches us, is not to provide our offspring with things, with luxuries or securities of any kind, but to raise them up, at the very least, to the minimum level where they can care for themselves, where they can meet what Abraham Maslow magnanimously spent so much time delineating for us: their hierarchy of basic needs for living in a state of economical and psychological well-being.[3] The fit survive. That we know. That is the moral lesson of evolution, one of its maxims. Less focused upon is the demise of the unfit. That story doesn't count for much.

This brings up a corollary of the "natural law." If you do not care for yourself, others must care for you. These others may be willing, at first, but soon most tend to resent it. In this way the unfit become victims of scorn, abuse, contempt, even exploitation. At best they are ignored, forgotten, passed by, abandoned. It is their own fault that they are losers. The operating idea is this: If they continue to receive the help of others, they won't help themselves. Why should they? Help ought to get them back on their feet and not reinforce their proneness. Help is for the *sake* of getting them to stand upright and get going. It is not for the sake of enabling them to do nothing and remain supine. They who choose prostration deserve their fate, no matter how miserable. Certainly this is what nature repeatedly and inexorably shows.

But in the human species this natural law is somewhat defied. Because we value the individual human soul and life, we become our brother's or sister's keeper—but this is usually conditional. The reason we value the life of another is because we value our own, and "There, but for the grace of God, go I," we say. We are gregarious. We know that. A life without other humans is no life at all. Next to death, solitary confinement is the greatest horror. People need people, we sing. We like to feel needed, not simply wanted. Being needed gives meaning and vitality to our existence. Being needed becomes especially crucial if no one would choose us for our own sakes, just because we are so fine, so great to be around. Then, serving those who demonstrate by their helplessness that they need us becomes our reason for living, a case of the needy meeting our need.

Based on the concept of community, that humankind survives best in a group, that "in union there is strength," we understand and even extol the idea of interdependence. Society, whether bright-colored satin or drab raggedy burlap, is a fabric woven of many strands. The survival of the unfit depends on the survival and prosperity of the fit. We live under human laws and an economic system based on this tenet. But the system wobbles and waffles over deciding *who* is unfit. The handicapped? Surely. Those whom fate strikes with disease? Certainly. Those born with less than functional mental equipment? No question. Absolutely. The poor and hungry? Hmmmmm. There is a question here as to whether they brought it upon themselves. The aged? Same question: Why didn't they provide for their own latter-day fate when they had the chance instead of squandering their early gains? The alcoholic? Same question. No one *forced* any alcoholic to get that way. Interdependence becomes qualified. It works best among equals who exchange services, or in a small group, in families bound together by strong ties, by blood and unbreakable oaths. In truth, anyone can be saved and helped to have all hierarchical needs fulfilled to the highest extent possible, if prosperous and able enough members of a support group pitch in and work for that end. We know this, too.

And just here is where all this affects counseling. Here's the rub. Practitioners, their names and addresses sold to mental health entrepreneurs by virtue of their membership in professional organizations, are bombarded with junk mail advertising the glories of the "new" ways to help clients: family counseling, networking, group activities of all kinds. They are made to feel that their efforts with individual clients won't be successful unless they pay heavy attention to the human context in which clients live and then diagnose and assess available "support systems," that catch phrase legacy of the 1970s that has made it into prime-time. They are urged to become family counselors, to learn the prevailing theories and methods, and, of course, the various dialects of the new vernacular, for curing whatever is wrong with clients by focusing on the group, the system, the interrelationships these clients have with the assemblage of significant others in their worlds. No person adequately survives alone. Ergo, there is a family, a support group, a network, a collection of some sort, cohesive or straggly, out there somewhere. The message is this: "Your client isn't out of step. The troop is. Remedy, or at least meliorate, what is going wrong in the troop."

For some counselors this message does duty as an escape clause: "The reason I can't get anywhere in helping this client is because she is trapped, held captive by a horde of loony bandits. I can't get the whole gang in here for counseling and there is no way I can help her to extricate herself. The loonies have all escape tunnels blocked. Confronted by this standoff, my powers are snuffed. I'm impotent. Oh, well. In her choppy sea of troubles I can at least hold her hand so she doesn't drown."

Back to the moral imperative. It is the *duty* (there is nothing "selfish" about this) of every person to "look out for Number One." It is the *duty* of everyone graced in life with equipment that is not dysfunctional to survive and, according to the All-American Dream, to prosper.

Where, in all of this, lies the counselor's duty?

THE POWER OF METAPHORS

The *VISA* bill comes in the monthly mail. Across the front of the envelope in large and flashy blue script, it says: "More Than a Charge Card." What could the advertisers mean?

Perhaps they mean:

- It makes a good companion in the tub when your soap runs out.
- It can be something to love, to kiss and hug on lonely wintry nights, when you experience an uncommon fit of despondency.
- You can wear it as an eyepatch to announce your affluence.
- It will improve your dreams if you stick it beneath your pillow at night.
- You can use it to scratch your arm or leg, when either is ashy or the sunburn is peeling and a lively itch beckons, without getting skinflakes under your fingernails.
- You can use it for a spare, when a card is missing from your pinochle deck.
- You can wave "Hello" with it.
- You can wave "Goodbye" with it.
- When you feel frisky, you can use it as an indoor Frisbee and can sail it around your bedroom.

No, they probably don't mean any of these things. Advertisers are in love with metaphors. They use them to suck you in. Probably what the *VISA* people mean is that you can borrow money with your charge card. No doubt they mean that you can do some similar things, too, such as use it for identification to establish credit when you take out another charge card. But whatever they mean, you may be certain it will cost you money.

When advertisers use metaphors, look out. They wouldn't do it if there were not a self-serving payoff in it. That's a reliable staple of American business and the free enterprise system. Metaphors work.

Why not let them work for you? Counselors can learn the tricks of advertising as well as anyone.

So can clients.

CLIENTS, CUSTOMERS, AND COUNSELEES

The author neither likes nor uses the word *counselee*. Not anymore. He used to use it, but he has found that recipients of counseling services don't like it. No one wants to be an "ee" of anything. Not counselee, helpee, trainee, or tutee. He supervised a doctoral student one time whose dissertation ended up bearing this title: *The effects of intergrade tutoring with group guidance activities on the reading achievement, self-concept, attitudes toward school and behavior of third and fourth grade tutors and on the reading achievement and behavior of first and second grade tutees.*[4] It was a good study, an important research effort in many ways, but he cannot read that title without laughing when he gets to the last word.

We put an "ee" sound at the end of a word to indicate "a little one," turning William into Billy, Deborah into Debbie, or Francis into Frankie, the way the French use the word-ending "ette." What we imply is some kind of second-class status, lesser importance, diminution. The "ee" ending not only diminishes, it belittles.

Albert Ellis once told the author, "Of course, you always choose weakies." The author flinched and Al caught it. Then Al zeroed in, using "ee" endings on a goosey gaggle of words. "Gives you a pain in the tummy, huh? That thought makes you feel weepy and whiny, does it?" The author got the point one whole bunch quicker than if Al had launched into a long and logical explanation. The author didn't like to hear it, but it was damned useful.

What *counselee* implies, whether a counselor means to do so or not, is that the person who gets counseled is less important than the counselor. After all these years of exposure to the "client-centered approach," no one in the business ought to feel that way. Yet, to the author's amazement, at least, some still do. They see clients as inadequate people. That may be important for certain counselors, especially if they themselves don't feel adequate. If by draping the robe-role of counselor around themselves they can move one step up in the pecking order at the expense of their clients, at least when they are in the counseling cubicle, we can suppose it makes some kind of sense, but such a reason is hardly defensible. "Keeping ahead of the Joneses" is an American social disease that is widespread, but counselors ought to develop a professional immunity to the temptation, is that not so? It's hard to see how anyone who thinks of clients as "counselees" is manifesting "unconditional positive regard."

The okay word is *client*. To be a client means that you are using the services of a professional, someone you are employing because that individual has been trained and has expertise in a given occupational area. Thus, we hire attorneys, accountants, architects, landscapers, interior decorators, fixers and mechanics, consultants of all kinds . . . and counselors. We are buying their services. Nor are we customers when we do this. It is okay to be a customer or a consumer when we buy things, not human services. When we purchase things, we know that we are not safe, we must shop around, and we must use our own judgment. If we get stung, we blame ourselves, for we all have had our minds imprinted with the caveat, "Buyer beware!"

It is *not* okay to be a *patient*. If *counselee* belittles, then *patient* devastates. The medical professionals have institutionalized the word as something to be feared. It means "sick person." And if you are a "mental patient," you are in deep trouble, as they say. You are "up the creek without a paddle."

In general our society abhors the mentally ill as much as nature does a vacuum. We blame them for their condition. We never trust them, not even years after they are certifiably cured. When Norman Mailer stabbed his wife in the heat of a family argument in 1962 and was taken into police custody, he was frantic lest the authorities label him legally insane or mentally incompetent, thereby impugning his credibility as an author and damaging anything he might subsequently write.[5] This is no less true of John Kenneth Galbraith who strictly shepherded a dark secret until he stepped out of public life and felt free to acknowledge a debt. In his memoirs he confesses:

> My depression got worse. Whiskey brought a brief moment of relief before dinner. Increasingly massive doses of Seconal were necessary for sleep. Classes became a struggle. In the growing darkness of the late Cambridge autumn I turned to a neighbor and friend who was also a brilliant psychiatrist. My visits were a beautifully guarded secret. I feared my credibility as an economist would suffer were it rumored that I was receiving such attention. I learned to my surprise that I had long been subject to cycles of euphoria and depression. These had been relatively mild—not far out of the plausible range of a normal reaction to good news and bad. The election campaign and its aftermath had merely increased the amplitude of the cycle. The excitements of travel and the hope of victory had enhanced the euphoric tendency; the defeat and its morbid prospect had taken depression to the depths. I doubt that I was the first person in politics so to suffer. Or the last. On discovery of my disorder, I turned my mind to tracing previous cycles. Presently the cloud lifted. Thereafter when it returned, . . . I could recognize it for what it was. This brief darkness I came to consider one of the more useful experiences of a lifetime, and I have not since minimized the services of a psychiatrist.[6]

Galbraith had well learned the lesson of secrecy. If he required any confirmation of what could happen if his secret were broadcast, it was provided by the very public expulsion of the vice presidential candidate from the Democratic ticket in 1972. The party's choice for president, George McGovern, dumped Thomas Eagleton as his running mate in mid-campaign because the senator from Missouri had, some 10 years earlier in his life, sought mental health services. In Galbraith's words, "A massive assault was immediately mounted on this excellent man centering on the treatment he had undergone for an unpleasant but by no means catastrophic or even exceptional episode of mental depression."[7]

There is no question that in this society we are suspicious of the mentally ill, of anyone who has been a bona fide mental patient. We are on guard, totally uncomfortable around them. So, as a counselor educator, the author cringes when he hears any apprentice use the word "patient." It is squeaky chalk. His suspicions usually turn out to be warranted: The user of the term is going after self-aggrandizement at the expense of his or her client. Such folks want to be seen as "doctors."

The counseling profession stands to be the winner in any rivalry between various competing groups to become the provider-of-choice in the future, the author believes, just because the seeker after mental health services is not stigmatized by having gone for counseling. Counseling is a service for everyone. At least the field hasn't yet lost that beneficial reputation. You don't need to be sick to go for it. Sickness is not the price of admission. If you get counseling, that doesn't mean you are abnormal. It still means that you are sensible, that you know some counseling will be helpful in difficult life situations where an honest and neutral person trained in human relations skills will put experience and critical acumen to work in your behalf. Or maybe you choose to go just to upgrade your general life-effectiveness, to become more personally masterful.

So let's junk the word *counselee.* That "ee" ending is a subtle force working against the heart of what it is that we are all about. In counseling sessions the author will sometimes say, at appropriate moments, those times when a divorce or a parting of ways between former intimates is in the offing, when the focus is upon this very painful likelihood, "it's better to be the leaver than the leavee." Aside from the difficult-to-swallow truth about psychological well-being encased in that sentence, it always produces a laugh. No one likes to be an "ee." We laugh at "ee's," almost with pity.

THERAPY

Patients, not clients, get therapy. All kinds of counselors take to calling themselves "therapists" as soon as they can get away with it, attempting to elevate and dignify who they are and what they do. Sometimes they will even announce that they are *psycho*therapists. Identification as a counselor isn't prestigious enough for them. When they are asked at cocktail parties or other social gatherings what they do for a living, they are worried that "counselor" won't sound as though it is the equivalent of lawyer or doctor or business manager. They would probably love to answer "psychologist," but not having the credentials, that might be risky.

How can "therapy" be a step up? It seems a whole lot harder to be able to counsel someone who is in need of no therapy of any kind. *That* is a challenge. After years of counseling many clients who have "been in therapy," whether such treatment was delivered by a psychologist, psychiatrist, or psychoanalyst, the author never fails to be amazed at what therapists do. Their clients spill the beans and reveal "the inside story," which turns out to be full of horrors. Many therapists are expert mostly at hanging onto their patients, at creating a dependency on the therapy. Helping those they serve to become independent operators in their own worlds frequently seems never to have been considered. Many such clients become astounded at the thought that they do not need to see themselves as "sickies."

This is not to say that there are no ethical, competent, effective, and honest therapists in practice. There are many. What it does say, unfortunately, is that folks who seek help ought to be customers before they become clients or patients. Some early comparative shopping will save time and often a satchel of hard-earned cash.

APPROACH

Also, it is high time the word *approach* stood up to some criticism. It is nebulous, amorphous, wishy-washy, and sloppy whenever it is linked with a brand of counseling. It's a cop-out. When we cannot pin down a collection of ideas, a set of assumptions and propositions about reality, we call the effort an approach.

"What counseling approach do you use?" is a frequently asked question.

There is an impulse to answer, "Do you want to know how I meet clients? Whether I lie in wait for them, sneak up on them, come in dancing, or whether I charge at them like a bull, headlong?"

The approach/avoidance syndrome, well documented in psychology texts, comes to mind, and in that context the word has some valid meaning. The questioner wanting to know "what approach" is seldom ready for a full exposition of a well-thought-through theory of counseling.

That person is content with and even expects to get a label: "client-centered, rational-emotive, behavioristic." Then the questioner can say, "Oh, I thought so," and amble away believing some meaningful thinking has taken place and the matter has been serviceably pigeonholed.

MORE ON THEORIZING

In the chapter on "Practical Counseling Theory and Research" it seemed to the author at the time of writing that there was no room for the following quotations. Besides, they might add more puzzlement to an argument that seemed puzzling enough in its general outlines. But the quotations are too splendid in their implications to ignore. These eminent thinkers and writers give comfort to anyone trying to make some sense out of what surely is a profound and troubling condition of a counselor's calling.

> *If by theory one means a tightly organized set of postulates from which rigorous inferences can be drawn, I certainly do not have one. Furthermore, I do not even want one. The aspects of human life in which I have taken the greatest delight are the spontaneous, the unexpected, the unpredictable. If overwhelming evidence for a comprehensive theoretical system compelled me to accept it, I should do so, albeit with reluctance. But in our vast intellectual universe, where many towering edifices of theory, many intricate philosophical patterns have been wrought from the stuff of reality, always leaving some of it unused when the work is complete, I have chosen to value openness above rigor, richness and suggestiveness above completeness.*
>
> *If by theory, however, one means simply the organized set of concepts by means of which one attempts to fit experience into a meaningful pattern, then I may call myself a theorist. The search for meaning—in books, in music, in the experiences of my own and other people's lives—has been continuous since childhood. Again and again organizing ideas have been adopted, tested, discarded, combined with other ideas. Out of this process a way of thinking about human nature and the function of counseling has emerged.*

> *—Leona E. Tyler*[8]

> *I think the first thing that led me toward philosophy (though at that time the word "philosophy" was still unknown to me)*

*occurred at the age of eleven. My childhood was mainly solitary
as my only brother was seven years older than I was. No doubt as
a result of much solitude I became rather solemn, with a great
deal of time for thinking but not much knowledge for my
thoughtfulness to exercise itself upon. I had, though I was not yet
aware of it, the pleasure in demonstrations which is typical of the
mathematical mind... Before I began the study of geometry
somebody had told me that it proved things and this caused me
to feel delight when my brother said he would teach it to me...*

*My brother began at the beginning with definitions. These I
accepted readily enough. But he came next to the axioms. "These,"
he said, "can't be proved, but they have to be assumed before the
rest can be proved." At these words my hopes crumbled. I had
thought it would be wonderful to find something that one could
prove, and then it turned out that this could only be done by
means of assumptions of which there was no proof. I looked at
my brother with a sort of indignation and said, "But why should
I admit these things if they can't be proved?" He replied, "Well, if
you won't, we can't go on."*

—Bertrand Russell[9]

*Perhaps the greatest change, stemming principally from the
revolutions in physics, is in our conception of what a theory is.
For Newton, inquiry was a voyage on the sea of ignorance to find
the islands of truth. We know now that theory is more than a
general description of what happens or a statement of
probabilities of what might or might not happen—even when it
claims to be nothing more than that, as in some of the newer
behavioral sciences. It entails, explicitly or implicitly, a model of
what it is that one is theorizing about, a set of propositions that,
taken in ensemble, yield occasional predictions about things.
Armed with a theory, one is guided toward what one will treat as
data, is predisposed to treat some data as more relevant than
others. A theory is also a way of keeping in mind a vast amount
while thinking about a very little... We now see the construction
of theory as a way of using the mind, the imagination, of
standing off from the activities of observation and inference and
creating a shape of nature.*

—Jerome S. Bruner[10]

*The "two cultures" controversy of several years back has
quieted down some... At one edge, the humanists are set up as*

*knowing, and wanting to know, very little about science and
even less about the human meaning of contemporary science;
they are, so it goes, antiscientific in their prejudice. On the other
side, the scientists are served up as a bright but illiterate lot, well
read in nothing except science, ... incapable of writing good
novels. The humanities are presented in the dispute as though
made up of imagined, unverifiable notions about human
behavior, unsubstantiated stories cooked up by poets and
novelists, while the sciences deal parsimoniously with lean facts,
hard data, incontrovertible theories, truths established beyond
doubt, the unambiguous facts of life.*

*The argument is shot through with bogus assertions and false
images, and I have no intention of becoming entrapped in
it, ... on one side or the other. Instead, I intend to take a stand in
the middle of what seems to me a muddle, hoping to confuse the
argument by showing that there isn't really any argument in the
first place. To do this, I must show that there is in fact a solid
middle ground to stand on, a shared common earth beneath the
feet of all humanists and all the scientists, a single underlying
view of the world that drives all scholars, whatever their
discipline—whether history or structuralist criticism or
linguistics or quantum chromodynamics or molecular genetics.*

There is, I think, such a shared view of the world. It is called
bewilderment. *Everyone knows this, but it is not much talked
about. Bewilderment is kept hidden in the darkest closets of all
our institutions of higher learning, repressed whenever it seems to
be emerging into public view, sometimes glimpsed staring from
the attic windows like a mad cousin of learning. It is the family
secret of twentieth-century science, and of twentieth-century arts
and letters as well. ... What we have been learning in our time is
that we really do not understand this place or how it works, and
we comprehend ourselves least of all. And the more we learn, the
more we are—or ought to be—dumbfounded.*

—*Lewis Thomas*[11]

MAKING LISTS

Have you ever been thumped on the head with the idea that list-making
is central to effective living? The author realized this over a decade ago
when he questioned why so many "how-to" books were successful. The
answer was simple enough. They are filled with lists. A how-to book

without lists doesn't cut it in the marketplace. People want ready-made prescriptions, recipes, lists of what to do, what steps to take. We are in love with lists. But we don't want to take out the time to make our own. That is work. We all make *some* lists, to be sure, because what to buy at the grocery store or what tasks must be done before company comes can't be done for us or found in a book.

What a heart-massaging and useful insight! It was like discovering some secret that is plain and obvious to every member of a whole society, like learning what every Eskimo already knows, that it is fun—even sexy— to rub noses, or if you're in Hawaii, that it makes life brighter and more fragrant to wear flowers around your neck.

People are generally in love with lists. It starts when they are mere tykes, at least whenever Santa Claus comes to town. "I'm making my list and checking it twice," goes the song. Not long after this insight into the obvious, *The Book of Lists*[12] became a best-seller. It topped the best-seller *list*. And, as we have come to expect in America, the imitators followed. We now even have *The Book of Sex Lists.*[13] These books simply *list* things ("Barbara Huttons's 7 Husbands," "3 Presidents with the Least Sex Appeal," "8 Facts to Prove That Sex is Big Business"[14]), only some of which are useful ("6 Things to Do When You Get an Obscene Phone Call," "15 Sex Therapy Clinics"[15]).

When you stop to think about it, we all rely on an array of lists. Every book, including this one, has its table of contents and index. Some books, after the telephone directory, the dictionary being perhaps the most vital in our lives, are nothing else than a long list. The card catalog in the library is the list we go to as soon as we enter. The calendar is a list of days, weeks, months. Where would we be without our lists?

What is crucial in this focus on lists, though, is not that they exist in such profusion, from encyclopedias to almanacs to new automobile manuals to the record books of sports, but that they are hard to make. It takes thought and time to make an inclusive list, and more time and thought to pare one down to essentials.

When Dr. Reuben published his book, *Everything You Always Wanted to Know About Sex—But Were Afraid to Ask,*[16] folks bought it in droves. But *everything*? Come now, Dr. Reuben, the book does not contain everything. There aren't enough pages. It's too skinny. The title is hype, of course. It's a tongue-in-cheek come-on. We smile before we even open the book. It is easy to make a liar out of Dr. Reuben, but who is going to do the *work* that would require. Let him play his little title game, his Reuben-rubrics.

There is the nubbin. It is too much work. People love lists. They are truly useful. They save time. But don't think. Not even to recall something. Just check the list. Let someone else make up the list.

What more useful service can a counselor provide than helping a client to produce a personally relevant list? Or to make one up for the client? Listing, it would seem, is essential to effective counseling, whether of significant others in the client's world, self-defeating behaviors, client goals, an agenda for a session, or a treatment plan.

This fiat ought to be high up on any counselor's list of what skills to acquire and refine: Get good at list-making.

SAYING "NO"

Learning how to say "No" and *mean* it is tough for many troubled individuals, "troubled" because they are taken advantage of so wantonly by practically everyone they know. An inability to say "No" with fervor is frequently what brings a client to counseling, or, at the least, is a common behavioral complaint.

The distinguished American writer, Edmund Wilson (1895–1972), beseiged with requests on all sides as his popularity grew, has gifted us with a "No" model that is hard to improve. When prevailed upon to do something, he simply mailed out the card he had printed up in boldfaced lettering.[17] His *list* is a dilly:

EDMUND WILSON REGRETS THAT IT IS IMPOSSIBLE FOR HIM TO:

READ MANUSCRIPTS,
WRITE ARTICLES OR BOOKS TO ORDER,
WRITE FOREWORDS OR INTRODUCTIONS,
MAKE STATEMENTS FOR PUBLICITY PURPOSES,
DO ANY KIND OF EDITORIAL WORK,
JUDGE LITERARY CONTESTS,
GIVE INTERVIEWS,
CONDUCT EDUCATIONAL COURSES,
DELIVER LECTURES,
GIVE TALKS OR MAKE SPEECHES,
BROADCAST OR APPEAR ON TELEVISION,
TAKE PART IN WRITERS' CONGRESSES,
ANSWER QUESTIONNAIRES,
CONTRIBUTE TO OR TAKE PART IN SYMPOSIUMS OR "PANELS" OF ANY KIND,
CONTRIBUTE MANUSCRIPTS FOR SALES,
DONATE COPIES OF HIS BOOKS TO LIBRARIES,
AUTOGRAPH BOOKS FOR STRANGERS,
ALLOW HIS NAME TO BE USED ON LETTERHEADS,
SUPPLY PERSONAL INFORMATION ABOUT HIMSELF,
SUPPLY PHOTOGRAPHS OF HIMSELF,
SUPPLY OPINIONS ON LITERARY OR OTHER SUBJECTS.

Might not a client be counseled to follow suit?

REAL MEN

In this world of cultural shifts where the crosscurrents of issues affect us all, where the pronouncements and manifestos from special interest factions fly overhead, their charges and countercharges billowing in the airwaves and generating the fallout we all breathe, our consciousness may become somewhat dulled or encrusted by what is in the air. We are often bemused at which way to turn, where we might position ourselves, and surprised at our own involvement when it was our intent to remain detached.

Just so in the cultural exchanges between the sexes that had at times raged, sirens blaring, and at times become the lowing of distant foghorns, the author had paid some intermittent mind, desultorily choosing to view a media event here or to read an accounting or argumentation in a magazine or a book there, dimly aware of all the fuss. Certainly it was neither in his nature nor in his professional demeanor to be a male chauvinist, and he sided with the feminists on most moot points, even cleansing his language where as a consequence of cultural osmosis it was oiled over with vestiges of unwarranted maleness. He was always the advocate of heterosexual counseling groups, pushing heterogeneity of every kind over more homogeneity, the better, he thought, for members to experience and learn from the cultural differences each brought to the happening.

So it was almost by accident that the author ended up being the counselor of an all-male group, three-fourths of whom had been alive for half a century. And what a group! These men were all successful in their chosen vocational areas, achievers, worldly-wise, a sense of being in charge pervading practically every aspect of their beings and lives—with one exception. They hardly understood women at all. The female psyche was a mystery, qualifying as one of the seven wonders of the modern world. Their relationship to women became the thematic center of every session, and their relationships with other men offset and afforded protection against the mystery, a mystery fraught with illogic and amorphous dangers, seemingly inexplicit, seemingly unknowable. They were struggling to get a handle on a core dimension of their lives, going back to childhood and how they were mothered on through the tentative sexual encountering of adolescence, thence on to mate selection, early marriage, parenthood, and the long haul of midlife domesticity and consolidation. They explored how they had related to women in their lives over the years and where they were in the present moment.

What the author learned was astounding. The group regenerated appreciations for male bonding he hadn't known since military duty in his youth. How important were the male jokes and clowning! How important it was that every male be able to formulate an *opinion* on every subject, no matter how remote from personal experience, to have a point of view, to be able to articulate a thesis! How important was the company of other males, the society of men in the workplace, the ongoing action of doing business with other males! These were all *real men*, so self-seen, unwilling to admit to anything less, not hard, not ruthless, certainly possessed of honor and integrity, and they really did not know how to surrender any of the manhood they had acquired so painstakingly. Vaguely they felt such surrender was what women wanted, and so were merely threatened; they were mystified, uncomprehending.

Primarily as a result of this professional experience, the author had agreed to participate on a panel at a convention and present his learnings. The topic was: "Group Counseling for Males in the 1980s."[18] For that even he preceded his more analytical commentary with the following list, his attempt to compress his learnings, to get the essence of the American (not for him to say that it is more international, more universal) male character:

REAL MEN

Real men know what is real. Real men know the score.
Real men understand what it is to be physical and when to become so.
Real men know that life is a game of chance. They understand gambling.
Real men understand drinking, what it is for.
Real men know what dirt and sweat are.
Real men understand work. As Hemingway said, "You do your work and
 survive."
Real men know that when you make your bed, you sleep in it.
Real men know that most things in this world are ridiculous, and they joke
 about it.
Real men don't complain, whine, nag, cry.
Real men aren't ratfinks, snitches.
Real men are cool.
Real men make love *and* war.
Real men have stiff upper lips, stomachs of iron, are two-fisted, and above all:
 they have balls.
Real men use real language. They swear.
Real men know how to die. They leave the world like Humphrey Bogart. They
 don't cop out in the eleventh hour and find God, like John Wayne.

Real men are hustlers.

Real men protect the family they were born into, their women, their offspring.

Real men take care of business.

Real men say, "Show me. Don't tell me."

Real men can stand the heat in the kitchen and they know where the buck stops.

Real men know on which side their bread is buttered.

Real men know the world is full of violence, crooks, con artists, competitors, enemies, and they are ready for anything.

Real men are movers and shakers.

Real men achieve. They get the job done. They know the world is full of boobs, nerds, and no-accounts: they just turn on the TV set and check out gameshow audiences to confirm this.

Real men know how to kick ass and take names.

Real men know exactly when and how to be real men.

Real men aren't soft-soapers, do-gooders, preachers, teachers, social workers, or counselors.

TRY TO TALK A REAL MAN INTO BEING DIFFERENT!

Somewhere shifting and drifting about in those crosswinds aloft, or so one would hope, there is a corresponding list for *real women*, but where does one go to find it? Perhaps real women, assured of their own integrated psyches, confident in their womanhood, have no call to make up such a list, or, as the men in that counseling group no doubt would prefer to think, the power of women would be compromised should they in any way abrogate the tenor of their mystery and deal in forthright revelation.

CONVERSIONS: PASSIVE AND ACTIVE

> *The Communists who joined the party as a result of having studied Marx can be counted on the fingers of one hand. They are first converted and then they read the Scriptures.*
>
> —*Albert Camus*[19]

Camus's remark, casually dropped into a footnote in his powerful treatise, *The Rebel*, stunned the present author when he first read it. For a time he sat silent and reflective, the shock and implications of recognition oozing into his consciousness. "How true," he said to himself, remembering all those instances where friends and relatives had been converted to religious and political faiths of one kind or another, and then how diligently they studied thereafter to shore up their wonderful newfound faith. The world opened up for them. Their way of being was lifted onto a higher plane. At first inspired, or even rapturous, they became transformed. They didn't want to lose the glory, to backslide, so they worked tenaciously to consolidate their faith.

The religious convert—who in a relatively short but intensely emotional period, which may or may not be accompanied by visions and hallucinations, blinding lights, visitations from the Deity or an angel, the physical shakes, a palpably-felt psychic rebirth, as William James details and closely examines in his *Varieties of Religious Experience*[20] where he presents testimonial account after account—is not that different from the rest of us. We all have the potential to become converts. The act of "falling in love" has all the same hallmarks, which Dorothy Tennov[21] has diagnosed and defined as "limerence," that state of ecstasy where the whole world becomes illuminated with rainbows of beauty because one's soul mate has at last been found, where one is protected from all of life's troubles and evils and is overcome by a feeling of buoyancy: One can "walk on air." Most people, if you ask around, have either "been there" or will claim to "know it" when "falling in love" happens to them. Nor is the political "radical," that person who "sees the light" and intensely, devotedly identifies with a righteous "cause" all that dissimilar.

Aside from the common phenomenon of shoring up one's faith after the conversion experience through study and other deeds, the newborn Christian reading the *Bible*, the Communist plowing through *Das Capital*, the limerent learning every last detail about and gifting her or his "love object," there is this characteristic element in such conversions: The subjects are all "saved" by external means or circumstances. Although we all may have the potential for such conversion, we all do not readily subscribe to an external "saving" element, to the promise of eternal life, a better world, or an uncritical and devoted beautiful life companion. Such conversions require a passive subject, one upon whom a drama (of sorts) can be enacted. If the only way out we see is from the inside, where we must lift ourselves "by our own bootstraps," we are less likely to experience the "passion" of the conversion syndrome. "If you should expose to a converting influence," says William James, "a subject in whom three factors unite: first, pronounced emotional sensibility; second, tendency to automatisms [post-hypnotic suggestions]; and third, suggestibility of the passive type; you might then safely predict the result: there would be a sudden conversion, a transformation of the striking kind."[22]

As counselors we strive to expose our clients to a "converting influence," namely our services, regardless of what form they may take. But we handicap ourselves from the start by insisting that the client do the work, take action, become the writer, director, and actor in whatever client-drama there is to unfold. We want to convert our clients from a belief system of "I can't: the world is against me," to one of "I can: My thinking has been erroneous: There are many actions I can take to improve my situation, make headway, and feel better." Although as counselors *we* are external to the client, perhaps even being seen as the saving grace, we feel we cannot ethically take over for the client.

So we search for that predisposition buried somewhere within our clients' minds that we can identify, affect, and build upon, somehow struggling to convert our clients from passive victims to active self-enhancers, from objects to subjects. The process is frequently long and involved, beset with many obstacles, but it is nevertheless what we try to do. When we are successful and conversion occurs, it is often marked by client euphoria, a "high" equal to falling in love or finding God or the true cause, except that the client falls in love with the self, finds God therein, and takes up his or her own cause.

Nor is counseling done with at this point. If conversion is to be sustained, the "scriptures" must be studied and the faith shored up. The true "way" of newborn living must be spelled out, the directions memorized, the actions owned—made into an integral and natural part of the client's life-after-rebirth.

CHANGE

Life is constant flux. Everything changes all around us, dramatically, all the time. The rate of change continues to accelerate, as Alvin Toffler has warned us in *Future Shock*,[23] and any modern Rip Van Winkle would wake to a world he could hardly have forecast. It is an express track culture we are traveling on, where quick adaptation to change is one of the most crucial abilities the young can acquire. Basic social institutions undergo major transformations in less than a generation. It requires almost a stubbornly stoic if not heroic individual to resist changing in reaction to the four-minute-mile, fast-lane pace of modern-day civilization. To get off the express track or be left behind is to speak of trauma and social pathology.

Psychologists continue to study human behavior and make inquiries into the dynamics of how people change with an eye to finding interventions that will result in controlling change in healthful directions, forestalling the negative, accentuating the positive. How do people change?

What are the essential personal components? Can we control our individual destinies? Can we control our development over the life span, shape ourselves into what we have earlier in life decided we want to become? If we are halfway successful, will we, as Rainer Maria Rilke observed in a trenchant moment, "find bitterness in our chosen thing?" What events are inevitable? What can we do beforehand in the face of their inevitability?

Counselors understandably tend to overrate their powers. It is natural that they would believe in the primal value of counseling; to be engaged in this service occupation and to be doubtful, have miniscule or no faith that their methodology works, would be tantamount to either being a quack or feeling the constant paralyzing earthquake tremors of cognitive dissonance. They strive to discover how a client changed in the past in order to determine what interventions would foster the client's change in the present and the future. Over time, if they are at all adept in biographical analysis, counselors learn how people change without any help from the normative generalizations of academics engaged in narrowly focused psychological inquiry.

People change when they must attract a new lover, and change even more when they find what they were supposedly looking for. People change in response to a dramatic shift of conditions in their work settings. People will change for the sake of money. They have their price. Pay them enough, lure them with enough, and they will do it. Group pressure will cause change: People want a psychological home in a social enclave. Almost any environment that demands new behaviors for adequate survival will bring about change. People change in prison, in the military service, in marriage, in schools, in a foreign country. If a counselor had the power to manipulate environments, causing change would be easy and counseling would seem silly, the last choice as a recourse. People are greedy, hungry for good things and good times, and they will spring onto bandwagons to find joy. As every con artist knows, greed can be tapped to ensnare people into making unprecedented and unnatural moves. People change as a result of dissatisfaction: If they hurt badly enough they will take action. They will even kill. Make the environment torturous enough, make people desperate enough, and they will eat human flesh, no doubt—if their teeth are in good shape—tearing it raw from the bones. They will become cannibals. What's more, future historians will recount how they became celebrities for their deeds.

> "Just a few moments of your attention I crave
> While I relate a sad death on the wave."

So began one of the ballads written about a macabre incident that took place one hundred years ago. Two highly respectable British seamen, on being cast adrift from the foundered yacht *Mignonette*, killed and ate a young shipmate in order to survive themselves. Their subsequent trial was a *cause celebre* at the time.

But this was no passing sensation . . . In *Cannibalism and the Common Law*, A. W. Brian Simpson has recreated not only the drama of the trial but the atmosphere of the Victorian era in which it unfolded. He has spun an absorbing tale of wrecks and heroism . . . He amplifies his story with legends and anecdotes—often laced with black humor—of other celebrated cannibals such as the American frontiersman, Alfred Parker, who is reputed to have eaten most of the Democrats in a Colorado county.[24]

Almost the last cause of change is logic and reason, including a realistic inventory of internal variables, an objective view of externals, an unimpassioned laying out of possibilities, and a field-testing program that involves operational options. People want payoffs, immediate—not delayed—gratifications. They have been conditioned to seek ends and seldom find their kicks in the process itself. If they were less future-oriented, there would be less future shock.

The most difficult kind of client is the one who feels no pressure to change, the one without envy, pain, avarice, exorbitant greed, desperation, or fear, the one who quietly decides to go about creating a new or improved self. But counselors infrequently see anyone fitting this description, even when they look in the mirror for such an image. Self-actualization is a rarity, a weird outcropping.

AUTHORITY

Authority is a word that over time has received a bad press. It has been doing duty to stand for "those in charge," the Authorities. When conceived in this fashion, implied about and attached to the term is the notion of power over others in almost a military sense: "On whose authority is this order issued?" The affiliation of authority and power is recognized in reference to "authority figures" and those who have difficulty dealing with same. This use of the word is equated with "father figure." If you had trouble dealing with the authority of your poppa, it is implied, then the chances are high that you will go through life having relational difficulties with whomever becomes your "boss." And the fact that Sigmund Freud incorporated the idea of the Oedipus complex into his systematic scheme of human development, describing how it can go off the track if unresolved, tends to back up this point of view with a thundering rationalization hard to ignore. Beyond this there are towering questions related to submission and obedience to the authority of the state, and even unto God.

But there is an older way to conceive of authority that is not associated with power, at least with the power to control and determine the fate of others. If power comes into this way of defining the word at all, it implies knowledge, or the power to make or do. Here the word goes directly to its roots, the authority derived from being the *author*, composer, designer, creator, inventor. The power to create and do by virtue of one's knowledge and capacity to perform versus the power to control others as a condition of one's role or position is implied in this older sense of the term. Such authority has to do with competence. Such authority can at any time demonstrate ability.

This kind of authority is what we associate with professionals in any field of endeavor, and effective counselors have sought and acquired it. They really know what they are purported to know, and they know that they know it. When called upon, they can author it.

CHEESE

> *If you put a rat in front of a bunch of tunnels and put cheese in one of them, the rat will go up and down the tunnels looking for the cheese. If every time you do the experiment you put cheese down the fourth tunnel, eventually you'll get a successful rat. This rat knows the right tunnel and goes directly to it every time.*
>
> *If you now move the cheese out of the fourth tunnel and put it at the end of another tunnel, the rat still goes down the fourth tunnel. And, of course, gets no cheese. He then comes out of the tunnel, looks the tunnel over, and goes right back down the cheeseless fourth tunnel. Unrewarded, he comes back out of the tunnel, looks the tunnels over again, goes back down the fourth tunnel again, and again finds no cheese.*
>
> *Now the difference between a rat and a human being is that eventually the rat will stop going down the fourth tunnel and will look down other tunnels, and a human being will go down the tunnel with no cheese forever. Rats, you see, are only interested in cheese. But human beings care more about going down the right tunnel.*
>
> *It is belief which allows human beings to go down the fourth tunnel ad nauseam. They go on doing what they do without any*

> *real satisfaction, without any nurturing, because they come to*
> *believe that what they are doing is right. And they will do this*
> *forever, even if there is no cheese in the tunnel, as long as they*
> *believe in it and can prove that they are in the right tunnel.*

> *—Adelaide Bry*[25]

Is it possible to read this analogy contrasting rats and human beings and not be moved by the truth it portrays? Of course, rats are only interested in cheese. And human beings do act that way: They pursue ends in order to be *right*. Humans justify their behavior, too. They are not rats. They have human minds. They believe in a "higher order" of behavior. What's *wrong* with being *right*?

But we smile as we read the analogy, too. It is like a "gotcha" game. You're *right*—but you didn't get the *cheese*. "Gotcha, dummy." You *want* the cheese, though, don't you? Or why did you go down the fourth tunnel in the first place? It has all the classic elements of a good con. When you didn't get the cheese, you placate your wounded ego by saying, "But I was in the *right* tunnel." You don't tear up the place demanding the cheese—or else! You suffer your losses of money, time, and energy and justify your behavior. Your motives were pure. You were right. And that's something.

How many millions of times in life is that everything? We're right. But we don't get the cheese.

What the difference between people and rats brings home to us, if we see the point, is not simply that we are conditioned to be *right* in our actions some of the time or even on important occasions. We have all grown up in a society that has a vast superstructure of morality governing practically all of our behaviors, because we do little that is not social. We do almost nothing that is so individualistic as to be of no concern to other people. We act in a context. For most of us, too, a moral system exists, an elaborate interlocking system of ideas about what is right and what is wrong, a system whose authority is seldom questioned. Like the streets and houses in the neighborhood, it is simply *there*. Perhaps it is prescribed by a religious philosophy thoroughly worked out before we were born. Then, too, there are family traditions of morality. And there are ethnic codes to follow. There are ethical codes in every job, every business, every institution. We learn from birth onward what ways are the *right* ones. There is a *right* way to do anything, and if you do it some other way someone will be sure to inform you that you did not do it right. It makes no difference that you got the cheese. What the difference between people and rats brings home is this: We are conditioned to do right on *all* occasions.

There is etiquette for everything we do. We are rule-dominated. Our education and training consists of learning all the rules and how to follow them in every domain of life. Once learned, we act accordingly. Programmed. We are predictable. We know what our conduct *should be*, and we conduct ourselves in ways that are approved. The *right* ways.

Breaking out of our programs, changing any little behavior we have acquired in life, is a major undertaking. No wonder B. F. Skinner sees humans as stimulus-response organisms. Given our conditioning to be *right*, we are patsies, pushovers, easily shepherded. We even blame ourselves for wanting cheese, and we get on our own cases when we don't resist the temptation to go for it. When we eat the cheese, we feel guilty.

There is much in the rats, people, and cheese story for any counselor to contemplate. How does a counselor help a client who is getting no cheese in life? How worthwhile is it to be *right*? How many clients cannot change their behaviors because to act differently means they won't be doing what is right? A counselor who doesn't address the morality of any considered behavioral change with a client is swimming against the current with 10-pound weights attached to each ankle.

FROM ANONYMOUS

Every book has to end somewhere, and this one ends on a note from that well known author, Anonymous. Often Anonymous seems to have absorbed all the handed-down wisdom of the whole human race and said it just right. Anonymous, it seems, is only after truth, never personal gain. There is no evidence, either, that Anonymous is prone to "writer's block." Perhaps that is because Anonymous is free of publishers and copyright restrictions and simply allows anyone to pass on whatever thoughtful gems come to mind. Anonymous's works are likely to turn up anywhere.

The following piece—call it a poem, if you like—was found in the newsletter of a Michigan-based professional organization.[26] Its unknown author, one might submit, knows a great deal about counseling powers and passions.

YOU LEARN

After a while you learn
the subtle difference

between holding a hand
and chaining a soul.
And you learn
that love doesn't mean leaning
and company doesn't mean security.
And you begin to learn
that kisses aren't contracts
and presents aren't promises.
And you begin to accept your defeats
with your head up and your eyes ahead
with the grace of a woman or a man,
not the grief of a child,
and learn to build all your roads on
today because tomorrow's ground
is too uncertain for plans
and futures have a way of
falling down in mid-flight.
After a while you learn
that even sunshine burns
if you ask too much.
So you plant your own garden
and decorate your own soul
instead of waiting for someone
to bring you flowers.
And you learn
that you really can endure,
that you really are strong,
and you really do have worth.
And you learn,
and you learn,
with every goodbye
you learn . . .

Thank you, Anonymous. Goodbye, my unknown friend.

NOTES

1. Lomax, J. A. (1946). In R. L. Woods, (Ed.). *A treasury of the familiar* (p. 609). New York: Macmillan.

2. Robbins, T. (1980). *Still life with woodpecker.* New York: Bantam Books, pp. 116–117.
3. Maslow, A. (1954). *Motivation and personality.* New York: Harper & Row; (1962). *Toward a psychology of being.* New York: Van Nostrand.
4. Gardner, W. E. (1973). *The effects of intergrade tutoring with group guidance activities on the reading achievement, self-concept, attitudes toward school and behavior of third and fourth grade tutors and on the reading achievement and behavior of first and second grade tutees.* Unpublished doctoral dissertation, Wayne State University, Detroit, MI.
5. Mills, H. (1982). *Mailer: A biography.* New York: Empire Books.
6. Galbraith, J. K. (1981). *A life in our times: Memoirs.* Boston: Houghton Mifflin, pp. 304–305.
7. Ibid., p. 524.
8. Tyler, L. E. (1970). Thoughts about theory. In W. H. Van Hoose, & J. J. Pietrofesa (Eds.), *Counseling and guidance in the twentieth century: Reflections and reformulations.* Boston: Houghton Mifflin, pp. 298–299.
9. Russell, B. (1956). *The autobiography of Bertrand Russell: 1872–1914.* Boston: Little, Brown, pp. 56–57.
10. Bruner, J. S. (1973). *The relevance of education.* New York: Norton, p. 15.
11. Thomas, L. (1983). *Late night thoughts on listening to Mahler's ninth symphony.* New York: Viking Press, pp. 156–157.
12. Wallechinsky, D., Wallace, I., & Wallace, A. (1977). *The book of lists.* New York: Morrow.
13. Gerber, A. B. (1981). *The book of sex lists.* Secaucus, NJ: Lyle Stuart.
14. Ibid.
15. Ibid.
16. Reuben, D. R. (1969). *Everything you always wanted to know about sex—but were afraid to ask.* New York: David McKay.
17. Wilson, E. (1977). *Letters on literature and politics: 1912–1972.* New York: Farrar, Straus, & Giroux, p. 690.
18. Delivered at the American Personnel and Guidance Association Convention in Detroit, MI, March, 1982. Significantly, or perhaps just coincidentally, in the autumn of that year Bruce Feirstein's little book. *Real men don't eat quiche* (New York: Pocket Books), enjoyed a brief popularity, its author appearing on the television talk shows to joke away the seriousness of being male.
19. Camus, A. (1956). *The rebel: an essay on man in revolt.* New York: Knopf (Vintage Books), p. 94.
20. James, W. (1902). *The varieties of religious experience: A study in human nature: Being the Gifford Lectures on natural religion delivered at Edinburgh in 1901–1902.* New York: Random House (Modern Library ed.)
21. Tennov, D. (1979). *Love and limerence: The experience of being in love.* New York: Stein & Day.
22. James, W. (1902). Op. cit., p. 236.

23. Toffler, A. (1970). *Future shock*. New York: Random House.
24. Quoted from an advertisement that appeared in *The New Republic*, June 4, 1984, p. 27. Simpson's book is published by the University of Chicago Press.
25. Bry, A. (1976). *est: 60 hours that transform your life*. New York: Harper & Row. (Avon Books ed.) pp. 15–16.
26. Taken from *MAAA Dispatch* (Michigan Alcohol and Addiction Association Newsletter), January, 1982, p. 5.

Index

About AACD. . . .

The American Association for Counseling and Development is a private, non-profit organization dedicated to the growth and enhancement of the counseling and human development profession. Founded in 1952, AACD is a membership association headquartered in Alexandria, Va. with more than 43,000 members in the United States and 50 foreign countries. It provides leadership training, continuing education opportunities and advocacy services for its members.

AACD has been instrumental in setting professional and ethical standards for the counseling profession. The Association has made strides in accreditation, licensure and national certification and represents members' interests with other professional associations, before Congress and with federal agencies.

AACD members work in education settings, from pre-school through higher education, in mental health agencies, community organizations, correctional institutions, employment agencies, rehabilitation programs, government, business, industry, research facilities and private practice. Association members participate in regional activities and in national divisions and affiliates organized around specific interest and practical areas. Each division publishes a journal and provides opportunities for professional development.

AACD and its members are committed to the continuing development of the counseling profession. Divisions and organizational affiliates include the following:

American College Personnel Association
Association for Counselor Education & Supervision
National Vocational Guidance Association
Association for Humanistic Education & Development
American School Counselor Association
American Rehabilitation Counseling Association
Association for Measurement & Evaluation in Counseling &
   Development
National Employment Counselors Association
Association for Non-White Concerns in Personnel & Guidance
Association for Religious & Value Issues in Counseling
Association for Specialists in Group Work
Public Offender Counselors Association
American Mental Health Counselors Association
Military Educators & Counselors Association

DATE DUE

FALL 90			
FAC			
APR 2 3 1993			
APR 2 2 1994			
FAC			
SPR 96			